PENGUIN BOOKS

THE BOHEMIANS

Ben Tarnoff has written for *The New York Times*, the *San Francisco Chronicle*, and *Lapham's Quarterly* and is the author of *A Counterfeiter's Paradise: The Wicked Lives and Surprising Adventures of Three Early American Moneymakers*. He was born in San Francisco.

Praise for Ben Tarnoff's *The Bohemians*

"Tarnoff's book sings with the humor and expansiveness of his subjects' prose, capturing the intoxicating atmosphere of possibility that defined, for a time, America's frontier."
—*The New Yorker*

"Tarnoff breathes fresh life into his narrative with vivid details from the archives . . . giving us a rich portrait of a lost world overflowing with new wealth and new talent. . . . [A] stylish and fast-paced literary history."
—*San Francisco Chronicle*

"Engrossing . . . By skillfully tracking the friendships and fortunes of this unusual quartet, Tarnoff narrates the awakening of a powerful new sensibility in American literature. . . . Tarnoff powerfully evokes the western landscapes, local cultures, and youthful friendships that helped shape Twain. He has a talent for selecting details that animate the past."
—*Chicago Tribune*

"Rich hauls of historical research, deeply excavated but lightly borne . . . Mr. Tarnoff's ultimate thesis is a strong one, strongly expressed: that together these writers 'helped pry American literature away from its provincial origins in New England and push it into a broader current.'"
—*The Wall Street Journal*

"Delightful . . . Adeptly wrapping a wonderful story around these young writers, Tarnoff glides smoothly along, never dwelling too long and never claiming too much. He stacks fifty pages of endnotes at the back of the book but such archival sweat doesn't show in the prose."
—*The Boston Globe*

"Tarnoff is a good storyteller and character-portraitist, with a deep knowledge of the West Coast."
—*The Washington Post*

"Meticulously researched and exhilarating . . . Twain may be the main draw of Tarnoff's book, but Tarnoff's writing about a few of Twain's contemporaries—Bret Harte, Charles Warren Stoddard, Ina Coolbrith—is just as engaging."
—*Minneapolis Star Tribune*

"Tarnoff successfully contributes to the compendium [of Twain scholarship] with a fresh take on Twain's San Francisco circle, which was akin to the Algonquin Roundtable in Manhattan or 'Lost Generation' of writers in Paris." —*The Kansas City Star*

"Lively . . . Tarnoff draws a vivid contrast between sardonic, sophisticated, and sartorially dapper [Bret] Harte, San Francisco's literary star, and the unkempt, uncouth Mark Twain who rolled into town in 1863, a scuffling newspaperman looking to move on and up from provincial Virginia City, Nevada." —*The Daily Beast*

"Tarnoff provides a fascinating snapshot of the era, when the city's prosperity and unique international character (he points out that in 1860 almost two-thirds of the city's adult males were foreign-born) brought about a thrilling, if chaotic, admixture of idealism and fun." —*The New Yorker's Page-Turner* blog

"Deftly written, wholly absorbing." —*The Oregonian*

"Tarnoff's glimmering prose lends grandeur to this account of four writers (Mark Twain, Bret Harte, Charles Warren Stoddard, and Ina Coolbrith) who built 'an extraordinary literary scene' in the frontier boom town of 1860s San Francisco. . . . The lively historical detail and loving tone of the interwoven biographies make a highly readable story of this formative time in American letters, starring San Francisco as the city that lifted 'Twain to literary greatness.'" —*Publishers Weekly*

"Tarnoff energetically portrays this irresistible quartet within a vital historical setting, tracking the controversies they sparked and the struggles they endured, bringing forward an underappreciated facet of American literature. We see Twain in a revealing new light, but most affecting are Tarnoff's insights into Harte's 'downward spiral,' Stoddard's faltering, and persevering Coolbrith's triumph as California's first poet laureate." —*Booklist*

THE
BOHEMIANS

Mark Twain and the

San Francisco Writers

Who Reinvented

American Literature

BEN TARNOFF

PENGUIN BOOKS

PENGUIN BOOKS

Published by the Penguin Group

Penguin Group (USA) LLC

375 Hudson Street

New York, New York 10014

USA | Canada | UK | Ireland | Australia
New Zealand | India | South Africa | China
penguin.com
A Penguin Random House Company

First published in the United States of America by The Penguin Press,
a member of Penguin Group (USA) LLC, 2014
Published in Penguin Books 2015

Illustration credits appear on page 321

THE LIBRARY OF CONGRESS HAS CATALOGED THE HARDCOVER EDITION AS FOLLOWS:
Tarnoff, Ben.
The Bohemians : Mark Twain and the San Francisco Writers Who Reinvented
American Literature / Ben Tarnoff.
pages cm
Includes bibliographical references and index.
ISBN 978-1-59420-473-9 (hc.)
ISBN 978-0-14-312696-6 (pbk.)
1. American literature—California—San Francisco—History and criticism.
2. Authors, American—Homes and haunts—California—San Francisco.
3. Twain, Mark, 1835–1910. 4. Harte, Bret, 1836–1902. 5. Stoddard, Charles Warren,
1843–1909. 6. Coolbrith, Ina D. (Ina Donna), 1841–1928. I. Title.
PS285.S3T37 2014
810.9'979461—dc23
2013028131

Printed in the United States of America
3 5 7 9 10 8 6 4

Designed by Gretchen Achilles

For Dad and
Grandpa Benny

CONTENTS

THE
BOHEMIANS

Telegraph Hill,
San Francisco, 1865.

INTRODUCTION

The Civil War began with an outburst of patriotic feeling on both sides and the belief that a few battles would result in a swift victory. It ended with the death of 750,000 soldiers and a nation shaken to its core. The wise men of an earlier era found themselves entirely unequal to the crisis. The great political and military leaders of the past—eminences like John Crittenden and General Winfield Scott, both born in the previous century—went into forced retirement, while younger, more modern minds like Abraham Lincoln and Ulysses S. Grant rose to the challenge. The Civil War destroyed old assumptions and rewarded radically new thinking. It triggered a cultural upheaval comparable to the one wrought a century later by the Vietnam War, a national trauma that made an older generation suddenly obsolete and demanded novelty, innovation, experimentation. The 1860s was bloody, bewildering—and, if you managed to survive, a magnificent time to be a young American.

If America belonged to the young, then its future lay in the youngest place in America: the Far West. The pioneers who settled it were overwhelmingly young, and untethered from traditional society, they built a new world without the benefit of their parents' counsel. If their encampments often reeled with postadolescent excess, they also offered opportunities unlike any that might be found in the colleges and countinghouses of the East. These new Americans were the "tan-faced children" of Walt Whitman's poem "Pioneers! O Pioneers," the vanguard of democracy:

> *All the past we leave behind;*
> *We debouch upon a newer, mightier world, varied world,*
> *Fresh and strong the world we seize, world of labor and the*
> *march,*
> *Pioneers! O pioneers!*

When Whitman looked West, he didn't just see a place. He saw an idea, rooted in a mystical tradition as old as the country itself. Thomas Jefferson had been its founding prophet. He and his disciples believed that American civilization would march inevitably toward the Pacific, and that the continent's limitless supply of virgin land would be settled by yeoman farmers who embodied the nation's egalitarian spirit. Of course, the reality was often more complicated. The region contained land that resisted cultivation, and Indians who resisted extermination. But as the line of settlement inched steadily forward—past the Alleghenies, then the Mississippi, then the Rockies—the Jeffersonian dream of a westward "empire of liberty" began to look like prophecy. Even Henry David Thoreau, when departing for his daily walk in Concord, felt drawn in a westerly direction. "The future lies that way to me," he wrote, "and the earth seems more unexhausted and richer on that side."

Mark Twain was born in 1835 and reached young adulthood at the best possible time, just as the country embarked on the most extraordinary period of change in its history. He was a westerner by birth, raised on the Missouri frontier. The outbreak of the Civil War forced him farther west, as he fled the fighting in his native state for the region beyond the Rockies. There he found another frontier—and a social experiment unlike any in the country. In 1848, the discovery of gold in California had triggered a swift influx of people from all corners of the world. As the gateway to the gold rush, San Francisco went from a drowsy backwater to a booming global seaport. Mostly the newcomers were young, single men—they hadn't come to stay, but to get rich and get out. They erected tents and wooden hovels, makeshift structures that made easy kindling for the city's frequent fires. They built gambling dens and saloons and brothels. They lived among the cultures of five continents, often condensed into the space of a single street: Cantonese stir-fry competing with German wurst, Chilean whores with Australian. On the far margin of the continent, they created a complex urban society virtually overnight.

By the time Twain got there, San Francisco still roared. It was densely urban, yet unmistakably western; isolated yet cosmopolitan; crude yet cultured. The city craved spectacle, whether on the gaslit stages of its many theaters or in the ornately costumed pageantry of its streets. Its wide-open atmosphere endeared it to the young and the odd, to anyone seeking refuge from the overcivilized East. It had an acute sense of its own history, and a paganish appetite for mythmaking and ritual. Even as the gold rush waned, and the miners' shanties became banks and restaurants and boutiques, the city didn't slow to a more settled rhythm. Rather, it financed the opening of new frontiers—in Nevada, Idaho, and elsewhere—and leaped from one bonanza to the next. Its citizens spent lavishly: on feasts of oysters and terrapin, on imported fashions and furnishings. They drank seven bottles of champagne for every one drunk in Boston. Long after the gold rush, they kept the frontier spirit of the city alive.

They also sustained a thriving publishing culture. California was always crawling with scribblers. The first generation wrote the story of the gold rush themselves, in letters and diaries and in the pages of the newspapers they started as soon as they arrived. San Francisco's printing presses cranked out pamphlets, periodicals, and books, relieving the loneliness and boredom of the frontier. By the 1860s, the city had spawned an extraordinary literary scene—a band of outsiders called the Bohemians. Twain joined their ranks, and the encounter would shape the entire current of his life.

Bret Harte was their leader. Immaculately dressed and witheringly ironic, he didn't mix easily with others. He held himself apart, and hated the mediocrity of most California writing. In the gold rush, he would discover material that met his exacting standards: tales of the frontier, infused with dark humor and colorful slang. These would feed the country's growing fascination with the Far West, and catapult him to the top spot in American letters. He drew other young Californians into his orbit, helping them grow into writers capable of seizing the national stage.

Charles Warren Stoddard needed the encouragement. Dreamy and frail, he always doubted himself. He was what his idol and sometime correspondent, Walt Whitman, would call "adhesive"—gay—and he struggled to square his sexuality with a world that offered few outlets for it. He buried himself in poetry and became the boy wonder of the Bohemians. But his real breakthrough came when he traveled to the South Seas, where he discovered a tropical paradise that sated his sensuality and inspired his best writing.

Ina Coolbrith also suffered for her secrets. A painful past had forced her to live outside the narrow mold of Victorian womanhood, and she was determined to make the most of it. She earned recognition from an early age for her poetry, and later became the first poet laureate of California. To the Bohemians, she provided companionship, sympathy, and support that proved indispensable to the growth of the group. She also gave them a place to gather, in the parlor of her parents' house.

The Bohemians were nonconformists by choice or by circumstance, and they eased their isolation by forming intense friendships with one another. San Francisco was where their story began, but it would continue in Boston, New York, and London; in the palace and the poorhouse; in success and humiliation, fame and poverty. They benefited from the disruptions of the 1860s, as the Civil War shattered the moral certainties of antebellum America and created rifts in the culture wide enough for new voices to be heard. At the same time, the war made America smaller. It connected California to the rest of the country with railroad track and telegraph wire, and fostered a spirit of nationalism that brought East and West closer together. San Francisco emerged from its seclusion, and its writers found a wider readership at a moment when the nation sorely needed new storytellers.

The Bohemians would bring a fresh spirit to American writing, drawn from the new world being formed in the Far West. If the old guard of American literature was genteel, moralistic, grandiose, then the Bohemians would be ironic and irreverent. They would prefer satire to sermons, sensuality to sentimentalism. They would embrace the devilish sense of humor that flourished in the communities of the frontier. Above all, they would help break the literary monopoly of the East. The Bohemians would prove that the Pacific coast could produce literature on a par with the Atlantic—that the Far West wasn't a backwater but a civilization of its own, capable of creating great art.

No Bohemian made better art than Twain. San Francisco gave him his education as a writer, nurturing the literary powers he would later use to transform American literature. He would help steer the country through its newfangled nationhood, and become the supreme cultural icon of the postwar age. But first, he would spend his formative years on the Far Western fringe, in the company of other young Bohemians struggling to reinvent American writing.

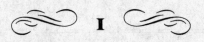

I

PIONEERS

Mark Twain

Mark Twain in 1863, taken on his
first visit to San Francisco.
He was twenty-seven.

ONE

What people remembered best about him, aside from his brambly red brows and rambling gait, was his strange way of speaking: a drawl that spun syllables slowly, like fallen branches on the surface of a stream. Printers transcribed it with hyphens and dashes, trying to render rhythms so complex they could've been scored as sheet music. He rasped and droned, lapsed into long silences, soared in the swaying tenor inherited from the slave songs of his childhood. He made people laugh while remaining dreadfully, imperially serious. He mixed the sincere and the satiric, the factual and the fictitious, in proportions too obscure for even his closest friends to decipher. He was prickly, irreverent, ambitious, vindictive—a personality as impenetrably vast as the American West, and as prone to seismic outbursts. He was Samuel Clemens before he became Mark Twain, and in the spring of 1863, he made a decision that brought him one step closer to the fame he craved.

On May 2, 1863, Mark Twain boarded a stagecoach bound for San Francisco. The trip from Virginia City, Nevada, to the California coast promised more than two hundred miles of jolting terrain: sleepless nights spent corkscrewing through the Sierras, and alkali dust so thick it caked the skin. These discomforts didn't deter the young Twain, who, at twenty-seven, already had more interesting memories than most men twice his age. He had piloted steamboats on the Mississippi, roamed his native Missouri with a band of Confederate guerrillas, and as the Civil War began in earnest, taken the overland route to the Territory of Nevada—or Washoe, as westerners called it, after a local Indian tribe.

Now he fell in love with the first and only metropolis of the Far West. "After the sage-brush and alkali deserts of Washoe," he later wrote, "San Francisco was Paradise to me." Its grandeur and festivity exhilarated him, and he gorged himself with abandon. He drank champagne in the dining room of the Lick House, a palatial haunt of high society modeled on the banquet hall at Versailles. He toured the pleasure gardens on the outskirts of town. He met a pretty girl named Jeannie, who snubbed him when he said hello and said hello when he snubbed her. He rode to the beach and listened to the roaring surf and put his toes in the Pacific. On the far side of the continent, he felt the country's vastness.

He hadn't planned to stay long, but a nonstop itinerary of eating, drinking, sailing, and socializing kept him too busy to bear the thought of leaving. In mid-May, he wrote his mother and sister to say he would remain for another ten days, two weeks at the most. By early June, another letter announced he was still in San Francisco, had switched lodgings to a fancier hotel, and showed no signs of slowing his demonic pace. "I am going to the Dickens mighty fast," he wrote, a taunt aimed squarely at his devoutly Calvinist mother. The city offered many after-dark amusements—high-toned saloons and divey dance halls, gambling dens and girlie shows—and Twain rarely returned home before midnight. He was never at a loss for companionship: he reckoned he knew at least a thousand of the city's 115,000 residents, mostly friends from Nevada. The city's main thoroughfare, Montgomery Street, where crowds and carriages swarmed under gleaming Italianate facades, reminded him of his hometown. "[W]hen I go down Montgomery street, shaking hands with Tom,

Dick & Harry," he wrote his family, "it is just like being in Main
street in Hannibal & meeting the old familiar faces."

Spring turned to summer, and still Twain hadn't left. Dreading
the inevitable, he clung on as long as he could. "It seems like going
back to prison to go back to the snows & the deserts of Washoe," he
complained. In July, he finally said farewell. He had been away
from Nevada for two months. Even after he had settled back into the
sagebrush on the dry side of the Sierras, the city lingered in his
mind. Over the course of the next year he would find many reasons
to return: first to visit, then to live. He would chronicle its quirks,
and hurt the feelings of not a few of its citizens. In exchange, San
Francisco would mold him to literary maturity. It would inspire his
evolution from a provincial scribbler into a great American writer,
from Hannibal's Samuel Clemens into America's Mark Twain.

ON FEBRUARY 3, 1863, three months before the carrot-haired rambler
roared into California, the residents of Virginia City, Nevada, awoke
to find an unfamiliar name in their newspaper. That day's *Territorial
Enterprise* ran a letter from Carson City, the nearby capital, about
a lavish party hosted by the former governor of California. The
reporter arrived in the company of a bumptious, ill-bred friend—"the
Unreliable"—and proceeded to drain the punch bowl and sing and
dance drunkenly until two in the morning. Several famous citizens
made cartoonish cameos. Affixed to the bottom of this waggish sketch
of Washoe society was a new name: "Mark Twain."

This debut didn't attract much notice at the time. Clemens had
written under a number of pseudonyms; it occurred to no one that
his latest, Mark Twain, would someday be the most famous alias in
America. The writing was clever, but only faintly colored by the bril-
liance that would later revolutionize American literature. He was
always a late bloomer; his gifts took time to develop, and to be understood. He entered the world on November 30, 1835, a pale and

premature child. "When I first saw him I could see no promise in him," his mother said.

The origins of his pen name remain a mystery. In one disputed account, Twain claimed to have stolen the pseudonym from a famous steamboat captain named Isaiah Sellers. On the Mississippi, the leadsman would mark the depth on the sounding line and call it out to the pilot; "mark twain" meant "two fathoms," a phrase that could signal safety or danger depending on the ship's location. To a pilot in shallow water, it meant the river was getting deeper, reducing the risk of running aground; to a pilot in deep water, it meant the river was losing depth, a cause for alarm. "Mark Twain" marked a boundary in the writer's life no less critical: the year his prose gradually began to find its true channel.

By 1863, he had been writing for more than a decade. He was a typesetter by trade, having begun his apprenticeship at age eleven. A "very wild and mischievous" boy, his mother remembered, he hated school and, on the rare occasions he attended, tormented his teachers. So she let him drop out to become a printer's devil, as apprentices were called, and he fulfilled the phrase to the letter. He smoked a large cigar or a small pipe while arranging movable type, and sang off-color songs. The shop became his schoolroom. He put other people's lines into print and composed a few of his own. He learned to think of words as things, as slivers of ink-stained metal that, if strung in the right sequence, could make more mischief than any schoolboy prank. At fifteen he began typesetting for his brother Orion's newspaper, the *Western Union*, and wrote the occasional sketch. When Orion left on a business trip and put his sibling in charge, the teenager lost no time in testing the incendiary potential of the medium. He ignited a feud with the editor of a rival newspaper, scorching the poor man so thoroughly that when Orion returned, he was forced to run an apology.

Twain's irreverence didn't just drive his comic wit; it also adapted him to an era of tectonic change, when technology was disrupting tradition on an unprecedented scale. The Industrial Revolution gathered fresh momentum at midcentury, just as Twain came of age. He watched steamboats make the Mississippi into a bustling commercial highway, and his hometown of Hannibal into a concourse for a lively cross section of humanity. Steam accelerated trade and travel. It annihilated distance. It built new networks along rivers and railroads and, crucially, sped the diffusion of the printed word.

By the time Twain became a typesetter, America's love affair with newsprint was growing fast. In 1776, the country had 37 newspapers. By 1830, it counted 715. By 1840, that number had doubled. Steam-powered machines made printing cheaper and faster; rising literacy fueled demand. A complex ecology emerged, with high-circulation city papers at the top, one-editor sheets at the bottom, and a diverse spectrum of typographical wildlife in between. Gardening tips shared space with sensationalized crime reports; serialized romances appeared alongside partisan hack jobs. "Story papers" delivered cheap thrills in the form of adventure tales; illustrated weeklies used detailed engravings to visualize the news.

The newspaper revolution created America's first popular culture. Twain belonged wholly to this revolution, and the world he discovered in the Far West was its most fertile staging ground. Newspapers helped colonize the Pacific coast. They stoked the gold rush by publishing letters from the mines and endorsements from powerful editors like Horace Greeley, and they carried ads for California-bound ships and stagecoaches. Since the price of a ticket was prohibitive to the very poor, the emigrants mostly came from literate backgrounds, and they began printing newspapers and books when they reached the Far West. By 1870, California had one of the highest literacy rates in the nation: only 7.3 percent of its residents over the age of ten couldn't write, compared with 20 percent nationwide. The region's wealth financed a range of publications and gave people the leisure to read them. As Twain observed, there was no surer sign of "flush times" in a Far Western boomtown than the founding of a "literary paper." Poetry and fiction mattered to miners and farmers, merchants and bankers. For them the printed word wasn't a luxury—it was a lifeline. It fostered a sense of place, a feeling of community, in a frontier far from home.

TWAIN ARRIVED IN NEVADA in the summer of 1861. The ostensible reason was to accompany his brother Orion, who had been appointed secretary to the territorial governor. With the Civil War roiling his home state, however, Twain had another motive: to avoid the Northern and Southern recruiters drafting Missourians of eligible age into military service. Missouri would be a battleground, split between Union and Confederate sympathies, and Twain had no desire to stay until the real bloodshed began.

So he climbed into a stagecoach and embarked on one of the greatest adventures of his life. In the prairies he saw coyotes and jackrabbits. In Nevada he found a desert full of enterprising young men angling for instant riches—and a social panorama that rivaled the Mississippi in its variety. "The country is fabulously rich," he wrote his mother soon after he arrived, "in gold, silver, copper, lead, coal, iron, quicksilver, marble, granite, chalk, plaster of Paris (gypsum), thieves, murderers, desperadoes, ladies, children, lawyers, Christians, Indians, Chinamen, Spaniards, gamblers, sharpers, cuyotès (pronounced kiyo-ties), poets, preachers, and jackass rabbits." It also boasted one of the wildest newspapers in the West, a far-flung outpost of America's print empire: the *Territorial Enterprise*.

After a failed stint at silver mining, Twain joined its staff. He arrived for his first day of work in September 1862 looking like a cross between a hobo and an outlaw: coatless, bearded, with a bedroll on his shoulder and a Navy Revolver in his belt. Fortunately, the *Enterprise* didn't scare easily. Its editor, a taciturn twenty-three-year-old named Joe Goodman, presided over a crew of hard-drinking hell-raisers that made Twain's Hannibal pranksters look like choirboys. Their offices were the epicenter of the human earthquake known as Virginia City, a Nevada settlement of no fewer than fifty-one saloons cut into the side of a mountain that held in its seams the richest stockpile of precious metals ever discovered: the Comstock Lode. "Virginny" lived at a perpetual tilt from reality. It swayed under the wind of frequent sandstorms; it shook with the constant blasting that burrowed mine shafts into the sloping earth. Its foundations were as fragile as the mental states of its inhabitants, who shot one another over the slightest insult, and squandered their lives on fantasies of wealth that rarely paid dividends.

Virginia City's lawlessness enabled the usual western vices. Young men at a certain distance from civilization tended to lose sight of Victorian values, and indulge urges they might've been better able to suppress farther east. The same freedom that facilitated a brisk trade in sex and booze also emboldened the *Enterprise* to take an especially far-out approach to frontier journalism. Goodman's writers didn't simply report the facts. They improved upon them. They sketched their extravagant surroundings with the fidelity of a funhouse mirror, creating a ruthlessly funny caricature. Their aim was to scandalize, to satirize, to sell papers, to settle vendettas, to boost their personal celebrity. One obligation that didn't weigh heavily on the herd of young heretics at the *Enterprise* was to the truth, which in the West had a tendency to mix freely with fable.

Virginia City taught Twain how to be a working journalist. He prowled the city in search of anything that might make for a column or two of entertaining copy, from the steps of the courthouse to the stock exchange. He became a sponge for rumor and hearsay. Despite his gift for observation, he discovered that dry facts bored him. He preferred to embroider and enlarge the truth, or ignore it altogether. Less than a week after joining the *Enterprise*, Twain published a hoax—"an unmitigated lie, made from whole cloth," he confessed in a letter—called "Petrified Man." It claimed that a "stony mummy" had been found in the mountains of eastern Nevada, perfectly preserved. Delivered in pure deadpan, the sketch combined Twain's absurdist sense of humor with his venomous taste for revenge. He wrote it to punish someone who had slighted him, a judge named G. T. Sewall, who appears in "Petrified Man" as a dim-witted magistrate who holds an inquest on the body.

Newspapers throughout Nevada and California reprinted the hoax. Some got the joke; others took it seriously. Twain recalled that he collected the clippings and mailed them spitefully to Sewall: "I could not have gotten more real comfort out of him without killing him." But the greater comfort doubtlessly came from his growing fame. With the *Enterprise* as his springboard, Twain became a Washoe personality. Goodman, recognizing the young Missourian's talent, gave him room to roam. Mining companies courted him, hoping for favorable notices. The legislators in Carson City paid tribute to his political dispatches with a resolution of thanks. "I am the most conceited ass in the Territory," he crowed to his mother and sister.

Yet his swagger disguised a deeper anxiety. As his prominence rose, so did his expectations. Excessive in most things, he always wanted more. Virginia City may have been an exhilarating introduction to the Far West, but it stood in the long shadow of imperial San Francisco. "Not a settler in all the Pacific States and Territories but must pay San Francisco tribute," wrote Henry George, the economist and reformer, "not an ounce of gold dug, a pound of ore smelted, a field gleaned, or a tree felled" without increasing its wealth.

The Comstock was no exception. The mining shafts that ran hundreds of feet into the Nevada earth were built by San Francisco barons; the gold and silver extracted lined their pockets. Virginia City wasn't a competitor. Like many outposts of the sparsely settled Far West, it was a colony. San Francisco's banks and docks and dry-goods houses ruled the region. The city was an unlikely monarch, built on dunes and declivities and other disincentives to human habitation, yet it compensated for its ludicrous terrain with an excellent location. Like Constantinople, it straddled East and West: linked by

sea to the Atlantic states and to Asia, and by land to the boundless
Pacific interior. It made gold into coins, trees into timber. It gave
form to the raw material of the Far West, and reaped the considerable rewards. Its newspapers commanded a readership far beyond
that of the *Enterprise*, circulating throughout the Pacific coast and
sent on steamers back East. In a nation obsessed with newsprint, San
Francisco outdid them all, boasting more newspapers per capita than
any other American city. Twain could rise only so far in Nevada. So
in May 1863, when he came to San Francisco for two months of high
living, in a sober moment among several wobbly ones, he performed
a small but significant piece of business. He arranged to become a
correspondent for the *San Francisco Morning Call*.

By the 1860s, San Francisco reigned over a flourishing economic
empire. The gold rush had faded, its diggings largely exhausted by
hordes of prospectors, but the Comstock boomed. Then came the
Civil War. The conflict that ravaged the rest of the country made
California richer. The disruption of trade with the eastern states
sheltered the state's industries from competition. Manufacturers
produced mining machinery like pumps and drills, and a range of
consumer goods to meet demand from the region's growing population. Agriculture also expanded, as wheat became a major export.
New mines in Nevada and elsewhere kept bullion flowing into San
Francisco's banks—$185 million of which would be sent to North-
ern coffers to help finance the Union war effort. Aside from this
hefty contribution, however, California's role in the conflict was
limited. No serious fighting reached the coast, and Lincoln never
applied the draft west of Iowa and Kansas, partly in a bid to keep
the Far West loyal.

The Civil War would be a boon to California: not only by increasing its wealth but by bringing the dream of a transcontinental
railroad closer to reality. Although a railway to the Pacific had been
debated for decades, Congress didn't lay the legislative foundations
until the war made it possible to sell the idea as a matter of military

necessity. The Pacific Railway Act of 1862 took the first step, charter-
ing two private companies to build the tracks, and subsidizing the
venture with land grants and federal bonds. The construction would
go slowly at first. Californians followed its progress closely. They
awaited the approaching triumph with an intensity verging on the
messianic. The railroad was more than a twisting trellis of iron and
wood: it represented the consummation of a spiritual tradition as old
as Columbus. It would unite East and West, and link the Atlantic
trade with the Pacific. California's current riches paled in comparison with its estimate of its future fortunes. While the East descended
into hell, the West strode confidently in the direction of its dreams.

ANY CITIZEN OF SAN FRANCISCO asleep at daybreak on July 4,
1863, might've thought, in a haze of half-broken slumber, that the
war had come to California. The cannon at Fort Point and Alcatraz
pounded the sky. Warships at anchor opened fire. Little boys lit
firecrackers in the street. The city celebrated the eighty-seventh
anniversary of American independence with an expenditure of
gunpowder that couldn't fail to evoke the smoky, sulfurous battlefields
thousands of miles to the east.

Elsewhere, Americans spent the holiday differently. On July 4,
Confederate general Robert E. Lee began his retreat from Gettysburg, Pennsylvania. The battle had killed or injured more than
forty thousand men of both armies, and broken Lee's momentum by
ending his invasion of the North. The same day, the Confederate
garrison at Vicksburg, Mississippi, surrendered to Union forces commanded by Ulysses S. Grant, a victory that helped restore the Mississippi River to Northern control. By the time San Francisco awoke
to the celebratory sounds of gunfire, the tide had shifted ever so
subtly against the South. The Civil War would grind on for another
two years, and claim many more lives, but in hindsight, the summer of 1863 would be decisive: the moment when, two years after

vowing to save the Union, Lincoln finally began to reverse the Confederacy's gains.

The news from the front wouldn't reach San Francisco for another few days. If it had come sooner, it might have lent some enthusiasm to the Independence Day parade, which lacked the numbers of previous years. People could be forgiven for not feeling particularly festive. Even Californians, who had been spared the Civil War's worst suffering, had begun to tire of the conflict. Their appetite for alcohol and entertainment remained intact, however, and they used the holiday as a pretext to indulge in both. The alcohol came by way of brewery wagons, which dispensed enough beer on July 4 to put thirty-five people in jail for public drunkenness. The entertainment took place at the Metropolitan Theatre on Montgomery, where a Unitarian minister named Thomas Starr King delivered the day's oration.

King knew how to draw a crowd. Within five minutes of the doors' opening, the Metropolitan had filled to bursting. Men, women, children, even Copperheads—those who sympathized with the South—turned out to see California's most popular preacher take the stage. Five feet tall and 120 pounds, King didn't look like much of a performer. Yet when he spoke, the sounds that flowed from his dainty frame were so robust, so heady with aphorism and humor, that they commanded rapt attention and thunderous applause. For the last two years King had crusaded tirelessly for the Northern cause, touring the state to proclaim the indivisibility of the Union. From the start of the war, a vocal minority had supported Southern secession, and even discussed turning California into an independent republic. That danger had passed, but pockets of pro-Southern sentiment persisted, along with a certain indifference to national politics that came naturally to westerners. Californians found it easy to forget they belonged to the United States, and King endeavored to remind them in the most emphatic terms.

Before speaking that day, King read a poem written by a local poet. Like Lincoln's Gettysburg Address four months later, it spoke of the current convulsions as another American Revolution: "these throes that shake the Earth / Are but the pangs that usher in the Nation's newer birth!" The house received the verses warmly. Strangely, their author was nowhere to be found. He was ill, the papers reported. A sturdier soul might've rallied for the rare opportunity to stand before such an audience. But anyone who knew the poet personally might suspect this was precisely the reason for his absence: that shyness, not sickness, had kept him away.

Not that he wasn't fond of being noticed. On the contrary: Bret Harte liked to be looked at. That season, as summer fog cooled the city, he might be seen in a stylish overcoat sporting a lamb collar,

Bret Harte around 1862, when he was just becoming famous. He was about twenty-six.

brightened by a felicitous flash of color—a crimson necktie, perhaps—
that set him apart from the rabble. Every fold, every fabric of the
young man's outfit would be as carefully arranged as those stanzas
delivered at the Metropolitan. On Montgomery Street, he flitted
through the human foliage like a brilliantly plumed bird. If your eyes
happened to meet his, he would smile; if he spoke a few words in
greeting, his voice would be agreeable. But there would be no yarn
spinning or rib splitting—nothing to remind one of that Washoe wild
man Mark Twain. He preferred to be admired from afar.

And there was much to admire. At twenty-six, Harte had become the leading literary light of the Pacific coast—no small feat in
a state where even the shaggiest miner aspired to bardhood, and
poets were pop stars, declaiming verses to cheering crowds at public
gatherings. Harte had powerful friends, a rising reputation, a wife,
and an infant son. Since 1861, he had worked as a clerk for the sur-
veyor general of California, then for a US marshal. In the summer
of 1863, he became the secretary to the superintendent of the US
Mint in San Francisco. His evenings didn't involve drunken romps
of the Virginia City variety. They centered on more domestic concerns, like how to keep baby Griswold from disturbing his study, or
his wife from dragooning him into household chores, so that he
might have a couple of quiet hours to write.

This shy, soft-spoken dandy must've seemed like an odd choice for
the Far West's literary spokesman. He didn't wield an ax or a revolver. He ridiculed the region's most cherished myths, especially the
cult of the pioneer. He hated philistines, sentimentalists, and hypocrites, and felt that California had all three in abundance. Where
others saw progress, he saw decline. The sea trade that made San
Francisco rich? The "vagrant keels of prying Commerce." The stately
City Hall of white Australian sandstone? A "district poorhouse."

Few things escaped "the corrosive touch of his subtle irreverence,"
as his friend William Dean Howells later observed. But Harte wasn't
just a destroyer. If he often felt disillusioned with California, this was

because he saw its true potential: as an infinitely original civilization with its own unique history and habits—a "singular fraternity" of Spaniards, Mexicans, Chinese, Europeans, Australians, Indians, and Americans living "free from the trammels of precedent" on the far edge of the world. Here was the "real genuine America" trumpeted by Walt Whitman, a world of raw literary possibility beyond the wildest imaginings of the country's reigning custodians of high culture— and, just possibly, the seeds of a new national literature.

HARTE HAD ALWAYS WANTED to write. Nothing in his early life suggested he would succeed. His first literary effort, at age eleven, ended in a trauma that nearly derailed him. He wrote a poem, which he submitted to a Sunday newspaper. All week he anxiously awaited the outcome. When the fateful day finally came, and he raced to the nearby newsstand and discovered his poem printed on the newspaper's first page, his heart leaped. He bought a copy to take home—only to learn, to his horror, that his family didn't share his enthusiasm. "It was unanimously conceded that I was lost," he recalled many years later. His father had been a schoolteacher, but aspired to literature. He had died two years earlier, leaving his wife destitute. The thought that the young Harte would take a similarly impecunious path prompted a harsh response from his family. In their New York home was a book of Hogarth illustrations, and one of the pictures, *The Distrest Poet*, summarized their fears: it showed a pathetic figure in a dingy garret, hounded by a milkmaid demanding payment of an overdue bill. "It was a terrible experience," Harte remembered. "I sometimes wonder that I ever wrote another line of verse."

But he did, even as he left school at age thirteen to go to work. The antagonism between art and commerce, between the Muse and Mammon, seems to have imprinted itself early on. Also the cruelty of other people: his fellow schoolboys teased him for the "girlish pink-and-whiteness" of his complexion, he later remembered, calling him "Fanny." Like many sensitive, misunderstood youth then and since, he developed a protective layer of irony to shield himself from the world's meanness. He wrote a tragedy in which, by his account, "Gilded Vice was triumphant and Simple Virtue and Decent Respectability suffered through five acts." For himself, he reserved the role of "Gorgeous Villainy."

It was a part he would play his whole life, in one guise or another. Less flamboyantly than Twain, perhaps, but with a defiance just as deep and a wit just as savage. In 1854, the seventeen-year-old Harte and his younger sister boarded a ship from New York for California, to join their mother in Oakland. She had gone West the previous year, and married a rich lawyer named Andrew Williams, who later became the mayor of Oakland. The young Harte came to California for no particular purpose, and with "no better equipment," he recalled, than an imagination fed by large quantities of books—an appetite he indulged by holing up in a small, skylighted garret on the top floor of his stepfather's house and reading voraciously. Like any self-respecting teenager, he refused to let anyone enter. Charles Dickens was his favorite.

He also loved *Don Quixote*. Like Quixote, he lived mostly in his mind. When he left Oakland to wander through northern California in the mid-1850s, he might as well have been riding through La Mancha in full regalia. He stood out. By then his fair skin had been badly scarred by smallpox, but his foppish dress and aristocratic airs were more than enough to make him a curiosity in backcountry California. A "somewhat pathetic figure," an eyewitness reported, "a gentleman of refined tastes with no means of support." He tutored, taught school, and, possibly, mined gold. Mostly he struggled. "He was simply untrained for doing anything that needed doing."

He always felt his outsiderness acutely. One New Year's Eve, while the rest of the country celebrated the coming of 1858—a year distinguished chiefly by the hardening of the political standoff that would eventually trigger the Civil War—he stayed in his room, submerged in somber reflection. He was living near Uniontown, a hamlet on Humboldt Bay a few hundred miles north of San Francisco. Here, in this unremarkable place, Harte made the most important decision of his young life. Writing in his diary, he reflected on his past and reached a firm conclusion about his future. He decided he had no choice but to "seek distinction and fortune in literature." "I am fit for nothing else," he wrote.

This declaration would be decisive. A decade after his humiliating first encounter, he pledged himself to the writer's life. If he ended up like Hogarth's poet, dead broke in a dilapidated attic, so be it: "Perhaps I may succeed—if not I at least make a trial." He had the desire and the discipline. All he needed now was the opportunity— and it came in December 1858, when the citizens of Uniontown started a newspaper called the *Northern Californian*. Harte joined its staff as a printer's apprentice. This was the same job once held by Twain; other distinguished alumni included Benjamin Franklin and Walt Whitman. The "poor boy's college," Franklin called it—a place where young men toiled at the dirty, tedious work of typesetting, sleeping on the shop floor, suffering the abuse of tyrannical editors, all for the opportunity to see their writing in print every so often. At twenty-two Harte had published poetry and prose in California papers, and even placed verses in a New York magazine. But the *Northern Californian* opened a new horizon. In its offices he learned how to build sentences the way Twain did: from the ground up, with nimbler rhythms than those taught in the classrooms of the eastern colleges. Harte's diligence endeared him to the editor, who let him contribute odds and ends to fill the columns. And he might've continued doing so for years, if tragedy hadn't intervened.

On the morning of Sunday, February 26, 1860, canoes filled with dead Indians began appearing in Uniontown. The victims numbered at least sixty and as many as two hundred. They had been hideously mutilated. They were mostly women, children, and the elderly. Some were still alive, and from the testimony of the survivors, Harte stitched together the story of what had happened. The night before, a band of white men had paddled to Indian Island, a marshy lump of land in Humboldt Bay where the peaceable Wiyots lived. Another tribe, thought to be allied with the Wiyots, had recently killed cattle belonging to white ranchers. In retaliation, the attackers murdered the Wiyots with axes and knives.

The massacre shocked Harte, and inspired his most powerful piece of writing to date. With his editor away on business, he sharpened his pen to its finest point. Uniontown preferred to shut its eyes to the slaughter. Harte's editorial would violently pry them open:

[A] more shocking and revolting spectacle was never exhibited to the eyes of a Christian and civilized people. Old women, wrinkled and decrepit, lay weltering in blood, their brains dashed out and dabbled with their long gray hair. Infants scarce a span long, with their faces cloven with hatchets and their bodies ghastly with wounds.

Here was the nightmarish underside of the Jeffersonian dream. America's westward march may have invigorated its democracy, but only at the price of provoking bloody collisions with the land's native inhabitants. In California, as elsewhere, these collisions came to be known as the "Indian Wars," a misleading term for what was essentially an extermination campaign waged with overwhelming force. State militia and local vigilantes annihilated whole villages on daybreak raids, forced survivors onto reservations, and enslaved the children as indentured servants—a practice sanctioned under California law, despite a clause in the state constitution prohibiting slavery. Americans had often extolled the virtue of freedom while depriving other people of it, and on the Far Western frontier, this tendency was especially stark. The hypocrisy disgusted Harte. He took the unpopular view that the "white civilizer" bore responsibility for the bloodshed, and condemned the "barbarity" of "white civilization." His moral convictions drew in part from a personal source: as the grandson of an Orthodox Jew—a fact he didn't advertise—he felt a special affinity for members of persecuted races. And when his conscience rebelled, those who knew him only as a wallflowerish young man would witness an extraordinary transformation. In print, the lamb became a lion.

Harte's impassioned broadside in the *Northern Californian* didn't exactly delight his neighbors. The young editor's life was "seriously threatened and in no little danger," one friend remembered. Within the month, he fled Uniontown. The butchers of Indian Island would never be held accountable for their crimes. They were businessmen and landowners, men of standing who enjoyed the support of their community. For Harte to challenge them in so public a venue, and with such implacable prose, took backbone. People had been calling him useless his whole life. Later, they would call him worse: insincere, arrogant, cowardly—"too much of a gentleman to quarrel and too much of a lady to fight." But the events of February 1860 proved that, under his refined exterior, Harte had as much courage as any leather-footed frontiersman.

The Indian Island massacre had one happy result: it brought Harte to San Francisco, where he ended his half decade of wandering. He arrived in the spring of 1860, and used his newly acquired typesetting skills to find a job at a newspaper. Fortunately, the city had at least fifty, and Harte landed at one of the best: the *Golden Era*, the most popular literary weekly on the Pacific coast. "Literary" was loosely defined: its editor, a universally beloved Long Islander named Joe Lawrence, printed everything from pulp fiction to farming intelligence. What he couldn't harvest locally he imported from abroad, poaching large portions from eastern periodicals and pirating European novelists like Dickens—turning the absence of international copyright laws to his advantage. The *Era* enjoyed an immense readership, especially among miners and farmers. Their favorite section was the "Correspondents' Column," which published verse written by readers. Within its densely printed lines, amateurs could play at being a Browning or a Burns—a sort of literary karaoke for people whose days were spent in the least literary ways imaginable, sifting for gold in freezing rivers or tilling soil under the hot sun. Often the *Era* couldn't resist poking fun at a particularly dreadful piece of work, and one suspects the column's readers loved these snickering asides as much as the uneven efforts that occasioned them. To frontier Californians, the *Era* was a cherished institution. "Many times the *Era* has gladdened my heart amid the rude mountains of the Sierra," wrote one rural reader, "when the whoop of the Digger-Indian, the growl of the fierce grizzly, or the screams of our emblem bird, the Eagle, were more frequent and familiar sounds than those of church bells."

The *Era* could count on the rural market. But its editor wanted more urban readers—the better-heeled sort who reflected the city's rising stature. By 1860, San Francisco had outgrown the gold rush. The makeshift houses of clapboard and canvas had given way to sturdier ones of stone and brick. The plush hotels Twain would patronize were about to be built, and in the ultrafashionable neighborhood of South Park, the wives of powerful men were serving seventeen-course dinners on teakwood tables to their corseted and crinolined guests.

Joe Lawrence hoped to capture a greater slice of this lucrative city market. To succeed, he would need new talent. Fortunately, he didn't have to look farther than the second floor of the *Era*'s offices, where the young fugitive from Uniontown had recently started setting type. The twenty-three-year-old may not have been brilliant at the type case—he set too slowly—but he could certainly write. He had already contributed to the *Era* while living up north; now he became a regular. Lawrence, whose grandfatherly warmth endeared him to all his writers, gave Harte every encouragement. Soon he was supplying poems, stories, and sketches—within the month he even had his own weekly column. His prose grew more playful, more propulsive. It revealed a mind nourished on long rambles through the city and an omnivorous delight in its peculiar customs and characters. What made the deepest impression were the trade winds, those whistling ocean zephyrs that kept San Francisco in perpetual motion. A legend grew up that Harte set his *Era* pieces into type directly, without first writing them down. Regardless, Harte conquered the *Era*. He struck "a new and fresh and spirited note," Twain recalled, "that rose above that orchestra's mumbling confusion and was recognizable as music." Before long, that music would find the ear of the most powerful woman in California, the matriarch who would pave the way for San Francisco's literary rise.

IF CALIFORNIA WERE A KINGDOM, Jessie Benton Frémont would have been its queen. From her Gothic cottage on Black Point, a steep prominence overlooking the city's north coast, she beheld the glittering breadth of San Francisco Bay like a sovereign surveying her realm. She loved the sea and the sky. And the sounds: the crashing surf, the fluttering sails, the plaintive warble of the fog bells. It was like living in the bow of a ship, she wrote. When she tired of the view, she took her carriage into the city—a "true city," she remarked to a friend, with "very good opera" and "lots of private parties." Beautiful, brilliant, and tremendously self-confident, she would've cut a conspicuous figure anywhere in the country. But in California she commanded special respect, on account of the two legendary men whose names she bore: Benton and Frémont.

Her father, Thomas Hart Benton, was one of the eminences of antebellum Washington, a five-term senator from Twain's home state of Missouri. A disciple of Thomas Jefferson, Benton thundered early and often in Congress on behalf of western expansion. He acquired such an outsized reputation that the hero of Twain's *The Adventures of Tom Sawyer*, after seeing the statesman in the flesh for the first time, comes away disappointed that he isn't twenty-five feet tall—"nor even anywhere in the neighborhood of it." During his three decades in the Senate, Benton urged the construction of an overland route to the Pacific. Cutting a path across the continent would "realize the grand idea of Columbus" by opening a western passage to India, Benton believed, enriching America with the Asia trade. But he saw more than the West's material advantages: he grasped its cultural potential as well. "The nations of Europe hold us in contempt because we are their servile copyists and imitators," he declared, "because too many among us can see no merit in anything American but as it approaches the perfection of something European." In the West, America could cast off the lingering influence of the Old World and blossom into a truly original civilization.

His daughter would carry this idea with her to California. Jessie inherited her father's grit and his undying faith in the future of the Pacific coast. She also absorbed his stubbornness, a fact starkly demonstrated by her decision, at age seventeen, to elope with a handsome army officer eleven years her senior named John Charles Frémont. Once the senator's anger subsided, and he reconciled himself to the match, he found an excellent partner in Frémont. An intrepid explorer, Frémont shared his father-in-law's enthusiasm for the West. With Benton's help, he embarked on several expeditions to the far side of the continent. He collaborated with his wife on the published reports of these journeys, crafting rip-roaring adventure stories that became hallmarks of American popular literature.

Furnished with thrilling vignettes and gorgeous scenery, Frémont's tales created the founding myths of the Far West. They also provided a wealth of practical information for westward emigrants in the 1840s, and became an indispensable guide to those traveling overland during the gold rush. Frémont himself was hailed as a national hero, known to Americans everywhere as the Pathfinder, after James Fenimore Cooper's frontier novel of the same name. A consummate self-promoter, Frémont won many symbolic victories, but relatively few real ones. On the eve of the Mexican-American War in 1846, he waved the Stars and Stripes within sight of the Mexican garrison at Monterey before retreating. A decade later, he ran for president as the Republican Party's first candidate, and lost. He never made much of a scientist, soldier, or politician; but as a storyteller, as a forger of useful fictions, he went a long way toward fulfilling Benton's fantasy of a peopled, prosperous West.

One can imagine Harte's reaction when, one day in 1860, he heard that the Pathfinder's wife wanted to meet him. He hadn't been in the city a year and was already rocketing into the upper reaches of California society. She had enjoyed his *Era* pieces, and requested his presence at her parlor at Black Point. He swallowed his social anxiety and accepted. He came on a Sunday, his only free day, and on many Sundays after that, with his manuscripts under his arm. "I have taken a young author to pet," Jessie confided in a letter. A gardener, she liked watching things grow. Now she had something new to nurture: a writer who, with the proper pruning, might redeem the promise of her father's beloved West.

As 1860 ground on to its catastrophic conclusion, with the election of Abraham Lincoln in November and the secession of South Carolina the following month, the mood at Black Point turned grim. For the Frémonts and their Republican abolitionist friends, the coming crisis marked the final breaking point after decades of deadlock over slavery. They feared for the Union's future, yet welcomed a struggle that would purify it of its founding sin. In the chaos of early 1861, as one Southern state after another seceded, Jessie mobilized to ensure California would remain steadfast. She enlisted another of her protégés to lead the crusade: Thomas Starr King, the Unitarian minister. In places like Missouri, the struggle over secession would be fought with guns. In California, it would be fought with words: in the pages of its newspapers and in the populist theater of its streets and saloons and tree stumps. "I do not measure enough inches around the chest to go for a soldier," King told Jessie, "but I see the way to make this fight." At her urging, he transformed himself from a slight, sickly preacher into a fiery evangelist for the Union cause. He gave Californians what they wanted: rhetorical fusillades to inflame them, bursts of wit to buoy them, and a vision of divine righteousness every bit as riveting as their favorite entertainments.

Harte, too, answered the call. The moral clarity of the moment exhilarated him. He made an American flag out of flannel, which he flew proudly from his house. He wrote patriotic poems, which King read aloud at pro-Union speeches throughout the state: stirring songs of battle feverish with "patriot pride" and "clashing steel." Together the two men made a good team. King understood poetry. At the height of the Civil War, he gave lectures on Henry Wadsworth Longfellow, James Russell Lowell, and other living legends of American letters. A product of New England, King knew many of these luminaries personally, and persuaded them to contribute original verses, which he then delivered to crowds of enraptured Californians. To be honored by these distinguished men, whose volumes graced their shelves, whose poems they memorized and recited as solemnly as Scripture, made westerners swell with pride. It served King's purposes brilliantly. "The state must be Northernized thoroughly, by schools, Atlantic Monthlies, lectures, N. E. preachers," he wrote James T. Fields, the editor of the nation's most powerful literary periodical, the *Atlantic Monthly*. These would build an unshakable foundation for national unity, King believed, and help realize the region's potential. In his sermons he praised the natural beauty of the Far West, and urged Californians to create inner landscapes as majestic as the ones outside. He exhorted them to build "Yosemites in the soul." Like Benton before him, he prophesied not merely a prosperous future but a transcendent one. When King told Californians they belonged to America, they listened. When he told them that they, too, could create great literature, they believed.

* * *

THIS REVELATION STRUCK one young girl more literally than most. On her way home from school, she crept into a shaded street to escape the Los Angeles sun. It was midsummer, and the heat made the pepper trees sink toward the ground. A gust of wind brought a torn scrap of newsprint fluttering to her feet. On the paper she found lines of poetry, and far more powerful than the verses themselves was the staggering realization that they had been written by a Californian: Edward Pollock, a popular poet of the pioneer days. The girl adored poetry, but always considered it something "wonderful and apart." She never imagined it could be created in California.

In later life, Ina Coolbrith would date her literary awakening to this moment. Rhyme came naturally to her, she discovered. Her face breathed poetry through every pore, from the melancholy eyes to the teasing mouth, an expression too enigmatic to unscramble but inexhaustibly interesting. "Her whole life has been a poem," a fellow poet said. Sometimes it strode with epic strokes; other times it skipped lightly along like a limerick. But its dominant key was what Sappho, the ancient Greek poet, called *glukupikron*: "sweet-bitter," the intermingling of love and loss—in Coolbrith's words, "half rapture and half pain."

Her first memories were those of mourning. She was too young to remember the funeral for her father, who died five months after she was born in 1841. But she remembered that of her sister, held when Ina was two. Death pervaded her childhood—not only in the form of illnesses and accidents but through violence of the most vicious kind. Her uncle was Joseph Smith, the Mormon prophet. Fourteen years before Ina's birth, he claimed to have found a set of golden plates engraved with the writings of ancient Israelites who had sailed to America centuries before Christ. Translated and transcribed, this text became the Book of Mormon—"chloroform in print," Twain yawned, ridiculing its cumbersome prose. Mormonism faced more

than just mockery, however. Smith's disciples suffered brutal perse-
cution, driven from one town after another. When Ina was three, her
uncle died in an Illinois jail, murdered by a mob. Ina's father had
embraced his brother's teachings but her mother's faith faltered as
the anti-Mormon atrocities grew worse. In 1846, she married a non-
Mormon named William Pickett and left the church. She promised
her husband to conceal her past and instructed her children to do the
same.

A dark secret: for Ina, now in her fifth year, it would be the first
of several. In 1851, her stepfather led the family West. He had read
reports of gold in California and, after waiting for the spring grass
to grow tall enough for the oxen to eat, piled his wife and children
into a covered wagon and wheeled off across the plains. The young
girl loved the colors of the landscape: what Twain, who made the
trip a decade later, called the "world-wide carpet" of the plains,
blooming in all directions. She hated fording rivers. The wagons
crossed by raft, while the oxen swam. The weaker animals didn't
have the strength to struggle through the current and, swept downstream, they drowned while Ina watched helplessly from the shore.
The memory tormented her forever.

At the foot of the Sierra Nevada came the most picturesque portion of the journey. The family met Jim Beckwourth, a freed slave
turned Crow chieftain and a renowned mountain man. Ina remembered him in dazzlingly romantic hues: "one of the most beautiful
creatures that ever lived," she wrote. He wore his hair in two long
braids, tied with colored string, and rode without a saddle. He had
recently discovered a path through the Sierras—the Beckwourth
Pass, a popular early trail—and wanted Ina and her sisters to be the
first white children to cross it. "Here is California, little girls," he
said when they came within sight of the other side, "here is your
kingdom."

Or so Ina remembered almost eighty years later. In memory, her
life acquired a more poetic coloring. But it was an adventurous

childhood by any measure. The family settled in Los Angeles in 1855. A town of about two thousand, its adobe-lined streets had changed little since its pueblo days. A wondrous and terrifying place, it boasted beautiful orange orchards and one of the worst murder rates in the country. Cowboys, crooks, and gamblers staged frequent shoot-outs. Racial animosity between Mexicans and Americans ran high. Lynchings were common. A minister from Massachusetts who arrived the same year as Ina tallied ten murders in his first two weeks. In his diary he recorded the sounds of an average Sabbath: children crying, dogs barking, men fighting and betting and blaspheming. "[T]his is nominally a christian town," he wrote, "but in reality heathen."

Yet there was another Los Angeles, to which Ina belonged. The old Californio families of Spanish Mexican descent who once ruled the region—the Sepulvedas, the Figueroas, the Picos—held glorious fiestas. The girl who crossed the continent in a covered wagon had grown into a glamorous woman, and she became a radiant fixture of local society. She also found fame as a poet, after publishing her first verses at fifteen in the *Los Angeles Star.* Her poetry oozed with trite sentiment—"a sorrow dwells in my young heart," read a typical line—but it made her a cherished figure in Los Angeles' tiny literary scene. Fortunately, the poet was nowhere near as gloomy as her verse. Her neighbors recalled a "warm, rich personality gladdening all about her." She sang, danced, and flirted. At seventeen, she fell in love.

In 1858, a Californian named Robert Carsley scored the crowning victory of an otherwise undistinguished life by persuading the pretty, popular poet—already hailed in newsprint as "a young girl of genius" with "an enviable reputation"—to marry him. He earned a living as an ironworker, and occasionally blacked his face with burnt cork to play in minstrel shows. On October 12, 1861, he returned from one such performance in San Francisco suffering from a murderous fit of paranoia. He accused his wife of imagined infidelities and called her a whore. Deranged with jealousy, he tried to kill her and her mother, and nearly succeeded. Luckily Ina's stepfather intervened, shooting Carsley in the hand, which had to be amputated. The divorce trial that followed only added to Ina's humiliation. Once the darling of Los Angeles, she had become another victim of its violence. Once an object of admiration, she now inspired pity.

Worse, she suffered another tragedy, one too painful for her to reveal. The details are obscure, but her relatives would divulge the secret long after her death: she gave birth to a child who died. A poem she published in 1865 called "The Mother's Grief" comes closest to expressing her anguish at the loss. She sees her "pretty babe" playing in an open door, trying to grab a beam of sunlight lying on the sill. Then she faces the shattering fact of his absence:

> *To-day no shafts of golden flame*
> > *Across the sill are lying*
> *To-day I call my baby's name,*
> > *And hear no lisped replying.*

Tragedy changed her. It bred a depressive streak that tempered the wilder impulses of her girlhood, made her reticent, yet also unusually solicitous toward people in pain. She loved Lord Byron, and her ordeal made her more Byronic: an outcast with a secret past. "Only twenty, and my world turned to dust," she later wrote. Like Byron, she went into exile, embarking for San Francisco in 1862. Her family decided to join her.

She became Ina Donna Coolbrith, taking her mother's maiden name. She buried her history and started over. Californians often reinvented themselves. "Some of the best men had the worst antecedents," Harte observed, "some of the worst rejoiced in a spotless puritan pedigree." Still, her past lingered. She made friends slowly and returned to verse only haltingly. She found work as an English teacher and helped her mother around the house. The change of scenery couldn't heal her grief, yet San Francisco supplied an endless stream of distractions. She read the *Golden Era* every week. She plundered the shelves of the Mercantile Library. On November 4, 1862, she saw Thomas Starr King speak for the first time, at a benefit for families of Union army volunteers. The occasion wasn't exactly somber: it featured fortune-tellers and "gipsy tents" and *tableaux vivants*. During his opening address, King read the poetry of his friend Bret Harte, as he often did—a writer Coolbrith had been hearing about since her arrival. Harte's pleas for national renewal couldn't fail to connect. America was being reborn: Coolbrith was ripe for a similar renaissance.

THAT FALL, the Unitarian minister could be seen all over town. Thomas Starr King was in perpetual motion, this erudite Bostonian who skewered Copperheads and quoted Seneca and spoke of California as the new Canaan. Jessie Benton Frémont had departed the previous year, after Lincoln summoned her husband to St. Louis to take command of the army's Department of the West. Now the burden of waging the propaganda war dreamed up in her parlor at Black Point rested on King's narrow shoulders—and his exertions had begun to take their toll. "I have worked the last eighteen months, within an inch of my life, in speaking, preaching, orationizing, travelling, organizing," he wrote in October 1862. Yet somehow he still found time to read the *Golden Era* closely enough to notice a new contributor whose poetry pleased him—Pip Pepperpod, the pixieish pen name of a nineteen-year-old bookstore clerk named Charles Warren Stoddard.

Chileon Beach's shop on Montgomery Street sold mostly religious books and Bibles. Inside, its clerk was constantly dusting. Not because he cared much for cleanliness, but because the monotony of the motion made it easier for his mind to wander. As he sank deeper into his daydream, the feather duster in his hands became a palm tree. He longed for the tropics. He had fallen in love with them eight years earlier, while crossing Nicaragua on his way to California. He remembered the syrupy taste of the oranges and the mist that sprayed when he broke their skin. He remembered the bright plumage of the birds, flickering against the relentless green of the jungle. Most of all he remembered the natives, who adorned their nearly naked bodies with necklaces and wreaths.

One day, California's most famous preacher appeared in the doorway, cutting Stoddard's reveries short. Celebrities had been in the shop before, but never one whom Stoddard held in such high esteem. "In my youth I was a hero worshipper," he later wrote, "and Thomas Starr King seemed to me the most heroic of them all." After a probing glance at the trembling clerk, King drew a scrap of newspaper from his pocket. "Did you write those lines?" he asked, pointing to his "Pip Pepperpod" poems. Stoddard said he did. The minister responded by reading them aloud—a voice perfect for poetry, rendering the verses as artfully as he did Harte's. He added words of encouragement to his favorite lines, and invited Stoddard to visit him with more work. He also presented tickets to his upcoming lecture series on American poetry, where he would be discussing those distinguished New Englanders whom Stoddard had read as a schoolboy. Then he vanished. "I was left speechless with wonder and delight," Stoddard recalled.

At first glance, the young poet might've reminded King of Harte. Both were slender and delicately built; both had large, expressive eyes—not unlike King himself. But Harte wrote painstakingly, while Stoddard's penmanship spilled merrily down the page, often illegible, the spelling atrocious. Harte kept most people at a distance; Stoddard held on to them for dear life. Stoddard was deeply lovable; Harte was not.

What people loved best about Stoddard was his vulnerability. His yearning for success, his dread of failure, the pain he felt when

criticized and the pleasure he felt when praised—these are the emotional undertow of any writer's life, and he experienced them more
openly than most. Twain concealed his insecurities with bravado
and wit. Harte hid behind a fastidious exterior and a hermetic home
life. Coolbrith remained guarded after her recent trauma. Yet Stoddard aired his passions in public—and they all loved him for it.
This was the true source of what Coolbrith would call his "invincible charm," the all-conquering warmth that made people lower
their defenses. They saw their struggles reflected in Stoddard's
childlike face.

There would always be one part of his personality they couldn't
possibly understand, however: his homosexuality. Like Harte, he
endured abuse from schoolyard bullies because he looked too feminine. Unlike Harte, he pursued close relationships with certain boys
for whom he felt an especially deep devotion. These "chums" and
"pals" rarely reciprocated his affections, and as a child he came to
expect their rejection, even to take a kind of pleasure in it. He loved
being in love—"The Love Man," Jack London christened him
many years later. Yet for someone who found solace in the written
word, he lived in a world with no words for what he was, where gay
love was not only forbidden but invisible—enciphered in metaphor,
perhaps, but never plainly discussed. The term "homosexual" didn't
appear in print until 1869, in a pair of anonymous pamphlets written by an Austro-Hungarian journalist. Later, Stoddard would be
relieved to discover Walt Whitman, whose "Calamus" poems in the
1860 edition of *Leaves of Grass* offered a thinly veiled celebration of
same-sex love. When Whitman wrote of "the pensive aching to be
together," Stoddard knew precisely what he meant.

Stoddard first came to San Francisco in 1855, at age eleven. His
father had found a job at a merchant firm, and the rest of the family
went West to join him. Stoddard loved the city's extravagance: "a
natural tendency to overdress, to over-decorate, to overdo almost everything," he wrote. The gambling houses beckoned: in their lush

interiors he discovered "enchanting music" and "beautiful women in bewildering attire." Sin surrounded him. Just a few blocks from his family's home had been the city's most notorious district, Sydney-Town, where many enterprising Australians lived, peddling sex and liquor. In May 1856, the murder of a newspaper editor triggered a vigilante uprising that came down hard on the neighborhood. The vigilantes lynched the killer, James Casey, along with another infamous character named Charles Cora, who had murdered a US marshal. Stoddard remembered seeing a pair of black-hooded figures with nooses around their necks, swinging into space.

A year later Stoddard's brother Ned fell ill, and a doctor recommended a long sea voyage. So Ned took a clipper ship around Cape Horn, and Stoddard tagged along to keep him company. On arriving in the East, they stayed at their grandfather's farm in western New York. Ned soon returned to San Francisco, leaving Stoddard at the mercy of their grandfather, a man whose infinite capacity for cruelty was rooted in a particularly grim Presbyterianism. He terrified his grandson with visions of God's vengeance and, on one grisly occasion, took him to a funeral for a boy his age, in the belief that seeing the corpse would cause him to find religion.

In California, the world had looked brighter. Stoddard couldn't wait to get back. Finally, his father sent money for his fare and he fled New York, returning to San Francisco in 1859. The city had grown in his absence. Thirteen thousand people arrived in that year alone. The gamblers and prostitutes were still there, but the new civic mood had forced them to become more discreet. Commerce, not vice, now reigned supreme. There were fourteen gristmills, eighteen breweries, nineteen foundries, eighty-four restaurants, seventeen banks, and one sugar refinery. New neighborhoods had sprung up on land once occupied by sand hills.

The fast-growing city kindled Stoddard's imagination. Its many newspapers offered a way to put his mind-pictures into print. The *Golden Era* was "the cradle and the grave of many a high hope," he wrote: not only for those backcountry bards scrambling to break into the "Correspondents' Column" but for the young urban aspirants who increasingly filled its pages. Stoddard didn't start contributing until September 1862. "No member of my family suspected that I was so bold as to dream of entering the circle of the elect who wrote regularly every week for the chief literary organ west of the Rocky Mountains," he recalled. He came up with a pseudonym to conceal his identity—"Pip" for the hero of Dickens's *Great Expectations*, "Pepperpod" for its alliterative sound—and set off for the *Era*'s offices on Clay Street. His heart beat frantically. He passed the mailbox at the door of the *Era* several times without pausing. He waited until he couldn't see a single pedestrian on either side of the street. Then he sprinted to the box, slipped his envelope through the slot, and ran away in a cold sweat.

After this harrowing initiation, he became an *Era* regular. Under King's guidance, his style improved. "It is because you have strong powers and good capacities that I speak of blemishes more than excellences," the minister wrote his protégé. He used his pencil like a scalpel, trying to toughen the timid young dream-builder into a more mature poet like Harte. He even encouraged Stoddard to return to school. The discipline would do him good, King insisted. So Stoddard submitted, entering City College in early 1863. An indifferent student, he had trouble concentrating. He fell victim to a range of extracurricular temptations, and soon found that "city life in combination with City College" didn't suit him. When the semester ended in May, he dropped out.

IF STODDARD PROVED especially prone to distraction, San Francisco in the spring and summer of 1863 was an especially distracting place. On the Montgomery Street promenade, Mark Twain could be seen visiting from Washoe, shaking alkali dust from the folds of his flannel, telling meandering stories in his signature drawl.

In the dining hall of the Lick House, directly across from Stoddard's old bookshop, he guzzled champagne. One evening he attended a party at the hotel, and penned a report for the *Territorial Enterprise* on the ladies' outfits. "Miss A.H." wore a scarf "garnished with ruches, and radishes and things," her hair held together by a "wreath of sardines on a string." Another lady's coiffure featured greenbacks. "The effect was very rich, partly owing to the market value of the material."

While Twain thumbed his nose at the intricacies of urban couture, another high-profile personality embraced them. Bret Harte presented a very different silhouette to the spectators on Montgomery. He dressed as formidably as might be expected of the city's fastest-rising literary star: a friend to King and the now-gone Mrs. Frémont, and a featured contributor to the *Era*. He could be seen shuttling between his office at the US Mint and the *Era*'s editorial sanctum one block away, where Joe Lawrence presided over a growing stable of brilliant young talent.

Lawrence's hopes for a more metropolitan *Era* were succeeding beyond his wildest dreams. In his sumptuously furnished offices—"simply palatial," in one visitor's memory—he oversaw the most varied gathering of writers the city had ever seen. Seated cross-legged in his chair, he looked a bit like Santa Claus, with his flowing beard and meerschaum pipe. His cheerful disposition aided the resemblance, as did his openhanded generosity, plying potential contributors with kindness and cocktails at the Lick House bar.

By the summer of 1863, Lawrence had built the *Era* into the flagship of the city's flowering literary scene. Harte and Stoddard both wrote regularly. Twain, who had just become the *Morning Call*'s Washoe correspondent, would soon join them. On June 7, the paper added another young writer to its roster: "Ina." More than a year since leaving Los Angeles, Coolbrith had mustered the courage to make her *Era* debut. Her poem "June" sang of a sun-soaked summer landscape alive with birds and squirrels and flowers.

No matter that a San Francisco summer brought mostly fog—the seasons of the heart were Coolbrith's true subject. After a long winter, she was ready to bloom. The same could be said of California. Bolstered by a steady stream of silver from the Comstock Lode in Nevada and the invigorating economic effects of the Civil War, the Pacific coast soared. Only a decade and a half earlier, the gold rush pioneers had imported everything. They lit their lamps with gas produced from Australian coal and chilled their liquor with Alaskan ice. They bought their flour from abroad, despite living near some of the country's most fertile valleys. They were in a rush to get rich, and couldn't be bothered with posterity. By the 1860s, however, California had learned to grow its own crops, and was busy building its own industries. Now, in the pages of the *Era*, it had begun creating its own culture.

Harte led the charge. He didn't swing a hatchet like Whitman's "tan-faced" pioneer, yet he staked out a literary region as rich as any riverbed. For his *Era* columns, which he started writing in 1860, he created a new personality for himself called "the Bohemian." Just as "Mark Twain" enabled Samuel Clemens to scrap his impulses toward respectability and cultivate a bad-boy image, the Bohemian enabled a mild-mannered clerk to moonlight as a literary vagrant. The Bohemian drifted through the city, visiting fairs, balls, theaters, hotels—anywhere the "street music" played at a lusty pitch. In unsparingly ironic prose, he showed Californians to be sillier, stupider, and generally more human than they considered themselves. He cracked a few memorable quips: "There are moments when quiet, timid, inoffensive young men like myself are led to feel acute regret that they have not at some period of their existence dipped their hands in human gore."

Harte made an unlikely Bohemian. The word referred to a tribe of penniless artists seen around the seedier districts of Paris and New York. They drank to excess, contracted venereal diseases. They shivered to death in drafty garrets, toiling over masterpieces that would never be printed. But in Harte's hands, "Bohemia" became more than just a byword for wild living. It came to represent a creative alternative to the mundane and the mercenary in American life, a way to overcome California's crude materialism and fulfill Thomas Starr King's call to build Yosemites in the soul. "Bohemia has never been located geographically," Harte wrote, "but any clear day when the sun is going down, if you mount Telegraph Hill, you shall see its pleasant valleys and cloud-capped hills glittering in the West like the Spanish castles of Titbottom."

To the young writers of the *Era*, Bohemia offered a home, albeit an imaginary one. Harte, Twain, Coolbrith, and Stoddard differed widely in lifestyle and literary technique. In 1863, their paths were about to intersect. Under the banner of Bohemia, these four writers competed, collaborated, traded counsel and criticism. Some remained friends their entire lives. Others became bitter enemies. What connected them was their contempt for custom, their restlessness with received wisdom. They belonged to Bohemia because they didn't belong anywhere else.

Virginia City, Nevada, in 1866.
This was Twain's home base for
his first few years in the Far West.

TWO

On September 8, 1863, Mark Twain laid siege to San Francisco for the second time. It had been only two months since his last visit, but he needed a break from Nevada. Virginia City had been spiraling into ever-greater insanity. In his first dispatch to the *Morning Call*, Twain grumbled about its "infernal racket": "O, for the solitude of Montgomery street again!" Overfull wagons clattered through heavy traffic. Residents exchanged oaths and gunfire. In July, Twain's boardinghouse burned down. He made a dramatic last-minute escape by jumping out the window, but the blaze consumed most of his belongings. The same day, he contracted a severe cold.

Twain made the most of it. He mined his misfortunes for material, played them for laughs. When his house went up in smoke, he joked about it in the *Call*. When he got sick, he spent two weeks at Lake Tahoe recuperating. A lively social life impeded his recovery—he arrived with "a voice like a bull frog," he wrote, and left with "an impalpable whisper"—but he kept his readers informed of his exploits, sending back bundles of deliriously kinetic prose. The fever dream of Washoe was in his bloodstream now. He felt invincible. When his mother implored him to settle down and find "a place at a big San Francisco daily," he retaliated with a furiously boastful response. "Everybody knows me," he gloated, "& I fare like a prince wherever I go."

He came to San Francisco by stagecoach, riding in the box beside the driver without an overcoat. By then, he had been ill for more than a month, and shivering in the brisk air of the Sierras certainly didn't help. Perhaps the thought of convalescing at the Lick House proved too tempting to resist, or he wanted to explore the city's countless professional opportunities. He knew San Francisco held the key to his career. During his last visit, he had signed on as the *Call*'s Nevada correspondent. In September he scored a bigger by-line, when Joe Lawrence recruited him for the *Golden Era*. Twain's first feature for the literary powerhouse of the Pacific coast, "How to

Charles Warren Stoddard in 1869,

when he was about twenty-six.

Cure a Cold," recounted all the remedies people had prescribed for his ailment over the last several weeks. They ranged from drinking a quart of salt water, which made him vomit, to spreading mustard on his chest. His style was spare, almost telegraphic. It had the clipped cadence of a man on the brink of madness, occasionally bubbling into hysterics before wrangling his demons back into the cupboard. Samuel Clemens had been writing as Mark Twain for seven months. He had faced adversity and used it as fuel to fly even higher. Intoxicated by the Far West, riding the crest of his rocketing ego, he unburdened himself of any obligation to be courteous or coherent.

FORTUNATELY, THE *GOLDEN ERA*'S EDITOR had ample experience dealing with eccentrics. The rogues' gallery of writers that passed daily through Lawrence's majestic offices included a number of odd characters. Charles Warren Stoddard was one of them. The blushing poet, still "Pip Pepperpod" to his readers, loved the city's literary scene. It kept him from his studies. Why study literature in a classroom when the real thing was happening right outside? But his mentor Thomas Starr King had insisted he receive an education. So Stoddard decided to try again.

In the fall of 1863, Stoddard went back to school. This time he chose somewhere more isolated: Oakland. The sleepy suburb across the Bay held fewer distractions, even for a mind as hyperactive as Stoddard's. Oakland was only an hour or so away by ferry. The passenger stepped off the plank and onto another planet: "a kind of wildwood and wilderness," Stoddard remembered, its principal street trafficked by more cows than carriages, "almost as quiet as a cloister." Around the first of August, he had arrived at Brayton Academy, located on the edge of town. Its eleven-member faculty taught a range of subjects, including a preparatory course for those wanting to enroll in the College of California—the privately owned predecessor to the University of California. Stoddard could study everything from botany to rhetoric, and put himself on the path to a university degree.

Before the semester began, he rented a room in a house near the Oakland Creek. It suited his aesthetic: vines threaded the veranda, oak trees swayed overhead. In the distance, the Alameda marshes stretched to the horizon. When he first visited, the landlady showed him a room with a view of the garden. A mop of honeysuckle pressed against the windowpane. Then she led him up a narrow staircase to see another room: a box-shaped garret illuminated by a small skylight.

"Harte used to have this room," she said. Nine years earlier, Harte had lived here as a teenager. This was where he had barricaded himself against the world and embarked on marathon binges of Dickens and other favorite authors. Later, he would undertake his quixotic ramble across the California countryside, and begin the apprenticeship that laid the foundation for his future fame. "Much as I longed to share in the inspiration that young Bret Harte may have found in that star-lit chamber," Stoddard recalled, he decided against taking the room. He chose the one with a view of the garden instead.

The two men first met in 1863. Stoddard recounted the episode later in life, although he neglected to mention whether it happened before or after he saw Harte's boyhood home. He had recently begun keeping an autograph album, and begged his elders at the *Era* to contribute. He was the youngest of the lot, and sought their sympathy and encouragement. King inaugurated the volume with a warm dedication to its "gifted owner," a key endorsement from one of California's most revered figures. As Stoddard remembered it, this helped persuade Harte when he approached him. "I might have met with a refusal had not his eye fallen upon the dedication," he recalled. Seven years older, Harte "seemed to look upon albums and their keepers with polite scorn." The precocious young poet with the pleading blue eyes no doubt made Harte uncomfortable. Stoddard seemed so soft, so exposed.

In time, they would become friends. But not yet: if Stoddard expected a glowing tribute for his album, he would be sorely disappointed. Instead of praising Stoddard, Harte ridiculed him—subtly, but unmistakably. For his inscription, Harte contributed a poem about a girl named Mary. Mary has an album like Stoddard's. Rather than filling it with words, she fills it with flowers. Later, she opens it to find the pages stained, the petals crushed, the fragrance gone:

> *O Mary, maid of San Andreas!*
> > *Too sad was your mistake—*
> *Yet one, methinks, that wiser folk*
> > *Are very apt to make.*
>
> *Who 'twixt these leaves would fix the shapes*
> > *That love and truth assume,*
> *Will find they keep, like Mary's rose,*
> > *The stain and not the bloom.*

This bit of cynicism, delivered by a writer all of twenty-seven years old, didn't dissuade Stoddard from his ongoing quest for autographs. He needed that album. Its chorus of voices cheered him— even if, as Harte suggested, the affection they expressed was only dead residue, the "stain and not the bloom." Harte's curmudgeonliness on this count reflected his need to "throw the shadow of sarcasm over his sentiment," Stoddard observed, so as not to seem sentimental.

Harte's inscription aside, the album would be a source of comfort to Stoddard as the school year began and familiar frustrations returned. He still couldn't concentrate. "I conned my text-book by the hour and honestly endeavored to make its contents all my own forever, yet in the end I seemed to have accomplished little," he remembered. Worse, he felt isolated from his fellow students. In the evenings he would walk by the dormitories and gaze achingly "at the long rows of lighted windows and wish myself a happy habitant."

Fortunately, there was the ferry, and the trip across the Bay, and the scenic approach by sea. He spent weekends in San Francisco. At a certain distance, the skyline resolved into distinct shapes: the old semaphore station on the summit of Telegraph Hill, the smoke-stacks of the ironworks puffing coal. Closer, the waterfront teemed with workers talking a babble of tongues, hauling boxes and barrels and crates from the wharves to the warehouses. The ferry from Oakland landed near the spot where traders once came ashore to buy hides and tallow from the priests of Mission Dolores, in the days when the coastline formed a cove. Now landfill rounded the shore, a row of piers split the water, and a student, happy to be home, weaved through the crowded port and into the roaring streets.

STODDARD AGONIZED OVER HIS FAILURES as a student. In fact, they were a blessing in disguise: they preserved him from the dangers of a formal education. His mercurial mind never lingered in one place long enough to be properly embalmed by his professors. The scholarship they patiently endeavored to hammer into his skull fled under the force of his restless imagination. He wasn't alone. Twain's schooling ended at age eleven, Harte's at thirteen. Ina Coolbrith probably stayed in school until seventeen, although an itinerant childhood often kept her from the classroom. "Education consists mainly in what we have unlearned," Twain remarked many years later.

By this standard, San Francisco offered the best education on either coast. Harvard and Yale may have produced more polished specimens, but the Bay boasted a more varied curriculum, and a more colorful visiting faculty. In 1863, a number of writers fled the war-torn East for peaceful, prosperous California. Their arrival greatly accelerated San Francisco's literary life. Chief among them was Charles Henry Webb, a former whaler and war correspondent from New York. The Civil War had sparked a boom in American journalism, as the newspapers created over the course of the past few decades rushed to meet the country's surging demand for information. This gave aspiring scribblers like Webb a chance to shine. He went to the front and wrote reports of the carnage, colored by the occasional flash of humor. "I was quartered for the night, or rather halved and sandwiched, between two Colonels," he wrote from a Virginia encampment.

In San Francisco he slept more comfortably, lodging at the upscale Occidental Hotel. Webb was a coveted import, and didn't lack for job offers. Joe Lawrence lured him to the *Golden Era* by promising the highest salary ever paid a contributor. For an outsider to capture the most lucrative post at the most prominent literary paper in California might be expected to make some people jealous. But Webb preempted whatever bitterness his presence might provoke with an irresistible personality that made friends of Harte, Twain, and Stoddard. A charming conversationalist, he loved puns and parodies. When he told a joke, which was often, his stutter made it sweeter. The "decorative impediment in his speech," Stoddard called it, a humanizing flaw that kept listeners hanging on his every word.

Webb began his *Era* column on July 24, 1863. A seasoned city dweller, he took his readers on meandering safaris through San Francisco's social world. The puns flowed unceasingly from his pen. His subjects didn't include just prominent citizens but fellow writers. In fact, the city's literati were his favorite topic. He chronicled their adventures and hyped their achievements and cheered the arrival of each newcomer from the East, playing impresario to the growing carnival.

No newcomer aroused nearly as much excitement as an actress named Adah Isaacs Menken. In August 1863, playbills with her picture began appearing all over town. Stoddard saw them in nearly every shop window. The image "caught the eye on the instant," he remembered: a beautiful woman with a boy's haircut, and a white throat enclosed by a tie of luxuriant silk. On August 24, she would be making her San Francisco debut at Maguire's Opera House, in what was slated to be the most spectacular premiere of the season. "[I]f she is half as good looking as her picture," declared the *Golden Era*, "her success is certain."

By the time the doors of the theater opened on the day of the first performance, people had been massing outside for hours. "We doubt if a similar audience was ever gathered together on a like occasion," remarked a reporter surveying the scene. Even Thomas Starr King at his most popular couldn't command such a crowd. A river of humanity surged through the streets, swept through the vestibule, scrambled for good seats under the gas-lit glare of the grand chandelier. When the curtain came up, the audience caught its first glimpse of the face that set San Francisco on fire.

Menken didn't disappoint. In *Mazeppa*, she played a Tartar prince who falls in love with the daughter of a Polish count. Performing a male role enhanced her sex appeal: liberated from confining women's fashions, she leaped around the stage like a gymnast, flaunting her athletic figure. The climax came when the count, having discovered the affair, ordered his soldiers to tie her to a horse and set it loose across the countryside. First, they stripped off her clothes—and Menken, in an inspired bit of costume design, wore skin-colored tights that made her look naked. The sight of Menken's muscular body laid bare before the footlights, writhing in sweet agony as the California mustang cantered offstage, whipped the spectators into frenzied applause.

Everyone went to see her. The critics praised her "grace"; the crowds whispered about her outfit. Men went to feast their eyes on her famed physique. Women went to find out "if the performance was a proper one for them to behold," in the judgment of one journalist. A few puritans made a fuss—"Prudery is obsolete," wailed the *Sacramento Daily Union*—but Menken played to a full house every night. Her show became required viewing. "People who have not been, and who do not intend to go, will be exhibited at the close of another week in glass cages," quipped the *Era*.

Menken so thoroughly dominated San Francisco that when Twain returned to town in September 1863, he discovered that no one talked of anything else. "Here every tongue sings the praises of her matchless grace, her supple gestures, her charming attitudes," he wrote in a letter to the *Virginia City Territorial Enterprise*. Yet when he joined the multitudes that descended nightly on Maguire's Opera House to see "the Menken" for himself, the performance left him cold. Instead of a goddess, he found a lunatic. She pitched forward like a "battering ram," worked her limbs like a "dancing-jack," and rolled on the ground like a "pack-mule after his burden is removed." "If this be grace," he concluded, "then the Menken is eminently graceful."

Stoddard felt differently. From the moment he saw her picture pasted in San Francisco's shop windows, Menken riveted him. It wasn't just her beauty. It was her strangeness: how far she ventured "out of the common run"—how exuberantly she demolished Victorian ideals of femininity. The masculine vigor of her performance, paired with the "willowy elasticity" of her figure, created what one reviewer called an "idealized duality of sex." Offstage, she smoked cigarettes and enjoyed an active sex life—by the time she came to San Francisco, she was on her third husband—yet remained indisputably, irresistibly feminine. Stoddard admired her "half-feminine masculinity," an ambiguity that mirrored his own. In a private notebook, he fantasized about inhabiting a woman's body, so that his "physique" could be "made whole."

Menken's sensuality wasn't the only reason she fascinated people. She also belonged to an infamous clique of writers and artists in New York that Californians had been reading about for years: the Bohemians. This was a group that gathered at a gritty German bar on Broadway called Pfaff's. Their patriarch was Henry Clapp Jr., an

exceptionally ugly man who diverted attention from his unfortunate face with a scorching wit. He started a weekly paper called the
Saturday Press that fulminated against moral hypocrisy, cultural
philistinism, and the deadening materialism of American society.
"It attacked all literary shams but its own," William Dean Howells
recalled, "and made itself felt and feared."

Menken joined the Bohemian circle on Broadway. Her favorite
Pfaffian was Walt Whitman, the Brooklynite who sang the body
electric in sinewy strokes of free verse. In the preface to the first
edition of *Leaves of Grass* in 1855, he spoke of America as a living
poem, written in the vernacular of its common people. Only the poet
liberated from "precedent," he believed, could innovate the "new
free forms" needed to bring this hymn into being. Menken worshipped Whitman. She brought his name West, championing his
poetry in the pages of the *Era* and trying to emulate his voice in her
own gushing bits of free verse. In life as in literature, she resisted all
restraint. "Swimming against the current is hard and dangerous
work," she wrote.

The New York Bohemians were already celebrities in San Francisco by the time she arrived. The *Era* had been writing about them
for years, praising those "fellows of infinite humor and rare fancy"
who met at Pfaff's, and Harte himself called New York the "Bohemian Capital." In raising the Bohemian flag on the Pacific coast,
Harte had hoped to create a literary scene like the one at Pfaff's. He
didn't want to spend hours in an underground cellar chugging cheap
beer, however, and he didn't share Stoddard's enthusiasm for Menk-
en's libertinism. But the Bohemian spirit appealed to Harte. The
irreverence, the contrarianism, the sense that precedents needed to
be overturned—these would shape his work, and the work of the
young writers around him.

There was also a generational element. Most New York Bohemians were in their twenties, the same age as Harte, Stoddard,

Coolbrith, and Twain. For this reason they felt more relatable than the older New England writers promoted by Thomas Starr King. The Bohemians of both coasts came of age with the Civil War, and their countercultural sensibility belonged to a broader breakdown in traditional values precipitated by the conflict. When the Civil War scattered the Pfaffians, several of them came to San Francisco. They discovered something Harte had known since 1860: that the city held many advantages for the young iconoclast. Its isolation didn't provide just a refuge from the war but a safe haven from the conventions of the eastern establishment. It was a city where "eccentricities cause no astonishment," in the words of Fitz Hugh Ludlow, a Pfaffian who took the overland stage to California in 1863.

The legacy of the gold rush gave the city an unsettled feel. The gender imbalance of the pioneer days persisted—by 1860, men still made up more than 60 percent of the city's population—and evidence of bachelor life was everywhere. In 1861, the *Era* noted the large numbers of "nomads" who lodged in the "vast beehives" of the city's many boardinghouses and hotels. And hotels, as Harte observed, were the Bohemian's "natural resting place," where he could drift with the rest of the "living tide" perpetually passing through. The large numbers of unmarried men lent San Francisco a looser moral tone. Fewer families meant fewer restrictions, and more freedom to crack coarse jokes or enjoy risqué entertainments.

If San Francisco's fluid social fabric helped foster Bohemianism, the city's robust newspaper industry helped finance it. In America, "Bohemian" also referred to a working writer. The New York Bohemians included many journalists who lived by their pen—and San Francisco, which sustained more professional scribblers in proportion to its total population than any other American city, gave writers plenty of opportunities to ply their trade. It also provided a steady stream of suitable material. Sometimes all Harte had to do was look out his window. A "small portion of the large world" passed below, he wrote. The gold rush had brought people from all over the globe; the decade that followed drew even more. By 1860, about two-thirds of the city's adult male citizens were foreign-born. Irish, German, Italian, British, Scandinavian, French, Hawaiian, Chilean, and Peruvian faces dotted the crowd. The Mexicans sported red sashes. The Chinese wore blue blouses. A "bustling, breathless, and brand-new life," as Harte remembered it—and a gold mine for the prospecting writer.

There was another factor that made the Far West fertile ground for good writing. The land itself inspired a new kind of seeing. To the first generations of settlers, the country beyond the Rocky Mountains was truly another world. Its strange weather, its monumental scale, the coloring of its sky and soil—all these were alien. In diaries and letters, people struggled to find the right words for what they saw. Writing to his mother from Nevada in 1861, Twain used analogies to describe the desert that surrounded Carson City. A shrub called greasewood grew "to about twice the size of common geranium," he wrote, and looked like a miniature live oak tree. But when he turned to the mountains, the comparisons broke down:

> I said we are situated in a flat, sandy desert. True. And surrounded on all sides by such prodigious mountains that when you stand at a distance from Carson and gaze at them awhile,—until, by mentally measuring them, and comparing them with things of smaller size, you begin to conceive of their grandeur, and next to feel their vastness expanding your soul like a balloon, and ultimately find yourself growing, and swelling, and spreading into a colossus,—I say when this point is reached, you look disdainfully down upon the insignificant village of Carson, reposing like a cheap print away yonder at the foot of the big hills, and in that instant you are seized with a burning desire to stretch forth your hand, put the city in your pocket, and walk off with it.

This was what the writer Wallace Stegner would call the "westernization of the perceptions" more than a century later. In trying to grasp Nevada's epic dimensions, Twain feels himself "growing," "swelling," "spreading"—seized by a new sense of proportion. The terrain demanded a different kind of vision, and this meant moving beyond inherited notions of scale and space.

The seemingly obvious idea that a new landscape required new ways of seeing was actually quite radical. It challenged a set of beliefs about the West that had remained remarkably persistent throughout American history. Ever since the first settlers had pushed into the interior, eastern elites had regarded the frontier with suspicion, condescension, and contempt. New Englanders, steeped in the Puritan theocratic tradition, distrusted a backwoods society unrestrained by religion and law. Even Thomas Jefferson, patron saint of western expansion, saw the pioneers as "semi-barbarous citizens" who existed in an intermediary state between the savage Indian and the civilized American of the Atlantic coast. According to this standpoint, America's geography recapitulated the stages of mankind's development, from the most primitive in the West to the most advanced in the East. As the West matured, it would rise to the level of Atlantic civilization.

This theory of progress precluded the possibility that the frontier, despite its lack of refinement, might be able to inspire original works of art. If the West was "semi-barbarous," it needed more churches and schools and courthouses before it could produce anything of artistic value. Thomas Starr King subscribed heartily to this view. The preacher worked hard to "Northernize" California for two related reasons: to keep the state loyal to Lincoln, and to help a region "struggling up to civilization." He nurtured San Francisco's writers and forecast a promising literary future for the Far West, one that followed closely in the footsteps of his beloved New England. He had a very specific model in mind. He gave lectures on poets like Lowell and Longfellow because he wanted California to grow its own Lowells and Longfellows.

These weren't unusual choices. Lowell and Longfellow were two of the most famous writers in the country. Along with William Cullen Bryant, John Greenleaf Whittier, and Oliver Wendell Holmes Sr., they were known as the Fireside Poets: a set of nationally loved northeasterners who wrote frequently for the Boston-based *Atlantic Monthly*, the country's most prestigious literary magazine. To King, they provided a gold standard against which the young aspirants of the Far Western frontier could be judged.

New England had dominated American letters for decades. In the 1830s, Ralph Waldo Emerson had started an intellectual movement in Massachusetts that molded America's first generation of literary greats. Emerson and his descendants failed in one major respect, however. They gave the young nation much to be proud of—yet they never quite overcame the postcolonial inferiority complex that, since the Revolution, had kept American writers in thrall to their European elders. In a famous address to Harvard's Phi Beta Kappa Society, Emerson called for the creation of a native national literature, liberated from the cultural imperialism of the Old World. "We have listened too long to the courtly muses of Europe," he said. It was a worthy aim, echoed in other quarters by Thomas Hart Benton—but New England's literary nobility remained too deeply indebted to transatlantic influences to achieve it. Their subjects may have been American, but their style was largely imported.

The Far West offered a possible path forward. On the frontier, the rudiments of a new kind of writing were beginning to take shape. It would succeed only on its own terms, not by slavish emulation of New England or the wholesale adoption of Atlantic tastes but by discovering the value of its local materials, by broadening its vision to see what was hiding in plain sight.

The New York Bohemians would help. They had a special loathing for the "solemn Philistines" of New England, and they provided an alternative to Thomas Starr King's influence. Still, San Francisco's Bohemians would never be as combative as their New York brethren. They continued to crave the approval of eastern elites, partly because they feared they might go unnoticed without it.

IN OCTOBER 1863, Harte published his first story in the *Atlantic Monthly* alongside pieces by Emerson and Thoreau. This triumph had been more than a year in the making. As early as January 1862, Thomas Starr King had recommended Harte to the *Atlantic*'s editor, his friend James T. Fields. "I am sure there is a great deal in Harte," King wrote, "and an acceptance of his piece would inspirit him, and help literature on this coast where we raise bigger trees and squashes than literati and brains." Nine months later, Jessie Benton Frémont added her endorsement. Harte possessed "a fresh mind filled with unworn pictures," she assured Fields.

A Californian writing for a New England magazine might be expected to glorify the Far West. Harte did the opposite. He wrote a revisionist tale about California's history that presented the American conquest as a tragedy, not a victory. He inverted the usual triumphalist narrative, making the pioneers villains, not heroes. In Harte's fable they come "pushing, bustling, panting, and swaggering" in search of gold, a "deceitful lure" sown by Satan himself.

As blasphemous as this might be to a California reader, it wasn't out of place in the pages of the *Atlantic*. In the same issue, Thoreau called the gold rush "the greatest disgrace on mankind," condemning the prospectors as coarse and immoral. Emerson had said much the same thing three years earlier when he described 1849 as "a rush and a scramble of needy adventurers," and "a general jail-delivery of all the rowdies of the rivers."

These patronizing appraisals belonged to a long tradition of New England's distaste for the frontier. Harte derived his dim view of California from a very different source. He spoke from the inside, as a westerner. His misgivings about the American settlement of the Pacific coast had personal roots. He had seen the mangled corpses of Indians murdered by white vigilantes at Humboldt Bay, and in his columns for the *Golden Era*, he took aim at the "bustling Yankee" wherever he appeared—the boosters who blindly worshipped progress, the philistines who put money above all else. Yet he also believed in California's promise. Here was a region rich with "romantic and dramatic possibilities . . . unrivalled in history," he later wrote.

Harte's *Atlantic* coup solidified his place at the head of the San Francisco pack. It didn't secure him a permanent place in the eastern press, however. When Mrs. Frémont tried to get more of her protégé's writings published, Fields balked. "Your young friend fails to interest," he wrote. "He is not piquant enough for the readers of the *Atlantic*." Fields wasn't wrong: Harte's early fiction fell flat.

Twain, on the other hand, had piquancy to spare. By the fall of 1863, the Virginia City troublemaker had become a fixture of the San Francisco scene. His September visit had brought fresh victories. Before returning home to Nevada, he published four features in the *Era*, enjoyed another heady dose of high society in the dining hall of the Lick House, and earned a nickname suited to his oversize personality: the Washoe Giant.

Harte and Twain may have met by this point, although their friendship didn't begin in earnest until later. They differed in almost every respect—clothing, literary taste, lifestyle—yet they would soon form a complex and highly competitive partnership, one that often strained under the weight of their intense ambitions. Together they would do more than anyone of the era to put the Far West on the national stage. In 1863, however, they still played very different roles. Harte strove to be the Pacific coast's conscience; Twain took great pleasure in being its provocateur. After a tumultuous summer, the Washoe Giant felt unstoppable. His reporting drifted ever further from fact; his sentences convulsed with antic energy. He was headed for a fall, and it came the same month Harte broke into the *Atlantic*: October.

On October 28, 1863, the *Virginia City Territorial Enterprise* published Twain's "A Bloody Massacre near Carson." The article reported gruesome murders committed by a man named Philip Hopkins: Two days earlier, Hopkins had split his wife's head with an ax and peeled off her scalp. He had bashed out the brains of six of his children with a club and knocked another two unconscious. He had mutilated and stabbed his eldest daughter.

The story caused an uproar. Newspapers in Nevada and California reprinted it—including the *Sacramento Daily Union*, one of the most powerful in the West. The next day, Twain published a retraction. The article had been a hoax. "I Take It All Back," read the headline. He said the purpose of the prank was to expose "dividend cooking," a common practice whereby the owners of certain California and Nevada companies overvalued their stock and sold out before their shareholders discovered the deceit. In "A Bloody Massacre," Hopkins becomes homicidal because he lost his savings in one such scheme. Twain used the gore to get people's attention. "The only way you can get a fact into a San Francisco journal is to smuggle it in through some great tragedy," he explained.

The reaction was swift. The *Virginia City Evening Bulletin* noted the "almost universal condemnation" of Twain's "really disgraceful sensation story," and denounced his retraction as even worse than the hoax. The *Gold Hill Daily News* slammed him for tarnishing "the already bloody reputation of our Territory." True to form, Twain refused to apologize. Instead, he counterattacked. He insulted the editor of the *News*, called the *Bulletin*'s writer "an oyster-brained idiot," and declared himself "without a pang of remorse." This only added fuel to the fire. Even the influential *Sacramento Daily Union* weighed in, blasting the *Enterprise* for abusing "the sympathies of its readers."

Although unrepentant in public, Twain brooded in private. "All this worried Mark as I had never before seen him worried," recalled Dan De Quille, a fellow *Enterprise* writer who lived with Twain in Virginia City. "I am being burned alive on both sides of the mountains," he remembered Twain saying. He had written hoaxes before, outrageous ones. Anyone with a fleeting familiarity with his work knew that he rarely told the unvarnished truth. Yet even in frontier journalism, there were limits. Predictably, the Virginia City press refused to let the matter drop. Newspapers kept on it for years. People had seen Twain's darker side, and found it hard to forget.

He was always prone to extremes. "He liked, beyond all things, to push an affair to the bitter end," William Dean Howells wrote, "and the end was never too bitter unless it brought grief or harm to another." He made a loyal friend and a ruthless enemy, as immoderate in his affections as he was in his resentments. Since boyhood he had delighted in feuds, and found no shortage of them in Virginia City, where rival journalists fought constantly, not only in print but in person. Twain liked the city's combative culture. He and his friends frequently went to a gym for an hour or two in the afternoon, and Twain grew especially fond of fencing. "In attack he was fiery and particularly dangerous," Dan De Quille recalled, "for the reason that one could not watch his eyes, which he habitually wears about half closed."

Since Twain's days as a typesetter for his brother's *Hannibal Journal*, he had excelled at making other people look stupid. He enjoyed being on the attack, and loved causing mischief. Before long, he would pull another ill-considered stunt, and be punished with an even fiercer backlash.

BY LATE 1863, San Francisco's writers were growing restless. The *Golden Era* had gone from being an amateurish frontier rag to a savvy competitor on the national scene. "As a literary paper it has no

equal on the Atlantic side," bragged the *Alta California.* Its editor, Joe
Lawrence, had cultivated illustrious newcomers like Charles Henry
Webb and homegrown talents like Harte. But as his regulars became
better known, they began to resent him for how shamelessly he
used their names to sell his paper. Webb teased Lawrence for
treating his top-tier contributors like prizefighters: not as "graceful
and elegant" men of letters but as carnival attractions, blazoned in
big letters and hyped by the *Era's* relentless publicity blitz. "[S]o
loudly is the poor paper made to blow its own trumpet," Webb wrote,
"that the popular impression will be that it is a Brazen Era."

This kind of puffery felt crass in light of the city's new sophistica-
tion. The past year had boosted San Francisco's prosperity and prestige. An influx of easterners had invigorated its culture. The Civil

Ina Coolbrith around 1871,
when she was about thirty.

War had made it rich, and set in motion the construction of the transcontinental railroad, whose western span workers began building that year. The *Era* had dominated the first phase; now a new periodical was needed, as San Francisco's Bohemians came into their own.

Building a better paper would bring Twain, Harte, and Stoddard closer together. They went from being acquaintances to friends, from colleagues in the *Era*'s crowded firmament to co-conspirators in a literary crusade of their own. Another writer joined them: Ina Coolbrith. She had stayed mostly out of sight since relocating from Los Angeles in 1862. She taught English at a language school from ten in the morning until three in the afternoon, and then returned home to help her mother wash dishes, scrub linens, and do the rest of the domestic work. She had trouble sleeping at night, persecuted by memories of her past. By the age of twenty-two she had endured an abusive husband, a humiliating divorce, and the death of her infant child. She remained wary of what she called an "unpitying world," and wrote bitter verses about suffering "the shafts of enmity and scorn." Yet she needed a way out: beyond grief, beyond the burdens of her dreary work and demanding family. In San Francisco's literary scene she would find friends, fulfillment, and, finally, a life worth living.

She first met Stoddard at the home of a mutual friend. A "slender, delicate, handsome" figure playing "dreamily" at the piano, his fingers skipping confidently across the keys, improvising a tune—this was how she remembered him some sixty years later. "We were little more than boy and girl," she recalled. He was only twenty, but his success had been swift. He no longer put poems in the *Era*'s mailbox and ran away in a cold sweat. He was now a fixture of Bohemian San Francisco: "petted and spoiled by everyone because of his youth, his physical beauty, magnetic personality," Coolbrith remembered. It helped that he looked the part: the "ideal Poet in appearance," she wrote, as "beautiful as Shelley." Especially poetic were his frequent mood swings, his soul-expiring sighs, his moments of "moonstruck vacuity."

Like the other friendships that formed what Coolbrith later called "the tribe," the bond between her and Stoddard took time to develop. Eventually they became like brother and sister: Coolbrith threatening to box his ears for some silliness, Stoddard acting puppy-ish and coy. Stoddard would always strike others as childlike, confined to the sorrows and solaces of a permanent adolescence. Coolbrith would always appear too mature for her years, having lived a lifetime by her early twenties. Neither would ever enjoy the comforts of a conventional adulthood. Both kept secrets that precluded traditional paths, and they never started families of their own. But they remained close their entire lives. "The friendship between us has been more to me than the love of any man," she once told him.

In December 1863, Coolbrith published her second poem in the *Era*. It struck a hopeful note, describing the "seedling" of spring, "growing to its slow / Yet sure fulfillment." She was steadily emerging from her shell, just in time to take part in California's latest literary experiment. In recent weeks, the *Era* had been buzzing with talk of a new periodical. "Bret and I laid our heads together over a Mint Julep the other day," Webb announced in his column, "and have determined to start a paper."

They shared a single purpose: to wage all-out war on mediocrity, materialism, and the middlebrow. They deplored California's "depraved intellectual condition," its preponderance of "nervous old dandies" and "silly young girls," its taste for clumsy melodrama and moralizing. The time had come for a new kind of journal, more discriminating in tone. The *Era* had been a good start, but the Bohemians had outgrown it. They needed a platform of their own—"a Bohemian's Protective Union," as Webb put it—modeled on more metropolitan papers like the defunct *Saturday Press*, formerly the organ of the New York Bohemians. They would enlist San Francisco's

best writers, at typically Bohemian rates. "Any author expecting pay
for anything which he contributes, is to be kicked down stairs in an
ignominious manner by the Washoe Giant, whom we intend to em-
ploy specially for that purpose," Webb declared.

In early 1864, Webb and Harte rented an office on Montgomery
Street, not far from the *Era* building, and began assembling their
first issue. Their ambitions were large. They wanted to publish not
only the best literary paper of the Pacific coast but the equal of any
on the continent. Before they got their venture off the ground, however, a sudden shock sent them reeling.

On February 26, 1864, Thomas Starr King ran into a friend on
the street. The preacher always appeared frail, but today he seemed
more fragile than usual. His bones ached, he said; his throat was
sore. He felt like a sponge squeezed dry. He feared he wouldn't be
able to preach on Sunday, and returned home to rest. The next day
he looked worse. He stayed in bed. His doctor came: the diagnosis
was diphtheria, followed by pneumonia. The symptoms grew more
severe. On the morning of March 4, he composed his will. He calmly
recited the Twenty-third Psalm—"I will dwell in the house of the
Lord forever"—and bade farewell to his two-year-old son. "Beautiful boy," he said, before the child was taken from the room, and he
closed his eyes and his breath became slower and then stopped
altogether.

Twenty thousand people came to his funeral. They gathered outside the church he had spent the last year of his life building in the
heart of the city, across from Union Square. The mourners filed
through its Gothic facade for a final glimpse of the baby-faced reverend lying serenely in an open casket at the altar. On his chest was
a bouquet of violets sent by Jessie Benton Frémont, who had learned
the tragic news by telegraph. Her dear friend was only thirty-nine
when he died. Never robust, he had worked himself to the bone on
behalf of the pro-Union campaign hatched in her parlor, and succeeded miraculously. He wasn't one of those saviors who prefer

humanity in the abstract to people in particular: in his busiest moments he still made time for targeted acts of kindness, like tracking
down a young bookstore clerk named Charles Warren Stoddard and
telling him how much he enjoyed his poetry. The grand gesture
came as easily to him as the small, intimate one, and when he died,
Californians mourned him as they would a close friend.

Of course, his actual friends felt special pain. The *Era* published
tributes from several of them. Stoddard dedicated a poem to his
memory. Coolbrith grieved the loss of her "gentle Teacher, and true
friend" in verse. Harte contributed "Relieving Guard," the best of
the lot. The poem describes a conversation between two soldiers. One
has been keeping watch during the night. When another comes to
relieve him, he says he saw a falling star, sinking in the western sky:

"A star? There's nothing strange in that."
"No, nothing; but, above the thicket,
Somehow it seemed to me that God
Somewhere had just relieved a picket."

A fitting eulogy for a man who said he didn't measure enough
inches around the chest to be a soldier, but saw a way to fight. "Every sufferer for the redemption of our land now is sacred," King once
told someone whose brother died in the Civil War. In death he, too,
became sacred. A mountain in Yosemite was named for him, and a
giant sequoia in the Calaveras Grove. In 1931, California honored
him with a statue in the US Capitol. It stood for nearly eighty years
before being replaced, in 2009, with one of Ronald Reagan. "I wasn't
sure who Thomas Starr King was," explained the legislator responsible for the change.

Fortunately for King, his legacy endured in other ways. To San
Francisco's writers he had been a patient father, scribbling edits in
the margins of their manuscripts and administering fortifying
doses of moral support. He taught them to take themselves seriously,

and helped kick-start a literary culture that, after his death, grew in directions he could have never foreseen.

TWO MONTHS AFTER SAN FRANCISCO lost its best-loved preacher, its favorite heretic returned. Twain's principal vice was pride, followed closely by greed and gluttony. He had been in Nevada for seven months, blistering from the heat of the desert sun, and he atoned for the long absence by splurging on the special charms of "the most cordial and sociable city in the Union." Feasts of fried oysters, salmon, and fowl. Parties of polka and other popular dances. He had sampled similar offerings before, but this time was different. The trunk that accompanied him across the Sierras in May 1864 held the sum total of his belongings. He had come to San Francisco to stay. "I had longed to be a butterfly," he later wrote, "and I was one at last."

Recently, Nevada had begun to lose its appeal for Twain. It wasn't just the steady diet of lager beer and Limburger cheese, or the sharp odor of sagebrush, or the dispiriting bleakness of the scenery. He had more urgent reasons for leaving. In the three years since he and his brother made the trip from Missouri in 1861, Twain had undergone a transformation. Virginia City had radicalized him, spurring him to greater wildness and defiance. His literary powers had grown precipitously in the pages of the *Territorial Enterprise*. But as he became a better writer, he had also become harsher, more inflammatory. "A Bloody Massacre near Carson," his bruising hoax from October 1863, had been an early sign. The eruptions that followed left even larger stains on his reputation, and helped hasten his exit from Virginia City.

The Civil War loomed large in all this. It drove him to Nevada in 1861 and now, through a tortured chain of events, triggered his departure. On May 5, 1864, the ladies of Carson City held a fund-raising ball for the US Sanitary Commission. This was a national charity that provided food, medicine, and other supplies to sick and wounded Union soldiers. Before his death, Thomas Starr King had raised more than a million dollars for the Sanitary cause. On May 17, 1864, readers of the *Territorial Enterprise* learned that the cash collected in Carson City wouldn't be sent to the commission's headquarters in St. Louis, but diverted "to aid a Miscegenation Society somewhere in the East."

This hoax delivered a painful blow. Twain had located a sore spot in the collective psyche and hit it as hard as he could. The idea of blacks and whites getting married wasn't simply taboo; it also tapped an anxiety about the ultimate aim of the Civil War. When the Emancipation Proclamation took effect in 1863, the Union formally committed itself to freeing the Confederacy's slaves. President Lincoln defended this as a war measure, intended to undermine the South's ability to fight, but it made many Northerners uncomfortable. They were fighting to keep their country in one piece, not to liberate the slaves. "Miscegenation" in particular meant something very specific in 1864. The term had been coined the year before, by two editors at a Democratic paper in New York. They had concocted a powerful political hoax: an anonymous pamphlet in favor of interracial marriage entitled *Miscegenation*, which they attributed to antislavery Republicans. Democrats seized on this to build momentum for their campaign to unseat Lincoln in the election of 1864, while Republicans disavowed the pamphlet and distanced themselves from such radical views. When Twain joked that the money meant for the Sanitary Commission would instead be used for miscegenation, he articulated an awful fear festering in white minds throughout the Union: that the war would result in full equality for blacks, who would soon be taking white jobs, white land, white women.

The fallout would be severe. The next day, the ladies of Carson City wrote the *Enterprise* an enraged reply. The article was "a *tissue of falsehoods*," they fumed, "made for *malicious* purposes." When the *Enterprise* refused to print the letter, the rival *Virginia City Daily*

Union ran it for three days in a row. What made the scandal especially embarrassing for Twain was the fact that Mollie Clemens, the
wife of his brother Orion, had helped organize the Sanitary ball.
When her friends learned she was Twain's sister-in-law, they ex-
pelled her from Carson City society. Three days after the hoax, he
wrote Mollie a halfhearted apology. "I am sorry the thing occurred,"
he conceded, as though through gritted teeth. It was all a drunken
misunderstanding: he had scribbled the joke when he was "not sober," and showed it to his friend Dan De Quille. They agreed it was
too offensive to publish, but he must've left the manuscript lying
around the *Enterprise* office by mistake. "I suppose the foreman,
prospecting for copy, found it, & seeing that it was in my handwriting, thought it was to be published." A public admission of guilt,
however, was out of the question. His pride wouldn't permit it. "I
cannot submit to the humiliation of publishing myself as a liar."

Meanwhile, Twain opened hostilities on a second front. Fancy
social functions weren't the only way westerners raised money for
the Sanitary Commission. A more eccentric method came from Reuel
Colt Gridley, a schoolmate of Twain's from Hannibal who owned a
grocery store in Austin, Nevada. Gridley carried a sack of flour to
nearby towns and "auctioned" it off repeatedly to benefit the Sanitary fund. The bidders knew that no one would ever win the sack:
the only prize was the pleasure of outbidding one's rivals, and in the
briskly competitive West, this proved a clever incentive to pry open
people's pocketbooks. On May 18, 1864, the day after the miscegenation prank, Twain leaped headlong into the flour-sack fray by accusing the *Daily Union* of outbidding the *Enterprise* at one of Gridley's
auctions and then refusing to pay. This was a lie, but the *Union* rose
to the bait, and soon the two papers were exchanging taunts, strut-
ting and crowing like a pair of fighting cocks. Twain hadn't picked
this particular fight so that it could fizzle into another amusing side-
show for the Washoe reading public, however. He wanted blood.

The inner devils of a man drawn to his own destruction, inflamed by large infusions of liquor and the company of violent men: this was Twain at his most menacing. On May 21, he wrote a furious letter to James Laird, the *Union*'s publisher, urging a retraction of the paper's "insulting" editorials. Laird referred him to J. W. Wilmington, the author of the offending items, who curtly refused. His bile rising, Twain called Laird a "cowardly sneak" for hiding behind Wilmington and demanded, "without alternative," the "satisfaction due to a gentleman"—in other words, a duel. Laird again deflected: "Mr. Wilmington has a prior claim upon your attention. When he is through with you, I shall be at your service." But Twain persisted and, after receiving another infuriating refusal from Laird, published their entire correspondence in the *Enterprise*, with a postscript lashing the *Union*'s publisher as an "unmitigated liar," "an abject coward," and a "fool." Twain's baiting, bullying stream of abuse had backed Laird into a corner. Then, on May 29, 1864, five days after publishing his last attack, the Washoe Giant disappeared. He boarded a stagecoach with his friend Steve Gillis, a typesetter for the *Enterprise*, and decamped for San Francisco.

The reasons are unclear. Perhaps his courage failed him, or he never intended to fight in the first place. Nevada had a strict law against dueling, stipulating a maximum penalty of ten years in prison simply for issuing a challenge. Twain alluded to this in a letter to his brother, written a few days before leaving Virginia City. Yet he was careful to make clear that he wasn't "afraid of the grand jury"—nor of Laird—but merely felt restless after three years in Nevada. He said he planned to stay in San Francisco for a month, sell some Nevada mining stock, and then return to the East. Boredom, not fear, motivated his departure: "Washoe has long since grown irksome." But his enemies didn't buy it. They proposed another possibility: shame. "The indignation aroused by his enormities has been too crushing to be borne by living man," suggested the *Gold Hill Evening News*. "Mark Twain's beard is full of dirt, and his face is black before the people of Washoe."

Not exactly a fond farewell. The sting of his self-inflicted wounds lingered. "It cannot be said he made many friends in Nevada," remarked one contemporary. In later writings, Twain finessed the infelicities of his Nevada years—the massacre hoax, the miscegenation mischief, the near-duel with Laird—either by omitting them entirely or applying a thick lacquer of lightheartedness.

But these blunders weren't his only reason for moving to San Francisco in the spring of 1864. The big city represented more than just a refuge from his mistakes; it also promised a larger canvas for his talents. Over the last year, he had cultivated his newspaper contacts there with nearly as much enthusiasm as he had indulged his appetite for shellfish and champagne. On his first visit, the *Morning Call* had hired him as its Washoe correspondent; on his second, he began writing for the *Golden Era*. Then, in late 1863, an esteemed visitor had given Twain's literary ambitions another crucial lift.

On November 8, 1863, the country's most famous comedian came to San Francisco. He called himself Artemus Ward, and counted Abraham Lincoln among his many fans. When the president presented the preliminary Emancipation Proclamation to his cabinet in 1862, he prefaced it by reading one of Ward's sketches aloud, presumably to lighten the mood before changing the course of American history forever. Artemus Ward was the pseudonym of Charles Farrar Browne, a typesetter from Maine who became America's first stand-up comic. A best-selling author, he built a booming career on the lecture circuit, wringing loud laughter from a nation that sorely needed comic relief. He was also a New York Bohemian, a regular at the beer-soaked gatherings at Pfaff's. Like his colleague Adah Isaacs Menken, whose salacious *Mazeppa* had premiered in San Francisco only three months before he came to town, Ward had a flair for publicity, and knew how to fill a theater to bursting. By the time he arrived in San Francisco, his manager had already been there for weeks, securing favorable notices in local papers and canvassing prominent citizens for their endorsements. Ward's promotions paid off. On November 13, the night of his debut, an overfull crowd packed into Platt's Music Hall. At eight o'clock, the show began.

A tall, thin man took the stage. He had a face ideally proportioned for the caricaturist's pen. His nose bulged; his hair flopped. He wore an elegant suit with white kid gloves, and spoke so softly that people in the back had trouble hearing. In his writings Ward played the part of the illiterate rube: misspelling words, mangling syntax. "Perhaps" became "praps"; "facetious," "faseshus." But under all the clowning ran a bracing current of Yankee common sense, and sharply observant insights into the foibles of his fellow Americans. Ward reprised this personality at the lectern, to tremendous effect. He often seemed to forget where he was, losing the thread of his argument. He remained solemn even when saying the silliest things. He rambled through murmured digressions that never seemed to conclude, made ample use of non sequiturs and awkward pauses. The weirder things got, the harder the audience laughed.

"The point of his lecture of course consists in having no point at all," observed the *Daily Evening Bulletin* the next day. It was a parody of traditional oratory, with none of the preachy moral pronouncements typical of the genre. Sitting in the darkened theater, Harte watched Ward closely. The secret to the showman's power, Harte intuited, lay in an unusual sensitivity to everyday American speech. Ward captured the "humor that belongs to the country of boundless prairies, limitless rivers, and stupendous cataracts," Harte wrote in the *Golden Era*—"that fun which overlies the surface of our national life, which is met in the stage, rail-car, canal and flat-boat, which bursts out over camp-fires and around bar-room stoves."

HARTE HAD HIT ON SOMETHING. Those "camp-fires" and "bar-room stoves" were the forums of the frontier. The "fun" that suffused them had a long history in American life. It dated back to the colonial era, when the West had meant the land beyond the Allegheny

Mountains, and the crude, combative men who settled it liked to taunt each other with wildly imaginative boasts. A backwoodsman might declare he had bear's claws and alligator's teeth and the devil's tail. His rival might respond in kind, with some equally bizarre bit of braggadocio, and so on, until they either started brawling or broke down laughing.

On the frontier, laughter was the great unifier. In a society of strangers, it created a sense of community. This wasn't the polite tee-heeing of eastern parlors but the knowing cackle, the cleansing guffaw of people engaged in the same daily struggle. They lived hard lives, in strange and often terrifying surroundings. Humor helped ease their gloom and isolation. They spun the unfunny facts of frontier existence into surreal comic fictions—"tall tales"—that let them laugh at themselves and bond over what they had in common.

Twain absorbed their stories. As a boy in Missouri, he had immersed himself in a particular strain of frontier humor that emerged in the Old Southwest—a loosely defined region including western Georgia, Alabama, Tennessee, Mississippi, Arkansas, and Louisiana. When Twain went to Nevada in 1861, he found plenty of Southwestern influences on the Pacific coast. The gold rush had drawn hordes of emigrants from the Mississippi River valley across the plains to the Far West—"Pikes," they were called, after the Pike County region of Missouri and Illinois. The Pikes brought their tall talk with them, and grafted the humor of past frontiers onto a new one. Their legacy could be felt everywhere, from the slangy chatter of the mining camps to the pages of the *Virginia City Territorial Enterprise*.

Artemus Ward also owed something to his Southwestern predecessors. But he managed to craft a brand of comedy with even broader appeal, becoming rich and famous on a scale unthinkable for an earlier generation of humorists. After his success in San Francisco in November 1863, he continued his western tour, working his way through California and Nevada. When he landed in Virginia City on December 18, 1863, for a pair of sold-out shows at the local branch of

Maguire's Opera House, the enfants terribles of the *Enterprise* gave him a hero's welcome. Over the next ten days, they treated him to a tour of the local sights. The bawdy, histrionic boomtown looked like something straight out of one of Ward's sketches. He loved it.

Twain and Ward liked each other instantly. They spent evenings drinking brandy and beer, cavorting with dance-hall girls, sampling Chinese liquors. Their friendship bloomed so fast that, by the end of their Washoe jaunt, Ward had taken to calling Twain "My Dearest Love" in their correspondence. Both had lost their fathers at a young age and found work as newspaper typesetters soon after. Both drew their inspiration from the inky populism of the printing room, and from frontier humor. Only one year older, Ward had pursued a parallel path, and his example gave Twain higher hopes for his own future. The famous comedian lent his new friend every encouragement. He recommended him to the editors of the *New York Sunday Mercury*, which published two of Twain's pieces in February 1864—his first appearance in the New York press. He even urged him to "leave sage-brush obscurity, & journey to New York," as Twain reported in a letter to his mother in January. When Twain fled Virginia City four months later, he didn't choose another mining town. He chose a metropolis, the kind where he could outgrow "sage-brush obscurity" and begin to build a national reputation. He soon discovered that San Francisco didn't lack for young writers with similar hopes, and that a giant in Washoe looked somewhat smaller among creatures his own size.

Montgomery Street in the 1860s.

THREE

"The birds, and the flowers, and the Chinamen, and the winds, and the sunshine, and all things that go to make life happy, are present in San Francisco to-day, just as they are all days in the year," Mark Twain wrote shortly after moving to the city in May 1864. For a man with an ear for language, the streets were a daily feast. Passersby spoke brogued, drawled, broken English, and a variety of different tongues. Signs cluttered the sidewalks, giving the names of stores and what they sold. Newspapers broadcast the price of money and mining stock, the latest troop movements by telegraph. It was a city in love with the sound of its own voice, and Twain made a noisy addition to the ensemble.

He benefited from good timing. A couple of days before he came to town, a new paper launched its inaugural issue. This wasn't uncommon: in publishing-mad San Francisco, newspapers rose and fell about as frequently as mining companies on the Comstock. But on May 28, 1864, a different sort of print product appeared on the booksellers' shelves. If many journals were migraine-inducing rags—the paper as murky as a miner's sluice, the type densely set and crooked— these pages were gloriously clean and crisp. They measured twenty-two inches across and thirty inches high, a size known in the industry as "imperial"—a word that aptly summarized the periodical's stately visual style. The letters ran level across three broad columns, easy to read without squinting. Along the top came the title, in full typographical flourish: *The Californian.*

For months, two men had been staining their fingers with newsprint at 728 Montgomery Street, racing to fill all sixteen pages of their maiden issue. Half a year had passed since Charles Henry Webb first revealed in the *Golden Era* that he and Bret Harte were planning to start a paper. They traded a few cracks on the subject but, by the spring of 1864, what began as a joke had grown dreadfully serious. The city's Bohemia had scaled upward rapidly over the past year, invigorated by eminent visitors like Artemus Ward. The *Californian* aspired to embody this new spirit, to rally the Bohemians around a single standard. Webb served as its founding editor; Harte collaborated closely. They wanted to give urban readers something worthy of the city's growing stature, and promised to enlist California's finest writers in the effort.

But creating a literary magazine from scratch, and doing it every week, turned out to be a grueling ordeal. Webb confessed the despair he felt at filling "forty-eight yawning empty columns" that swallowed everything he threw at them and "seemed no fuller than before." Harte did a pair of pieces for the front page; Webb contributed a lengthy column. In his frantic rush to get the paper to press, however, Webb failed to recruit nearly enough writers to produce original work. As a result, he loaded up on "selected" material—excerpts lifted from other newspapers, books, even encyclopedias. Padding columns with plagiarized material was a common practice in those days. Yet it also made the *Californian* a blander, less bracing read. Fortunately, the paper didn't take long to find its footing. Webb continued to rely heavily on pirated content, but the original writing improved. Over time, he and Harte honed the paper's editorial voice to an exquisitely sharp point.

The *Californian* belonged firmly to the Bohemian school of satire and suspicion pioneered by Harte in the pages of the *Golden Era*. Readers expecting tales of honest miners, or lyrical tributes to California's landscape, would be disappointed. Like Harte himself, the *Californian* took pleasure in puncturing clichés. It could be populist or aristocratic, radical or conservative—but always contrarian. Its tone was sharper than anything in the *Era*, tinged with condescension and a dandyish self-regard. This greater fearlessness came from several sources. The rising self-confidence of Bohemian San Francisco was one. The darkening mood of the Civil War was another.

PROGRESS HAD ALWAYS been an article of faith among Americans, but the barbarism of the Civil War made it look like a cruel joke. The gap between the rhetoric of combat—the stirring hymns, the lofty speeches—and its putrid, soul-killing reality inspired no small amount of cynicism. As the *Californian* observed in 1864, human civilization had ascended to such magnificent heights as to be able to guide a "bullet to a man's heart, at a distance of half a mile," and land an artillery shell on his house three miles away. Americans might well wonder whether they were becoming more civilized or more savage. Harte often asked this question on the Far Western frontier, where settlers swindled each other, massacred Indians, and despoiled the countryside—all in the name of progress.

Reading the reports from the front, Ina Coolbrith had two reactions. The first was simple: she felt grateful for her family's safety. However hard they worked to stay afloat, however tedious her job as a teacher, none of her loved ones would ever go to war. But this happy thought came burdened with a sadder one: that other people's loved ones were dying in large numbers. She had no illusions about the heroism of violence. She knew that a death didn't end with a person dying, but rippled outward in waves. Every corpse meant grief for "some desolate house-hold," she wrote in a poem, and a lifetime of mourning for the mother—a pain she understood intimately.

Against this bloody backdrop, patriotic songs about "the splendor of battle" rang hollow. "Could those battle fields open," she wrote, "[a]nd *show* what their trophies *are*."

Life in San Francisco presented more mundane challenges. The most urgent was always money. When one of her half brothers needed a job, she tried to find him work. She knew that Charles Henry Webb, formerly of the *Golden Era*, had started a new paper: she had even published verses anonymously in its pages. Perhaps he needed another printer. But when she visited the *Californian*'s office to inquire, Webb wasn't in—"a great relief to me," she later recalled, "for only necessity could have urged me on such an errand." She left a note, and something else: a poem. Days passed without a word. Then one afternoon Webb appeared at her house unannounced. Coolbrith, whose shyness had only recently begun to recede, was scared "almost to death." Webb, too, likely felt a bit tense, with a lovely young woman staring at him anxiously through the doorway. He had a face neither handsome nor homely but "on the whole rather pleasing," she decided, framed by bright blond hair. He spoke with a stutter, and said very strange things. Nearly fifty years later, she recalled their conversation:

"About your brother," he began. "Has he ever set type? I need some help in the office . . . but is he a rat?"

"A rat?"

"Yes," he said, "a r-r-at! Y-you know the-the pr-printers have a-a un-union, and all ou-outsiders are ca-called r-rats."

As it happened, Coolbrith's half brother wasn't a rat: he was too young, which meant Webb could hire him as an apprentice. The conversation turned to another topic.

"A-and now a-about your p-p-poem," Webb said. "I have seen your n-name and know s-s-something of you, b-but you are r-rather y-young, and this v-v-verse of yours, is . . . ac-ccepted, of course, but h-have you a-any others?"

What Webb feared, he later confessed, was that Coolbrith had stolen the poem. He didn't mind poaching from other papers, so long as he attributed his "selections" properly; ripping off other writers, however, was unforgivable. Because of her youth and beauty, or simply because she was a woman, people always doubted her talent. As a schoolgirl in Los Angeles, she had written a poem for her composition class that the teacher refused to believe was her own. The little poet burst into tears. Her mother brought other specimens from home to persuade the school's principal that the lines were genuine, and the ordeal had a happy ending: the principal sent the verses to the editor of the *Marysville Express*, who published them.

The meeting with Webb went well. Coolbrith began writing regularly for the *Californian* and, despite the awkwardness of their first encounter, warmed to its editor. "He had a mother at home whom he devotedly loved," she remembered, "and I had a mother whom I devotedly loved." Family was sacred to Coolbrith, and she valued it in others. Webb began spending more time at her house, writing in her parlor. With his irrepressible good humor and stammering wit, his captaincy of the *Californian* and his stature in the city's Bohemian scene, he helped undo the defensive shielding that had insulated her for years. The kinder, funnier woman within began to filter through the cracks.

Coolbrith would bring a distinct sensibility to the Bohemians of the Pacific coast. Her style had evolved since her Los Angeles days. Her language had acquired a certain compacted precision, as in her portrait of a pouty girl:

> *Cheeks of an ominous crimson,*
> > *Eyebrows arched to a frown*
> *Pretty red lips a-quiver*
> > *With holding their sweetness down.*

She had tamed the breathlessness of her early verse, and replaced it with a more measured rhythm. Still, her poetry was stuck in a single gear, dogged by an unrelentingly mournful tone that made it feel monotonous. Her writing contained little of the keen irony that defined her personality, and made her such a valued addition to the Bohemian circle. She would never indulge her comic impulses as freely as her *Californian* colleagues. In fact, she despised puns and parodies. To her, Artemus Ward represented rock bottom for American culture: his ungrammatical "buffoonery" pandered to a "tawdry and vitiated" public taste. But while she hated humor writing, she could muster withering blasts of wit—as when, in her first prose piece for the *Californian*, she ridiculed those "model wives" who passed their lives in meek devotion to their "lord and master." She would never know the supreme bliss of darning her husband's socks. She would never accept the idea that "puddings rather than poetry" were "the proper sphere of woman."

By remarrying, she might have escaped the drudgery of earning a living at the schoolhouse and the hours spent helping her mother at home. But singledom had its rewards. For one, it freed her to pursue intense friendships with men without facing scrutiny from a jealous spouse. And San Francisco was full of interesting men. She met many through Webb. She almost certainly encountered Twain around this time, although they never became close. He left no record of her, and evidence for their friendship is scant. Her relationships with the rest of the Bohemians would be far more memorable.

One day while out walking, Webb and Ina paused outside the stout brick building that housed the *Californian*. As they stood talking, the door opened and a young man stepped across the threshold. In Coolbrith's memory he appeared "slightly built," with "large brownish gray eyes, slightly drooping at the corners," and skin pitted with smallpox. They moved aside to let him pass, but then Webb thought better of it.

"Wait a m-moment," he said. "Ina, this is Fr-Frank: Frank, th-this is I-na. N-now you b-be g-good to her."

Francis Brett Harte—"Frank" to his friends—was a name that

she knew. It was Harte's full name, which he still used to sign his pieces. By the end of the decade his byline would shrink to Bret Harte, and it was by this name that he became most famous. The first time Coolbrith saw Thomas Starr King speak, he had read Harte's poetry aloud. He led a charmed life, earning a comfortable income from his sinecure at the mint that gave him time to refine his work through a stern regimen of rewriting. No one could possibly be harder on Harte than he was on himself. The countless drafts that filled his wastebasket revealed a writer for whom one false note would be a humiliating defeat. He seemed to embody California's hopes for itself as its fortunes rose with the Civil War. With his distinguished dress and quiet courtesy, he suggested a future beyond the frontier, a metropolitan maturity to follow the Far West's gunsmoke-and-whiskey adolescence.

Coolbrith found him attractive. He was "manly," she later said, though not in the traditional sense. His masculinity was of a mellower sort. After their introduction, they corresponded about her poems for the *Californian*. For a man with a caustic literary edge and relentlessly high standards, he treated her with exceptional kindness. He once replied to a selection of her verses with the flattering remark that they were all so good he had trouble choosing which to publish. And when he didn't like one, he provided gentle criticisms to help her improve. "Every man has sometime in his life said something good," he told her. "[I]t is the habit of being smart that makes the good writer or poet, and the power of carrying a thought or fancy to completeness that makes the article or poem." Art was hard work: it demanded consistency. Guided by Harte, Coolbrith grew. The *Californian* meant the beginning of something better, when she found a path out of her imprisoning past and into a brighter future.

BY THE SUMMER OF 1864, San Francisco no longer needed visitors from the East to feed its creativity: it now generated heat of its own.

Since appearing in May, the *Californian* had become, in the words of its editor, an "established fact." The press embraced it. The *Morning Call* praised the paper's "charming repose, easy address, and delicacy of perception." The *Alta California* called it a "welcome visitor in every house." The *Sacramento Daily Bee* named it the "best looking paper ever printed in the State." "It is not of the wishy-washy, sentimental, sickly order of publications," wrote the *Marysville Express*, "but one which we hope Californians will be proud to recognize as one of our coast."

The *Californian* made people feel proud to be Californian. It was a triumph: gorgeously printed, ambitiously edited, a periodical for an ascendant Pacific coast. Webb encouraged this impression, advertising the *Californian* as a paper devoted to "the best interests of California." Yet on closer inspection, its pages carried little to inspire local pride. On the contrary: the picture of California that emerged from the *Californian* was largely harsh and unflattering. An undertow of contempt touched topics trivial and profound: California's climate was too mild, its people too ignorant, its culture too crude. This was the paradox at the heart of the paper. It benefited from California boosterism even as it skewered California. It serialized "sensation novels" by best-selling genre hacks like Mary Elizabeth Braddon while mocking them for being poorly written. It criticized pulpy melodrama while using it to lift sales. When Webb republished the report of a child sacrifice in Haiti, he insisted it was only for educational purposes: not "to pander to the popular appetite for horror" but to shed light on a dangerous superstition. The real reason, of course, was economic. The *Californian* cost money to run, and needed to cater to popular taste to survive.

Charles Warren Stoddard published his first poem in the *Californian* in July 1864. It described, in tender language, the process of death by drowning. If these suicidal verses offered any indication, the young poet had hit a breaking point. That summer, he had finished his first year at Brayton Academy in Oakland. School had

become a daily nightmare of fear and humiliation. Academic success eluded him. As soon as he stopped reading a book, its contents
drained from his memory like water. Nothing he did could make his
brain a better container.

By the end of the semester he was a "nervous wreck," he wrote.
Brayton Academy had broken him. His family brought in a doctor,
who suggested a change of scenery. Long trips to faraway places
were thought to be therapeutic. So in August 1864, Stoddard set sail
for the Sandwich Islands, as Hawaii was then known. His parents
had friends in Honolulu, and Stoddard felt deliriously grateful to be
going. Ever since seeing Nicaragua as an eleven-year-old boy, crossing the isthmus on his way to California, he had longed to return to
the tropics. His daydreams were populated by monkeys and parrots,
mango trees and coconut palms. The journey to Hawaii would do
more than just reunite him with this landscape; it would alter "the
whole current" of his life, he later said. In the farther frontier of the
Pacific Islands, he found a way to live without wanting to die.

BY THE TIME Stoddard left San Francisco, Twain had settled in. He
had begun the typical way after arriving in May 1864, blowing his
money on assorted extravagances and rooming at the luxurious
Occidental Hotel—"Heaven on the half shell," he called it. Within
days, however, the honeymoon ended and a sobering reality set in.
Twain had expected to earn a fortune by selling the mining stocks
he acquired in Nevada. But as their value plummeted, and his
prospective riches shrank to a more modest sum, he realized he
wouldn't survive as a speculator. He needed a job.

Once, in a vainer moment, Twain had told his mother he could
work for a San Francisco paper whenever he wanted. He was right.
Within a week of arriving, he had joined the *Morning Call* as a local
reporter. He already knew the editors from his stint as the *Call*'s
Nevada correspondent. And, despite the recent uproar in Nevada

over the miscegenation hoax, he still enjoyed broad popularity in the California press. On June 12, 1864, when a group of prominent citizens gathered at Maguire's Opera House to honor an army engineer who had salvaged a sunken warship, they asked Twain to deliver the opening address. He nailed it, delivering a mock-pompous monologue that would've made Artemus Ward proud.

In San Francisco he lived with Steve Gillis, the *Territorial Enterprise* typesetter who came with him from Virginia City. In their first four months, they moved seven times. Gillis was a short, sinewy southerner with a feared reputation as a barroom brawler, and he shared Twain's prankish bent. For fun they played billiards, or lobbed empty beer bottles onto the tin roofs of their Chinese neighbors and got cursed out in Cantonese.

These diversions aside, life in San Francisco proved harder than Twain expected. The *Call* made him miserable. His days began at the courthouse at nine in the morning, collecting material for the local column. After enduring hours of testimony—an old man claimed a woman whacked him with a basket, but he only spoke German and was too deaf to hear anything the lawyers said—he visited the city's six theaters, lingering just long enough to scribble a few notes on the half-dozen performances. Around eleven at night, he returned to the *Call*'s office to sift through his notebook's dreary, doodled expanses for a kernel of presentable copy.

It's hard to imagine a profession less suited to Twain's personality than daily journalism. Four decades later he still shuddered at the memory of its "soulless drudgery." Satisfying his nightly quota caused him endless suffering: it was "awful slavery for a lazy man," he recalled. Worse, the *Call* wanted him to report facts. At the *Enterprise* he had enjoyed wide latitude with the truth, roaming freely. At the *Call* he strained against a much shorter leash. He was no longer "Mark Twain," but an anonymous hack, churning out unsigned items for each morning's edition.

To console himself he employed a few tricks from his *Enterprise* days. He managed some mild hoaxing, and sparked a feud with a rival reporter at the *Alta California* named Albert S. Evans, who christened Twain the "sage-brush Bohemian." But Twain couldn't antagonize everyone equally. Certain targets were off limits. After seeing a pack of thugs throwing stones at a Chinese laundryman, he wrote an angry account of the incident—only to have it killed by his editor. "He said that the *Call* was like the New York *Sun* of that day," Twain remembered. "It gathered its livelihood from the poor and must respect their prejudices or perish." The Irish read the *Call*, and despised the Chinese. The paper couldn't afford to offend them.

Discouraged, Twain almost abandoned writing altogether. A friend who recalled running into him during his *Call* days said he planned to leave California and resume his career as a steamboat pilot. The Mississippi meant freedom: an "unfettered and entirely independent" existence, plus a generous salary. His friend begged him to reconsider. "You have a style of writing that is fresh and original and is bound to be popular," he said. "If you don't like the tread-mill work of a newspaper man, strike up higher."

Twain took the advice to heart. If he had put down his pen in 1864, he would've been rapidly forgotten. He might be vilified for his hoaxes or admired for his cleverness, but sooner or later his name would fade, along with the other minor-league wits who enlivened the era's newspapers. Instead, he stayed in San Francisco and struck up higher. It would be a rocky ascent. The city humbled him often. It pushed him to the brink of bankruptcy and suicide, and inspired moments of difficult soul-searching. But in the process he grew more profound, more perceptive. His satire became more socially astute. His humor developed a lacerating moral edge.

San Francisco broadened him. The city was considerably more complex than the one he had left behind in Nevada. In the court-room where Twain spent his mornings for the *Call*, so many differ-ent languages were spoken that the official interpreter knew "fifty-six Chinese dialects," he later quipped in his autobiography.

Daily journalism gave him a swift education in this cosmopolitan social world, and plenty to stir his moral outrage. He met crooked officials and lazy, brutal cops, and watched society reward the strong and the shameless.

But San Francisco's greatest gift to Twain was its Bohemia. He had been a visiting member for the past year, and returned in 1864 just as the *Californian* made its celebrated debut. The stylish new paper impressed him. He cheered the "sterling literary weekly" in the *Call* and singled out Harte for special praise. "Some of the most exquisite productions which have appeared in its pages emanated from his pen," Twain wrote, "and are worthy to take rank among even Dickens' best sketches." This was an unusually generous judgment from a writer who never missed a chance to draw blood. The *Californian* marked a new stage in the evolution of the literary West, and Twain desperately wanted to evolve along with it.

He soon had his chance. The *Call* shared a building with the branch office of the US Mint where Harte worked. As Harte remembered, the *Call*'s editor brought Twain downstairs one day to introduce him. The scruffy stranger made an impression. "His head was striking," Harte recalled. "He had the curly hair, the aquiline nose, and even the aquiline eye—an eye so eagle-like that a second lid would not have surprised me—of an unusual and dominant nature." His eyebrows were "bushy," his dress "careless." He exuded "supreme indifference to surroundings and circumstances."

To Twain, Harte presented a different picture. He had a "distinctly pretty" face, despite his smallpox scars. If Twain dressed like a tramp, Harte was at the other end of the sartorial spectrum: always "more intensely fashionable than the fashionablest of the rest of the community," Twain noted. He often wore a brightly colored necktie—"a flash of flame under his chin . . . [or] indigo blue and as hot and vivid as if one of those splendid and luminous Brazilian butterflies had lighted there." However hard Twain tried to feign indifference, Harte had the upper hand. He was not only California's most important writer, but had recently become editor of its most important literary paper, the *Californian*, while Webb was away. He held the keys to the kingdom, and his first encounter with Twain probably had the air of a job interview.

It was a miracle they were able to communicate at all. Twain "spoke in a slow, rather satirical drawl," Harte recalled. He himself had a smooth, silvery voice, perfect for a lady's parlor. In their writing they sounded even less alike. Since childhood, Twain had been listening to people tell stories, from the slaves of the antebellum South to the boatmen of the Mississippi. The mongrel infinities of American English played in his ear, inspiriting his writing with the spontaneity of living speech. Harte took a more bookish approach. His references were literary, the result of many lonely hours spent reading, and he composed his prose with as much prickly care as his clothing. Later, after the relationship between the two men soured, Twain would see Harte's fastidiousness as evidence of his insincerity: both his dress and his writing belonged to the same cynical stagecraft, Twain fumed, the affectations of a hollow man. At the time, however, the *Call*'s local reporter admired the *Californian*'s editor and star contributor. The dapper young writer behind the desk at the US Mint had polish, discipline, and prestige, precisely the qualities Twain lacked.

The meeting went well: Twain got the job. "I have engaged to write for the new literary paper," he told his mother and sister on September 25, 1864, burying any anxiety he felt under a barrage of smugness. "I quit the 'Era,' long ago," he wrote. "It wasn't high-toned enough." His new gig promised a less provincial readership. "The 'Californian' circulates among the highest class of the community, and is the best weekly literary paper in the United States."

He would soon have more time for his literary labors, after the *Call* fired him in mid-October. "It was true that we had long desired to dispense with Mark's services," recalled one of his superiors, "but had a delicacy about bluntly telling him so." They tried dropping "broad hints to that effect," without any result. Finally, the *Call*'s editor, George Barnes, took Twain aside and suggested he resign. Barnes liked Twain, and he went about it in the friendliest possible way. "It was like a father advising a son for his good," Twain remembered, "and I obeyed." Even so, it hurt. Forty-two years later, when the *Call* building burned during the earthquake and fire of 1906, the former reporter couldn't conceal his pleasure at his long-delayed revenge.

Losing his job at the *Call* did more than wound his pride. It also did serious damage to his pocketbook. He had recently reduced his hours, earning $25 a week. By contrast, the *Californian* paid him $50 a month—half his former salary. Thus began a long period of barely keeping his head above water. "It was a terrible uphill business," observed his old boss Barnes, "and a less determined man than him would have abandoned the struggle and remained at the base." But when Twain committed to a task, he brought a terrifying amount of energy to it. "Mark was the laziest man I ever knew in my life, physically," said his roommate Steve Gillis. "Mentally he was the hardest worker I ever knew."

For the next two months, Twain undertook his most ambitious writing to date. From October 1 to December 3, 1864, he published nine pieces in the *Californian*. They reflected a writer who, though still frisky with liquor and frontier humor, had begun to make a deeper investment in literary craft. He did a series of finely chiseled parodies of popular newspaper genres, spoofing advice columnists, theater critics, and local reporters. The moral dimension of his work began to mature. He still told lies, but for better reasons: small, funny lies meant to illuminate large, unfunny ones. These were fictions in pursuit of the truth, and they enabled Twain to probe the distance between what people said and what they did, between how America saw itself and what it actually looked like. He took aim at the sentimental romance story with "Whereas," a tale about a woman whose fiancé loses all four limbs to gruesome accidents, an eye to disease, and his scalp to an Indian. Despite being "deeply grieved to see her lover passing from her by piecemeal," she wonders whether she should still marry him. It was a viciously funny assault on the idea that love conquers all, with the specter of the Civil War lurking between the lines. The fiancé's slow dismemberment echoed the mutilating violence of the battlefields back East. In both cases, a delusion—the glory of war, the invincibility of love—had been deflated by a bitter reality.

Before Twain could dig deeper, extraliterary considerations put his writing on hold. In late November 1864, Steve Gillis beat a bartender within an inch of his life. He was arrested, and then released on bail after Twain signed a $500 bond. Gillis decided to flee before facing charges, and Twain, who would now be required to pay hundreds of dollars he didn't have, followed suit. Gillis returned to Virginia City, while Twain traveled to Tuolumne County, where Gillis's brother Jim owned a cabin in the heart of California mining country. There, among the gulches of the old Mother Lode, Twain would make an astonishing find: in a region already stripped of its resources, a wealth of literary material existed. For the next twelve weeks, his notebook swallowed it whole.

IF GILLIS HADN'T smashed a beer pitcher across a bartender's head, Twain might never have spent nearly three months in the Sierras. Such were the "queer vicissitudes" of life in the Far West, as he called them. A man might lose his fortune on the stock market and make it back at the faro table. An earthquake might periodically rearrange people's houses. At any point one's circumstances might change, radically.

In December 1864, soon after Twain hightailed it out of San Francisco, Stoddard returned home after four months away. The trip to Hawaii had transformed him. He had stayed with a family friend outside Honolulu, and spent many blissful hours lying in a hammock and browsing the shelves of the local bookstore. The thick, slumberous air soothed the grim memory of his failed year at Brayton Academy. He met fellow expatriates like Enoch Wood Perry Jr., a San Francisco painter. Together they took a trip to the Big Island, where Perry wanted to sketch the scenery.

Touring the island on horseback, they spent a week in the home of a missionary at Hilo. Each afternoon, Stoddard visited a nearby waterfall. A mountain stream skated across a sheet of volcanic rock, vaulted off a cliff, and fell into an oasis fifty feet below. Floating in the water were naked brown bodies—young natives on their daily swim—and this was the real reason Stoddard went: to admire "angels in liquid amber," arching "their lithe length in ecstasy." One of the bathers, Kane-Aloha, became his companion. "Friendship ripens quickly in the tropical sunshine," Stoddard recalled.

Perry strongly disapproved. Twelve years older, he presumably felt responsible for his young, eccentric friend. But Stoddard outsmarted him. He persuaded Perry to enlist Kane-Aloha as their guide, and then lost his "chaperone" in the bush. "I cut loose from the gentleman who was nobly striving to restrain me," he remembered, "and became an easy convert to the un-trammelled delights of barbarians." Kane-Aloha led him through the jungle, feeding him freshly picked fruit. "We reveled in riotous living," Stoddard remembered. "We had certainly transgressed the unwritten law but we were not in the least sorry for it."

What kind of transgression, Stoddard never said. He and Kane-Aloha were almost certainly lovers, and their parting, as he reminisced in a later sketch, was an emotional one. Long after Stoddard left, the tropics remained engraved in his mind: a landscape of kaleidoscopic color, the cure to the monochrome Presbyterianism of his childhood. Like Paul Gauguin three decades later, Stoddard saw the Pacific Islands as a refuge from civilization. He considered the people primitive, unembarrassed by their sexuality, uncontaminated by the shame that weighed so heavily on him. This fantasy

sustained his lifelong obsession with "barbarianism." He infan-
tilized the natives—partly to make his affection for them more in-
nocent, partly because he felt more comfortable with children, being
childlike himself.

Back home, he nerved himself for another semester in Oakland.
It wouldn't take long for him to realize, once again, that he would
"never become a student worthy of the name." Fortunately, he had
an extracurricular source of sanity: the *Californian* still wanted his
poems. These were no longer the semi-saccharine warblings of Pip
Pepperpod, the parlor tricks of a precocious child hoping for another
pat on the head, but the tighter lines of a more mature poet, signed
under his full name: Charles Warren Stoddard.

He couldn't have asked for better company. As 1865 dawned, the
Californian entered its finest year: the moment when it finally fulfilled its promise to be the best literary paper of the Pacific coast
and the equal of any on the continent. Bret Harte, Mark Twain, Ina
Coolbrith, and Charles Warren Stoddard made regular appearances.
Eastern newspapers lifted liberally from its pages. Webb, who had
returned as editor, protested loudly about the practice, although he
undoubtedly loved the attention. In fact, plagiarism was the least of
his problems. The *Californian* suffered from a permanent shortage
of cash. As Webb put it, the paper "nearly bankrupted" him "in an
inconceivably short space of time." By April 1865, he had run out of
money to pay his contributors and moved the offices into an alley off
Montgomery Street.

But the future of California literature could wait: that spring,
momentous news came tapping over the telegraph wire. Ulysses S.
Grant and William Tecumseh Sherman were tightening the Union's
stranglehold on the South. Four years after the first shot at Fort
Sumter, the Civil War was almost over. On April 3, 1865, the Confederate capital of Richmond fell to Union forces. When the report
reached San Francisco, people took to the streets to celebrate. On
April 9, Robert E. Lee surrendered. Thomas Starr King's dream had

come true: the Confederacy crushed, the Union triumphant, and California standing proudly on the winning side. The Pacific coast would never again see America as something separate: the abstraction of national life had become a living Union, fused in the crucible of war, bound not only by geography but by bloodshed, myth, and the terse eloquence of Lincoln.

AT 10:20 P.M. ON APRIL 14, 1865, John Wilkes Booth put a bullet in the brain of the president. Lincoln spent nine hours in a coma and died at 7:22 a.m. the next day. That afternoon, as mournful streams of Morse code crisscrossed the continent, 150 citizens of San Francisco assembled at the corner of Montgomery and Clay. They marched to the offices of the *Daily Democratic Press*, broke into the building, and demolished the composing room. They stormed another anti-Lincoln paper, and another, before a squad of fifty policemen and the city's military commander persuaded them to disperse.

That night, the army kept the peace. San Francisco looked like an occupied city of the defeated South, with troops in formation, cavalry rattling the pavement. The evening passed without incident, and by Wednesday, April 19, the city had found a more dignified way to express its grief. A funeral procession fifteen thousand strong snaked through the streets. Six white horses shrouded in black drew a casket emblazoned with LINCOLN in gold letters, surrounded by soldiers, clergymen, foreign consuls, and toward the rear, a large number of black men. They stopped at Union Square, where a fraction of them fit in the crowded pavilion and the rest remained outside to listen until the services ended and everyone sang "The Battle Hymn of the Republic."

I have read a fiery gospel writ in burnished rows of steel: Harte, a patriot who had written many pro-Union poems, found his pen paralyzed at the news of Lincoln's death. A reality too terrible to render in words, it shattered his composure and brought a demoralizing sense of uncertainty. In an article for the next issue of the *Californian*, printed with heavy black borders between its columns to commemorate the fallen president, Harte tried to focus his thoughts. Lincoln didn't just lead the nation, Harte reflected: he embodied it. The landscape of the West lived through him: his tall, lanky frame relayed the "continuity of endless rivers and boundless prairies," his "eloquence and humor" drew its power from "the easy intercourse of the pioneer."

Everyone knew that Lincoln was a westerner. He had been born in a log cabin on the Kentucky frontier, planted crops on his father's farm, and practiced law on the prairies. Supporters revered him as "the rail-splitter," the ax-swinging pioneer who built fences from split wood, and he still had enough backcountry in his blood to laugh heartily at Artemus Ward during the darkest days of the Civil War. But Harte's point went deeper: Lincoln did more than save the Union. This "simple-minded, uncouth, and honest" westerner liberated America from the cultural choke hold of New England—those Anglophilic Brahmins with their "crisp and dapper style of thought," which had for so long "retarded the formation of National character." Decades earlier, Thomas Hart Benton had predicted that a new, original civilization would sprout on western soil. Lincoln prepared the ground for this flowering. He tilted the continent's center of gravity: not only from South to North, but from East to West, fulfilling a long line of Jeffersonian prophecy.

But the Civil War, like all revolutions, didn't change everything all at once. Politically, America emerged from the conflict transformed; culturally, it hadn't fully absorbed the shift. American literature still awaited its Lincoln. The Bohemians of San Francisco offered a promising alternative to New England, but so far had yielded little on a par with Emerson or Thoreau. The *Californian*, despite its tasteful typography and metropolitan polish, still felt young: the work of writers in their twenties, quicker to criticism than to creation. Its strongest suit was always parody—parody as a petri dish for the budding writer: a way to study style, to digest influences, to ventriloquize different voices.

In the summer of 1865, Harte began publishing his "Condensed Novels" in the *Californian*. These were artful pastiches of famous novelists, with each writer's idiosyncrasies amplified to the point of absurdity. His victims included writers he loved, like Dickens, and those he didn't, like the popular sensationalist Mary Elizabeth Braddon. James Fenimore Cooper, whose *Leatherstocking Tales* had cast a sickeningly genteel glow over the American frontier for decades, came in for an especially satisfying shellacking. The "Condensed Novels" succeeded because of Harte's freakishly precise ear for word music, for how subtle shifts of language produced different chords of meaning.

He showed less enthusiasm when it came to producing compositions of his own, however. He wrote no fiction during his years at the *Californian*, abandoning the narrative vein that had produced his debut in the *Atlantic Monthly*. Perhaps he preferred to put his energy into parodies; perhaps certain domestic developments made it harder to concentrate. His second son was born on March 5, 1865: Francis King Harte, named for the late Thomas Starr King. Harte took fatherhood seriously. A visitor to his house might find the distinguished writer on all fours, wearing a feather duster on his back, pretending to be a funeral hearse while his children delightedly took part in the procession.

His friends admired his devotion. When Webb came over one day, he discovered his friend lying on the floor, using his feet to catapult one of his boys into the air, "turning the little fellow over like a butter-ball, and making him throw all sorts of [somersaults] and hand-springs." Then, abruptly, the fun ended. "A summary stop was put to the amusement when Mrs. Bret entered the room," Webb observed, "and from the rapidity with which the curtain fell on the performance, I've an idea that she does not wish to see her children made a circus of." Webb had stumbled upon the central friction of

Harte's home life. Fatherhood made him happy; marriage made him miserable.

Anna Griswold Harte may not deserve the scathing descriptions left by her husband's friends over the years, although the sheer number of them suggests there is some truth to their collective portrait of her as jealous, tyrannical, pretentious, stubborn, sullen, and shrewish. At the very least, Mr. and Mrs. Harte had little in common, as their grandson tactfully put it decades later. Photographs reveal a woman with low-lidded, unplayful eyes and a thin mouth firmly set in its grooves—"positively plain," in the judgment of William Dean Howells's wife, Elinor. She came from a wealthy New York family, a fact flamboyantly transmitted by her expensive tastes and faultless posture. Whether she considered her husband's literary calling insufficiently aristocratic, or coveted the time it took, she interfered with his writing at every opportunity. Their marriage became a lesson in low-intensity warfare, a game of sabotage and subversion. She conducted constant insurgencies to destroy his peace and quiet, and the struggle only intensified as his success grew.

The *Californian* helped keep him sane. It offered an alternative family: looser knit, but no less in need of a father figure. He couldn't clown around on the floor with its contributors, perhaps, but he could enjoy the subtler satisfactions of nurturing their talent and watching them succeed. He spent time with Twain, helped Stoddard with his poetry, cultivated a closer acquaintance with Coolbrith. She was everything his wife wasn't: smart, sympathetic, beautiful. Her eyes were large and gray, her voice soft and deep. Her skin had the color of olives or, in Stoddard's words, "the ripe glow of the pomegranates." If Anna Griswold was a creature of the Northeast, Coolbrith "might easily have been mistaken for a daughter of Spain," Stoddard said: the dark eyes, the flushed skin, "the contralto voice," streaked with "gentle melancholy," always "Spanish and semitropical." She also had a sense of humor. Harte loved to tell funny tales about his children, and recite the limericks he wrote for them. "We used to shout with laughter at these child-stories and verses, recounted in his inimitable manner," she remembered.

Coolbrith gave Harte the female companionship he couldn't find at home. In return, he provided something equally valuable: a supportive mentor. By 1865, she had begun to reveal more of herself in her writing. In March, she published "The Mother's Grief" in the *Californian*, a poem that hinted at her long-hidden heartache over her dead child. About the same time, she showed another, fiercer side in a pair of meandering essays. In one, she sneered at the Victorian domesticity that Anna Griswold Harte and other American women embraced:

> Unfortunately, I seldom attend balls and merry-makings, being a very quiet, stay-at-home little body; in fact, one of those model wives, of which the newspapers are forever preaching, who pass their lives in a most exemplary devotion to the members of their own households, alternating between the bliss of mending husband's stockings and feeding "Mrs. Winslow's Soothing Syrup" to a teething baby.

Coolbrith would never make a model wife. If she ever felt shame at this fact before, it had by now become a badge of pride. This was the root of her Bohemianism: not the supercharged sexuality of Adah Isaacs Menken, who married four men in ten years, but a refusal to play the game. Even later in life, when marriage might have saved her from financial hardship, she held firm. "Why doesn't some rich man fall in love with me, and give me a chance—to refuse him!" she told Stoddard. In 1865 she was twenty-four. Instead of "mending husband's stockings," she rode the streetcar to the end of the line and strolled along the sand at North Beach, not far from where Jessie Benton Frémont once lived on Black Point. "How grand the Bay looks with its white waves dashing on the shore," she rhapsodized in the *Californian*, "and stern old Alcatraz yonder, standing like a tried and faithful sentinel keeping watch and ward over the hidden treasures of the deep."

It was the same view that Harte had seen in 1860 when he first met Mrs. Frémont at her house, in that unimaginably distant day when James Buchanan sat in the White House and no American had ever filed an income tax return or fired a Gatling gun. Thomas Starr King was still an unknown preacher, often joining Harte in Jessie's parlor for conversations on poetry and politics and how to steel California for the coming conflict as the South inched closer to secession. In the half decade since, the country had been split and brutally sutured. California had prospered. King had shown heroism in life and been deified in death. Harte had gone from setting type for the *Golden Era* to co-editing the *Californian*, and now led a literary scene vastly more sophisticated and self-aware. Writers of proven talent had materialized from the primordial soup of the Far Western frontier. And Twain was on the verge of a discovery that would eventually enable him to eclipse all of them.

A replica of Jim Gillis's cabin on Jackass Hill, 1947. "The headquarters of all Bohemians visiting the mountains," Dan De Quille called it.

* * *

ON DECEMBER 4, 1864, Twain arrived at Jackass Hill in Tuolumne County, where Steve Gillis's brother Jim had a cabin. The contrast with San Francisco couldn't have been more complete. During the gold rush, the area overflowed with prospectors. Now only a handful remained: a "forlorn remnant," Twain wrote, human ruins in a lunar landscape. These raw, desperate men had no hope of becoming millionaires. The boom was over: they were lucky if they gleaned enough gold from the exhausted earth to cover their grocery bills. These were the survivors of 1849, the ones who hadn't sailed home, or destroyed their bodies with overwork, or died of delirium tremens in dilapidated boardinghouses, or been shot or stabbed in street fights. In their clay-stained faces, the myth of the heroic pioneer met harsh reality.

The cabin at Jackass Hill presented a cheerier picture. It was a hallowed spot in the literary geography of the Far West: the "head-quarters of all Bohemians visiting the mountains," in the words of Twain's friend Dan De Quille. Harte had stayed there in the mid-1850s, absorbing the scenes of mining country that would later infuse his fiction. He came "ragged and hungry," Jim Gillis remembered, and sullen with despair over his yet-unacknowledged genius. Jim let him stay a week before putting $50 in his pocket and sending him back to San Francisco. Years later, after Harte became famous, he treated his former host so rudely that Jim demanded his money back.

Twain was in a bad mood when he arrived. The weather didn't help. The winter rain fell constantly, turning the soil to sludge. He shared the cabin's damp, narrow confines with three men: Jim Gillis, Jim's brother Billy, and their mining partner Dick Stoker. After San Francisco, Twain's new surroundings almost certainly came as a shock. Here he ate beans, not shellfish. Worse, the "high-toned" literary career he had spent the last two months cultivating—producing weekly pieces for the *Californian*—came skidding to a halt. For fifteen weeks, he published nothing in the San Francisco papers.

But rural California had its rewards. Jim Gillis was one of them. A native of Mississippi, he bridged the two worlds of the Far West, fusing Bohemian brains with backwoods brawn. He knew how to mine gold, and how to read Latin and Greek. He stocked his shelves with Byron, Shakespeare, and Dickens. Best of all, he told stories. Decades later, Twain recalled how Jim would "stand up before the great log fire" and soberly deliver "an elaborate impromptu lie." He studied Jim's special genius: how he made it up as he went along, "enjoying each fresh fancy," not caring "whether the story shall ever end brilliantly and satisfactorily or shan't end at all." It resembled the storytelling of the slaves Twain heard as a boy, and drew heavily on the Southwestern humor that had shaped him as a writer. As he watched Jim solemnly conjure "monstrous fabrications" from thin air, the literary possibilities of this soggy patch of California began to unfold in Twain's mind.

In Angel's Camp, a decrepit mining town seven miles from Jackass Hill, Twain struck an even richer vein. He and Jim traveled there on a prospecting trip in late January 1865. By all accounts, Twain never had any luck digging for gold. He preferred lounging at the local tavern, observing the society of "marooned miners" who gathered by the stove. He sketched them in his notebook—"T.—Age 38—stature 6, weight 180"—and recorded snatches of overheard dialogue. He catalogued the meals: "beans & dishwater" most days and, on special occasions, four kinds of soup known as "Hellfire, General Debility, Insanity & Sudden Death." He heard tall tales, including one about a jumping frog. On February 6, he scribbled the following:

Coleman with his jumping frog—bet stranger $50—stranger had no frog, & C got him one—in the meantime stranger filled C's frog full of shot & he couldn't jump—the stranger's frog won.

The story involved a contest between two frogs. One man wagered his frog could jump higher. Another man accepted, and then secretly stuffed a handful of quail shot into the other frog's mouth to make him too heavy to jump. As with Jim Gillis, the storyteller delivered these particulars with unsmiling sternness, as if he were relating "austere facts." Neither he nor his listeners laughed. He "was not telling it to his hearers as a thing new to them," Twain noted, "but as a thing which they had witnessed and would remember."

Quite possibly they did remember it, since the story was a popular one. Its basic plot had been around for decades, in oral and written forms. Twain himself may have recognized it from the versions printed in California newspapers. He may have heard it in Missouri or along the Mississippi, told by black or white voices. In the oral literature of the frontier there was no original, only variations. Tall tales mutated constantly, molded by new regions and narrators. By the time the jumping frog landed at the tavern at Angel's Camp, it had traveled a considerable distance through the streams of western folklore.

Twain adored the story. Later, he remembered it as the "one gleam of jollity that shot across our dismal sojourn in the rain & mud." He and Jim Gillis often "quoted from the yarn & laughed over it." When he returned to San Francisco a few weeks later on February 26, 1865, he shared the tale with Harte. The US Mint's offices on Commercial Street, where Harte received him, represented a radically different California than the one on display at Jackass Hill and Angel's Camp. Harte himself had little love for miners. He despised their vulgar materialism, their propensity for unpleasant place-names like Poker Flat and Murderer's Bar—"offences against public decency," he called them in the *Californian*. Even so, Harte was fascinated by Twain's sojourn in the Sierras. "He said the men did nothing all day long but sit around the bar-room stove, spit, and 'swop lies,'" Harte recalled. When Twain recounted one of those lies, he "half unconsciously dropped into the lazy tone and manner of the original narrator." "It was as graphic as it was delicious," Harte observed admiringly.

Twain mimicked the timbre of Angel's Camp brilliantly. To reach a wider audience, however, he would need to render that voice in writing. This meant translating a piece of music with its own special rhythms into the silent, linear script of the printed page—a daunting task. The undertaking became more urgent when he discovered a batch of letters from Artemus Ward waiting for him at the Occidental Hotel, postmarked more than three months earlier. The comedian wanted Twain to submit a sketch for an upcoming book on Ward's trip to Nevada in late 1863, when the two had first met. Twain dashed off a reply, suggesting the story of the jumping frog. "Write it," came the response from New York. "There is still time to get it into my volume of sketches."

Even with the deadline looming, Twain dragged his feet. He didn't usually suffer from writer's block, but this particular bit of prose would pass from his pen about as easily as a kidney stone. In the meantime, he had to make a living. The financial strain of surviving on a freelancer's salary in San Francisco hadn't gotten any easier while he was away—and he presumably still owed $500 from forfeiting the bond when Steve Gillis jumped bail back in December 1864. Luckily, Twain had a large appetite for work, and a pathological fear of the poorhouse. After almost three months away, he flung himself back into the literary life of the city.

He wasn't the same writer as before. The change could be felt in his first piece for the *Californian* after his return to the city, "An Unbiased Criticism," published in March 1865. Ostensibly a review of a new art gallery on Montgomery Street, it swiftly unspooled into a long digression about life in Angel's Camp. He wove his memories of the miners into an affectionate burlesque of the world he had left behind. He parroted how they spoke: rambling from one subject to the next, getting lost in dense thickets of extraneous detail.

He was experimenting. The jumping frog kept rattling around

his head while he procrastinated with other journalistic pursuits, like parody and social satire. In June 1865, he began writing a letter for his old editor at the *Virginia City Territorial Enterprise*. As a reporter for the *Morning Call*, Twain had gotten a firsthand look at the corrupt machinery of criminal justice. Now, in his *Enterprise* pieces, he laid into the city's cops with new zeal. He hammered them for being shiftless, cruel, inept—for clubbing a man and throwing him in jail and letting him die of a head wound, for never arresting the racist Irish rowdies who threw stones at the Chinese. The city's police chief retaliated with a libel suit against the *Enterprise*, and his men even jailed Twain overnight for public drunkenness. These efforts at intimidation didn't work: as late as February 1866, he hadn't let up. "Mark Twain is still on the war-path," noted the *San Francisco Examiner.* "He is after the San Francisco Policemen with a sharp stick."

Twain had always hated hypocrites, snobs, blowhards, and bullies. But the longer he spent in San Francisco, the shrewder his analysis became. He criticized not just people but institutions; not just isolated cases of bad behavior but broader patterns of injustice. By 1865, he had earned a new nickname: the Moralist of the Main. His morality wasn't of the priggish, temperance-society sort. It was the conscience of the individual against the crowd, the same morality that later made Huckleberry Finn refuse to betray his friend Jim. Society taught him that runaway slaves should be returned to their owner. His heart told him different. If that meant eternal damnation, so be it: "All right, then," Huck says, "I'll *go* to hell."

As a prankster and a social critic, a parodist and a folk philosopher, Twain had never been better. In 1864, he had come close to abandoning writing and resuming his piloting career on the Mississippi. By 1865, he was cranking out large quantities of prose on any topic he liked. Under the influence of Harte and the *Californian*, his style evolved. He no longer dropped bombs like the miscegenation hoax of May 1864—his firepower had found a narrower bore, and more deserving targets. His mischief hadn't become any milder, only more discerning. Nevada's *Gold Hill News*, which had blasted Twain during the miscegenation uproar, now praised his work for the *Californian*.

He also earned accolades from the Atlantic coast. On September 9, 1865, the *New York Round Table* singled him out as the "foremost" writer "among the merry gentlemen of the California press"— significant praise from a prestigious literary paper. Eastern editors had been reprinting his *Californian* pieces for months; now the critics had started to take notice. Charles Henry Webb took it as an omen. "To my thinking Shakspeare [*sic*] had no more idea that he was writing for posterity than Mark Twain has at the present time," he wrote, "and it sometimes amuses me to think how future Mark Twain scholars will puzzle over that gentleman's present hieroglyphics and occasionally eccentric expressions."

Webb was joking, but someday he would seem oddly prescient. In late 1865, Twain finally finished the story from Angel's Camp and sent it east. The manuscript held nothing less than the Fort Sumter of American letters, exploding in the annihilating blaze of a jumping frog.

II

BONANZA AND BUST

Gold miners in Tuolumne County
in the 1860s, around the time that
Twain visited Jackass Hill.

FOUR

The American frontier was a magical place. Daniel Boone wrestled bears in Kentucky and Davy Crockett battled a twelve-foot catfish in Tennessee. In Utah, grasshoppers grew so big they were barbecued like steaks, and in Arkansas, the corn grew so fast that a seed planted under a sleeping sow sprouted a stalk that speared the poor creature before sunrise. The frontier marked the outer limit of the ordinary. It was a "borderland of fable," the historian Bernard DeVoto once wrote, an alternate reality where fact merged with fiction and a young, practical nation indulged its yearning for myth.

The frontier always lived vividly in people's minds. On the map, it was harder to place. In theory, it represented the line between wilderness and civilization. In practice, it was a porous, imprecise boundary between two different Americas: the populous East and the populating West—not one continuous front of white settlement but a patchwork of conquest and compromise spanning a vastly diverse region. The frontier improvised a society from many competing strands. Indians, northerners, southerners, blacks, Europeans, Chinese, and Mexicans overlapped and collided. Certain rules were suspended, others rewritten entirely. In these communities,

America outgrew the colonial legacy of the Atlantic coast and created something new.

This evolution could be heard in the stories people told. In taverns and trading posts, stagecoaches and steamboats, they traded funny, fantastic yarns that reflected the new realities of western life. Tall talk was a kind of realism: a magnified portrait of actual speech, characters, and settings. It was also uncompromisingly coarse, the product of a male-dominated frontier. It broke all the rules of respectability, embracing vulgarity, violence, drunkenness, depravity, even ugliness. The heroes were hideous, and often hideously cruel. The language was exuberantly ungrammatical, composed in regional dialects that stretched and scrambled proper English into gorgeously expressive new forms.

These forms found their way into print via the nation's journalists. Reprinted from one newspaper to the next, popularized by periodicals in eastern cities, frontier humor became a national phenomenon, forming a "low" vernacular alternative to the high-cultural effusions of New England. Those "semi-barbarous citizens" described by Jefferson hadn't waited for their raw societies to become civilized before creating their own culture. They went ahead and did it anyway, using the materials at hand. The result wasn't just quirky spellings and quaint anecdotes. It was America's first folk art, a mortal threat to the literary dominion of the Atlantic coast. The revolt had been brewing for a while. On November 18, 1865, Mark Twain fired the first shot by publishing "Jim Smiley and His Jumping Frog" in the *New York Saturday Press*.

The path to publication had been anything but easy. Ever since returning to San Francisco from the Sierra foothills in February 1865, Twain had struggled to write the story he had heard at Angel's Camp about a jumping frog. He produced at least two incomplete drafts, trying to find the right tone, but he couldn't get this slice of frontier storytelling done to his satisfaction. He still hoped to send the piece to Artemus Ward in time for it to appear in his upcoming book. But time was running short: with each passing month, that opportunity receded.

What made the jumping frog such a difficult birth wasn't just style or structure. The real problem involved a crisis of faith. Despite a prolific output and rising recognition, Twain had grave doubts about his future. Even as he developed a supremely confident writing voice, pummeling the San Francisco Police Department and other crooks and charlatans, he suffered serious misgivings about his chosen profession. As 1865 came to a close, the insecurities that he had long concealed under a swaggering exterior came painfully to the surface.

Money always made Twain crazy, even in those moments when he had enough of it. His father, John Marshall Clemens, had been a man of honesty, ambition, and appallingly bad business sense. He had started out as a lawyer, but it was his disastrous career as a speculator and entrepreneur that kept his family poor. The constant flutter of financial panic that Twain felt came partly from a fear of repeating his father's failures. Wealth meant more than just fancy things—it promised a bulwark against chaos and uncertainty. Poverty, by contrast, represented something far worse than material scarcity: it brought shame and self-loathing. Throughout 1865, money problems kept Twain's anxiety keyed to a constant pitch. He began sending daily letters to the *Virginia City Territorial Enterprise* in October, earning $100 a month. He made another $40 writing for the *San Francisco Dramatic Chronicle*. He still contributed to the *Californian*—although after the summer, his pace dropped to about once a month—and placed a couple of parodies in the *San Francisco Youths' Companion*. In all, he earned the same income as he did as a reporter for the *Morning Call*, doing work he hated. But his wages couldn't keep pace with his debts.

In *Roughing It*, his later narrative of these years, he would describe this as his "slinking" period. "I slunk from back street to back street to back street," he wrote. "I slunk away from approaching faces that looked familiar." It took a terrible emotional toll. "I felt meaner, and lowlier and more despicable than the worms," he re-called. His former colleagues at the *Call* poked fun at his distress. "There is now, and has been for a long time past, camping about through town, a melancholy-looking Arab, known as Marque Twein," the paper joked in October. This nomad wore ratty clothes, drank heavily, and changed lodgings whenever he reached "the end of his credit." "Having become familiarly but painfully known to all the widows in town who let out rooms, he finds it expedient to move again." A darker view was provided by Twain himself four decades later: driven to despair, he almost committed suicide. "I put the pistol to my head but wasn't man enough to pull the trigger," he confessed. "Many times I have been sorry I did not succeed, but I was never ashamed of having tried."

Unhappiness forced him inward. In November he would turn thirty. He was poor, unmarried, unsure of himself and his prospects. He grew reflective, philosophical. On October 19 and 20, 1865, he wrote a letter to his brother Orion and his sister-in-law Mollie:

I never had but two **powerful** ambitions in my life. One was to be a pilot, & the other a preacher of the gospel. I accom-plished the one & failed in the other, **because** I could not supply myself with the necessary stock in trade—*i.e.* religion. I have given it up forever. I never had a "call" in that direc-tion, anyhow, & my aspirations were the very ecstasy of pre-sumption. But I *have* had a "call" to literature, of a low order—*i.e.* humorous. It is nothing to be proud of, but it is my strongest suit, & if I were to listen to that maxim of stern *duty* which says that to do right you **must** multiply the one or the two or the three talents which the Almighty entrusts to your keeping, I would long ago have ceased to meddle with things for which I was by nature unfitted & turned my atten-tion to seriously scribbling to excite the **laughter** of God's creatures. Poor, pitiful business! Though the Almighty did His part by me—for the talent is a mighty engine when supplied with the steam of **education**—which I have not got, & so its pistons & cylinders & shafts move feebly & for a holiday show & are useless for any good purpose.

This epiphany marked a turning point. It was the moment when he decided to "drop all trifling, & sighing after vain impossibilities" and consecrate himself to the writer's life. It was the moment when he accepted his inheritance as a child of the frontier: as a "low" humorist "scribbling to excite the laughter of God's creatures." Instead of trying to become someone he wasn't, he would make peace with the person he already was.

His new self-knowledge didn't solve anything in the short term. "I am utterly miserable," he revealed at the end of the letter. "If I do not get out of debt in 3 months,—pistols or poison for one—exit *me.*" Yet he also felt a pinprick of hope: the *New York Round Table* had praised him for his *Californian* pieces, and the acclaim made waves when it reached San Francisco. "It is only now, when editors of standard literary papers in the distant east give me high praise, & who do not know me & cannot of course be blinded by the glamour of partiality, that I really begin to believe there must be something in it," he wrote.

Out of this crisis came the courage to face the jumping frog. Eight months after he heard the tale at Angel's Camp and promised to write it for Artemus Ward, it remained unfinished. Now he wrestled the manuscript into its final form and sent it to New York. By the time Twain's contribution arrived, however, it was too late: Ward's book had already gone to press. The publisher, George W. Carleton, passed the item along to Henry Clapp Jr.—a New York Bohemian who had once held court at Pfaff's with Walt Whitman—and on November 18, 1865, "Jim Smiley and His Jumping Frog" appeared in Clapp's *Saturday Press*. This wasn't another sarcastic squib of the Bohemian school: it was a fable of the frontier, drawing laughter deep from the country's diaphragm, changing the course of American literature forever.

HUMOR IS HARD TO DEFINE. It thrives on context, and suffers in translation. What makes people laugh in one time and place often doesn't make sense in another. "Jim Smiley and His Jumping Frog" still reads brilliantly, but it's not as funny now as it was when it first appeared. Americans loved the story because it offered something at once familiar and strange: frontier humor, drawn with an unusual degree of detail. Twain took a world usually depicted in broad, buffoonish strokes and gave it sharp focus. The comedy came less from what he said than how he said it: how he rendered the lazy drawl and matter-of-fact tone that Bret Harte, listening to Twain's tale in his office at the US Mint, had found so irresistible.

Twain modeled the story on the Southwestern humor sketches that filled the newspapers of his Missouri youth. That genre's key feature was the "frame," which involved using a refined, socially superior narrator to introduce and interpret the tall-talking back-woodsmen for the reader. It kept the frontier at a safe distance. It acted as an enclosure, the literary equivalent of those split-rail fences that marked the first signs of white settlement in the West.

At first, "Jim Smiley and His Jumping Frog" appears to use the standard Southwestern frame. The narrator is educated, well-spoken. He arrives at a mining camp looking for a reverend named Leonidas W. Smiley. He asks an old man at the tavern named Simon Wheeler, who says he doesn't know Reverend Smiley—but he does know a gambler named Jim Smiley. This starts Wheeler on a long, rambling digression that culminates with a tale of a jumping con-test between two frogs—the kernel of the original entry in Twain's notebook from Angel's Camp.

The narrator is baffled by Wheeler. He can't keep his soliloquy moving in a straight line, and never once smiles at the ridiculous things he relates. He talks in the Pike County dialect native to Missouri, and transplanted to California by migrating southwesterners. Yet he is by far the smarter of the two, despite his lack of education. He isn't some dumb yokel presented for the reader's ridicule, but a savvy storyteller, painting pictures with words as vividly as Dickens. Unlike the narrator, who speaks the humdrum idiom of eastern respectability, Wheeler skips along in a richly imaginative vernacular. His similes are especially graphic: a dog's jaw sticks out like "the fo'castle of a steamboat," his teeth "shine savage like the furnaces." The jumping frog goes "whirling in the air like a doughnut," and lands "flat-footed and all right, like a cat." These are the melodies of the frontier, the lyrical realism of a region recording itself.

Twain inverts the typical Southwestern frame. The joke is no longer on the frontiersman, but on the flummoxed narrator who can't quite follow him. The frontier is no longer a lower stage of development struggling up toward the level of Atlantic civilization, but a universe all its own.

"Jim Smiley and His Jumping Frog" made Twain a household name. The story "set all New York in a roar," reported the *San Francisco Alta California*, and spread swiftly across the country. "I have been asked fifty times about it and its author, and the papers are copying it far and near." "No reputation was ever more rapidly won," raved the *New York Tribune*.

The tale's deeper significance, however, wouldn't become clear until later. The jumping frog spelled the beginning of the end of the old guard in American letters: the decline of a genteel elite that looked to Europe for its influences, and the rise of a literature that drew its inspiration from more native sources. In 1865, Twain started down the path that would later produce masterpieces like *Adventures of Huckleberry Finn*. In the "low" frontier, he found the makings of an authentic American art—a force powerful enough to exorcise the ghosts of the Old World and redeem the literary promise of the West.

Thomas Starr King had been an early believer in this promise. Before his death in 1864, he had encouraged California's writers, and urged them to follow the example of his native New England. But the Bohemia that sprang up in San Francisco strayed from his blueprint. It entertained eccentric visitors like Artemus Ward, and refused to adopt anything like a house style. San Francisco's Bohemia took all kinds. It let a boy named Charles Warren Stoddard set his daydreams to verse, and a poet named Ina Coolbrith rail against the restraints of Victorian womanhood. At its helm was the unlikeliest Bohemian of all: a salaried employee of the US Mint and devoted family man, who expressed contempt for the conventions of California life while taking part in nearly all of them.

By the end of 1865, Harte had hit a wall. The *Californian* soared, his parodies sparkled, and a cluster of obscure writers had solidified into a well-defined clique centered on him, Stoddard, and Coolbrith. But his creativity had stalled. He wrote clever burlesques of famous novelists, but no good literature of his own. He attacked the literary aristocracy of New England as "an English graft," while scorning California for its crudeness.

Twain found a way forward. He moved from critique to creation—no longer simply lampooning New England but surpassing it. Instead of ridiculing a place like Angel's Camp for its coarseness, he saw what made it special. Harte's disdain for the rougher colors of the region had blinded him to their artistic potential; Twain used them to build a new kind of literature. This was the source of his genius, the quality that would ultimately distinguish him from his Bohemian brethren. He wasn't the most meticulous writer, or the most disciplined. But he had an eye for the extraordinary in ordinary American life, for the unsung sublimities of the continent's language, geography, and myths, and "Jim Smiley and His Jumping Frog" gave an early glimpse of that power.

No one recognized the story's revolutionary importance at the time, least of all Twain. He enjoyed his newfound fame but felt ambivalent about where it came from. In a letter to his mother and sister in January 1866, he expressed surprise that "those New York people should single out a villainous backwoods sketch to compliment me on." But the success clearly lifted his spirits. The gnawing doubts of the previous year had faded under a fit of manic energy. He was now bursting with book ideas, eager to capitalize on his popularity.

Harte followed Twain's ascent closely. He had laughed at the jumping frog long before anyone in the East. "[I]t will never be as funny to anyone in print as it was to me, told for the first time by the unknown Twain himself on that morning in the San Francisco Mint," he recalled decades later. Harte reprinted the story in slightly edited form in the *Californian* in December. By January, they were talking about writing books together. "Though I am generally placed at the head of my breed of scribblers in this part of the country," Twain told his family, "the place properly belongs to Bret Harte." They planned to collaborate on two projects, he said: a collection of sketches, and one of burlesques. "I wouldn't do it," Twain added smugly, "only he agrees to take all the trouble."

Harte had his reasons for wanting to publish something soon. A book with both of their names on it would sell very well—owing not only to Twain's recent celebrity but to Harte's. In December 1865, while Twain basked in the glow of the jumping frog, Harte also came under intense scrutiny. This wasn't for anything he wrote but for a book of poetry he edited. With one stroke, Harte had ignited a controversy that outdid Twain at his most inflammatory.

It began innocently enough. A Montgomery Street bookseller named Anton Roman wanted to publish a volume of California verse called *Outcroppings*, and asked Harte to edit it. This would be a showcase for the Far West's finest writers, a chance to astonish the East with the literary riches of the Pacific coast. Such a project had special significance. Poetry wasn't just something that happened in the pages of the *Californian*, or in the red-plush parlors of rich neighborhoods like Rincon Hill. It belonged equally to the mining camp and the metropolis, to the worlds of Angel's Camp and Montgomery Street. Californians recited poetry at public gatherings. They scribbled verses and sent them to their local papers. They took a personal interest in the literary fortunes of their state, and as soon as they heard of Harte's anthology, they swamped him with submissions. Each morning another infusion littered his desk. Sometimes the "chill wind from the Bay" came in through the window and blew one of the poems outside, Harte remembered—"attaining a circulation it had never known before." The aspirants included "practical business men, sage financiers, fierce speculators, and plodding traders, never before suspected of poetry, or even correct prose." They touched on similar topics: the Golden Gate, Yosemite, California flowers.

These happened to be precisely the sort of subjects Harte hated. He had zero patience for the pastoral and the picturesque. The book he completed in time for Christmas 1865 reflected his exacting taste—and inflicted a wholesale humiliation on the writers of the Far West. *Outcroppings* included only nineteen poets. Many were Harte's friends: Coolbrith and Stoddard contributed four poems each. In the preface, Harte attacked California literature, blaming the state's "monotonous climate" for the generally bad poetry it produced.

Predictably, *Outcroppings* provoked a furious response. "Bret Harte has given the world to understand that of the 1300 poets of California, there are less than twenty whom [*sic*] come up to the austere standard of his fastidious taste," wrote the *San Francisco Dramatic Chronicle* on December 7, 1865. "The rejected 1280 will probably take his scalp." In the coming weeks, the prediction proved painfully accurate. Especially angry were the rural writers who fumed at the spectacle of an effete city dweller passing judgment on their state. As the *Sacramento Union* observed, the poems in *Outcroppings* could've been written anywhere: it "contains as little of the spirit, sentiment and imagery of California as might be expected from one who frankly avows his mean opinion of the country and its bards." The *Virginia City Territorial Enterprise* put it less tactfully: *Outcroppings* was "the very trashiest of the trash."

Harte had started a culture war. On one side were San Francisco's Bohemians. On the other were the provincial pastoralists. "One of the most astonishing characteristics of the San Francisco Bohemian is the importance he attaches to his metropolitanism— considering its recent date," scoffed the *Territorial Enterprise*. To their critics, the Bohemians were poseurs: former bumpkins dressed up in fancy clothes. "He affects to scorn everything provincial before he has scraped the mud of the country from his feet or its dirt from his face." The Bohemians struck back, assailing the backwater bards for their hackneyed verse. In a parody for the *Californian*, Harte imagined a volume called *Tailings* made up of poems rejected from *Outcroppings*: "Methinks I see the swaddling clothes of mist," ran one representative line.

The two camps had more in common than they cared to admit, however. The Bohemians weren't nearly so urban, and their enemies weren't nearly so rustic. San Francisco's writers frequently drew their inspiration from the countryside, and *Outcroppings* included poems about farmers and birds. The anti-*Outcroppings* crowd, on the other hand, didn't live in a landscape of sylvan simplicity. California's mines and farms increasingly resembled little cities, with industrial machinery, well-capitalized companies, and complex regional economies.

The struggle over *Outcroppings*, then, reflected a divide more imagined than actual. But this didn't diminish the ferocity of the

fight. At stake was more than just rival styles of poetry. The real issue concerned California's public image. As the state grew closer to
the rest of the nation, it became more mindful of the impression it
made. The transcontinental telegraph, completed in 1861, didn't just
bring eastern news west, but western news east. Harte recalled that
California papers suppressed reports of unsavory local incidents
because they didn't want them to end up in the eastern press. A
negative story might impede the westward flow of people and capital, and threaten California's economic future.

Outcroppings' critics feared the book would present a distorted,
and possibly damaging, picture of California to the country as a
whole. Ironically, the collection had originally been conceived along
boosterish lines: its publisher hoped "to foster Eastern immigration
by an exhibit of the California literary product," Harte wrote. The
final product didn't make much of an advertisement, however. Not
only did it fail to include any local color, it openly insulted the state's
intellect.

Yet the eastern press liked it. Critics in Philadelphia, New York,
and Boston gave *Outcroppings* high marks. Meanwhile, the wailing
of the western papers ensured excellent sales. Harte appeared to
enjoy his new role as the villain of the Pacific coast. In a letter he
boasted of being "abused beyond his most sanguine expectations,"
and he fanned the flames at every opportunity. When the anti-
Outcroppings camp announced its intent to publish its own book of
verse, Harte teamed up with Twain to plan a parody. "We know all
the tribe of California poets, & understand their different styles, & I
think we can just make them get up & howl," Twain told his mother
and sister. He loved the backcountry's fibbers and fabulists, but felt
no sympathy for its "poetical asses."

By early 1866, he and Harte had become the literary giants of the
Far West. In person and in print, they made an unlikely pair. The
same papers that revered one ravaged the other. When the *Sacramento Bee* learned that Twain wanted to write a book, it suggested a

title: "'Deep Diggings,' in contradistinction to the 'Outcroppings,' that have been crushed by the entire press, and found to yield 000 to the ton." Yet the two men liked each other, and respected one another's work. Harte embraced the jumping frog; Twain publicly defended Harte for his "rare good taste" in editing *Outcroppings*. Their affinities ran deeper than their differences. Both felt restless with the Pacific coast, and anxious for a wider audience. They wrote with one eye eastward, hungry for bigger victories. They had grown up with the West, and now they were in danger of outgrowing it.

IN 1866, California turned sixteen. It was a young state, self-conscious and arrogant. Its best writers were thirty or under, and they wrote with an irreverence native to the West and to the young. They no longer gathered in the offices of the *Golden Era*, or those of the *Californian* a few blocks away. Those were the places where, for the past six years, the literary seams of the Pacific coast had been prospected, extracted, refined. Now Bohemia found a new berth, farther from the city center.

Inside a quiet house on Russian Hill was a parlor that smelled of fresh violets or lavender. Marble busts lined the mantel. Books lay everywhere. Through a curtained window came a view of the neighbor's garden, with statues of Cupid and a swan, and a fountain that made soothing music. This was Ina Coolbrith's home, and in it she hosted a salon that formed the core of literary San Francisco for the next several years. "She was the center of a little world," recalled a visitor—no longer the shy girl who came from Los Angeles four years earlier, but a woman of growing confidence and wicked humor. "Those eyes of hers were wondrously changeful and reflective," another observer said, equally given to sympathy and scorn. Harte admired her verse, and featured it prominently in *Outcroppings*. The ensuing uproar spread her name farther than ever before. "Miss Coolbrith is one of the real poets among the many poetic

masqueraders in the volume," wrote the *Nation*—a major acknowl-
edgment from the eastern press.

Her parlor gave the Bohemians a place to meet. Russian Hill
made an especially scenic setting, rising three hundred feet above
the city. The houses looked fragile from this height, row upon row
clinging precariously to the hills: the Italianate of the imperial
present, the wood-frame dwellings of the recent past, and in the
distance, the adobe Presidio of Spanish prehistory. In a later poem,
Coolbrith called it a "hill of Memories."

Harte came often. The rarefied air of Russian Hill offered a refuge from the ceaseless mercantile buzz below. It also gave him an
excuse to get out of the house—the domestic battleground where
his unpleasant wife, Anna Griswold Harte, kept up a perpetual
stream of distractions to derail his writing. By 1866, Harte had lost
the center of his literary life: the *Californian* was sinking. Its
founder, Charles Henry Webb, briefly resumed control but couldn't
revive the paper's flagging fortunes, and he sailed for his native
New York in April 1866. He had been in San Francisco for only three
years, and his writing never quite won the audience he wanted.
Keeping the *Californian* alive had been a constant struggle. Like all
things Bohemian, the periodical had burned brightly and for a brief
period. Its decline left a vacuum in the city's literary fabric, one
filled by Coolbrith's salon.

Charles Warren Stoddard also became a regular on Russian Hill.
"I was nowhere more at home than there," he recalled: high praise
from someone who felt at home almost nowhere. In December 1865,
he had finally left Brayton Academy in Oakland after two excruciat-
ing years. "It was now evident to me the world was my school and in
it I must learn all that I hoped to know," he wrote. Coolbrith's "restful room" was a good start. Harte gave editorial guidance: "He
would jump upon my faults quite frankly, and was equally open in
appreciation." Coolbrith provided personal advice. "In mood he was

as variable as a San Francisco summer day," she remembered. "I used to say to him, 'Charloway, if there were as many legs as there are sides to you, a centipede would not be in it!'"

Outcroppings brought them closer. Stoddard recalled "the abuse which was heaped upon us," and in particular upon him. The delicate, unmanly poet represented everything the countryside critics hated about the city, and thus made a big target for the book's enemies. The *Territorial Enterprise* slammed his poems as "the worst specimens of this imperfection." Since boyhood he had been bullied for being too girly, and he never learned to insulate himself with irony or pride. His work gave him "no satisfaction," Coolbrith observed. "It was in reality his despair." Negative criticism only confirmed his inner sense of worthlessness. He needed other people's approval, and went to extraordinary lengths to obtain it.

In 1866, shortly after the *Outcroppings* saga, Stoddard mailed copies of his poems to his favorite authors. He had kept an autograph album for years, asking his friends for inscriptions. Now he took it a step further, fishing for compliments from the most famous writers in the English language. These included the literary lords of New England—Emerson, Longfellow, Holmes—and British eminences like Alfred Tennyson, Charles Darwin, and Anthony Trollope. Once the letters went out, the trembling set in. "I was hoping against hope," he recalled, madly nervous, ashamed of his presumptuousness in begging "the attention of the immortals."

Incredibly, most replied. Emerson enjoyed his poems: "I am much touched with them, and I think so well of their superior skill and tone that I would hear with pain that you had discontinued writing." Tennyson offered fainter praise: "I have read your verses & I liked them." Herman Melville, whose novels of the South Seas helped awaken Stoddard's love for the tropics, said he had been "quite struck" by one of the items. Others gave less favorable feedback. John Stuart Mill urged him to publish only poetry "of the very highest quality." Oliver Wendell Holmes warned him not to use writing as "an apology for neglecting humbler and more steadily industrious pursuits."

But Stoddard was unfit for more industrious pursuits. High-strung and hopelessly impractical, he had made a terrible student and an indifferent bookstore clerk. He would never outgrow what Coolbrith called his "ethereal unreality." He was "as much out of place in this very material country as Pegasus in a quartz mill," Harte said, and he meant it as a compliment. By age twenty-three, Stoddard had tried and failed to fit in. He now decided to make a bold concession to his nature: to embrace his literary calling by pub-lishing his first book. In 1866, he and Harte began selecting poems for it. This would be his chance to prove he was a real poet.

Twain could relate. He, too, had recently come to terms with his calling: not poetry, but the "[p]oor, pitiful business" of "scribbling to excite the laughter of God's creatures." He, too, had struggled with doubt, and wanted approval from faraway critics not "blinded by the glamour of partiality." The quality that Twain most prized in people—loyalty—Stoddard had in abundance. His love, once fas-tened, never came undone. Coolbrith recalled telling Stoddard that a friend had been bad-mouthing him behind his back. "I loved him," Stoddard replied. "I cannot unlove him." This was the kind of unwavering devotion that Twain missed in more distant men like Harte. "He was refined, sensitive, charming, gentle, generous, hon-est himself and unsuspicious of other people's honesty," Twain remembered.

By 1866, he and Stoddard had something new in common: Ha-waii. Stoddard's visit two years earlier had been unforgettable, and he longed to return. In January, the California Steam Navigation Company started regular steamer service between San Francisco and Honolulu. Its directors invited Twain on the maiden voyage aboard the *Ajax*. He turned it down because he was still writing a daily letter for the *Territorial Enterprise*, a job he couldn't afford to lose. "I am so sorry now," he wrote his mother and sister afterward. Here was a perfect subject for his pen: fifty elegant San Franciscans, "the cream of the town," traveling two thousand miles into the heart of the unknown. "Where could a man catch such another crowd together?"

He wouldn't make the same mistake again. When the *Ajax* made its second voyage in March 1866, he was on board. He had persuaded the editors of the prestigious *Sacramento Union* to pay him to write correspondence from the islands. The trip came at an opportune time: Twain had been getting sick of California and the indigent, itinerant life he led there. Despite the success of his jumping frog story, he remained a poor freelancer. "I am tired being a beggar," he wrote his brother, "tired being chained to this accursed homeless desert." In Hawaii he hoped to find a new world to explore, and the chance to capitalize on his recent triumph.

In his four months in Hawaii he wrote twenty-five letters for the *Union*, watched a volcano erupt, saw native girls skinny-dip in the sea, ate horrifying amounts of tropical fruit, and tried and failed to surf. The contrast with San Francisco exhilarated him: here he walked on coral, not cobblestone, and smelled jasmine and oleander instead of offal and sewage. Like Stoddard, he found the balmy, beautiful setting deeply relaxing: during five weeks in Maui, he took a much-needed holiday. "I have not written a single line, & have not once thought of business, or care, or human toil or trouble or sorrow or weariness," he wrote his sister-in-law. But Hawaii wasn't purely a vacation: it also gave Twain invaluable training in travel writing, the genre that would produce his first major book, *The Innocents Abroad*. He took *Union* readers on a galloping tour of a kingdom rife with lurid customs and costumes, rich with sugar and whales, infested with British, French, and American interlopers, and governed by the last of the great Hawaiian kings, Kamehameha V.

In the midst of this came Twain's first big scoop: a journalistic coup that amply repaid the *Union*'s investment in him. On May 3,

1866, the USS *Hornet* sank off the coast of South America on its way to San Francisco. On June 15, fifteen survivors washed ashore on Hawaii's Big Island. They had spent the last forty-three days in a longboat, subsisting on dwindling rations of salt pork and sea biscuits and the occasional dolphin. At the time, Twain was in bed, recovering from a bad case of saddle sores. But when eleven of the *Hornet*'s sailors arrived at the Honolulu hospital, he arranged for a friend to carry him there on a stretcher. One invalid to another, he interviewed the men about their ordeal and wove their answers into a suspenseful tale. The *Union* published it on July 19, 1866. The first account of the shipwreck to appear in the American press, it caused a sensation. Less than a year after the jumping frog made the nation howl with laughter, Twain tried a different key—drama—and scored another hit.

He was on fire, and he knew it. As soon as he returned to San Francisco in August 1866, he set about milking the *Hornet* saga for everything it was worth. He traveled to the *Union*'s offices in Sacramento to demand $300 for the scoop, and then turned around to expand the story into a magazine-length piece that he sold to *Harper's Monthly*. But by far the most important outcome of his Hawaii adventure was his debut as a public speaker: a decision that, more than any others, would eventually seal his ascent into the upper stratosphere of national stardom.

His motive, as always, was money. He recalled Artemus Ward, whose San Francisco debut on November 13, 1863, had taken in more than $1,000 at the door. Ward had leveraged his popularity as a writer into a lucrative career on the lecture circuit, and now Twain hoped to do the same. His writing gigs paid irregularly, and neither of his collaborations with Harte had panned out. He wanted to turn his *Union* letters into a book, but devoting himself to the manuscript would require covering his living expenses. So he started writing a lecture on his latest area of expertise: Hawaii.

One rainy evening, Twain stopped by his old office at the

Morning Call to ask for advice. He "entered in a sort of uncertain way, clad in a thin black frockcoat—his only protection from the storm," recalled George Barnes, his former boss. He laid a damp manuscript on an editor's desk and demanded his opinion. "I've been to Harte and Stoddard, and the rest of the fellows, and they say, 'Don't do it, Mark; it will hurt your literary reputation.'" The editor read the lecture while Twain dried his soaked clothes by the fireplace. "Mark," the editor asked after an interval, "which do you need most at present, money or literary reputation?" "Money!" Twain replied. "Then go to Maguire, hire the Academy of Music on Pine street, and there deliver the lecture. With the prestige of your recent letters from the Hawaiian islands, you will crowd the theater."

Happily, Twain obeyed. He booked the city's largest venue for the night of October 2, 1866, and launched a marketing campaign complete with handbills and newspaper ads. These were vintage Twain: hoaxing, wry, sliding between sharply different registers:

A SPLENDID ORCHESTRA
Is in town, but has not been engaged.
ALSO,
A DEN OF FEROCIOUS WILD BEASTS
Will be on exhibition in the next Block.
MAGNIFICENT FIREWORKS
Were in contemplation for this occasion,
but the idea has been abandoned.
A GRAND TORCHLIGHT PROCESSION
May be expected; in fact, the public are privileged
to expect whatever they please.

The doors opened at seven. "The Trouble to begin at 8 o'clock."

Twain's promotional push set off a wave of advance sales. "We have no doubt the house will be crowded," declared the *Call*. "Those who wish to get seats will do well to go early," counseled the *Evening*

Bulletin, "for the indications of a grand rush are unmistakable." The rumor mill went into high gear: Twain would talk about mermaids, or perform native dances. Nobody wanted to miss what promised to be one of the biggest premieres on the San Francisco stage.

Several years later, Twain remembered feeling deathly afraid as the night drew near. He couldn't sleep. He couldn't eat. He was "the most distressed and frightened creature on the Pacific coast," reviewing his lecture notes until all of the humor drained from them. "I grieved that I could not bring a coffin on the stage and turn the thing into a funeral." Yet he had already committed himself to making the show a success by hyping it relentlessly. Now all that remained was to deliver a performance worthy of his promises.

On the evening of October 2, 1866, the Academy of Music swelled to capacity. From the footlights to the family circle, the house was packed. "It is perhaps fortunate that the King of Hawaii did not arrive in time to attend," cracked a journalist, "for unless he had gone early he must have been turned away." The fashionable men and women of "the regular opera 'set'" turned out in full. The wife of the current California governor, Mrs. Frederick Low, sat in a box. Even Harte came to show his support. He arrived with "a big claque," an observer later recalled, almost certainly with Stoddard in tow.

At eight o'clock, the crowd started stomping its feet. When Twain appeared in the wings, they broke into thunderous applause. He ambled forward with a lurching, graceless gait, his hands thrust in his pockets. "I was in the middle of the stage," he recalled, "staring at a sea of faces, bewildered by the fierce glare of the lights, and quaking in every limb with a terror that seemed like to take my life away." For several moments he stood silently staring, as the energy in the house ripened to an unbearable pitch. Then the words came: slow and deliberate, quirky and crude—the voice of the frontier, drawing its listeners under.

For seventy-five minutes, they laughed, clapped, and cheered. A "brilliant success," raved the next day's *Evening Bulletin.* Twain met the demands of a "serious" lecture by covering the islands' economy, politics, history—yet he deftly interwove these with a current of comic tension that kept his audience on a hair trigger, primed to ignite at any moment. An absurdity might slip discreetly into the stream of his story, and then another, sparking laughter that rose and crested just as he suddenly shifted gears, delivering a passage of such heartfelt eloquence that the house fell solemn and silent. This was more than humor: it was "word painting," said a reporter, a tapestry of anecdotes and images recorded by Twain's all-seeing eye.

Twain later in his lecture career. Drawing by Thomas
Wrist, from the New York Daily Graphic, *October 26, 1874.*

He didn't just make people laugh. As with "Jim Smiley and His Jumping Frog," he brought a faraway place to life.

Ever since Twain first began writing, he had tried to give his words the flavor of living speech. Dashes, italics, phonetically transcribed dialect—these were meant to make readers hear a speaker's special vibrations, the glottal tics of different tongues. Onstage, he could do this directly, breaking free of the filter that confined his written voice. He could feel out his audience, refine his rhythms. Unlike the spiritualists, suffragists, and fake scientists then sweeping lyceum halls across the country, he didn't declaim in the usual authoritative style. He took a more intimate tone. He wanted to connect. He gazed at people's faces. He played with his hair, kneaded his hands. He looked nervous, and dressed carelessly. He wasn't a smooth performer, and this was the key to his peculiar charm. He didn't hold himself apart; he talked plainly, unpretentiously. He brought people inside the joke. He made them feel like he belonged to them.

Even Harte came away impressed. He had warned his friend not to degrade himself by perpetrating an act of popular entertainment, and been proved wrong. At least he had the honesty to admit his mistake. In a glowing review for a prominent eastern paper, the *Springfield Republican*, Harte said Twain "took his audience by storm." He couldn't resist offering a few criticisms, faulting the lecture's "crudeness," "coarseness," and "plainness of statement." But he also discerned a deeper virtue in Twain's performance: its Americanness. Twain's humor belonged to "the western character of ludicrous exaggeration and audacious statement," Harte wrote, "which perhaps is more thoroughly national and American than even the Yankee delineations of Lowell." James Russell Lowell, the former editor of the *Atlantic Monthly*, had depicted the dialect of rural New England in a famous book called *The Biglow Papers*—yet it paled in comparison to Twain, who achieved a much richer rendering of the American vernacular.

He captured not only the patterns of everyday speech but their spirit: not only how Americans talked but how they thought. That night at the Academy of Music, he premiered a personality that, by the end of the century, would be enshrined in the national psyche. It was especially well suited for the modernizing nation that emerged after the Civil War: quotable, photogenic, endlessly self-aggrandizing. It would flourish in the first age of mass media, live perpetually in the public eye. It wasn't entirely the man himself but an amplified, embroidered version—and on October 2, 1866, this character took its first step into the spotlight. "I think I recognize a new star rising in this western horizon," observed Harte, with a tinge of envy.

Twain's total take, after expenses, came to $400. Not bad for a night's work, but he hoped to do better. So he took his show on the road, embarking on a hastily organized tour of California and Nevada. He stormed Sacramento, and then cut deep into mining country, conquering a string of one-horse hamlets in quick succession: Marysville, Grass Valley, Red Dog, You Bet—former boomtowns in slow-motion busts, desperate for theatrical distraction. Twain kept expectations high, plastering each town with advance publicity and indulging in offstage antics that enhanced his personal myth. Papers ran reports of the performer guzzling gallons of beer in a single sitting, preparing for lectures with gin and relaxing afterward with whiskey, smoking cigars and telling stories in his trademark drawl until dawn.

The climax came in Virginia City, where Twain staged a glorious homecoming. On October 31, 1866, he played to eight hundred people at Maguire's Opera House—the same place where he had seen Artemus Ward perform a few years earlier—and won them over before saying a word. A "hurricane of applause" greeted him as soon as the curtain lifted, recalled Steve Gillis, who came to cheer for his old roommate. The *Territorial Enterprise* embraced its native son, hastening to take credit for his triumph: after all, Twain's famous pen name first appeared in its pages. If Twain inspired pride among his friends, he also found forgiveness among his enemies.

During his stay in Virginia City, he received an invitation to lecture in nearby Carson City. The letter was signed by more than a hundred leading citizens—including two husbands of the Sanitary Commission ladies whom Twain had wounded with his miscegenation hoax back in 1864. He heartily accepted, and atoned for his past wickedness before a roaring crowd at the Carson Theater.

Back in San Francisco on November 13, Twain was as popular as ever—and as poor. He wanted to go East but couldn't afford to. His creditors claimed most of his profits from the tour, and when he performed at Platt's Music Hall on November 16, the city courts demanded a share of the proceeds in payment of an old debt: the bail bond he had signed for Steve Gillis two years earlier. Adding to his frustration, his second lecture fizzled. He incorporated new material that pushed the bounds of propriety, and told jokes too vulgar to "be heartily laughed at by ladies," observed the *Dramatic Chronicle*. That "coarseness" noted by Harte had gotten out of hand; if he wasn't careful, he might squander his soaring reputation.

Fortunately, he soon found the solution to his financial woes. While never a brilliant businessman, he had a knack for negotiation. He had convinced the *Sacramento Union* to send him to Hawaii, and now he persuaded another big paper, the *Alta California*, to give him an even broader assignment. He would be its "traveling correspondent," a commission he hoped would carry him through Europe, Asia, and beyond. He would take a steamer to New York, pitch his Hawaii book to a publisher, ride his rising star to greater fame in the East, and plan his pilgrimage around the world. But first, he would say good-bye to San Francisco.

On the evening of December 10, Twain delivered one last lecture. This time he repeated his original talk from October, and met with vociferous approval. He concluded with a sincere farewell to the city he loved. He praised its generosity, its "good-fellowship." After five years in the Far West, he confessed his qualms about returning East. The country he once knew had become an "unknown land," wasted by war, dotted with premature graves. Time never stood still, and it wouldn't in California either. In his absence, he expected the state to continue its rapid ascent. Channeling the rhetoric of Thomas Hart Benton and legions of local boosters, Twain waxed lyrical about California's prospects. "She stands in the center of the grand highway of the nations," he declared. "[S]he stands midway between the Old World and the New, and both shall pay her tribute." The approaching transcontinental railroad would unite East with West, connect the traders of Europe with the raw riches of Asia, and bless California with a boundless prosperity and population. "Has any other State so brilliant a future? Has any other city a future like San Francisco?"

Five days later, he departed for New York aboard the steamship *America*. He left behind more friends "than any newspaper man that ever sailed out of the Golden Gate," he wrote his family wistfully. Never again would he find such a "fraternity" of young writers like Harte and Stoddard—yet he would remain close to both men, and indissolubly linked to the city that had lifted him to literary greatness. In a few short years, San Francisco had honed the Washoe Giant into a writer of exceptional intensity. By the time he went East in 1866, all the colors of his palette were in place: the slashing wit, the moral urgency, the comic realism. He would be returning to a nation in desperate need of new voices. The country was in flux. The Civil War had unglued it from its past; in the years that followed, a fast-growing industrial economy sped it toward a bewildering future. In the midst of this came an outsider from the West to help America find its footing, a folk artist of improbable talent and originality who became, in the words of William Dean Howells, the "Lincoln of our literature."

Broadway on a Rainy Day
by Edward & Henry T. Anthony,
c. 1865.

FIVE

It had been thirteen years since Mark Twain last saw New York. When he stepped off the pier onto the city's icy, congested streets on January 12, 1867, he hardly recognized the place. Here was the nerve center of the new economy, full of buyers and sellers, plutocrats and paupers. The Civil War had unleashed Northern industry. Manufacturers who got rich making Union munitions now made consumer goods, and shipped them by rail to ever-expanding urban markets. In Manhattan, Twain detected a new tempo to everyday life. People didn't have time to be friendly: they were always in a rush. When a lady got on a crowded streetcar, no man stood up to offer his seat—"no man dreamt of doing such a thing," Twain wrote, watching America's most populous city backslide into "original barbarism."

Twain had a talent for taking the national temperature. The "fidgety, feverish restlessness" he felt in New York was a symptom of something larger: the new economic world that emerged after the Civil War. America was becoming modern. Among other things, this meant larger concentrations of capital and a starkly Darwinian approach to social relations. Also the compression of time and space, as a swiftly consolidating nation knitted itself together by rail.

While Twain elbowed his way through Manhattan's crowds, a similarly frenetic scene unfolded in the Sierras, as thousands of Chinese workers laid track for the transcontinental railroad. They worked at a frantic pace for pitiful wages, braving blizzards and avalanches and rockslides. Five years after Lincoln signed the Pacific Railway Act of 1862 into law, they did the backbreaking labor required to realize such an ambitious idea. The bill had stipulated two spans, each to be built by a different corporation: the Central Pacific would be responsible for the western half, starting from California, and the Union Pacific would oversee the eastern, starting from the Missouri River. The federal government subsidized the construction with bonds and land grants, awarded per mile of completed track. In theory, this would encourage the work to go faster. In practice, the companies bribed and manipulated lawmakers into making the incentives more generous, funneling an ever-larger share of public resources into private hands. What had once been envisioned as a patriotic endeavor to bind up a nation threatened by disunion became a feeding frenzy of government largesse.

Meanwhile, California anxiously awaited the moment when the rails would meet. The state's vanishing isolation would inspire large changes in its literary life. From Ina Coolbrith's parlor on Russian Hill, the Bohemians looked out over a new national landscape. A smaller country meant they could penetrate eastern markets more directly. Writers everywhere were in high demand. Surging literacy, the plummeting cost of printing, the rise of cities, and the growth of rail networks all conspired to produce a reading boom after the Civil War. The masses were ravenous for the printed word in all its bound and broadsheet varieties, and California helped sate the hunger. By 1867, Coolbrith had started publishing her poems in high-profile New York magazines like the *Galaxy* and *Harper's Weekly*. Bret Harte was writing columns for a pair of Massachusetts papers. Charles Warren Stoddard was preparing his first book.

Scaling the heights of the national literary scene wouldn't be

easy for any of them. It would inflict new anxieties and insecurities—
and Stoddard, still the baby of the Bohemians at twenty-three,
would feel these most acutely. By the spring of 1867, he was a mess.
The ordeal of publishing a book was shredding his nerves. As he
assembled his manuscript, the jittery streak that made him moody
and impulsive bloomed into full-scale panic. Harte offered a steady
hand, helping to collect the poems and read the proofs, but delays at
the printing office kept postponing the publication date. Finally,
Anton Roman, the enterprising local publisher, came to the rescue.
He agreed to take on the project, with one caveat: Stoddard would
go to Yosemite for the duration. There the author would sit tight
until the book was out and the press was singing his praises.

Before leaving for the valley that summer, Stoddard received an
encouraging note from a faraway friend. "Your book will be a
success—your book *shall* be a success—& I will destroy any man
that says the contrary," Twain wrote from New York in April 1867.
"I will back up your book just as strong as I know how. Count on me
to-day, to-morrow & *all the time*." Stoddard had sent his autograph
album for an inscription, and four days later, Twain returned it
with another ringing endorsement. "My Young Friend," he wrote,
"you stand now upon the threshold of the grand, mysterious Future,
and you are about to take the most momentous step in the march of
your life."

Twain's sympathy for Stoddard drew partly from the fact that he
knew exactly what the poor poet was going through. On the opposite coast, Twain was struggling with the same agony of bringing
his first book to print. He had landed in New York in early 1867
with a stack of clippings in his suitcase, eager to sell a manuscript
based on his Hawaii letters. But there were unforeseen obstacles,
like the heavy traffic that made traversing Manhattan all but impossible and the winter that made him shiver and curse like any
good Californian. Fortunately, he found a friend to keep him company: Charles Henry Webb, the founder of the *Californian*, who

had recently returned to New York and resumed his literary life there, writing for various papers and magazines. Webb lived only a couple of blocks from Twain's hotel, and he invited the frostbitten humorist over to his apartment for booze and a bit of advice. He suggested Twain shelve the Hawaii project and instead build a book around "Jim Smiley and His Jumping Frog." The still-famous story would be the collection's centerpiece; the rest would consist of sketches from the *Californian* and the *Virginia City Territorial Enterprise*. Webb even set up a meeting for Twain with Artemus Ward's publisher, George Carleton, to pitch the idea.

In February 1867, Twain descended on Carleton's offices at 499 Broadway, manuscript in hand. He expected the appointment to be little more than a formality: soon he would sign his first book contract, and be flying up the literary ladder he had come East to climb. In the anteroom, the clerk behind the counter greeted him warmly. When he learned Twain had come to sell a book and not to buy one, however, he did everything he could to discourage him. Undeterred, Twain penetrated this perimeter and reached the inner sanctum where Carleton sat. Twain walked in swaying and drawling like a drunk, his wild crop of red hair spiraling off his head in all directions. Carleton eyed this savage and could barely conceal his contempt. "Well, what can I do for you?" he demanded.

When Twain mentioned his book, Carleton "began to swell." He "went on swelling and swelling and swelling until he had reached the dimensions of a god of about the second or third degree," Twain recalled. Then came an eruption as violent as a volcano, an angry rush of words that "fell so densely that they darkened the atmosphere." "Books——" Carleton yelled, "look at those shelves! Every one of them is loaded with books that are waiting for publication. Do I want any more? Excuse me, I don't. Good morning."

This encounter inspired Twain to spend the next twenty-one years fantasizing about killing Carleton in "increasingly cruel and inhuman ways," until the delicious day when, on vacation in Switzerland, the publisher approached the now-famous writer to apologize. "I refused a book of yours, and for this I stand without competitor as the prize ass of the nineteenth century," Carleton said—or so Twain recalled in his autobiography, savoring the sweet pleasure of this "long-delayed revenge."

Carleton had a rough touch, but he wasn't alone in his initial opinion of Twain. He later said he spurned the strange visitor because he "looked so disreputable," and many people agreed. Twain was a western import, vulgar in dress and diction, and this made the path to eastern success steeper than he expected. He needed to prune his less palatable aspects while retaining enough of what made him distinctive—a delicate negotiation that would preoccupy Twain for decades. Carleton's rejection wouldn't be the last. But what made that day in February 1867 especially painful was another humiliation that Twain neglected to mention in his autobiography: around the same time that Carleton declined to publish Twain's first book, he agreed to publish Harte's. From the publisher's point of view, Harte was surely a safer bet: less "disreputable," more agreeable to good taste. His manuscript, like Twain's, consisted of previously published pieces, including his "Condensed Novels" for the *Californian*.

Twain was furious when he found out. Harte had always seemed one step ahead. Now, three thousand miles away, the dapper Bohemian was outmaneuvering him once again. "How is Bret?" Twain wrote Stoddard in April 1867. "He is publishing with a Son of a Bitch who will swindle him." "I don't know how his book is coming on—" he added spitefully, "we of Bohemia keep away from Carleton's." Twain had every reason to resent Harte's advantages: despite the national renown of "Jim Smiley and His Jumping Frog," Twain still bore the stigma of the "low" frontier. His competitiveness with Harte only grew sharper in the coming years, as he strove to break free of that label.

Eventually Webb offered to publish Twain's book himself, after more publishers declined it. Twain revised the manuscript, swapping out words that might offend or bewilder eastern readers: "hell" became "hades," "bully" became "jolly." This self-editing would be crucial for Twain's career: by smoothing his rougher edges, it ultimately helped him infiltrate American culture and not remain forever at its fringes. At first glance, the volume that appeared in May 1867 looked like a well-polished piece of work. *The Celebrated Jumping Frog of Calaveras County, and Other Sketches* made a gorgeous addition to booksellers' shelves: bound in cloth, it featured a golden frog on its cover, leaping into space.

Sadly, the pages inside presented a less distinguished appearance. To Twain's horror, the text was full of typos, errors, and last-minute editorial changes. He had spent March back home in Missouri, and hadn't read the proofs before they went to print. Webb, after persuading Twain to do the book in the first place, had let him down. The book sold poorly. The popularity of the jumping frog story wasn't enough to make people buy it. Twain put on a good face in public, bragging in his letters to the *Alta California* about the collection's "excellent style." In private, however, he admitted the scale of the disaster. "It is full of damnable errors of grammar & deadly inconsistencies of spelling," he wrote Harte on May 1, 1867. "[B]ut be a friend & say nothing about these things." Confessing his failure to a man whose success he keenly envied only added to his embarrassment.

Fortunately, he was far too ambitious to pin all his hopes on one project. The powerful dread of the poorhouse that kept him working even at his darkest moments carried him forward once again. In the same letter to Harte, he revealed his next undertaking: bringing his Hawaii lecture to New York. In typical Twain fashion, he picked the biggest hall in town: Cooper Union. This was the site where, in 1860, Lincoln had delivered the speech that helped pave his way to the presidency—a diatribe against the expansion of slavery into the West and a defiant response to the threat of Southern secession. That night, Lincoln had premiered the oratorical prowess that over the

next five years would make him America's storyteller-in-chief, the
man who gave meaning to the Civil War, who saw in its terrible rush
of events the potential to fulfill the nation's founding promises.

Seven years later, another western storyteller took the stage.
More than two thousand people crammed inside Cooper Union on
May 6, 1867, to see him. They had been lured there by newspaper
ads, handbills, posters, even a free ticket giveaway—all orchestrated
by Frank Fuller, an old friend whom Twain had enlisted as his manager. At seven thirty, the performer appeared—nattily dressed in a
tailored suit, at Fuller's insistence. He walked to the edge of the
stage, stared at his spectators, and set about making them howl. "For
an hour and fifteen minutes I was in Paradise," Twain recalled.
"From every pore I exuded a divine delight." The reviews the next
day reported a great hit. "It was certainly peculiar and original,"
ventured the *New York Tribune*, adding that Twain's style "needs to
be seen to be understood."

That night, Twain proved he could bring his Pacific personality
to an Atlantic audience; that, like Lincoln, he could find the fila-
ment that wove one corner of the country to another. He might've
capitalized on this insight to embark on a lecture tour throughout
the East, earning money and fame. But by the time Twain took the
stage of Cooper Union in May, he already had something bigger
in mind. That summer, an old Union navy ship called the *Quaker
City* would set sail across the Atlantic with a well-feathered flock of
Americans aboard. This would be the first organized pleasure cruise
in the country's history. The prospectus promised an ambitious
itinerary—Europe, the Holy Land, Egypt, the Crimea—and the
press gossiped about the star-studded passenger list, said to include
celebrities like Henry Ward Beecher and William Tecumseh Sherman. Naturally, Twain was itching to join. "Send me $1,200 at once,"
he telegraphed his editors at the *Alta California*. "I want to go
abroad." They acquiesced, paying his fare. After several delays, and
the withdrawal of Beecher, Sherman, and many other marquee

names from the trip, the *Quaker City* finally churned its enormous side wheel through New York harbor on June 8, 1867. The ship dropped anchor near Brooklyn to wait out a storm, lingering for two days before continuing on to the open sea. Twain was comfortably installed in an upper-deck cabin, eagerly awaiting his next adventure. He would be visiting the cradle of Christian civilization—not as a humble colonial, worshipping at the altar of the Old World, but as a new kind of American: skeptical, confident, vigorously independent. It would be a reverse pilgrimage of sorts, going to distant countries to discover his own.

TWAIN'S IMPATIENCE SERVED HIM WELL. Instead of dwelling on his hatred for Carleton, his jealousy of Harte, and his exasperation at Webb for botching his first book, he sprinted headlong into his next endeavor. "A man has no business to be depressed by a disappointment," he later wrote. "[H]e ought to make up his mind to get even."

In the summer of 1867, Stoddard could've used this advice. While Twain sailed across the ocean, the poet sat in Yosemite, counting down the days until his book appeared. Buoyed by the encouragement of his friends, he prayed for a victorious debut. For the past half decade, Stoddard had been Bohemia's golden child. Now came the moment to fulfill the bright future everyone had forecast for him. In early September 1867, when his *Poems* finally came off the presses, he emerged from his leafy seclusion to face the public.

Even at his gloomiest, Stoddard could never have predicted the bloodbath that broke out upon his return. Back in San Francisco, he stepped right into the firing line. Reviewers pounced on his *Poems*, ridiculing him as "the pet of the literary 'Ring'": the pampered brat of a pretentious, cliquish elite. The resentments surrounding the *Outcroppings* saga were still raw, and Stoddard had a bull's-eye on his back simply by virtue of being a city boy. The soft, sensuous grain of his verse didn't help. The response from eastern critics was equally disappointing: although not uniformly hostile, they didn't exactly swoon either. A couple of prominent papers delivered especially harsh judgments, the kind that inevitably stuck in an author's mind. The *Nation* called his poems "imitation spasms." The *Round Table* lamented "the incubus of imitation which paralyzes the wings of his muse."

Unlike Twain, Stoddard didn't get angry and swear revenge. He didn't fantasize about killing his critics—he agreed with them. They confirmed what he had long suspected: that he wasn't a poet after all; that his poetry, as he put it, was the "mere wind-fall of unripe fruit." This discovery depressed him. Since boyhood, poetry had been a way to endure the other unhappiness in his life. If he couldn't hold down a job or succeed in school or find a young man to reciprocate his love, at least he could write verse. Poetry provided a role to play, an identity to inhabit. Without it, he was adrift.

Stoddard needed a new place of safety. He found it in the baptistery of St. Mary's Cathedral at two o'clock in the afternoon on November 2, 1867, where a priest wetted him with holy water and sealed his conversion to the Catholic faith. He had been mulling over the decision for at least a year, but the fiasco of his first book stoked his need for spiritual renewal. "From the steps of that altar I seemed to rise a new being," he remembered. He had always felt a sense of incompleteness, and a longing to be filled. He had tried Presbyterianism, Unitarianism, Methodism—but none of these plugged the hole in his heart as completely as Catholicism. It brought a more permanent version of the peace he had experienced in Hawaii a few years earlier. "I couldn't be anything else than a Catholic," he later said, "—except—except a downright savage, and I wish to God I were that!" His Catholicism and his infatuation with the "primitive" cultures of the Pacific belonged to the same impulse. Both satisfied his love of beauty, his taste for pageantry and ritual. Both offered alternatives to the drab materialism of American society.

Catholicism also helped Stoddard make sense of what he called his "temperament," and what later generations would call homosexuality. The sinfulness of the flesh, the consolation of confession, the possibility of forgiveness—these were useful concepts for a man always at war with himself. In the church, he obtained a purer outlet for his passions, a way to indulge his tenderheartedness without fear of rejection. Unlike many other men over the years, Christ would always return his love. "Shun all Humans," he wrote in his diary, "look straight to God and all is sure."

This was easier said than done, especially for someone as incurably human as Stoddard. Each Sunday he attended Mass and let his spirit take flight. Afterward, he walked to Coolbrith's house on Russian Hill to resume his earthly entanglements. The two friends traded "pleasant gossip of our familiars" in her parlor, she recalled, or took day trips to far parts of the city. They went to the beach below the Cliff House, and scoured the rocks at low tide for algae to add to Coolbrith's collection. They went to the coast along Fort Point, cooked lunch over a driftwood fire, and returned home "with too fragrant a spoil of sea-mosses, radiantly tired, in the gloaming." Weekends were precious to Coolbrith—her only free time away from teaching school and helping run her family's household—and she liked spending them with Stoddard. He made her laugh: often his "wit would break out" unexpectedly, she remembered, "as if he feared to appear too earnest."

Their time together also had a more melancholy side, and by early 1868, this would have been especially apparent. Stoddard's religious awakening helped settle his spirit but did little for his professional life. Within the brick-walled stillness of St. Mary's, he found peace; in the noisy world without, he still struggled to find his place. The disappointment of his *Poems* unmoored him, and left him anxious about making a living. If he wasn't a poet, then what was he?

While looking for the answer, he decided to give acting a try. His friend managed a theater company that would travel to Sacramento that spring, and Stoddard, despite his extreme sensitivity to criticism, had much to recommend him as a performer: a rich, deep voice and large, evocative eyes. He took the river steamer to Sacramento and, on March 13, 1868, made his theatrical debut. He played a minor character in a forgettable melodrama but acquitted himself admirably enough to impress the *Sacramento Union*, whose critic called him "natural and self-possessed."

Unfortunately, his talent for self-sabotage swiftly intervened. The day after his premiere, a pair of boys recognized him on the street. "That feller made his first appearance last night," one said to the other, "and he done bully!" This embarrassed him, and revealed a downside to being an actor: if he stood in one spot for any length of time, strangers would start talking to him. He hated it. The sort of stardom that Twain relished, Stoddard recoiled from. Soon an even bigger hurdle emerged: he couldn't learn his lines. Touring companies often performed many plays over a brief period, and the memorization proved too much for Stoddard's feeble powers of concentration. At night he tied a wet towel around his head to keep himself awake for long hopeless hours spent studying his script, and prayed the words would be in his brain by morning.

His friends did their best to support him. The letters they sent to Sacramento conveyed their sympathy and devotion. "Follow your own guidance," Coolbrith counseled, a couple of days before Stoddard first took the stage. She had just celebrated her twenty-seventh birthday, and missed him desperately. "I could not help wishing for a glimpse of your face," she wrote. Her correspondence reflected how intimate they had become, how much she relied on him as her confessor and confidant. Birthdays always brought her down: "They remind me too forcibly that life is passing to no purpose." She was widely known in San Francisco, but largely unknown everywhere else. She had seen her poetry praised in the *Nation* and published in a pair of popular New York papers, yet these were the sum total of her exposure in the eastern press. She couldn't help feeling "as if I had wasted, wasted utterly, every year and hour and moment of my life." She didn't have any suggestions for how Stoddard might resolve his latest difficulty; if anything, she found herself suffering from a similar crisis.

Harte wasn't much help either. "I've much to say but nothing to advise," he wrote Stoddard on March 16, 1868. "Whatever you do— short of arson or Chinese highway robbery, which are inartistic and ungentlemanly—I am, my dear boy, always yours." Harte, too, was feeling demoralized—although he had too fine a sense of decorum to confess this in his letter. By early 1868, the biggest name in the literary West had succumbed to the same feelings that had lately infected one after another of his friends. The contagion took many forms—Twain's frustrations with his first book, Stoddard's anguish over his, Coolbrith's more diffuse despair—but it shared a single root.

All four writers had recently seen rising success. But this brought rising expectations, and with it, more potential for disappointment. Harte was long thought to have the most promising future, and thus the most to lose by failing to fulfill it. As he readied his first book, he appeared poised to succeed where Twain and Stoddard had fallen short. George Carleton, the New York publisher who had humiliated Twain, would bring Harte to an eastern market. His prospects for a brilliant debut seemed assured.

When Harte's *Condensed Novels and Other Papers* appeared in October 1867, however, Twain could take vengeful pleasure in the result. It looked awful: poorly printed, on cheap paper, and marred by comic illustrations commissioned by Carleton. These engravings horrified Harte. They were caricatures, broadly drawn, and they skewed the book's tone too "low." Despite the high polish of Harte's prose, the pictures gave his pages a crude feel. As Twain had learned with *The Celebrated Jumping Frog*, presentation mattered— especially for western writers repackaging themselves for an eastern audience. Harte felt compelled to write letters to friends and potential reviewers disavowing Carleton's changes, but he couldn't entirely undo the damage. Even favorably inclined critics couldn't fail to notice them. The *Atlantic Monthly* praised his "charming parodies" but denounced the images as "vulgar and inappropriate."

Harte hated his first book. A "deformed brat," he called it, "malformed in its birth" by Carleton. What made the defeat harder to bear was a tragedy that hit Harte the same month: on October 27, 1867, his third son died. The child lived for only eight days. For a man who took pride in fatherhood, who parented his children with an affectionate intensity rarely seen in the rest of his life, his grief can only be imagined. He never discussed it. The loss certainly compounded the bitterness of his recent literary misfortune, and contributed to the gathering gloom that threatened to entirely submerge him by early 1868.

For the past eight years, Harte had wrestled with California. Their relationship was never easy. He didn't mind taking unpopular positions when he felt the dictates of conscience or good taste required it, as when he narrowly escaped being lynched after defending the Indians of Humboldt Bay, or braved the ire of the country bards excluded by *Outcroppings*. A loner since childhood, Harte saw independence as a virtue. His favorite writers were those who stood apart. He liked Stoddard's poetry because it resisted the groupthink of the "tuneful mob," and rose above the "hardness, skepticism and Philistinism of life on this coast." The pitiful reception of his friend's *Poems* could only confirm Harte's low opinion of local culture. "The curse of California," he wrote in February 1868, "has been its degrading, materialist influences which have reduced man and woman to the lowest working equivalents." For nearly a decade, Harte had done battle with these forces. Now he began to lose faith the fight could be won. Perhaps the "twitter, whirl and excitement" of the region would never settle into a rhythm conducive to deep thought. Perhaps Californians would never put art above commerce. Perhaps the East held more opportunities. He considered moving his family across the country to find out.

Just as Harte was getting ready to wash his hands of the West, however, something changed his mind. This would be the luckiest break of his life—the boon that rallied him from his slump and catapulted him to the attention of the postwar reading public. It would reunite him with Twain, and lift Stoddard and Coolbrith at the moment they most needed it. In retrospect, 1868 would be a turning point: the year when the long literary wave of California finally crested.

HARTE HAD ALWAYS THOUGHT California needed to outgrow its mercenary instincts to sustain a true literary culture. He had it backward. The only reason the region boasted so many writers to begin with was because it could afford to. The wealth generated by agriculture, mining, and trade created a market for local literature and gave people the leisure time required to read it. Harte could inveigh against California's "degrading, materialist influences," but those same influences subsidized his creativity. The cultural and economic fortunes of the state were inextricably linked.

Anton Roman understood this. The Bavarian-born bookseller had come to California during the gold rush, and made his fortune peddling books to bored miners. More recently, he had cashed in on the Bohemians by publishing both *Outcroppings* and Stoddard's *Poems*. No one had a better vantage point on the local literary scene, and by 1868, Roman felt California was on the verge of a breakthrough. The manuscripts piling up on his desk showed a new depth to local talent. Never before had he seen such a surplus of good writing. So he came up with an idea that most people must have seen as suicidal: a monthly magazine that printed only original work. There would be no pirated items of the kind that padded out most literary papers—and, astonishingly, he would pay cash for each contribution. Roman's name for his venture reflected his bullish faith in its success: the *Overland Monthly*, a transcontinental challenger to the mighty *Atlantic Monthly*.

First he needed an editor. Harte was the obvious candidate. Roman had his reservations. He worried Harte might "lean too much toward the purely literary"—a subtle way of saying he worried Harte might be too anti-Californian. The publisher wanted "a magazine that would help the material development of this Coast" by boosting its cultural profile among a national audience, and he hesitated to hand control to a man who made a point of spotlighting California's flaws.

Predictably, Harte didn't thrill to the idea either. He "threw cold water on the project" in their early meetings, Roman recalled. Harte doubted California had enough talented writers to make such a project possible. The collapse of the *Californian* lingered in his mind, as did the uproar over *Outcroppings*. But Roman believed. He felt it "in his bones," a friend observed, and once he had decided Harte should be his editor, he applied his considerable energies toward achieving that goal. One can picture the gregarious publisher parrying Harte's concerns, one after another. Roman had already extracted advertising pledges from local merchants to cover the *Overland*'s start-up costs. He also promised to supply a portion of the content himself, with selections drawn from his ever-growing stack of manuscripts.

But the most memorable moment of their negotiation, as Roman remembered, involved a geography lesson. A map hung on the wall of Roman's office. He showed Harte "the central position of San Francisco" between the hemispheres. The transcontinental railroad would be completed in a year. The Pacific Mail Steamship Company had recently started regular service from San Francisco to Japan and China, accelerating transpacific traffic. Once the coasts were connected by rail, California hoped to become a nexus for global trade, bridging Asia with America and Europe. This was the basis of

Roman's unshakable optimism: the belief that the railroad would make San Francisco the center of the world.

Harte accepted. He was still skeptical of the magazine's survival but couldn't pass up the chance to continue his cultural crusade. "I am trying to build up a literary taste on the Pacific slope," he explained to a friend. "I want to make a good fight while it lasts." The outcome was anyone's guess. "The *Overland* marches steadily along to meet its Fate," he wrote Stoddard, "but what [it is] I know not." In the spring of 1868, Roman took his editor on a trip to help answer this question. They brought their respective families, and spent nearly three months touring the countryside south of San Francisco. The two men had much to discuss before the unveiling of the *Overland* that summer.

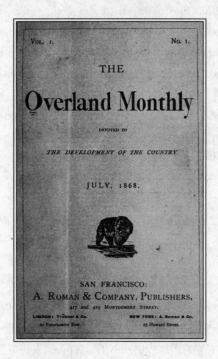

The cover of the first issue of the
Overland Monthly.

Their differences ran deep. Roman admired the pioneers of California's past and felt confident of its golden future; Harte ridiculed the former and felt ambivalent about the latter. Roman was a booster, Harte a Bohemian—yet, somehow, they found a way to build a mutually beneficial relationship that brought the *Overland* to life.

When the first issue landed in July 1868, its cover carried an engraving that neatly illustrated the constructive tension at its core. Originally, the design had featured a grizzly bear, a symbol of California. Then Harte drew two parallel lines under it, to represent the approaching railroad. This simple image offered a complex commentary on the Far West's future. It showed the miracle of steam and steel awaited by Roman and many others—yet its tone was hardly triumphant. As Harte himself explained, the bear "recognizes his rival and his doom" in the "coming engine of civilization and progress." Their encounter would be violent. It would involve the annihilation of the primitive past by the industrial future—a microcosm of the economic forces overhauling the country as a whole.

Twain loved the engraving. He later called it the "prettiest fancy" that "ever shot through Harte's brain." He could congratulate the *Overland*'s editor in person: in a typical feat of good timing, he had swept back into San Francisco on April 2, a few months before the magazine's launch. He hadn't set foot in the city for more than a year, and had been breathtakingly busy in the interval. His voyage aboard the *Quaker City* in 1867 had succeeded beyond his wildest dreams. For five months, he had watched a horde of American tourists overrun the Old World's holiest and most historic sites, and captured the comic spectacle in fifty letters for the *Alta California*. In the spring of 1868, the San Francisco–based paper published the last of them.

Twain's dispatches didn't just circulate in California. They also caught the eye of a Connecticut publisher named Elisha Bliss Jr., who offered to turn them into a book. The author enthusiastically agreed. After the anticlimax of *The Celebrated Jumping Frog*, he leaped at the chance to mount another assault on the publishing world. There was only one problem: the *Alta* owned the copyright to the letters. When the paper's editors got wind of Twain's plans, they shot off a telegram reminding him of this fact in no uncertain terms. They had bankrolled his overseas adventures, and didn't like losing their investment to another publisher. Twain brushed them off, but the editors soon raised the stakes. They threatened to pre-empt Twain's book with their own collection. Twain swallowed his pride and tried asking their permission nicely. When the editors again refused, he boarded a steamer for San Francisco to talk face-to-face. This was what brought him West at the same moment that Harte was assembling the *Overland*: a deadlocked copyright dispute that threatened to torpedo his next book. "Mark Twain has got a scrape on his hands," howled the *Marysville Appeal*.

Those hoping for blood would be disappointed. Twain didn't come to California "to break somebody's head," as the *Appeal* presumed. He came to negotiate. Whatever his flaws as a businessman, he excelled at the bargaining table. In the spring of 1868, he strode into the *Alta*'s offices in San Francisco and faced off with one of the paper's owners. Somehow, Twain walked away with everything he wanted: the *Alta* wouldn't publish its book; he would go ahead with his. On May 5, 1868, Twain gave Bliss the good news. "The Alta people, after some hesitation, have given me permission," he wrote. "I am steadily at work, & shall start east with the completed manuscript about the middle of June."

This gave him little more than a month. He had a tremendous amount to do. The letters alone weren't enough to sustain a whole book. Written on the fly, they made a scattered, uneven chronicle of his trek through Europe and the Middle East. He promised Bliss to "weed them of their chief faults of construction & inelegancies of expression." He needed to build a continuous story from their diverse parts, one that could appeal to a national audience. This meant not merely punching up the prose but eliminating regional references that only made sense to Californian readers. It also involved purging the profanity, irreverence, and mean-spirited mockery that occasionally made his *Quaker City* correspondence too risqué for mainstream tastes.

Twain had recently been reminded of how much he could benefit from this sort of self-censorship. Barely two weeks after stepping off the steamer, on April 14, 1868, he had played a sold-out show in San Francisco and was eviscerated by the critics. Entitled "Pilgrim Life," the lecture gave highlights of his time abroad, in the same comic-travelogue vein that produced his first Hawaii talk. Only this time, the jokes had a nastier flavor, particularly in his merciless portrait of the other *Quaker City* sightseers and his general contempt for Christianity. The *Morning Call* upbraided Twain for "carving the sconces of proper folk." The *California Weekly Mercury* deplored his "sacrilegious allusions." His treatment of the Holy Land invited special outrage, as when he cast doubt on the Second Coming by saying Christ wouldn't dare return to so dreary a part of the world as Palestine. Soon the pulpits joined the papers in condemning such blasphemy. "The most straight-laced of the preachers here cannot well get through a sermon without turning aside to give me a blast," Twain complained.

If he wanted his book to be a hit, he would have to tone it down. For help, he turned to an old friend: Harte. The fellow writer had long helped Twain tame his wilder impulses, ever since their days together at the *Californian*. Now, in the spring of 1868, Harte took time from his busy schedule to wade through Twain's unwieldy manuscript. Many of the pages had been composed in manic all-night writing binges. They included cut-and-pasted letters from the original newsprint, with revisions penned in the margins, plus entirely new passages. Twain later estimated that he had worked from eleven or twelve in the evening until dawn the next day for an entire month. The result was a mishmash of reheated and freshly cooked copy, just the sort of literary mélange that could use Harte's meticulous editorial eye.

For Harte to undertake such a task while also preparing the first issue of the *Overland Monthly* demonstrated true devotion. Whacking a path through Twain's shaggy draft would be hard work. Happily, Harte had no scruples about cutting with a wide stroke. He "told me what passages, paragraphs & *chapters* to leave out—& I followed orders strictly," Twain later said. This would be Harte's greatest act of friendship, and Twain, all competitiveness aside, felt grateful for it. He credited Harte with transforming him from "an awkward utterer of coarse grotesquenesses" into an author suited for the national scene. Harte wouldn't be the book's only editor, but he left a sizable mark. A comparison of the *Alta* letters with the book manuscript offers hints of his influence. The language grew tighter, the storytelling more coherent. The slang vanished; the diction matured. "Jackass" became "donkey"; "fooled" became "deceived." Most important, the humor softened. The insolent digs at religion and his *Quaker City* shipmates mellowed into gentler gibes.

By early summer, Twain had a deliverable text. "[T]he book is finished," he wrote Bliss on June 17, 1868, "& I think it will do." He planned to return to New York by the end of the month but couldn't resist extending his stay for one final lecture. On the evening of July 2, an immense crowd cheered his return to the San Francisco stage. He spoke on Venice, blending humor and memoir and history in a gripping performance that lasted nearly two hours and included "no slang & no inelegancies," as he boasted to a friend. The critics loved it: "wit without vulgarity," declared the *Dramatic Chronicle*. He had redeemed himself. Instead of cracking off-color jokes about the Savior, he gave gondolas in the Grand Canal by moonlight. He described a Venetian Republic that, centuries ago, had ruled the rich trade between Europe and Asia—a perfect subject for San Franciscans, who expected the railroad to bestow similar privileges. Four days later, he sailed for New York. He would never again return to the city that raised him as a writer. He didn't need to: it had already given him what he wanted. When he first came seesawing down its streets in 1863, he was mostly unknown. By the time he left for the last time, he carried the manuscript that would forever make him famous.

THE SAME MONTH TWAIN WENT EAST, Harte debuted the *Overland*. Both men were on the brink of glory, and helped each other across the threshold. In exchange for Harte's heroic edits, Twain gave him four excerpts for the magazine. When the inaugural issue appeared in July 1868, it included the first of these—a preview of a highly anticipated project by one of the Far West's best-loved writers. It was a brilliant coup by Harte, an early sign of his editorial shrewdness. Whatever his initial doubts, he put his whole heart into making the *Overland* soar. It offered a gleam of hope after the disaster of his first book and the death of his infant son. It drew him out. A man who rarely socialized in the street now waylaid his writers when he saw them. If they dodged him, his letters would follow them home, one after another, until they surrendered and sent him pages.

Then the real work began: out came the editor's pen, for Harte to start chiseling the raw text into something that met his standards. He wasn't timid, although he treated his writers with enough tact to dull whatever pain they felt at his incisions. They knew that he made the same demands on his own writing as he did on theirs. He also had a gift for making them feel as if they were in it together: as if the hundred-odd pages of essays, poetry, and fiction that filled the *Overland* each month were a collaboration, and not just the product of one overworked genius.

The day after the *Overland* launched, Harte invited Stoddard and Coolbrith to the magazine's offices above Roman's bookshop. The summer of 1868 found both in a fragile place: Stoddard had recently slunk back home after ditching his stage career in Sacramento; Coolbrith felt stagnant and blue. Harte would help deliver them from their collective funk. They would become his star contributors, and his copilots: the crew he relied on to keep this glittering new flagship of the literary West afloat. "He called us his children," Coolbrith remembered. "[W]e were almost like members of one family." He gave them keys to the *Overland* sanctum. They would meet there, or climb the hill to Coolbrith's house to take tea in her parlor and talk over the next issue's table of contents.

They became inseparable: the Overland Trinity, as they came to be known. It was a hefty title for such a delicate-looking group. Anyone who caught them rushing down Montgomery Street with bundles of proofs under their arms could be forgiven for not realizing these three were the all-powerful arbiters of literary taste in California. But they had certainly earned it. For years, they had watched the coast grow, and had grown along with it: from the *Golden Era* of its infancy to the *Californian* of its adolescence. Now came the *Overland Monthly* to usher in its adulthood, on the eve of the railroad that would complete California's coming-of-age.

"We were critics, editors, poets, authors, type-setters," Coolbrith recalled. "Each and any duty, any one of us was ready to perform, and we worked for one common end, the success of Bret Harte's— nay, our—magazine." But Harte didn't just edit the *Overland*: he also wrote for it. In fact, the magazine carried his finest writing to date, the work that finally brought him national acclaim.

It all began with "The Luck of Roaring Camp" in the *Overland*'s second issue, a short story about the gold rush. The subject wasn't a new one for Harte. He had tried writing fiction about the pioneer era before, using place-names and slang and other touches of local color to create a distinctively Californian setting. What made "The Luck of Roaring Camp" different was its use of irony— the ingredient that enabled him to unlock the creative power of the Pacific coast.

"The Luck of Roaring Camp" opens in a California mining town in 1850. In a cabin at the edge of a clearing, an Indian prostitute is giving birth. A hundred miners stand outside, waiting. These broken, barely human men have names like Stumpy and Kentuck, and are missing fingers and toes and ears and eyes. Instead of feeling sympathy for the woman's suffering, they make bets on whether she will survive.

She dies, but the baby lives. The miners adopt it as their own. But child rearing doesn't come easily to them: the best they can manage is a weird parody of parenting. They shower the child with wildly inappropriate gifts, like a revolver and a tobacco box. They christen it in a "burlesque of a church service," complete with a choir and "mock altar." They name it "The Luck," out of the belief that it brings them good fortune in the gold ditches, and even begin to worship the child as a little god. Then winter comes, and the snowmelt causes the water to rise. A flood overruns the camp and The Luck drowns.

Harte had discovered what frontier yarn spinners had long known: that the West was a darkly funny place. What elsewhere would happen naturally—raising a child—becomes a ridiculous farce in the upside-down world of Roaring Camp. The miners try to civilize themselves for The Luck's sake, but the most they can muster is an absurd caricature of normal society. They don't know the first thing about traditional institutions like family or religion. Luck is their only faith: a belief in fortune, and the knowledge that it can change. The same water that washes gold down the Sierras also destroys the camp. "Water put the gold into them gulches!" exclaims one of the miners. "It's been here once and will be here again!" Their story isn't a triumphant epic of western conquest, but a sick joke, the ironies heightened by the narrator's slyly satiric tone.

Not everyone saw the humor. "The Luck of Roaring Camp" found detractors early, starting with the proofreader at the *Overland*'s printing office. She was a pious woman, a "vestal virgin" in the opinion of one *Overland* staffer, and she bristled at the impropriety of Harte's tale: particularly the use of a prostitute as a character and the expletives uttered by the miners. Anton Roman later recalled riding valiantly into this "great hullabaloo" to override the proofreader and order the story published. Harte remembered it a bit differently: Roman got cold feet, fearing the tale might "imperil the prospects of the magazine," prompting a showdown between editor and publisher. Harte "writhed under it, even to the point of resigning," Coolbrith recalled. But at length he prevailed, Roman yielded, and "The Luck" went to press.

Locally, the critics shrugged. A "pleasant little sketch," yawned the *Alta California*. In Harte's recollection, the religious press had a harsher verdict. "Christians were cautioned against pollution by its contact," he later wrote. "[B]usiness men were gravely urged to condemn and frown upon this picture of California society that was not conducive to Eastern immigration." These halfwits might have had the last word, if the August 1868 issue of the *Overland* hadn't reached the Atlantic coast and touched off a tidal wave of applause that came crashing across the continent that fall. "[O]ne of the best magazine articles that we have read in many months," gushed the *Nation*. A "genuine California story," proclaimed the *Springfield Republican*. Nothing from Harte's pen had ever landed quite like this. The *Atlantic Monthly*'s editor, James T. Fields, rated "The Luck" so highly that he offered to publish anything its author wrote. This amounted to a blank check from America's most prestigious literary paper, a windfall that would make most writers fall weeping out of their chair. Not Harte. "I'll try to find time to send you something," he replied. "The *Overland* is still an experiment," and "should it fail . . . why I dare say I may be able to do more."

Harte knew exactly where his loyalties lay: at the head of the Overland Trinity, alongside the friends who had shared his frustrations at the story's hard path to print and now shared his joy at its breakout success. He was right: the *Overland* was an experiment. It tested a hypothesis long pondered on the Pacific coast: whether the Far West could produce a national literary platform on a par with the *Atlantic*. By the fall of 1868, the results were in. Eastern papers had embraced the *Overland*'s "Far Western flavor," its "Pacific freshness." "It is by no means a mere copy of Atlantic or European habits of thought and style, but smacks of its native soil," noted the *New York Home Journal*. These strange new tastes arrived at an opportune time, as America's rapidly growing readership fueled an expanding market for print. The novelty-hungry masses helped

A building at Clay and Battery Streets
damaged in the 1868 earthquake.

make the *Overland* a hit. Within its first two years, the magazine's circulation in the eastern states would be the same as in California, Nevada, and Oregon combined.

Yet Harte, instead of being hailed as a hero, remained a controversial figure in California. "The Luck of Roaring Camp" found favor with local critics only after their eastern counterparts praised it. "Since Boston endorsed the story, San Francisco was properly proud of it," Harte explained. This dynamic wasn't difficult to explain. "The Luck" showed California in a distinctly unsentimental light. From a purely promotional point of view, it was bad publicity. Harte didn't care: he liked being the flea in the region's boosterish hide, and in the fall of 1868, he would routinely play that role in the pages of the *Overland*.

ON THE MORNING OF October 21, 1868, a violent earthquake shook San Franciscans out of their houses and into the streets. Panic prevailed. "Many acted as if they thought the Day of Judgment had come," one journalist reported. When the dust settled, people found their city in ruins, wrecked by the worst tremor since the American conquest of California. The earth had cracked open in many places, and sank several feet in others. Many major buildings suffered severe damage, including City Hall. Areas built on landfill, like the business district east of Montgomery Street, looked especially postapocalyptic. Toppled chimneys, shattered glass, and loosened chunks of masonry littered the pavement.

In an eerie coincidence, Harte had recently written about earthquakes in the *Overland Monthly.* "The nineteenth century is unfortunately no more superior to earthquakes than was the ninth," he said, and the disaster that followed would offer terrible evidence of that fact. Despite all the advances of modern technology—"electric telegraphs, photography, chloroform," to name a few—temblors could still strike whenever they pleased. It was a lesson that would've been obvious to an earlier era of Californians, back when people regularly lost their homes to fires and floods, or their money to the faro table. Life during the gold rush was full of sudden reversals of fortune, the sort dramatized by "The Luck of Roaring Camp." But to the rising capitalist class of San Francisco, who envisioned a more solidly prosperous future fixed to the coming railroad, the earthquake of 1868 was profoundly embarrassing. It exposed a frightening instability beneath the veneer of civilization they had worked hard to create. It showed that no matter how much progress the city had made since 1849, some dark undomesticated wildness endured—that San Francisco was still a gambler's paradise, if only because it sat on such incorrigibly quaky soil.

The city would be rebuilt. But its businessmen feared for its reputation. If San Francisco became permanently branded as an earthquake town, it might kill future investment and immigration. Within hours of the disaster, the Chamber of Commerce held an emergency meeting to discuss ways to prevent this. Moments after the first shock, reports of the destruction had gone out over the transcontinental telegraph. The chamber needed to take control of the narrative. So its members drafted a telegram, to send to eastern and European cities. They substantially underreported the damage and blamed the collapsed buildings on poor construction. Over the coming weeks, most of the city's papers repeated these lies. Knowing their words would reach the rest of the nation by wire, they trumpeted the idea that "criminal carelessness" was the culprit—not immutable natural forces of the sort that might make San Francisco inhospitable to development.

Harte couldn't have asked for a bigger slice of boosterism to sink his satirical teeth into. In the next *Overland*, he ridiculed the notion that the earthquake could've been avoided "with a little more care and preparation on our part." His defiance stirred the wrath of the "dignified dons of the city," a friend recalled, who didn't enjoy seeing their public-relations campaign exposed as a fraud.

Harte couldn't help himself. Bolstered by the success of "The Luck of Roaring Camp," he felt freer to indulge his contrarian impulses. In October 1868, he edited an article that offered a more sustained critique of California. Its author was Henry George, a local printer and journalist who had published a handful of literary sketches in the *Californian*. In the *Overland*, he showed a more polemical side, training his cantankerous eloquence on a topic of supreme urgency to all Californians: the transcontinental railroad. The result, "What the Railroad Will Bring Us," was one of the most important pieces ever published in the magazine. It forecast a disaster worse than any earthquake, and one too large for San Francisco's leading citizens to sweep under the rug.

George began with a simple question. "What is the railroad to do for *us?*—this railroad that we have looked for, hoped for, prayed for so long?" The Central Pacific and the Union Pacific were nearing their junction in the Utah desert, to be completed within a year. This long-awaited link would hopefully give California greater prosperity and population, and make San Francisco the seat of a commercial empire. And yet, within this apparently favorable turn of events lurked an awful threat. "The locomotive is a great centralizer," George wrote. "It kills towns and builds up great cities, and in the same way kills little businesses and builds up great ones." The economic forces unfettered by its arrival wouldn't benefit everyone equally—on the contrary, it would concentrate wealth in the hands of the few, and make life harder for the rest. Mass immigration would force real estate prices up and wages down. The railroad barons, big landholders, and factory owners stood to gain an ever-greater share of land and capital, while ordinary people found it harder to earn a decent living. California's relatively egalitarian society would disappear, fractured by the growing gulf between rich and poor already seen in the industrializing East. San Francisco would have its own Astors and Vanderbilts—and its own scenes of ruthless poverty to match those of Massachusetts mill towns and

Manhattan slums. "When liveries appear," George wrote, "look out for bare-footed children."

Later, George would expand on these insights to produce his 1879 best seller *Progress and Poverty*. He would become a godfather of American progressivism, an inspiration to those who sought to create a more humane alternative to the jungle capitalism of the late nineteenth century. In the pages of the *Overland*, George took his first step in that direction. He sounded a dissonant note of caution among the chorus of California's optimists. Not everything he predicted would come to pass, but the pessimistic thrust of his argument would be largely borne out by the years that followed. He realized the scale of the coming changes, not just to California's economy but to its soul—a society born in the gold rush, brought up by the Civil War, and now on the verge of losing its roots. "In California there has been a certain cosmopolitanism, a certain freedom and breadth of common thought and feeling, natural to a community made up from so many different sources," he noted. This quality had sustained San Francisco's literary scene. It had nourished Harte, Stoddard, Coolbrith, and Twain, and given them a sandbox to romp around in. The locomotive would eventually flatten this culture, iron out its idiosyncrasies. It would bring a grimmer era, blighted by economic uncertainty and social upheaval. In 1868, George caught sight of the bust at the end of the bonanza.

Chinese railroad workers in Bloomer Cut, 1860s. Bloomer Cut was a corridor through the Sierra Nevada, built for the transcontinental railroad.

SIX

The connection couldn't be completed on time. Heavy rains and a labor dispute caused a delay. The railroad would take two more days to finish. On May 8, 1869, the two halves of the transcontinental track were to meet in Utah, and San Francisco was ready to celebrate. No single moment in its short history had been more keenly anticipated than this—and neither the bankers nor the stevedores nor any of the ethnic societies, fraternal orders, labor leagues, army battalions, marching bands, or unaffiliated revelers planning to take part wanted to postpone what promised to be the party of the century. So they did what westerners often did when inconvenient facts threatened to spoil a good story line: they ignored them.

At sunrise, cannon woke the city. By ten, the streets overflowed. A telegram came from Sacramento announcing the railroad's completion—a fake message, intended to serve as the parade's starting signal. The procession lurched forward in reply. Horse-drawn floats made a tableau of the city's many tribes: German gymnasts swung from parallel bars, ironworkers brandished a newly built locomotive. Artillery, steam whistles, and church bells blared. Under the springtime sun, people of all classes and colors staged a performance worthy of the occasion. At night they lit bonfires and sent five hundred rockets sputtering into the night sky.

By the time the Central Pacific and Union Pacific finally met at Promontory Summit, Utah, on May 10, 1869, San Francisco had been partying for two days straight. That morning, the wire ticked with the real signal—done. The city gave one last roar. The guns at Fort Point boomed, the fire alarms rang, and the rest of the country, informed simultaneously by telegram, burst into cheers. Omaha, Chicago, New Orleans, New York—the continent rejoiced. Four years after the end of the war that had almost cut the Union in two, "Uncle Sam's Waistband" girded it tighter than ever before. A journey that lasted about twenty-four days by stagecoach from St. Louis to San Francisco, and often even longer by steamer from New York, now took a week from coast to coast. It was "a victory over space," declared one San Francisco newspaper, a shrinking of the West's epic scale. Californians felt confident that great things would result.

BEFORE LONG, THE JUBILANT MOOD would fade. In retrospect, the story followed the typical western pattern: delusion, then disappointment. The greenhorn goes to the mines to become a millionaire and dies broke in a boardinghouse: this is the seed of California humor, the collision of romance with reality. The arrival of the railroad would close a chapter in California history, inflicting radical changes on the social world that had sustained the decade's Bohemian experiment. At the time, however, it took an especially prescient pair of eyes to see this coming—what most people saw was a gleaming monument to the new American industrialism, a marvel of modern engineering that connected the nation both physically and culturally.

The railroad didn't just carry people and goods. It carried books, newspapers, ideas. It carried the June 1869 issue of the *Overland Monthly*, with new fiction by Bret Harte. In the ten months since

"The Luck of Roaring Camp," the magazine's esteemed editor had continued to feed his growing fan base with stories of gold diggers, gamblers, and whores. Eastern papers reprinted them; James T. Fields, the editor of the *Atlantic Monthly*, even offered to collect them into a book. They arrived at an ideal moment, just as the railroad stoked the country's curiosity about the West and a postwar publishing boom created more print products to satisfy it.

Dime novels were the lowbrow equivalents of Harte's tales: lurid morsels of frontier melodrama, wrapped in cheap paper and popular in eastern cities. They offered parables of rugged individualism and wide-open spaces to urban readers whose lives were increasingly absent of both. They appealed to an era in which tenements and factories and corporations and bureaucracy were aggregating human beings into a mass of interchangeable parts. They provided a national epic of conquest, of white settlers subduing the wilderness and the Indians, to men whose masculinity seemed to be crumbling under the assault of the machine age. As the nineteenth century wore on, America's infatuation with the "Wild West" would only grow.

This set the scene for Harte's success with eastern readers. What distinguished his stories from their pop-cultural competitors wasn't just the quality of the writing. It was his wit—the mischievous streak that sizzled just beneath the surface. Harte had come to absorb the lesson of his friend Mark Twain: that frontier humor was the resin in which the peculiar power of American speech was caught and crystallized. Those wacky yarns told by the barroom stove held the promise of a national literature liberated from "the trammels of English literary precedent," Harte later wrote, the "inchoate poetry" of a unique American vernacular. Twain had inaugurated this revolt with "Jim Smiley and His Jumping Frog"; now, in the pages of the *Overland*, Harte tried to bring the spirit of the frontier to short fiction.

He did so subtly: not just with California settings and characters but with finely calibrated nuances of tone. Harte's best stories, like the man himself, relied on a measure of deception. Just as his fashionable clothes belied a sneering Bohemian wit, his fiction wore a polite disguise that let it pass easily into respectable company. At first glance, Harte's stories appeared to satisfy the tender pieties of good taste. He laced them with bits of pathos—like orphans and hookers with hearts of gold—calculated to yank at the reader's heartstrings. Yet on closer inspection, these were parodies of the sentimentalism they pretended to embrace. They came laden with the kind of ironic reversals familiar from everyday life on the frontier. A man stranded in the wilderness kills himself to leave enough food for his friends to survive—they die anyway. A father reunites with his estranged son—only to find out he's an impostor. These follow the contours of frontier humor: the setup, then the "snapper," as Twain called the punch line that concludes a comic tale.

The *Overland* stories that began traveling east by transcontinental rail in 1869 would create an infinitely richer picture of the Far West than the one painted by pulp fantasy. They showed a place of paradox and incongruity, where conventional rules of sentiment and syntax broke down, and humor overlaid everything. They confirmed Harte's calling as a humorist, and his identity as a westerner. Despite his relentless criticism of California, he loved its indigenous irony—"the Western predilection to take a humorous view of any principle or sentiment," as he later called it. As a boy, he had developed a wry exterior to deflect the cruel taunts of other children. By the time he was thirty-three, this facade had grown virtually impregnable. His voice always hovered uncertainly between sincerity and sarcasm, his meaning as elaborately layered as his dress. He was as shifty as a frontier fabulist, as slippery as a confidence man hustling a watch off your wrist. "You could never be sure of Harte," William Dean Howells later said. "He was a tease."

Yet there were a select few who cracked this armor. In 1869, as the *Overland* took flight, Ina Coolbrith became one of them. They had been friends for years, and had collaborated closely on the premier literary paper of the Pacific coast since its debut the previous summer. But it wasn't until the abrupt departure of the third of the Overland Trinity—Charles Warren Stoddard—that their relationship really began.

Ever since the failure of his first book in 1867, Stoddard had struggled. The poet had been promised a glorious career from an early age. Now twenty-five, he seemed in danger of never achieving it. His conversion to Catholicism brought a measure of peace, as did the founding of the *Overland*, which provided a place to publish under Harte's patient tutelage. "He was an exacting and relentless critic," Stoddard recalled, and those honest critiques did immeasurable good for a writer too often coddled by his literary elders.

But sharp editing alone couldn't solve his problems. His real enemy was the manic energy that spun his nerves into knots or left them unspooling in long stretches of lethargy. He hated being alone, and compulsively sought the company of others. "Why do you waste your time among these people?" he remembered Harte saying. "They encourage you in idleness when you should be hard at work." Yet the harder he applied himself, the more his mind resisted. It fled to other places, like Hawaii, and the memory of the naked native boys he had found there four years earlier. He longed to return, and when the opportunity arose, he seized it. His sister had recently married a rich American in Maui, and they invited him to visit. He finagled a traveling commission from the *San Francisco Evening Bulletin* to pay his way, and set sail in October 1868 for eight indulgent months in the islands.

His friends hated to see him go. "Harte says one end of our triangle is too far removed from the other two, and ought to be drawn nearer," Coolbrith said in a letter in January 1869. She was gazing out the window of her house on Russian Hill as she wrote, watching the sun between the clouds. A light rain fell, and, in the neighbor's garden, a bird bathed its feathers. "I'm sure it's our bird," she told Stoddard. She felt saddened by his absence, even more so by his silence. He was never one for staying in touch, and she couldn't help feeling hurt when he disappeared for months without a word. "Of all of your friends am I alone to be forgotten?" But at least it had one happy result: the rest of the Overland Trinity grew closer. "Harte is not as formidable as I imagined him; we get on very nicely."

Harte, she discovered, was hilarious. He could tell a joke with a look or a gesture, "a born actor of the subtlest, most refined type." But beneath this performance was another Harte: petty, delicate, the boy whose pink skin struck his classmates as too girly and then grew hideous with smallpox scars, who felt the sting of every unkind word and always preferred the company of books to people. This was the Harte whom Coolbrith came to know while Stoddard cruised the Pacific thousands of miles away. Meanwhile, a different image of the author began to take shape in the nation's mind on the strength of the stories that circulated widely in the eastern press. By 1869, Harte had begun his final ascent. It would put new pressures on his personality, and punch holes in the composure he worked hard to maintain.

One day Coolbrith found him in the *Overland* office, seething. There would always be a certain class of critics who condemned him for writing about scoundrels and tramps. He wrote stories, not sermons, and this outraged many self-described Christians, beginning with the proofreader who gagged on the impiety of "The Luck of Roaring Camp." Mercifully, these prudes were in the minority. But they still got under his skin. "I tried first to comfort, then to laugh him out of his mood," Coolbrith remembered. When that didn't work, she took out a piece of paper and wrote five lines:

> *There was a young writer named Francis*
> *Who concocted such lurid romances*
> *That his publishers said*
> *You will kill this firm dead*
> *If you don't put a curb on your fancies.*

As he read, a "laugh twinkled in his eyes, which he tried to conceal." Then Coolbrith scribbled another stanza, and he cracked. "I am almost tempted to box your ears!" he cried. "But instead, like a good Christian I'll proceed to heap coals upon your head." Limericks began flying across the table:

Here is the young Sapphic divinity
Number one of the Overland Trinity
Who uses the muses,
Pretty much as she chooses,
This dark-eyed poetic divinity.

They took care of each other. "Harte was good to me—good as a brother should be to an only sister," she said. He knew her finances were precarious, subsisting as she did on a schoolteacher's salary. He knew her time was scarce, consumed by endless hours spent scrubbing and cooking and cleaning for her family. So he came over to her house on Russian Hill and helped shell peas and hull strawberries. He kept his ears open for any paid writing work, and when the Society of California Pioneers asked him to compose a poem for its anniversary, he insisted she do it instead, earning her $50.

Most important, he edited her. She wrote for almost every issue of the *Overland*, at Harte's insistence. He was relentless. "I was quite disappointed at not receiving the poem this morning, but I suppose the weather was unpropitious for your muse," one of his letters read. "Is it because the Muse is feminine that she is dilatory?" read another. He went to her house on a Saturday afternoon and rang and rang and rang. Sometimes he sent a messenger instead, with instructions to wait until she produced pages. "I must have my best contributors," he explained.

He was equally diligent in his revisions. He suggested a new title here, an extra syllable there. Coolbrith responded by immersing herself in her craft. Certain themes grew clearer. The plaintiveness that had always predominated in her verse became more openly an obsession with death, even a longing to die herself:

> *What do I owe the years, that I should bring*
> > *Green leaves to crown them King?*
> *Blown, barren sands, the thistle, and the brier;*
> > *Dead love, and mocked desire,*
> *And sorrow, vast and pitiless as the sea:*
> > *These are their gifts to me.*

Harte always wanted more. She saw him at his best and worst, at his most compassionate and his most childish. Once, he greeted her in the street with a red face and a menacing voice, demanding to know why she had passed him twice that day without saying hello. She hadn't noticed him, of course—why would she snub him? But he refused to drop it. "You've been having a row with someone," she said at last, "and are vexed with everyone." This hypersensitivity "to any slight, real or fancied," would only grow more acute as his national reputation rose. Instead of taking solace in his success, it made him shrill and defensive, with terrible consequences for those whom he felt mistreated him.

Yet the one person who mistreated him the most never seemed to make him angry. Anna Griswold Harte dropped by the *Overland* offices at regular intervals to bark orders at her husband in full earshot of others. He obeyed these without protest, halting his work at a moment's notice to join her on a shopping trip, or indulge whatever whim she had concocted to break his concentration. "How my heart aches for the poor boy," his mother confessed to an *Overland* staffer. "Through the day, in his office, he is always interrupted—he is never alone, and when he comes home at night, she . . . just wears the life out of him." The emotional energy he expended on her surely sapped his patience with others, and contributed to the widening cracks in his usually cool demeanor.

In June 1869, when the *Overland* changed owners, Harte's arrogance came out with a vengeance. Anton Roman, the founding publisher, had decided to sell the magazine. It was Roman who first conceived the venture and persuaded Harte to come aboard. But in the year since, the editor had made it entirely his own. When a businessman named John H. Carmany bought the *Overland* from Roman, Harte took the opportunity to flex his editorial muscle. He greeted the new publisher with a list of demands. He wanted a new office and a salary of $200 a month, plus a written guarantee of his sole sovereignty of the *Overland*. "Of my ability to be trusted with the exclusive control of the magazine," he declared, "the *Overland* of the past year must be the judge." He was dictating terms, not negotiating. "If I do not hear from you by tomorrow 10 a.m. I shall consider myself at liberty to enter into other negotiations."

Carmany surrendered. Harte would have his office, and enough money to quit his sinecure at the US Mint and devote himself to the *Overland* full-time. The editor's fast-inflating ego had made him formidable at the bargaining table. The publisher would live in fear of Harte, anxious to keep him at the *Overland* as his national popularity grew. But Harte's surging confidence also had some unfortunate side effects. The sense of entitlement, the prickliness over any perceived ingratitude—these could be damaging. Fame would make him ornery and overbearing, even to the point of self-sabotage. It would've been a good subject for one of his stories: a man who played his hand perfectly, until he shot himself in the foot.

IN 1869, as the *Overland* thrived, Twain watched admiringly from the opposite coast. "The Eastern press are unanimous in their commendation of your new magazine," he told the *Alta California* in July 1869. "I have heard it handsomely praised by some of the most ponderous of America's literary chiefs." But whatever pride he felt at the rising profile of the Pacific coast was offset by his envy of the man leading the charge. Harte's short fiction had made him a star. Twain needed to catch up.

It had been one year since he sailed out of San Francisco for the last time, with the manuscript he hoped would make him famous. He had landed in New York on July 29, 1868, and delivered the text to his publisher Elisha Bliss Jr. six days later. Then the waiting began. By March 1869, the book still hadn't appeared. Bliss cited production delays, and even got bogged down in a battle with his board of directors, who raised a sanctimonious stink about the impertinent tone of Twain's writing. They backed off, but by July 1869, Bliss had more bad news: publication would be postponed again, this time until the fall. Twain had exercised remarkable restraint over the past several months. Now he went ballistic:

> After it is done being a fall book, upon what argument shall you perceive that it will be best to make a winter book of it? And—
>
> After it is done being a winter book, upon what argument shall you perceive that it will be best to make another spring book of it again? . . .
>
> All I desire is to be informed from time to time what future season of the year the publication is postponed to, & why—so that I can go on informing my friends intelligently—I mean that infatuated baker's dozen of them who, faithful unto death, still believe that I am going to publish a book.

Bliss got the message. That month, Twain's long-awaited comic romp through Europe and the Holy Land finally appeared. *The Innocents Abroad* was as prodigiously proportioned as the personality that produced it: a brick of a book, 651 pages and 234 illustrations wedged between covers of black cloth—four continents, two years, and any number of revisions in the making. Harte's edits had been invaluable. He "trimmed & trained & schooled me patiently," Twain gratefully recalled. But the book also bore traces of another influence, closer to his heart: a twenty-three-year-old girl named Olivia Langdon with whom he had fallen madly in love.

In a typically Twainian coincidence, the same trip that produced *The Innocents Abroad* also led him to "Livy." He had met her in late 1867 through her brother Charley, a fellow passenger aboard the *Quaker City*. By the summer of 1868, he had proposed. It wasn't an obvious match. For one, she didn't share his sense of humor. His wit ricocheted right off her, even when delivered in his rollicking drawl. She was meek where he was manic, pious where he was profane. She came from a rich, respectable family in Elmira, New York, and grew up in a cocoon of Victorian gentility entirely insulated from the frontier society that created Twain. To imagine this graduate of the Elmira Ladies' Seminary having anything more than a passing acquaintance with the whiskey-swilling westerner was about as farfetched as a barroom yarn about giant grasshoppers or jumping frogs.

Predictably, her answer was no. But he wouldn't give up: he wrote her some 184 letters over the next seventeen months in which he tried to sound like the man she might want to marry. He quoted Scripture. He scrubbed his language of anything western. He presented himself as a sinner, sorely in need of her civilizing influence, and disowned the parts of his past she might find unpalatable. "*Don't* read a word in that Jumping Frog book, Livy—*don't*," he wrote. "I would be glad to know that every copy of it was burned, & gone forever."

All these saintly noises sounded a bit strange coming from Twain's pen, but it wasn't as uncharacteristic as it looked. He loved Livy sincerely, with a passion that cut past his usual irony and tapped an emotional current of true intensity. She also belonged to a world he desperately wanted to join: the upper stratum of American society. Over the last several years, he had inched his way up, from Virginia City to the more sophisticated precincts of San Francisco. Now he was in the East, about to publish a book he hoped would be taken seriously by members of Livy's social class. He wanted the acceptance of America's elites, despite his tendency to ridicule and bewilder them. Livy offered access to this aristocracy, and he set about grooming himself for the role of her suitor.

Fortunately, it never quite fit. He would never be a proper gentleman, or a credible Christian, or speak sentences uninflected by the drawl that gave his voice its remarkable melody. He couldn't get rid of the West if he tried: it was in his blood, inoculating him against bad, boring writing, inspiring the rhythms that would realign American literature. But he cleaned up enough for Livy, who finally said yes to him in late 1868. "I am so happy I want to scalp someone," he roared to a friend. He hadn't gained just a fiancée but a partner in crime, a highly educated companion who could edit his work. As page proofs of *The Innocents Abroad* began arriving in the spring of 1869, she took it upon herself to revise them—to "scratch out all that don't suit her," in Twain's words. Like Harte, she helped trim the manuscript's rougher bits to create a product that would be agreeable to the reading public of postwar America.

It worked. *The Innocents Abroad* sold 82,524 copies in its first eighteen months, earning Twain $16,504 in royalties—or more than $217,000 in today's dollars. It would be his biggest best seller by far, the book that gave him a permanent place in the culture. Reviewers loved it. Even the *Atlantic Monthly* approved. "There is an amount of pure human nature in the book that rarely gets into literature," wrote the magazine's assistant editor, William Dean Howells. "[E]ven in its impudence it is charming."

The *Atlantic*'s support was a bit surprising, considering the book was an attack on everything it stood for. Livy had helped Twain temper his irreverence—but all the Livys in the world couldn't change the fact that *The Innocents Abroad* was a bullet in the heart of America's literary establishment. It began with how the book was sold. It was published by subscription, which meant that traveling salesmen went door-to-door peddling it to consumers. This was a popular way to sell cookbooks and Bibles, but no self-respecting literary writer would ever dream of distributing his work this way. The polite thing to do was to put your book on the shelf and wait for it to sell, not run into people's houses demanding they buy it.

Subscription publishing had ancient roots—Napoleon Bonaparte and George Washington had both worked as book canvassers—but it flourished after the Civil War. The rapid growth of railroads enabled salesmen to travel farther and faster. Elisha Bliss's American Publishing Company belonged to this new generation of subscription houses, enlisting agents to trawl for customers throughout the country.

Twain loved the model. It let someone of his unorthodox talents bypass the gatekeepers of traditional publishing, and gave him a more direct route to his core audience: the middle class. His readers were doctors, lawyers, businessmen—the rising bourgeoisie of the new industrializing nation. They didn't care if subscription publishing lacked high-culture cachet. They wanted to satisfy their growing curiosity about the rest of the country and the world. The *Quaker City* sightseers came mostly from their ranks. *The Innocents Abroad* was their story.

Upscale Americans had been going to Europe for decades. But in the years after the Civil War, as transatlantic travel became cheaper, a new kind of creature began crossing the ocean en masse: the Middle American. He didn't have the polish of his predecessors. He spoke atrocious French and mangled the pronunciation of foreign names. Faced with the glories of Europe, he wavered between head-scratching incomprehension and enraptured reverence for things he didn't understand—"old connoisseurs from the wilds of New Jersey who laboriously learn the difference between a fresco and a fire-plug," as Twain put it. Worst of all, he had an insatiable need for souvenirs. In Egypt, Twain spotted a relic hunter crawling up the Sphinx, hammering a memento off its face. "The gentle reader will never, never know what a consummate ass he can become, until he goes abroad."

The familiar spectacle of watching one's fellow Americans make fools of themselves in a foreign country—Twain captured it perfectly. But parody wasn't his only point. There was pride too. Like him, these bourgeois barbarians were emissaries of a newly confident nation that had just passed through the bloodiest war in its history. America was coming of age—and the moment was ripe for an Oedipal reckoning with its Old World roots. Twain didn't go abroad to swoon over a superior civilization. On the whole he found Europe and the Holy Land dirty, dilapidated places, trapped in the past. Even their most cherished treasures often failed to impress. Leonardo da Vinci's *The Last Supper* was a "mournful wreck," he wrote; like much else he saw on his journey, it had grown decrepit with age. The lesson of *The Innocents Abroad* was that Americans should stop venerating the corpses of dead cultures. Their barbarianism was infinitely preferable to the decadence of a region well past its prime. They belonged to the country of the future: an innovative, economically ascendant nation with a style all its own.

This declaration of independence struck deeply at the Eurocentric sympathies of America's ruling intellectual class. It came from the same insurrectionary vein as "Jim Smiley and His Jumping Frog." The roots of this revolt lay in the West, and *The Innocents Abroad* was unmistakably a work of western humor. Most of the slang had disappeared in the revisions, but the frontier could still be heard in the book's rich irony and rambling flow—what Howells, in his *Atlantic* review, called its "continuous incoherence." Like any good backwoods storyteller, Twain never told a tale straight, but zigzagged his way downstream via all possible digressions. If *The Innocents Abroad* proclaimed America's liberation from the Old World, its prose suggested the form that freedom might take.

It made for a great book. But a great book isn't guaranteed to sell. The other half relies on hustle, and happily Twain had this quality in large supply. By November 1869, he was back on the lecture trail, playing more than fifty towns over the course of the next few months.

He also wrote to various newspaper editors personally, angling for good reviews. His publisher promised to send out as many as two thousand advance copies to ensure widespread press coverage.

One would of course go to Harte, who had played such a key role in the *Innocents'* creation. "He praised the book so highly that I wanted him to review it *early* for the Overland," Twain explained. But then something went wrong: the book's western distributor inexplicably refused to provide a review copy. An earlier Harte might've shrugged it off and politely waited for the issue to be resolved—but the new Harte, the exalted author of "The Luck of Roaring Camp," courted by the *Atlantic*, revered far and wide, threw a fit. He "wrote me the *most daintily contemptuous & insulting letter you ever read*," Twain said, "—& what I want to know, is, where was *I* to blame?" Suddenly the old friends were no longer on speaking terms.

Yet Harte still wrote an admiring review of *Innocents* for the *Overland* in January 1870, calling it "six hundred and fifty pages of open and declared fun." And when Harte's book of short stories appeared in April under the title *The Luck of Roaring Camp and Other Sketches*, the newspaper that Twain now co-owned and edited, the *Buffalo Express*, joined virtually every other periodical in the country in praising it. If their friendship had fallen off, at least it hadn't deteriorated into open warfare—yet.

A worse collision was coming, and Harte's bad attitude wasn't entirely to blame. The two men had always been competitive. But now they were competing for something more than fame: the power to define the Far Western frontier in the American imagination. As the pioneer era of the Pacific coast faded, swept away by the railroad and the Civil War, it would pass into myth—mined for cheap thrills by dime novels and other pop pleasures, adapted for more literary ends by writers like Harte and Twain. What Twain would come to hate most about Harte, apart from the insufferable superciliousness of a writer swollen with his own success, was the picture he drew of the Far West.

Sometime in the early 1870s, Twain marked up his copy of *The Luck of Roaring Camp and Other Sketches*. His margin notes included much praise: the title story, for instance, he found "nearly blemishless." But he also noticed several false notes: misused gambling slang, inauthentic snatches of dialect. One passage he felt was too indebted to "Dickens & an English atmosphere." Over time, as his hostility for Harte grew, these criticisms became more severe. He would vilify Harte as a literary swindler: "showy, meretricious, insincere," a master of "artificial reproduction," the originator of "a dialect which no man in heaven or earth had ever used." It no doubt angered him how easily Harte had seduced the eastern critics. The *New York Times* applauded Harte's "truthful pictures of early Californian life"—but what did a New York newspaperman know about early California life? In the summer of 1870, Twain signed the contract for his next book. This would be *Roughing It*, a memoir of the Far West—and an implicit rebuke of what he saw as the phoniness of Harte's fiction.

Of course, *Roughing It* would hardly be an objective portrait of the Pacific coast. No such thing existed, thank God: a region so thoroughly steeped in fable couldn't possibly be described without a fair amount of fictionalizing. Twain's account would be as artificial as Harte's. But Harte had an easier time selling his version of the West to the mandarins of eastern culture, owing to his greater polish. Despite the *Atlantic*'s favorable notice of *The Innocents Abroad*, Twain remained a lowbrow author: published by subscription, packaged for a popular audience. The heady air of frontier humor that made his work irresistible to the masses didn't endear him to the guardians of "serious" literature.

Sometimes this bothered him; sometimes it seemed to give him satisfaction. Yet there was one member of the eastern elite whose opinion would always matter to him: Livy. His long courtship hadn't just involved convincing her to be his wife, but persuading her parents to accept him as their son-in-law: an undertaking that, in

Twain's recollection, included providing the names of "six prominent men" from San Francisco as character references. To his horror,
these didn't exactly further his case. "The friends I had referred to
in California said with one accord that I got drunk oftener than
was necessary, & that I was wild, & godless, idle, lecherous & a dis-
contented & unsettled rover & they could not recommend any girl
of high character & social position to marry me," he lamented in a
letter to his old friend Charlie Stoddard. Fortunately, Livy "did not
believe it, & would not believe it if an archangel had spoken it."
Their nuptials would proceed as planned.

On February 2, 1870, they were married in the parlor of her parents' house. Twain sent the wedding announcement to Stoddard, the
text tastefully engraved on pink-tinted card stock. He had finally
won the girl he loved and ended his long vagabondage. He had written a best seller and made his name in the East. Yet he couldn't shake
the taste of a bitter thought lingering in the back of his mind. "Tell
me," he scribbled on the inside of the envelope, "what is the matter
with Bret Harte?—why all these airs?"

STODDARD WOULD STAY OUT OF IT. His nonconfrontational nature
precluded him from taking sides in any standoff; his loyalty to both
men made it inconceivable. He loved Twain, but felt forever grateful
to Harte, who "did more for me and my work than any other man."
For years, the elder Bohemian had steered him through his long
literary apprenticeship. Now he would help him achieve his
breakthrough as a writer.

By 1869, San Francisco's Bohemian scene had become a victim of
its own success. Twain had gone on to greater things in the East;
Harte was contemplating his own exit from California. Both had
found their national niche by embracing their regional roots. But
Stoddard had no special talent for writing about the West. He would
need to find a different route to an eastern readership.

In the summer of 1869, he returned to San Francisco after eight months in the Hawaiian Islands. He had roamed the countryside, visiting villages, spending nights with native boys. "You will easily imagine, my dear sir, how delightful I find this life," he wrote Walt Whitman. Two years earlier he had sent his idol a copy of his *Poems* and heard nothing back. "Now my voice is stronger," he declared in his new letter, and Whitman agreed. "Those tender & primitive personal relations away off there in the Pacific Islands, as described by you, touched me deeply," the great poet replied, recognizing a kindred spirit.

Stoddard, in his own way, was coming out. Not that he would've understood it in those terms. But rather than feeling anxious and ashamed about his failure to fulfill certain expectations—to succeed in school, hold down a job, get married—he had begun to embrace what made him different. In 1867, critics had slammed his *Poems* for being unoriginal. In 1869, he found a more distinctive literary voice by writing about an aspect of his life that had long remained hidden—not in verse, but in playful, intimate prose that conveyed much of the sweetness that people loved about him in person.

"A South-Sea Idyl" appeared in the September 1869 issue of the *Overland Monthly*. Those who knew Stoddard only for his poems might be surprised to see him transformed into the gloriously indolent sun worshipper who narrated this tropical tale. For a week or two he lived with a Hawaiian boy. They played in the ocean, frolicked naked along the beach. They spent hours watching wild poppies in the wind. They shared a bed—and somehow, Stoddard managed to make the eroticism obvious without crossing the line. When he described being "petted in every possible way," Whitman surely knew what he meant. But the coyness of Stoddard's tone kept him safely within the bounds of propriety. He could play at "barbarianism" without his readers realizing how serious he was. He could talk about "hating civilization" and pretend he was kidding.

Harte loved the piece. "Now you have struck it," he told Stoddard.

"Keep on in this vein and presently you will have enough to fill a volume and you can call it *South Sea Bubbles*!" In prose, Stoddard found the original sound that had eluded him in poetry. It was laced with a distinctly western irreverence for the pieties of proper society—what William Dean Howells later called his "mustang humor," born of a frontier even farther off the map than the California mining camps. At times Stoddard sounded positively Twain-like: "If you want to do any thing particularly, I should advise you to do it, and then be sufficiently sorry to make it all square." He also owed a debt to Adah Isaacs Menken, whose example had exhilarated him back in 1863. In her poetry and her performances, Menken had been someone "who dared to live up to her nature," he wrote admiringly. But his approach remained closest to Whitman, whose coded celebrations of gay love in verse had inspired Stoddard to do something similar in prose. When he sent Whitman a copy of "A South-Sea Idyl," the poet replied warmly, praising the piece as "beautiful & soothing."

Harte wanted the *Overland* to publish more in the same vein. Stoddard obliged. Other sketches followed, with titles like "Barbarian Days" and "How I Converted My Cannibal." These might add up to a book with real national potential, if only Stoddard could summon the discipline to stay the course. "It's time . . . you began to work with a long aim," Harte advised.

Of course, the long aim never came easily to Stoddard. He had barely landed in California before he wanted to get back on a boat for the tropics. Writing about the Pacific paled in comparison to the pleasures of actually being there. He might follow this new literary path to glory in the East. Or he might abandon all ambition and enjoy a more fulfilled life in a faraway place. In the islands he could be himself, but never famous; in America, he might be famous, but never himself. This was a difficult dilemma for an already indecisive mind, and it accounted for the stormy emotional weather that spun him like a top.

He anchored himself anywhere he could: in the companionship of the Overland Trinity, the pleasant air of Coolbrith's parlor, the solemn ceremonies of Catholicism. By 1870, he had found another mooring: a twenty-eight-year-old Union war veteran named Ambrose Bierce. Bierce had come West as a member of a military fact-finding and surveying tour. In California he resigned his post, found a job at the San Francisco Mint, and began writing. Stoddard had a weakness for pretty, unusual men. "Biercy" fit the bill in every particular. Infernally handsome, he stood nearly six feet tall, with curly blond hair and bright blue eyes. His animal magnetism earned him admirers wherever he went. Coolbrith liked him. So did Harte— high praise from a man usually reluctant to accept newcomers.

In print he was less lovable. Bierce wrote a weekly column for the *San Francisco News Letter and Commercial Advertiser* that vandalized virtually everything San Franciscans held sacred. It recalled Bohemia's bomb-throwing days, back when the *Californian* loved to antagonize the local establishment. Bierce could do social satire as brilliantly as Harte and Twain. But he also went after babies, baseball, and Yosemite—whose idyllic scenery so revolted him that he called for its destruction with gunpowder. He wielded his pen like one of those modern weapons that mowed down whole columns of his comrades in the Civil War. If he occasionally hit a genuine villain, he also injured many innocents.

This ruthlessness reflected an unusually modern mind. Like the Middle Americans of *The Innocents Abroad*, Bierce was a creature of the new industrialism. He had seen the fruits of Yankee ingenuity up close: guns that shot straighter and artillery that shot farther, built by the Northern factories that now powered the postwar economic boom. He understood that the technological revolution was also a moral one: that it rewrote the rules of what was permissible, whether on the battlefield or in the boardroom, whether in the "hard war" tactics of William Tecumseh Sherman or the robber-baron entrepreneurialism of Jay Gould. Bierce had seen a barbarism far, far

bleaker than Stoddard's romanticized savagery. It was the barbarism of the future, the mechanized cruelty of a civilization with
more efficient ways to kill people and fewer scruples about doing so.
"To the amiable maniac who believes in a tolerably rapid rate of
human progress toward a tolerably stupid state of human imperfection through cumulative accretions of brotherly love," he wrote in
an article for the *Overland*, "the events of the past few years must
seem singularly perverse, if not wildly wayward."

Bierce's background made him uniquely skeptical of the promises of progress. This came in handy in California, as the optimism
of the 1860s wilted in the harsher economic weather of the 1870s. He
rose to prominence just as San Francisco's literary scene was scatter-
ing, and the world that shaped Twain, Harte, Stoddard, and Coolbrith
was disappearing. The years ahead would bring profound changes to
California: not only to its economy and society but to its self-image.

The gold rush had created the idea of California as a land of opportunity, and this persisted long after the original diggings ran
dry. The Civil War kept the region broadly prosperous. Flush times
kept people employed; a perennial labor shortage kept wages high.
In the 1870s, however, a new reality set in. The remaining goldfields
had become industrialized: complex, capital-intensive ventures that
looked like eastern factories. Farms had become organized along
similar lines. "Wheat barons" owned estates hundreds of square
miles in size, using intensive, single-crop agriculture that depleted
the soil and made harvests more vulnerable to drought. Heavy immigration from the East drove wages down. Frenzied speculation
drove land prices up. The Jeffersonian fantasy of the West as a republic of independent freeholders was vanishing; in its place emerged
monopoly, wage labor, and big business. A select few would make
obscene amounts of money. The rest would endure a decade of
disappointment.

No single event marked the shift from the rich, hopeful 1860s to
the stagnant, gloomy 1870s more than the transcontinental railroad.

The messianic rhetoric that greeted its completion had begun to fray almost right away. In November 1869, six months after the rails met in Utah, the Suez Canal had opened in Egypt. Gone was the possibility of dominating the lucrative Asia trade—Europe now had a faster route to the Far East.

There were bigger difficulties ahead. Before 1869, California's relative isolation had sheltered its economy from eastern competition. San Francisco had enjoyed a profitable stranglehold on regional commerce: everything passed through its port. Now the interior, connected to the rest of the country by rail, could buy more cheaply from firms farther east. Local industries suffered, just as the thousands of laborers who built the railroad streamed into San Francisco looking for work. Wages fell; unemployment rose. By early 1870, San Francisco was in a slump. Seven thousand of its citizens were out of work, and that number would soon grow.

The heads of the Central Pacific—Collis P. Huntington, Mark Hopkins, Leland Stanford, and Charles Crocker—fared better. In 1862, the federal government had awarded their company the contract for the western span of the transcontinental railroad. They used this commission to create the most powerful corporation on the Pacific coast. The Central Pacific snapped up smaller railroads, secured generous loans from the government, acquired large tracts of public land, extracted tribute from towns along its routes, and generally made its imperial presence felt in ways that couldn't fail to recall Henry George's prophetic warnings in the *Overland Monthly*. The "Big Four" flaunted their wealth, spending conspicuously. By the end of the decade, they would be building kingly mansions on San Francisco's Nob Hill.

Meanwhile, the slow death of the California dream made the rest of the city a depressing place. One observer noted the abundance of "social wrecks"; more dangerous were the hoodlums who prowled the streets looking for easy prey. The ugliest symptom of the economic malaise came in the form of attacks on the Chinese. These were nothing new, yet they grew more vicious in the 1870s. The Central Pacific had imported thousands of laborers from China to work for low wages. Many of them moved to San Francisco after the railroad was built, and clashed with the city's largely Irish working class. Acts of racist violence ensued, which Bierce regularly spotlighted in his column for the *News Letter*. For all his antihumanitarian impulses, Bierce despised racial prejudice. When the body of a murdered Chinese woman appeared on the sidewalk one morning, he used it as ammunition against the cruel delusion of white supremacy. "The cause of her death could not be accurately ascertained," he wrote, "but as her head was caved in it is thought by some physicians that she died of galloping Christianity of the malignant California type."

The rising tide of anti-Chinese rage also stirred the conscience of California's leading writer. For years Harte had written eloquently against racism. In 1870, even as his thoughts increasingly turned

An illustration by Joseph Hull from the pirated Chicago
edition of Harte's The Heathen Chinee, *published by the*
Western News Company in 1870.

away from the Pacific coast to the prospect of life in the East, he decided to deliver another withering satire on the subject. The result was a poem called "Plain Language from Truthful James." According to Bierce, Harte first sent it to the *News Letter*—but Bierce insisted it belonged in the *Overland*, where more readers would see it. He was right. The poem appeared in the September 1870 issue and swiftly became the most popular thing Harte ever wrote.

"Plain Language from Truthful James"—or "The Heathen Chinee," as it came to be known—tells the story of a card game between a Chinese man named Ah Sin and a pair of white men. Everyone is cheating, but Ah Sin cheats better, and wins. When his opponents discover his trickery, they are outraged. "We are ruined by Chinese cheap labor," one of them cries. This is the punch line, a delicious inversion of a phrase already popular among anti-Chinese agitators, appropriated by Harte to expose the hypocrisy of white racism. The Chinese "did as the Caucasian did in all respects, and, being more patient and frugal, did it a little better," he later recalled. They weren't any more or less deceitful, only smarter. They had learned the white man's game, and beat him at it.

"The Heathen Chinee" penetrated American culture with terrific speed. It caused "an explosion of delight whose reverberations reached the last confines of Christendom," Twain remembered. Newspapers and magazines around the country republished it. Its lines were recited, quoted, parodied, set to music, reprinted and resold on city streets. John H. Carmany, the *Overland*'s publisher, claimed that his clients in the East "doubled their orders" of the magazine because of the poem. Fields, Osgood, and Company, the *Atlantic*'s publisher, had just released Harte's *The Luck of Roaring Camp and Other Sketches* in April 1870. Now it rushed to produce a collection of Harte's poetry for the Christmas market, with "The Heathen Chinee" as the centerpiece. The book sold out its first six editions within five days, and went on to be Harte's biggest seller.

Within months, Harte had become one of America's most

famous writers. "Harte *does* soar, & I am glad of it, notwithstanding he & I are 'off' these many months," grumbled Twain in November 1870. His rival's most recent triumph came at an inopportune moment, just as Twain was struggling with the manuscript for *Roughing It*. Once again, he felt he was falling behind. Harte had somehow conquered both sides of the cultural divide: admired by the highbrow elite, adored by the middlebrow masses.

Yet he didn't seem especially happy. Harte "was no less chagrined than amazed" by the national frenzy set off by "The Heathen Chinee," Coolbrith observed. He complained about it to her and Stoddard. He said he wanted to be known for his "finer, higher work," not a crude bit of doggerel. But he had another reason to regret the poem. Many readers misinterpreted its message: ignoring the ironic tone, they read it as an endorsement of anti-Chinese racism. What Harte intended as satire, they took seriously. A pirated edition of the poem published in Chicago made this painfully clear. It featured drawings of a slant-eyed Ah Sin getting attacked by a mob of whites, without an ounce of irony.

This was only the beginning. In the coming years, "The Heathen Chinee" would become a rallying cry and a recruiting tool for the crusade against Chinese immigration. When the poem appeared in 1870, the "Chinese question" was still more of a western issue than a national one. Harte helped make it real for the rest of the country. Easterners who had never seen a Chinese person before now carried Ah Sin around in their heads, and before long, this nasty caricature would pay disastrous political dividends. In 1875 Congress passed the Page Act, the first of many laws aimed at restricting Chinese immigration. The following year, both the Republicans and Democrats added "Heathen Chinee planks" to their party platforms, wooing voters with bigoted rhetoric.

Harte had every reason to hate "The Heathen Chinee." Later, he would call it the worst poem he ever wrote. On the other hand, he didn't hesitate to take advantage of the huge benefits it conferred on his career. By the time the poem appeared, he was already being courted by several eastern periodicals eager to lure him away from California. He treated his suitors to the same petulant personality he had displayed the year before while renegotiating his *Overland* contract. When *Putnam's Magazine* wanted him as its editor, he demanded $5,000 a year plus full creative control—refused. When the *Galaxy* wanted him as a contributor, he shamed it for submitting "the lowest and least advantageous offer which I have yet had the honor to receive from any one." He could afford to be choosy. "I have propositions for more copy than I could possibly furnish."

The most intriguing offer came from Fields, Osgood, and Company: owner of the *Atlantic* and publisher of *The Luck of Roaring Camp and Other Sketches* and his forthcoming *Poems.* In June 1870, it invited Harte to become an exclusive contributor for its magazine group, at an annual salary of $5,000. This was the same sum he had just demanded from *Putnam's,* but his price had already gone up. Powerful Californians, in a bid to keep Harte on the Pacific coast, wanted to make him a professor at the new University of California, temporarily in Oakland while its campus in Berkeley was being built. "It has long been tolerably well known in literary circles that Mr. Harte could not afford to remain in California—where there is a conspicuous lack of the sense necessary to the appreciation of genius—unless he were bribed with a lucrative sinecure," Bierce cracked in his *News Letter* column. The position would bring Harte's total income to $6,000 a year. What he wanted to know from the *Atlantic* camp was simple: "Can you do as well for me, and how?"

The timing worked perfectly: the same month Harte sent his reply, "The Heathen Chinee" broke. Suddenly he had all the leverage he needed to extract whatever deal he wanted. Meanwhile, the university appointment was held up by one of the regents, who remembered Harte's role in ridiculing the hushed-up coverage of the 1868 earthquake and still hadn't forgiven him for it. No doubt this stung the author's pride, because even after the regent was reconciled, Harte declined the post.

By late 1870, he had made up his mind. This would be his last year as *Overland* editor. He didn't know where exactly he would end up, only that he would leave San Francisco. The Far West had created him. But its time had passed. In a letter to an eastern editor, Harte declared the region "played out." "The tourists have already exhausted superficial California and what is below is hard, dry and repulsive," he said.

Harte urged his friends to follow him across the continent. "[H]e was constantly formulating plans whereby Charlie [Stoddard] and I might join him in the East," Coolbrith remembered. "What kind of an instrument would a triangle be with only one angle?" she recalled him saying. "When I would speak of the impossibility of my leaving my invalid mother, 'Bring her with you,' he would answer; and then when assured that she would not leave her boys, he would conclude, 'Well then, I see no other way than to marry the whole family!'" Coolbrith couldn't go East: she had domestic duties, relatives to support. She gave Harte a portfolio of her poems, in the hopes that he might show them around, and possibly even land her a book deal with a big house in Boston or New York. She would need his help: despite publishing dozens of poems in the *Overland*, her national career had gone nowhere. Harte and Twain had taken off. Stoddard had won new attention from the eastern press for his Pacific prose sketches. But she had languished, still largely a local phenomenon after all these years. Her verse didn't distinguish itself strongly enough to find a wider readership. Ultimately, her contribution to the Bohemian scene had been less literary than personal: a backstage role that earned her less recognition than the rest. When a Cincinnati paper reported on a new issue of the *Overland*, it misspelled her name as "John D. Coolbrith."

Someday, perhaps, she might get famous enough to escape California. Until then, she would fondly remember "that dear old circle" shattered by Harte's departure: the hours spent in her parlor poring over page proofs or swapping limericks or that one time in the *Overland* office when Stoddard spontaneously broke into song—a dreadful sound, full of "unprecedented sharps and flats" and "sudden soaring into the upper impossibles"—until Harte entered with a horrified look on his face and all three of them died laughing. The Overland Trinity had been her other family, the one that made her feel free instead of trapped, and its dissolution left a permanent pain in her heart.

Unlike Coolbrith, Stoddard could leave San Francisco anytime he liked. He, too, hoped Harte would help him in the East. Yet he also felt drawn in another direction: toward the Pacific. "I know there is but one hope for me," he wrote Whitman in the spring of 1870. "I must get in amongst people who are not afraid of instincts and who scorn hypocrisy." In July he decamped for Tahiti for three months. He ran out of money and ended up sleeping in a chicken coop until the American consul put him on a ship home—but not before he gathered more material for his future book of South Seas sketches. His taste for travel grew as San Francisco's appeal faded. The city had been "'railroaded' to the depths of the commonplace," he later wrote, deprived of the special privileges that made it rich and the frontier isolation that made it distinctive. He couldn't blame the *Overland* editor for clearing out. "No one who knows Mr. Harte," he said, "and knew the California of his day, wonders that he left it as he did."

On February 2, 1871, Harte boarded a parlor car of the *Overland Express* with his wife and two sons. It had been eleven years since he first climbed to the top of Telegraph Hill and saw Bohemia laid out below, back when he was an eccentric newspaperman barely off the typesetter's bench, taking lonely walks through a city marvelously remote from the rest of the country, possessed of its own peculiar culture, accessible only to those young or fit or foolish enough to endure the long journey by steamer or stage. Now he departed in a blaze of glory, carried by the locomotive that made San Francisco seven days from New York. He hadn't been East since 1854, and would be seeing the new America for the first time: a steam-fed leviathan of cities, slums, mansions, machines, monopolies, and a media-hungry middle class eager for the next offering from the author of "The Heathen Chinee." Expectations were high. Twain would be watching.

III

EXILE

Portrait of Harte published on
the cover of *Every Saturday*,
January 14, 1871.

SEVEN

America greeted the news of Bret Harte's departure from California in 1871 with an enthusiasm verging on the hysterical. The nation had an endless appetite for novelty. The roaring capitalism of the postwar era was demolishing the old and making a religion of the new, and now a writer from the younger half of the Union arrived to give fresh life to American letters.

Mark Twain felt his mercury rising. The spotlight properly belonged to him, and he knew it. He was the true westerner, not this foppish city slicker who looked like he just stepped off Savile Row—a dandy with little direct knowledge of the mining camps, who wouldn't be caught dead in a flannel shirt and a slouch hat. Twain had plenty to be pleased about—*The Innocents Abroad* was selling well—but his star shone nowhere near as brightly as Harte's. Harte didn't capture just the middle-class demographic that loved Twain, but also those vicarish high-culture types who tended to be stingier with their praise. "Do you know who is the most celebrated man in America to-day?" Twain fumed to a friend, "—the man whose name is on every single tongue from one end of the continent to the other? It is Bret Harte . . . All the cities are fussing about which shall secure him for a citizen."

He was right: every city wanted Harte. From the moment the former *Overland Monthly* editor boarded the train in San Francisco in February 1871, the country breathlessly beheld his transit. The telegraph tracked his every move. Newspapers from Idaho to Ohio chattered about where he might choose to live.

Chicago felt good about its chances. The city was America's railroad hub, a gateway between the urban East and the rural interior. Its merchants and manufacturers had followed the transcontinental track to the Pacific, poaching markets once loyal to San Francisco, and now Chicagoans hoped to lure Harte to the shores of Lake Michigan to take the editorship of their *Lakeside Monthly*. Soon after he and his family arrived on February 7, several prominent citizens invited him to dinner to discuss the offer.

Inexplicably, he failed to show. This rudeness outraged his hosts, and their indignation grew when they learned the reason for it: apparently Harte had expected a carriage to be sent. This embarrassing revelation unleashed the scorn of the local press, and wormed its way through papers around the country—the first hiccup in Harte's princely progress. Yet Harte may have concocted the carriage excuse to cover up a domestic squabble, according to a story told years later by a friend. In Chicago the family stayed with Mrs. Harte's sister. When Mrs. Harte discovered the *Lakeside* dons hadn't invited her sister to dinner, she angrily announced that none of them would go.

Whether Bret's ego or Anna's temper or some other symptom of their toxic marriage produced the Chicago fiasco, it suggested a darker margin to the storybook romance between America and the author of "The Heathen Chinee." But it didn't do enough damage to dampen the enthusiasm generated by his trip across the country. The Hartes left Chicago on February 15, briefly visiting Syracuse and New York City before continuing to Boston, where the next phase of the wooing would begin.

The assistant editor of the *Atlantic Monthly* met them at the station. William Dean Howells had a simple mission: to get Harte to sign the exclusive contract that his employers had wanted to finalize for months. After he heard what happened in Chicago, he hired the best carriage available. He felt terribly anxious, and not a little intimidated. When Harte appeared, Howells took his first look: "a child of extreme fashion," he decided, arrayed in fabrics far more conspicuous than anything one might find on Howells's short, fat frame. Then the celebrated author "pressed forward with his cordial hand-clasp," and Howells's fears faded: Harte, he was relieved to discover, was completely charming.

Over the course of the following week, that charm would be put to the test, as Howells took Harte on a tour of a social galaxy unlike any he had ever seen. Chicago had heart, but Boston was "the Hub": the high temple of the New England intellectual tradition that Harte, only six years earlier, had ridiculed as "an English graft" in the pages of the *Californian*. To Harte's mind, the Bohemian scene had produced more indigenous fare, like "The Luck of Roaring Camp"—leaner, truer to life—and it wouldn't be long before he let slip a few disparaging digs at his surroundings. He and his family stayed at the Howells residence in Cambridge a half mile from the Harvard campus, surrounded by famous writers. "Why, you couldn't stand on your front porch and fire off your revolver without bringing down a two-volumer," Harte cracked to his host. Literary eminences weren't the only things nearby: pretty girls flocked to the Howells home when they heard Harte was inside. They dawdled outside in stylish dresses, hoping to catch sight of him. His engraved portrait had recently appeared on the cover of *Every Saturday*: a glamour shot showing him with windswept hair and voguishly long sideburns. The artist omitted Harte's smallpox scars, making him look far handsomer than he did in person. It set off "a perfect furore in cultivated society," reported Howells's wife, Elinor. "All the young ladies are in love with him."

Harte induced nearly as much swooning at the Saturday Club, a monthly gathering of all the big-name Brahmins. He attended on February 25, 1871, his first full day in town. In an oak-paneled room on the second floor of a Boston hotel, the wizened monuments of American letters lined up to meet him: Ralph Waldo Emerson, James Russell Lowell, Henry Wadsworth Longfellow, Oliver Wendell Holmes Sr. Even Twain would have been intimidated by such company. But if Harte felt the slightest bit starstruck, it didn't show. On the contrary: he "had a spice of irreverence that enabled him to take them more ironically than they might have liked," Howells observed. The westerner didn't defer to his eastern elders, but held his ground, tweaking them with a subtly teasing wit and telling stories about rattlesnakes and prairie dogs. And they loved it: for the duration of his stay in Boston, Harte was a coveted caller, escorted from one function to another by Howells.

The main event came on February 28, when Mr. and Mrs. Howells held a dinner at their house in Cambridge. At a table set with fine china sat a large sampling of the local intelligentsia—"so many we knocked elbows," wrote the philosopher John Fiske. A twenty-seven-year-old Henry James came. So did a young Harvard professor named Henry Adams. Harte didn't disappoint, telling Lowell that he found certain of his verses "overliterary." Once again, everyone seemed to take it in stride. "I was so wined and dined by the literary folk whom I used to scalp in the *Overland* that between remorse and good liquor I hardly knew where I stood," Harte gloated in a letter to Ambrose Bierce.

The hostess felt triumphant. "*[T]he party!*" Elinor gushed in a letter. "How shall I do justice to it?" It wasn't just the catered meal, followed by chocolate ice cream, cake, and coffee, or a guest list that boasted Boston's best minds. It was the sense that she and her husband had finally earned their place in high society. Harte's visit had cemented Howells's stature at the moment he needed it most. In five months, he would inherit the editorship of the *Atlantic*. The task ahead was daunting. Although the *Atlantic* remained America's most prestigious literary periodical, it had fallen on hard times. Circulation had dropped sharply under competition from New York magazines like *Harper's* and *Scribner's*—lavishly illustrated monthlies that catered to the less rarefied tastes of the rising middle class. The golden age was over: Hawthorne and Thoreau were dead; Emerson had entered his long senescence. The magazine needed more modern voices to survive. Some of these Howells would find in the next generation of northeasterners, like Henry James and his brother William. Along with Henry Adams and Oliver Wendell Holmes Jr., they belonged to a wave of postwar writers who helped sweep away the tired intellectual legacy of the antebellum era and innovate new ideas in law, literature, history, and philosophy.

This experimental spirit would transform New England in the coming decades, and yield valuable items for the *Atlantic*. But Howells would also look farther afield, to Bohemian newcomers from the Far West. He understood the West as few Bostonians could, being a westerner himself—a midwesterner, to be exact. He was born in Ohio, and his father had been a country printer, his uncle a steamboat pilot. Like Harte, Twain, and many other young Americans of modest means and large ambition, he had gotten his start as a typesetter and wrestled up through the ranks. If his scrappy background always made him a bit of an outsider among the Brahmins, it also gave him a special respect for those frontier scribblers coming East from California. He wrote a glowing review of Twain's *The Innocents Abroad* when it appeared in 1869. And in Harte, he saw not just a popular writer who could revive the *Atlantic*'s flagging finances, but "the earnests of an American literature to come."

What would this literature look like? Howells hoped it would outgrow the "intense ethicism that pervaded the New England mind"—the moralizing that made writers like Emerson, Hawthorne, and Thoreau a little too preachy for his taste, as much as he admired them. In a word, he wanted realism: closely observed studies of everyday American life, offered for their own sake, not to prove a point. Harte's gold rush tales gave California in its native colors, without sermons or sentimentalism. They sprang from the "soil" and "air" of "the newest kind of new world," Howells wrote, and confirmed the editor's belief that the "finest poetry is not ashamed of the plainest fact." This would be precisely the sort of thing Howells would promote in the *Atlantic* upon his ascension in 1871: stories of America in the particular, set in the mining camps of the Mother Lode or the drawing rooms of Beacon Hill or the steamboats of the Mississippi.

On March 6, 1871, Harte agreed to write exclusively for the *Atlantic*. He would publish no fewer than twelve pieces a year and his employers would pay $10,000 for the privilege. This was twice what they had offered back in the summer of 1870, before "The Heathen Chinee" sent Harte's stock soaring. It was also twice the annual salary of a congressman, and a shocking amount of money by literary standards. The *Atlantic* had made Harte the highest-paid writer in America, and Boston felt proud to be bagging him. The city "may still claim the proud distinction of being the literary metropolis," declared a local poet when she heard of Harte's decision. "He tarried in Chicago. He investigated New-York. He came to Boston, he saw, he was conquered."

Howells welcomed the news. It helped that he liked Harte. For a week he had enjoyed the "witchery of that most winning presence," right up until the moment when he drove his guest to the station and put him on the train to New York, where the Hartes were planning to live. The men spent their final minutes together in the parlor car, talking and laughing the way they had the past several nights. Then Harte remembered: he had forgotten to buy cigars. They ran to go get them. By the time they returned, the train was moving down the track and Harte had to scramble up the steps of the last car. Howells followed to see his friend aboard before jumping back to the ground—just missing an archway that would've killed him if he had held on a moment longer. He looked up to see Harte waving, cigar in hand, a look of "mock heartbreak" on his face. It was an image that remained permanently imprinted on Howells's brain, perhaps because it came so soon after almost dying, perhaps because it seemed an ominous sign of things to come.

TWAIN HAD A PLAN. "I must & will keep shady & quiet till Bret Harte simmers down a little," he wrote his brother Orion in March 1871. "I will 'top' Bret Harte again or bust. But I can't do it dangling eternally in the public view." He was flattering himself: he wasn't in danger of dangling in public view. Two years had passed since *The Innocents Abroad.* He now lived in Buffalo, where he co-owned and edited a newspaper called the *Express.* He had taken the job to appease Livy's parents, to prove he was ready to settle down. But the responsibilities of running a daily paper couldn't possibly satisfy someone of his temperament. The decrepit editorial offices—laced with cobwebs, heated by old coal stoves—must have felt like a tomb to a man accustomed to the livelier pace of western papers. While Harte triumphed, Twain languished.

How had it happened? How had the Washoe Giant, the feared hoaxer and humorist of jumping frog fame, become a burgher of Buffalo? His new domestic life was anything but tranquil. In November 1870, Livy had given birth to Langdon, their first child. Born prematurely like his father, the baby struggled to survive. Three months later, Livy came down with typhoid fever. The household slid into chaos: doctors and nurses descended while Twain sank deeper into despair. "You do not know what it is to be in a state of absolute frenzy—desperation," he wrote his publisher Elisha Bliss. Langdon exercised his little lungs at every opportunity, to the dismay of his sleepless father. "I believe if that baby goes on crying 3 more hours this way I will butt my frantic brains out & try to get some peace."

Needless to say, he couldn't write. He had told Bliss to expect

Roughing It, his book of western adventures, months before. But the work went slowly, with no end in sight. "In three whole months I have hardly written a page of MS," he confessed in March 1871. His nerves were shot, and not only on account of the trouble at home. In January, the Boston magazine *Every Saturday* announced that Twain had written a parody of Harte's "The Heathen Chinee" under another pseudonym. Being upstaged by Harte was bad enough; now he was being accused of imitating him. He wrote the editor an angry letter demanding a correction. "I am not in the imitation business," he snapped.

Anger made him mean; fear made him frantic. He was afraid Livy or Langdon might die; that Harte's dazzling rise meant his own inevitable decline; that *The Innocents Abroad* marked a professional high point he could never repeat. Three years after leaving San Francisco for the last time, he was afraid he would never be fully embraced in the East. The evil sprites of self-doubt that always harassed him in low moments made his solitary moments away from the screaming baby and his sick wife all the more miserable, and sapped the confidence he needed to write.

One thing was certain: he had to get out of Buffalo. Livy agreed. In March, they put the house on the market. They wanted to move to Hartford, Connecticut, a flourishing city of fifty thousand halfway between Boston and New York. Its downtown was a major piece of the postwar economic machine, home to insurance companies and gun manufacturers and subscription publishers like Twain's very own Elisha Bliss. It also had an extraordinary suburban enclave on its western border: Nook Farm, a close-knit community of liberal intellectuals who occupied a cluster of gorgeous mansions surrounded by meadows and ponds. Harriet Beecher Stowe lived there. So did Joseph Hawley and Charles Dudley Warner, co-editors of the *Hartford Courant*. This paradise of progressive politics and erudite conversation was where Twain longed to settle down. Here he might finally obtain a solid foothold in the eastern aristocracy, and put an end to the rootlessness that had so far defined his life.

But first, the family would spend the spring and summer at Livy's childhood home in Elmira, New York, where she could convalesce under her mother's care. Her condition had gotten worse. By the time they left Buffalo on March 18, 1871, she couldn't sit or stand, and had to be transported on a mattress. Twain prayed the move to Elmira would bring happier days; or, at the very least, nothing worse than the nightmare that preceded it: "I had rather die twice over than repeat the last six months of my life." He also hoped to break through his writer's block. "I want to get clear away from all hamperings, all harassments," he told Bliss. "I am going to shut myself up in a farm-house alone, on top an Elmira hill, & *write*."

The farmhouse belonged to Livy's sister Susan Crane and her husband, Theodore. It stood on a 250-acre estate called Quarry Farm, perched on a hill three miles from the Elmira home. This would be Twain's writing retreat. He walked there several times a week. He loved the cool air, the quiet, and the views of the valley below, brightened by the occasional burst of summer lightning—"a foretaste of heaven," he later called it. In this majestic setting, his brain became unstuck; the words began to flow. The agonies of the last several months faded; his fanatical work ethic returned. He immersed himself in his memories of the Pacific coast, and powered ahead on the manuscript that would restore him to the public eye. *Roughing It* would be part fiction, part fact: the story of the six most formative years of his life, beginning with that fateful day in 1861 when he boarded a stagecoach with his brother Orion and fled the Civil War for the far frontier beyond the plains.

He relied on several written sources for inspiration, including a pile of his clippings from western papers and some notes scribbled by Orion. Help also came in the form of an old friend: Joe Goodman, the editor of the *Virginia City Territorial Enterprise*, who appeared in Elmira on March 24. Nine years earlier, Goodman had given Twain his first job in Nevada journalism, witnessed the birth of his pen name, and nurtured his emerging talent. Now the newspaper-man was taking a trip through the East, and dropped by at just the right moment: with Twain knee-deep in *Roughing It*, sorely in need of guidance from someone who knew the Far West as well as he did. They rambled around Quarry Farm, reminiscing. They remem-bered old Washoe, its vulgar grandeur and boozy mayhem. Good-man would do for *Roughing It* what Harte did for *The Innocents Abroad*. He supplied the eye of a veteran editor, and the encourage-ment of a close friend. An anecdote later recorded by Albert Bigelow Paine, Twain's official biographer, gives a glimpse of their time to-gether. One day, Goodman read the manuscript while Twain fidgeted nearby. The author's anxiety steadily rose, until it erupted: "I knew it! I knew it!" he cried. "I am writing nothing but rot. You have sat there all this time reading without a smile, and pitying the ass I am making of myself." "Mark," Goodman said, "I was reading criti-cally, not for amusement, and so far as I have read, and can judge, this is one of the best things you have ever written. I have found it perfectly absorbing. You are doing a great book!"

Goodman's visit lifted Twain. By early April, he could report to Orion that the book was "booming along." Meanwhile, Livy slowly recovered: in late April, she rose from her sickbed and took her first few steps. The baby was healthy. Springtime came to Quarry Farm, greening its fields of clover and oak. Twain fell into a trance, crank-ing out pages at a superhuman pace. By mid-May, he was two-thirds done, and crowed to Bliss that he was writing with "a red-hot interest." His mood had swung from one manic extreme to the other. "Nothing grieves me now—nothing troubles me, bothers me or gets my attention—I don't think of anything but the book, & don't have an hour's unhappiness about anything."

All this confidence came through in the writing: *Roughing It* would be his most radical work to date. In *The Innocents Abroad*,

Twain had softened his westernness to appeal to an eastern audience. This time he let it rip, with glorious results. *Roughing It* follows the picaresque tale of a young rogue discovering the "curious new world" of the pre-railroaded Far West: a kind of living spoof of American society, where the usual rules break down and become parody. Here the banker and the gambler belong to the same social rank, outlaws with names like Six-fingered Pete murder dozens of men and are revered as local royalty, and everyone suffers from the delusion that a fistful of worthless mining stock might at any moment transmogrify itself into a tidy pile of cash. Unsurprisingly, Twain gives an embroidered account of his experiences. He says little about San Francisco, and almost nothing about the Bohemian circumstances of his literary upbringing. The *Golden Era*, the *Californian*, and Bret Harte get barely a few sentences. As usual, factual accuracy isn't his concern. Instead, he offers something far more interesting: a sprawling masterpiece of western storytelling, loosely woven from yarns collected over the years or freshly cut from whole cloth. *Roughing It* has the rhythms of his spoken voice, that inimitable flow where one story stumbles drowsily into another, and the populist polyphony of frontier dialect comes drawling and hollering off the page in snatches of phonetic prose.

The book's freewheeling form wasn't purely a matter of choice. Subscription publishers like Bliss needed to publish big tomes, so their salesmen could persuade the frugal residents of Middle America that the product peddled on their doorstep was worth the price. In a rush to meet the required word count, Twain loaded his manuscript with all kinds of filler, including several chapters on his trip to Hawaii. He made little effort to stitch these strays into a tight narrative arc; rather, he trusted himself to perform each bit piece brilliantly enough to keep people reading. Twain was a miniaturist. Both onstage and in print, he worked best in short bursts, stringing anecdotes together without much thought for the overall shape. This elastic structure gave him room to wander, to improvise, to probe those serendipitous places inaccessible to more formal writers like Harte. The result was a fuller portrait of the Pacific coast than anything to be found in Harte's fiction, and a wistful remembrance of the region that had made him a writer:

> It was a driving, vigorous, restless population in those days. It was a *curious* population. It was the *only* population of the kind that the world has ever seen gathered together, and it is not likely that the world will ever see its like again.

BY THE FALL OF 1871, Twain was back on track. He was wrapping up *Roughing It.* He felt bullish about its prospects. He planned another lecture tour. Livy was pregnant again. In October, they left Elmira for Hartford, renting a house while preparing to build one of their own. And he had finally begun repairing his relationship with Harte.

It's unclear who made the first move. But by mid-1871, the two men were talking again. Their official reunion came in early November, over beefsteaks at a fancy Boston restaurant. The occasion was a lunch hosted by Ralph Keeler, a minor writer from San Francisco. The other guests were more distinguished: William Dean Howells, now editor of the *Atlantic Monthly*; its former editor, James T. Fields; and Thomas Bailey Aldrich, editor of *Every Saturday.* For Twain, this wasn't just about reconnecting with Harte. It also marked his social debut among the New England literati. He had already met Howells back in 1869, when he swung by the *Atlantic*'s offices to thank the young editor for his generous review of *The Innocents Abroad.* But Twain was still very much an outsider. With his strange voice and swaying gait, his slangy diction and sealskin coat, he faced an uphill road to eastern respectability.

Fortunately, this was a forgiving crowd. The conversation consisted of "nothing but careless stories, carelessly told, and jokes and

laughing, and a great deal of mere laughing without the jokes,"
Howells recalled. It was an unbuttoned, unpretentious affair, with
the guests exchanging good-natured taunts across the table. One of
these came at Twain's expense, when Harte couldn't help noticing
how much pleasure his old Bohemian colleague took in his first
taste of Boston society. "This is the dream of his life," Harte said
mockingly, placing a hand on Twain's shoulder.

Later, Howells claimed Twain took it in stride, giving a look that
"betrayed his enjoyment of the fun." But Twain never took ridicule
well, especially when it touched on a sensitive subject. Harte was
pulling rank. He was reminding his fellow westerner that, although
both writers came from the same Bohemian milieu, only one of
them had gained access to America's most exclusive literary club.
This wasn't the same Harte who had patiently mentored Twain,
who had published him in the *Californian* and edited *The Innocents
Abroad*—this was someone darker, more aloof. And more anxious:
Harte's hold on the eastern elite had recently grown more tenuous,
owing to a series of embarrassing failures.

Only nine months had passed since Harte's transcontinental
crossing. The expectations surrounding him had been intense, and
he acquitted himself well during his whirlwind week in Cambridge
with Howells as his host. While "not quite au fait in everything,"
Elinor Howells concluded, he still made a satisfying addition to eastern literary society. But he would have to be more than just a good
dinner guest going forward: he needed to become a public figure.
People had seen his dashing portrait; now they wanted to see him
speak. This wouldn't be easy. Harte didn't have Twain's electric stage
presence. He "was not much of a talker," Howells recalled: his charm
came in small, intimate doses, not the celebrity-sized ones America
wanted.

His first test came in May, when the Army of the Potomac asked
him to read at its reunion in Boston. "You could hardly find a worse
reader than myself," he told the organizers. So he sent his friend

James T. Fields in his stead, with an atrociously bad poem that took him only an hour to write. He admitted the verses lacked the "dignity and fitness" demanded by the occasion, and even apologized to Fields. In June he had a chance to redeem himself, when James Russell Lowell invited him to read at the annual Phi Beta Kappa gathering in Cambridge.

This time, Harte went. He marched through Harvard Yard in a procession led by university president Charles William Eliot, and took his seat in the crowded Unitarian church across the street. When it came time for him to speak, no less a personage than Richard Henry Dana Jr.—whose classic memoir *Two Years Before the Mast* gave American readers their first glimpse of California in 1840—rose to introduce him. Spirited applause greeted Harte as he took the stage. His clothing made a sharp contrast to the somber-suited men around him: he wore green gloves and a gaudy suit. This foppishness might have been forgiven if what happened next hadn't been so unpleasant. He bent his head and shoulders and spoke straight down, like a teenager mumbling some sullenness he hoped his parents wouldn't hear. Hardly anyone could understand him, and when people asked him to talk louder, he ignored them. He recited an old poem of his from the *Golden Era*: "a jingle so trivial, so out of keeping, so inadequate that his enemies . . . must have suffered from it almost as much as his friends," Howells wrote. "The thoughtful portion of the audience were disgusted," reported a correspondent for a Washington paper. The press hammered him for weeks. "Bret Harte's 'Fizzle' at Harvard," read a representative headline.

These disappointments put a dent in Harte's reputation. They suggested he might not fulfill his anointed role as America's next literary savior—a suspicion confirmed by the July 1871 issue of the *Atlantic*, which included Harte's first story since signing his $10,000 contract. "The Poet of Sierra Flat" told the oddly autobiographical tale of a young man who publishes a poem in a country paper and becomes an overnight sensation, before botching an attempt at public speaking and falling from public favor. Yet the writing felt slack, toothless: those sharp grains of frontier humor that serrated Harte's earlier gold rush fiction had become blunter, less precise. It was the work of a writer straining for effect, closer to the slapstick West of the "horse operas" and other pop theatricals performed on Broadway than to the nuanced ironies of the region's better storytellers. The critics weren't impressed. "[S]carcely as striking as expectation demanded," wrote the *Philadelphia Inquirer*, and most others agreed.

May, June, July: in three months, Harte had done a heap of damage to his career, and he still had further to fall. What bothered people weren't just his failures, but how indifferent he seemed to them. He had shot to the top of the literary totem pole in record time, and now was in danger of sliding off it nearly as fast. He maintained his ironic exterior throughout, as if the vagaries of his professional life were too trivial to take seriously. Another writer might be motivated to make amends by working harder. Not Harte: in August, he published nothing at all in the *Atlantic*. "It is a serious damage to both of us that you should not appear in the August number," wrote the magazine's publisher, James R. Osgood. He had kept the issue open longer than usual to accommodate a last-minute offering from his star contributor, and was angry when it didn't appear.

Beneath his insouciant facade, Harte felt confused. He had expected to love the East. He thought of his trip as a homecoming, Howells wrote: an "exodus from the exile" of the Far West after seventeen years, and he told anyone who would listen how happy he was to be free of dusty, provincial California. But he couldn't adjust. He seemed "bewildered by the strangeness of his new surroundings," a friend said. First he tried living in New York—"this noisy yet lonely city where they set such infinite values on finite and valueless things"—and hated it. Then he looked for a house in the countryside, and found the landscape entirely changed from the one he remembered. "[W]hat have become of all the farms I knew as a boy? Where are the farm yards—meadows, barns, orchards?" he wrote Howells despairingly. He found temporary refuge in Newport, Rhode Island, where he rented a place for six months, staffed it with a cook and a maid, and sauntered around town in a velvet waistcoat, attending picnics and sailing parties, hobnobbing with luminaries like George Bancroft and Julia Ward Howe—and hemorrhaging money at a terrible rate. When he returned to New York, he "left Newport in debt to the butcher, the baker, and the rest," Twain recalled. That $10,000 from the *Atlantic* had gone fast, and it wouldn't come again. His mediocre output hadn't measured up: publisher Osgood later complained that never in his career had he "gotten so little out of a contributor."

All of Harte's misfortunes drew from a simple fact: his muse had fled. He couldn't write. He was a foreigner in the East, a man out of context. By the time he reunited with Twain in Boston in November 1871, his best years were behind him. "There was a happy Bret Harte, a contented Bret Harte, an ambitious Bret Harte, a hopeful Bret Harte, a bright, cheerful, easy-laughing Bret Harte, a Bret Harte to whom it was a bubbling and effervescent joy to be alive," Twain remembered. "That Bret Harte died in San Francisco. It was the corpse of that Bret Harte that swept in splendor across the continent."

NEITHER CHARLES WARREN STODDARD nor Ina Coolbrith heard anything from Harte after he left. They heard nothing about the connections he promised to make for them, nothing about Chicago or Cambridge or New York—nothing to imply the three of them had ever been friends. For years, he had mentored them. He had given them a platform, a Bohemia to belong to. Then he went East and slammed the door shut behind him.

Coolbrith never recovered. "I had my own heartache when he went away and seemed to forget his old friends in San Francisco," she later said. She had always felt doomed, and the coming years confirmed her fatalism. As boredom and bad luck made her life bleaker, the memory of her Bohemian days grew brighter. She took comfort in the past, in the nostalgia that made her present feel strangely posthumous. She hadn't lost just a literary circle but a fraternity that "toiled and suffered together; sorrowed and despaired and hoped together." The offices of the *Overland Monthly* had been an expanding universe; her family's home felt more like a prison. "[My] duties . . . leave me no time to scribble my miserable little verses, except what I steal from sleep," she told Stoddard. She wrote at night, by lamplight, composing a commencement ode for the University of California in the summer of 1871 and continuing to publish in the *Overland* under its new editor, William C. Bartlett. Her poems reflected her mood: "The sorrow infinite / Of earth; the closing wave / The parting, and the grave."

She couldn't help it: "I cannot sit in the shadow / Forever, and sing of the sun." The worse thing would be not to sing at all—to be too tired, or not have the time. In January 1872, a poet friend named Joaquin Miller deposited his teenage daughter on her doorstep. The girl needed a home while Miller traveled the world, and Coolbrith agreed to take her. By then, Coolbrith had inherited the household: her father had mysteriously disappeared. Relatives later said he returned to Los Angeles, or went prospecting somewhere. Reports differed, but the result was the same: Coolbrith now had sole responsibility for her aging mother. As her domestic burdens grew, her dream of someday leaving California for a literary career in the East faded. She would be forced to remain while her friends roamed free—and no one roamed more freely than her closest friend, Stoddard. She envied his freedom and his free time, those languorous stretches spent roving the South Seas, and the more focused moments writing about them. She felt like a relic, she told him:

The last of the brood, left alone in the old nest . . . Do you think of that, and of how lonely it is to be?—Now that all are flown over the seas and away, and how gladly I would follow you if my wings were not clipped so closely, and so heavy a burden about the poor little throat, that has grown too tired even to sing? You see how I seek consolation in self-pity. Alas! No one else pities me.

Stoddard was no stranger to self-pity. He had indulged in it his whole life, usually after being spurned by a love interest or dismembered by an unkind critic. He, too, felt hurt at Harte's silence, at the bewildering snub from his literary sage. But he didn't let it derail him. His skin had grown thicker in recent years. With Harte's help, he had discovered his talent for prose, publishing tales of his tropical adventures in the *Overland*. By the spring of 1871, he had his first piece accepted by the *Atlantic*: "A Prodigal in Tahiti," a comic account of his recent trip. Howells adored it: "infinitely the best thing of the kind that I ever read," he told Stoddard. He wouldn't be able to publish it for more than a year, owing to a hefty backlog of articles inherited from his predecessor, but he wanted more: "Do send us something else in the same vein, and believe, if you can, my promise that it will be promptly printed."

Encouraged, Stoddard powered ahead. In February 1872, he boarded a schooner for Samoa—but after a hellish sea voyage, he opted to remain in his beloved Hawaii, where he wrote more stories of island life. By now he had enough for a book. After returning to San Francisco that summer, he began looking for a publisher. He wanted a prestigious house, one that would give him a proper launch in the East. Fortunately, he had found a friend in Howells, who helped him pitch *Atlantic* publisher James R. Osgood. "I have spoken to Osgood about it, and I know that it will have a fair and favorable chance," Howells wrote Stoddard in early 1873. "At any rate it shall not lack my friendship." Howells didn't disappoint: Osgood agreed to do the book. He gave it a title—*South-Sea Idyls*—and scheduled its release for October.

South-Sea Idyls would be an anti-travelogue in the tradition of

Twain's *Roughing It*. In its sixteen sketches, fact and fiction freely intermingle; disquisitions on local history are mercifully absent. The narrator is a parody of the white colonizer, a Robinson Crusoe in reverse. He doesn't come to conquer, but to be converted. "[B]arbarism has given me the fullest joy of my life," Stoddard once told Walt Whitman, and *South-Sea Idyls* is delirious with the thrill of that discovery. A hidden current of homoeroticism runs throughout. What Stoddard didn't have to hide was how relieved he felt to find a place that didn't make him feel like a freak. He loved the islands not just for their naked boys and their scented frescoes of foliage but because they let him inhabit more of himself. They let him be lazy and mischievous, sleazy and spiritual; above all, to speak in his own voice instead of perpetually imitating everyone else's.

This voice was distinctly Californian, as reviewers of *South-Sea Idyls* recognized. In the *Atlantic*, Howells noted the similarities between Stoddard and Harte and Twain: "[T]hey have each deeply received the same California stamp," he wrote, "and their humor, broad or fine, has the same general character." This included a "careless, audacious irreverence" and an intimate, uninhibited tone— qualities that liberated Stoddard's style, and led to his first major success on the national scene. *South-Sea Idyls* established his bona fides as a western writer. It also represented a farewell of sorts before he followed in the footsteps of his more famous colleagues and left California. He headed East in August 1873, the month he turned thirty. He planned to explore Europe, paying his way with weekly dispatches for the *San Francisco Chronicle*.

Coolbrith was in Los Angeles visiting her sister when she got the news. "When I received your goodbye it seemed as if our long companionship had suddenly ended," she wrote Stoddard, "and with my living eyes I was to see you no more forever." He had skipped town many times over the past several years, but usually returned after a few months. This trip would take him farther and last longer. "You cannot avoid meeting Harte," she continued. "Don't mention me to him please, and if he should ask of me, which is not probable, say nothing of my poems. The subject has ceased to be other than ridiculous."

Stoddard would remain a faithful friend but an inconstant correspondent. He rarely remembered to write. Coolbrith could follow his progress in the *Chronicle*, as he traveled from Salt Lake, where he heard a Mormon sermon, to Chicago, where he saw a thousand shrieking trains, to New York, where the crowds wore him out and the beggars made his heart bleed. He didn't see Harte. But he did meet Howells. "I shall be among the first to welcome you," the *Atlantic* editor had written him, and the two hit it off. Stoddard's face expressed everything Howells liked best about his writing. The dainty lips, the soulful eyes, the receding hairline revealing the ovoid shape of his skull—it was the face of a man-child, vague and sweet and sad. "More delightful than either his prose or his verse was the man himself," Howells recalled.

Stoddard liked the East but couldn't linger. His *Chronicle* editors wanted European correspondence, and on October 3, 1873, he departed for England. Ten days later he landed in Liverpool, took the train to London, and read in the paper that Mark Twain was in town. Stoddard found his old friend in a suite on the third floor of the Langham Hotel: bored, restless, and happy to see someone from his San Francisco salad days. They would spend the winter together in London, enduring a season of especially thick fog—not the damp, purifying mists they remembered from San Francisco, but the choking particulate haze of an industrial city burning millions of tons of coal, the kind that clogged the lungs and made the days so dark that people needed lanterns at noon.

TWAIN HADN'T CHANGED. He had the same rumpled hair, the same owlish eyebrows. But his fame had grown considerably since Stoddard last saw him in San Francisco. By 1873, he had finally begun to overtake Harte as America's favorite western writer. For years, Twain had lagged behind. Now, as Harte's fortunes kept falling, Twain's continued to climb.

A big boost came from *Roughing It*, his chronicle of the Pacific coast. Twain had agonized over its reception: while confident of its commercial potential, he feared the critics would tear it apart. After all, *Roughing It* was an unrepentantly western piece of writing, steeped in a woolly vernacular that might prove indigestible to the eastern press. To limit the damage, Twain instructed Elisha Bliss to send out review copies only to a select few, compared with the two hundred they had used to hype the release of *The Innocents Abroad*.

Twain had nothing to worry about. Not only did *Roughing It* sell—more than seventy-five thousand copies in the year after it appeared in February 1872, earning the author more than $20,000 in royalties—it got good reviews. In the *Atlantic*, Howells praised the book's "grotesque exaggeration" and "broad irony." He recognized that these hallmarks of frontier humor were in fact forms of realism: "the truest colors" available to describe the Far West. This was because the region itself had the air of "an extravagant joke, the humor of which was only deepened by its nether-side of tragedy." Twain didn't just try to make readers laugh, in other words. He had a higher aim: to give a true portrait of a particular part of America.

Twain felt relieved when he read the review. "I am as uplifted & reassured by it as a mother who has given birth to a white baby when she was awfully afraid it was going to be a mulatto," he wrote Howells. This stamp of approval from the editor of the country's most eminent literary paper had real significance. *Roughing It* was a bigger risk than *The Innocents Abroad*—a purer dose of frontier folk art—and its critical success suggested that Twain had finally begun to infiltrate the inner sanctum of elite opinion. Howells would be his most important ally in that campaign. The *Atlantic* editor had a weakness for western talk. He knew that Americans didn't speak dictionary English, but a variety of local idioms rich

with homespun metaphor and slang. In Twain, Howells found someone who could turn these native sounds into art. He found what he
had hoped to find in Harte: the torchbearer of a new national literature that spoke the language of ordinary people.

He also found a friend. They grew closer in the months after
their literary lunch in Boston with Harte and others. They discovered the affinities beneath their obvious differences. Twain wore
outrageous outfits that made him stand out. Howells wore conservative suits that made him invisible. Twain's mustache swept like a
lightning bolt across his upper lip. Howells's hung walruslike over
his mouth. But they were both westerners in the East: self-taught,
hugely hardworking. Born two years apart, both began as typesetters
and came of age while sitting out the Civil War: Twain as a Bohemian on the Pacific coast, Howells as the American consul in Venice.
Both worked to expose the nation's moral shortcomings, especially
the injustices of its postwar economy and the unfinished business of
emancipation. But mostly, they liked each other. They never ran out
of things to talk about, whether sitting up late drinking Scotch or
writing long, chatty letters. It was a perfect marriage of two comple-
mentary personalities: the intense, wiry Twain and the stumpy, genial Howells, teaming up to make one of the most important literary
alliances in American history.

Over the years, Howells would earn accolades as an editor, an
author, and a critic. But his most public role would be as the country's
chief tastemaker—the "Dean of American Letters"—and he threw
his considerable cultural weight behind Twain. At first this meant
helping the "low" humorist gain acceptance in New England. Eventually it meant something more: to champion Twain as the representative writer of modern America, the "Lincoln of our literature."
Howells validated the radicalism at the root of "Jim Smiley and His
Jumping Frog." He saw Twain as an incomparable artist of everyday American life, an evangelist for "the superiority of the vulgar."
His support enabled Twain to become a transformative figure, the

wild-haired prophet who led the country away from the European-
ized gentry of the Atlantic coast and into the western interior.

But that was later. When *Roughing It* came out in 1872, Twain
and Howells were still in the courtship phase. Meanwhile, Howells
and Harte were halfway through a slow, bitter breakup. Relations
between the two men had taken a chilly turn. The poor quality of
Harte's *Atlantic* pieces was one reason. His unforgivable laziness was
another. Harte had "a queer absent-minded way of spending his
time," an observer noted, and what few hours he still devoted to
writing yielded only feeble imitations of his former glories. The critics were willing to go easy on him at first. But as the afterglow of his
eastern arrival wore off, and the media heat generated by "The Heathen Chinee" and "The Luck of Roaring Camp" cooled, they lost
patience. In March 1872, the *New York Evening Post* called Harte's
latest *Atlantic* offering a "catastrophe."

No one could've foreseen that America's hottest literary property
would promptly self-immolate after relocating across the country.
The large-hearted Howells felt sympathy for his struggling contributor, as his warm reminiscences of the man make clear. But Harte
wouldn't go down gracefully. He once bragged that he had "burned
his ships" after leaving California, and his flameout in the East
would produce another pile of wrecked friendships. The same month
the *Evening Post* pilloried Harte's story, the beleaguered author sent
Howells a new poem called "Concepción de Argüello." When Howells made a few editorial suggestions, Harte spat back a snarling reply. The poem dealt with the Spanish history of California, and
Howells had apparently consulted his Cambridge friends to help
fact-check it. Harte was indignant. He patronized Howells as "my
dear boy," and insisted those "Yankee Professors" had no idea what
they were talking about. "I am careless in *composition* at times," he
snapped, "but I am *never* careless with my facts, general outlines,
details or color."

Even the affable Howells found this hard to take. He wrote an angry response, and Harte, recognizing he had crossed a line, quickly backtracked with an apologetic follow-up. They reconciled, and the *Atlantic* published the poem. But the damage was done. Harte finished out his contract, but it wouldn't be renewed. He was every editor's nightmare: sloppy in his writing, sluggish in his habits, hostile to revisions. A photograph from 1872 showed him with bags under his eyes, staring into the middle distance. The fashionable necktie and sideburns were intact, but his face had the absent look of an actor who had forgotten his lines. These days he played the role of the writer more than he actually wrote, and his most important performances involved persuading rich men to lend him money. "He was utterly destitute of what is sometimes called 'the money sense,'" said a friend. This meant he spent freely, even while living on borrowed cash. But he couldn't stay afloat on credit forever. He needed to rekindle his career. So he turned to an old friend for help.

ON JUNE 13, 1872, Harte went to see Twain in Hartford. It was a hard time for the household to have visitors: eleven days earlier, Twain's firstborn had died of diphtheria. Always sickly, baby Langdon had grown weaker after the birth of his sister Susy in March. He was only a year and a half old. Livy dropped into a profound depression. Twain blamed himself.

One cold morning, Twain had taken his son for a drive in an open carriage to give him some air. He wrapped the child in furs, but grew distracted, and didn't see that the blankets had slipped off. Langdon's legs were exposed. When the coachman finally noticed, he told Twain, who rushed the baby back to the house and felt wholly to blame for what followed. "Yes, I killed him," he once told Howells, although nobody shared this opinion and the facts didn't support it. He felt responsible for Langdon's death, just as he had felt responsible for the steamboat accident that took his younger brother's life fourteen years earlier. When tragedy struck, he made himself the scapegoat. Guilt was how he grieved. "I have always felt shame for that treacherous morning's work," he reported in his auto-biography more than three decades later.

He went to the grave believing he had betrayed his only son. For Twain, treachery was the worst sin, and loyalty the supreme virtue. This explained why, despite their checkered history, Twain gra-ciously hosted Harte at such a challenging moment. Harte himself had lost a son five years earlier. He showed little empathy during his visit, however. He had often mistreated Twain, most recently by hu-miliating him at their Boston literary lunch. And even now, in Hart-ford, Harte couldn't resist dispensing "sparkling sarcasms about our house, our furniture, and the rest of our domestic arrangements," Twain remembered. But their friendship could survive these strains. It had deep roots, dating back to their Bohemian days. Harte had helped make Twain a writer. Now Harte needed a favor. He was broke. He couldn't even pay his rent. So Twain lent him $500—certainly knowing it wouldn't be repaid—and promised to cajole Elisha Bliss into giving him a book contract. This kindness wouldn't go unappreciated. When Harte returned to New York, he composed a grateful letter that reflected the renewed warmth between the two men. "Tell Mrs. Clemens I deputize you to kiss the baby for me," he wrote. "You ought to be very happy with that sweet wife of yours . . . It is not every man that can cap a hard, thorny, restless youth with so graceful a crown."

Harte's own conjugal crown was a constant headache. Illness made his unhappy marriage harder. His wife had been unwell since coming East, and their daughter Jessamy, born in May, nearly died in infancy. In July 1872, the family moved to Morristown, New Jer-sey, to escape the summer heat. The climate was healthier, but Harte faced a familiar problem: he couldn't write. The "sleepy *dolce far niente* air" made work impossible, he told Twain. "Could not you and I find some quite rural retreat this summer where we could establish ourselves . . . in some empty farm house a mile or two away from our families, and do our work, with judicious intervals of smoking, coming home to dinner at abt. 3 p.m.?"

Perhaps Harte felt some sliver of nostalgia for the collaborative spirit of San Francisco, for the camaraderie of the *Overland* offices and Coolbrith's parlor. But Twain couldn't help. He couldn't hole up in a farmhouse at the moment. He had something else in mind. *Roughing It* had been out for months. He needed a new project, and felt confident he would find it abroad.

On August 21, 1872, Twain sailed for England. He went alone, leaving Livy behind with the baby. "I do miss him so much," she confessed to a friend. But she knew the trip would be good for him: "England is a subject that he will get inspired over." Inspiration wasn't the only reason for Twain's trip: he also hoped to protect his work from unauthorized printing by English pirates. Still, the literary possibilities of England seemed endless. A country obsessed with caste and custom would be easy prey for Twain's pen. He could play the American barbarian, and produce another pillaging narrative like *The Innocents Abroad.*

What he didn't expect was how much he would love the English—and how much they would love him. He arrived to find himself hugely famous. Everyone knew his books, thanks to the pirated editions that sold for a shilling or two apiece. Most surprising, his readers came from all classes. In America, the masses embraced him but the elite still kept their distance; in England, both high and low delighted in him. He became a darling of the British press, and a featured attraction at London's swankest gatherings. At a state banquet attended by nearly a thousand of the empire's ritziest citizens, he walked arm-in-arm with the lord chancellor while the wigged minister, accompanied by a servant holding the train of his gown, explained how much Twain's work meant to him. At a dinner held by the sheriffs of London, 250 guests broke into spontaneous applause when Twain's presence was announced. "I was never so taken aback in my life," he wrote Livy. "I did not know I was a lion."

The English craze for American humor owed much to Artemus Ward, who had traveled to London in 1866 and achieved terrific success before succumbing to tuberculosis the following year. The press hailed Twain as his successor—the best specimen of the "peculiar humor invented by our American cousins." The English infatuation with him wasn't purely a fascination with the exotic frontier regions of their former colony—although that certainly played a part. It went deeper, recognizing Twain's shrewd intelligence, and his original contributions to the language they held in common.

Flattered wasn't the word. Twain was giddy. Never in his life had he enjoyed the praise of such powerful men—and in his letters home, he trembled with pure childlike joy at the honors heaped on his head. Long days spent socializing and sightseeing left little time for his book project. "Too much company—too much dining—too much sociability," he told Livy. He visited the Tower of London and Westminster Abbey. He saw Handel's *Messiah* performed at the Royal Albert Hall. In the pages of the *Spectator*, he publicly shamed John Camden Hotten, the pirate publisher who had capitalized on the absence of international copyright to print Twain's books without paying him any royalties. He loved every minute, but he wished Livy were there to share it with him. "I am not going abroad any more without you," he wrote. "It is too dreary when the lights are out & the company gone."

He kept his promise. By November, he was back in Hartford. Six months later, in May 1873, he returned to England—this time, with the whole family. Livy had never left the country before. She wouldn't be going as an ordinary tourist, but as the wife of Mark Twain, the great American humorist. She would be seeing things she had long imagined, like the thatched roofs of English cottages and Shakespeare's tomb in Stratford-upon-Avon. She would also be seeing things beyond imagining, like the sight of her husband surrounded by lord mayors and ministers and Robert Browning and Anthony Trollope. When she had agreed to marry him in 1868, she

never could've predicted that, within five years, the ill-dressed westerner would be the most sought-after man in London.

No wonder Twain loved England: it gave him the legitimacy he
always wanted. The irony was that his work could get a fairer hearing here than in his home country, where most of New England's
literary nabobs still scorned him. The English could see the genius
of their "American cousin" more clearly than the elite of his own
country. It would be a while before Boston realized its mistake. In
the meantime, London offered a foretaste of his future eminence.

American Humour, by Frederick Waddy, for *Once a Week* (London), December 14, 1872. "California has developed a literature of its own and its proudest boast is the possession of Mark Twain," declared the accompanying article.

EIGHT

By October 1873, Livy was done with London. "I am blue and cross and homesick," she announced—and newly pregnant. Adding to the urgency, a disaster had broken out back home. In September, a major investment bank went bust, sending a shock wave through the financial system. Railroads were hit especially hard. The stocks and bonds that financed their construction had also helped power the postwar boom, and when their value plunged, a substantial chunk of the postwar American economy came tumbling down with it. Credit contracted, prices fell, and the country entered a six-year depression.

One night after the Panic of 1873 began, Twain sat up smoking in his London hotel room. He couldn't sleep. He had already spent more than $10,000 satisfying his expensive tastes abroad—closer to $200,000 today. As the crisis spread, triggering a wave of bankruptcies, threatening his and Livy's investments, he decided to shore up his finances by booking a brief lecture engagement in London. In mid-October, he delivered six performances to admiring crowds. He did a seventh in Liverpool on October 20—drawing so much traffic that he shut down the streets around the hall—before yielding to his wife's wishes and getting on a boat to New York.

He wouldn't be gone for long. He would see his family all the way to the door of their home in Hartford, and then retrace his route back to England. He didn't mind the travel—he loved lying in his berth, reading late into the night alongside a porthole filled with the passing ocean—but he did hate to be separated from Livy. By the morning of November 20, 1873, he was back in his comfortable corner suite at the Langham Hotel, eating his breakfast of bacon and eggs, staring out the window, missing his wife.

He had returned to London to oversee the English edition of his next book. This wasn't the one he wanted to write about England, which never materialized, but a novel about contemporary America, coauthored with his friend and neighbor Charles Dudley Warner. Composed at breakneck speed over four months in Hartford, it drew a bleakly funny portrait of the country as a gambler's paradise populated by knaves and fools and sycophants. Its title gave a name to the postwar era whose financial fragility had just been exposed by the Panic of 1873: *The Gilded Age*, suggesting a thin layer of prosperity disguising a deeper decay. If *The Innocents Abroad* and *Roughing It* showed a young country struggling up to adulthood, *The Gilded Age* would be the story of its growing pains.

Ever since moving East in the late 1860s, Twain had noticed a new shamelessness in American life. Nearly every day the papers carried reports of widespread corruption, from the endless scandals of Ulysses S. Grant's sleazy administration in Washington to the thuggery of Boss Tweed's Tammany machine in New York. Private greed and public crookedness conspired to create "an era of incredible rottenness," in Twain's phrase. Politicians bought elections, stole taxpayer dollars, and cut backroom deals with plutocrats. The country was becoming one big boomtown, an economic frontier of fast, ungovernable prosperity, and everyone wanted in on the bonanza.

Twain's relationship to this dynamic was complex. From living in the Far West, he knew what rapid growth did to a community, how certain moral considerations got lost in the general rush for riches.

He knew the mind of a speculator, being one himself. He loved risky ventures, whether betting on mining stock in Virginia City or his own books on the subscription market. Yet he also felt disgusted by the postwar free-for-all. He hated the sleaze and rapacity of the new industrial order, how capitalism corroded people's sense of right and wrong and perverted the mechanisms of democracy. He fulminated against the era's tycoons and politicians—and also admired and befriended many of them. He understood the Gilded Age from the inside: not merely as a critic, but as a participant and beneficiary. The economic forces accelerated by the Civil War created the conditions for his commercial success. They supported a rising middle class and a broadening publishing culture that enabled him to connect to a popular audience. *The Gilded Age* would be the first novel to be sold by subscription, and Twain threw his usual entrepreneurial zeal into making it a hit.

This was why he was back in London by November 1873: to sell his book. He wanted to supervise its publication in England by Routledge & Sons, and secure an English copyright to preempt the pirates. But first he had to wait for Elisha Bliss to publish the American edition, and, as always, this took longer than expected. Fortunately, he had lined up some companionship for the season. He knew he would be lonely without Livy. So when his old friend Charles Warren Stoddard came to London as a roving correspondent for the *San Francisco Chronicle*, Twain persuaded him to move into his suite at the Langham Hotel and stay the winter as his private secretary.

Stoddard had little to recommend him for the role. His handwriting was frightful, his spelling even worse. But it didn't matter: "I hired him in order to have his company," Twain later wrote. Stoddard remembered it more vividly: "He seized me at once and said how nervous and miserable he was." Twain was about to return to the London lecture stage. He was feeling moody, introspective, and less social than before. Instead of partying with aristocrats, he wanted to hunker down with his fellow Bohemian and reminisce—to indulge in "long, long talks about old times in the New World and new times in the Old," Stoddard said. The secretary made a good companion. He was gentle and patient and kind. Over the next several weeks, he would spend nearly every waking minute with Twain, and get as close to him as anyone ever would.

On December 1, 1873, Twain began performing at the Queen's Concert Rooms in Hanover Square. He and Stoddard settled into a daily rhythm. They slept late. At twelve thirty, a servant brought breakfast. Stoddard sorted the morning mail, declining countless invitations to croquet and suppers and garden parties. Afterward they took a walk or visited an art gallery. A heavy coal fog covered London that winter. It greeted them the moment they left the hotel, burning their eyes, depositing bits of soot on their cuffs and collars. Streetlamps barely penetrated the murk; carriages moved at a crawl. The sunless gloom "nearly broke my heart," Twain told Livy, and it doubtless sped the onset of the crankiness that descended on him each day around three in the afternoon, as the hour of the lecture drew closer. Stoddard did his best to keep Twain distracted as he grew anxious and irritable, right up to those last agonizing minutes backstage at the Concert Rooms with the performer pacing in full evening dress, threatening to rush onstage early so he could get the damn thing over with.

Finally, the time came. Stoddard escorted Twain to the steps leading to the platform and watched him wobble out. He walked slowly to the footlights at the edge of the stage and rubbed his hands—one of his trademark tics. Then he began to speak, and the dread that had been building unbearably for the last five hours melted away. "The moment he heard his own voice he began to feel better, and I knew he was all right," Stoddard said. It wasn't a voice English audiences were accustomed to hearing: the deadpan drawl of the American West, enlivened by what one critic called the "delicious dialect of California."

He opened with his very first lecture, the one he had debuted seven years earlier in San Francisco: "Our Fellow Savages of the Sandwich Islands," based on his Hawaiian adventures. After a week, he switched to a new one about Nevada, drawn from *Roughing It*. The room always reacted differently, Stoddard observed. A joke could kill one night and bomb the next. Even the laughs came in various kinds: the big ones that broke out everywhere at once and the slow ones that started in one corner and gradually spread. Twain's listeners never quite knew when he was joking, because he never smiled. He loved how they sat "still as statues, for fear they might miss a word," and how their composure crumbled when his drolleries became too ludicrous to resist. He remembered their faces: the fat lady who laughed so hard she cried, the young girl who seemed to be having a seizure in the second row. "Bully audiences," he told Livy.

Lecturing energized him. When they got back to the hotel, he bounced around the suite, hammering out a Negro spiritual on the piano, fixing cocktails at the bar. His taste for liquor hadn't subsided since becoming a family man. Neither had his skill in preparing it: he "knew the art to perfection," Stoddard reported, concocting masterly creations of Scotch mixed with sugar and lemon and bitters. After they drank one, Twain demanded that Stoddard make the next. "With fear and trembling I'd make an effort," remembered the secretary, and the result always fell short. But it gave Twain an excuse to keep drinking. "Yours was so damned bad I'll have to make another one to take the taste out of my mouth," he said.

Twain was a born performer. He performed onstage, and in the street. He lived as a character of his own creation, blurring the line between his public and private selves, and between his life as he imagined it in his books and as it actually happened. Even with Livy he played roles: the adoring husband, the scoundrel in need of reform. But during those long nights with Stoddard in the winter of 1873, shut up in "gorgeous seclusion" with a cozy fire crackling in the hearth, Twain let his many faces fall away and something more intimate emerge. He spoke, and Stoddard listened:

Very, very often these nightly talks became a lament. He was always afraid of dying in the poorhouse. The burden of his woe was that he would grow old and lose the power of interesting an audience, and become unable to write, and then what would become of him? He had trained himself to do nothing else. He could not work with his hands. There could be no escape. The poorhouse was his destiny. And he'd drink cocktails and grow more and more gloomy and blue until he fairly wept at the misery of his own future.

This wasn't the stand-up comic that left posh Londoners in stitches. This was a man of great vulnerability, prone to apocalyptic bouts of fear and sadness. His dread of poverty came partly from the painful memory of his father's financial failures, and his alcohol-fueled confessions involved detailed recollections of his past. Twain discussed "his youth with a charm and a freshness that was positively fascinating," Stoddard wrote—and with a stamina that wore out his secretary. As the church bells chimed one, two, three, Twain's speech got slower and Stoddard got sleepier, until he couldn't stay awake any longer. He remembered Twain following him to his room, "now talking so slowly that the syllables came about every half minute and the last picture I'd have as I dropped off to sleep was of Mark bending over me, glass in hand, uttering the second syllable of a word he began a full minute ago."

A vivid panorama of Twain's personal history emerged from these sessions. "I could have written his biography at the end of the season," Stoddard said, and he wasn't exaggerating. He had seen Twain as a poor Bohemian in San Francisco, and as a rich celebrity in London. Now he struggled to stay awake as Twain's manic brain churned through the material that would supply the next and greatest phase of his artistic evolution: his childhood.

By 1873, Twain was in the midst of a fit of remembering. As a boy he had soaked up his surroundings and stored them in the

marrow of his developing mind. In his thirties, these memories began to resurface. He described the process in a letter to Will Bowen,
his best boyhood friend from Hannibal, Missouri. "The fountains of
my great deep are broken up," he wrote, borrowing a line from the
book of Genesis to convey the scale of the flood carrying him back
in time. His past wasn't a museum of musty relics but a living tissue
of "faces," "footsteps," "hands," "voices," "songs." It was a place he
experienced in the present tense; a place he heard, touched, tasted.

These remembrances didn't just set him off on drunken rambles.
They also opened a new field for literary creation. This possibility
first came into view when *The Gilded Age* finally appeared in late
December. The book flopped: sales were disappointing, and the critical response was mixed. William Dean Howells chose not to review
it for the *Atlantic Monthly*. Privately he called the novel "dyspeptic,"
blaming it for failing to digest "the crude material with which it is
fed"—a fair criticism, given the baffling array of characters and plot-
lines that glutted its six-hundred-plus pages. Yet for all its faults, *The
Gilded Age* represented a major step forward for Twain. It was his
first novel, and his first published attempt to put his boyhood memories into a full-length work of fiction. Flashes of his biography—
Mississippi steamboats, small-town life in the Old Southwest—give
the book its best scenes. His uncle's slave makes a cameo as Uncle
Dan'l. His mother's cousin shows up as Colonel Sellers, a frontier
hustler forever on the verge of getting rich. "I merely put him on
paper as he was," Twain explained.

He didn't have to look very far to find suitable fuel for his fiction:
the universe of his youth furnished everything he needed. In the
1860s, he had found the building blocks of his art in the Far West.
He had used a tall tale about a jumping frog to open a new path for
American literature, inspired by the raw, tuneful voices of the frontier. But these voices had been with him his whole life. In the 1870s,
emboldened by his success, he turned inward to recover them. He
remembered Hannibal, Missouri, and this remembering would

enrich his writing immeasurably. It would lead to Tom Sawyer and Huck Finn, and give him a deeper perception of what made America distinctive. In Hannibal, he would discover a microcosm for the nation as a whole, a place where the particular weave of American society could be made visible.

In London, Stoddard saw this development in its early stages. Twain's all-night reminiscences revealed the makings of his future masterpieces. "I trust I am betraying no confidence when I state that a good deal of the real boy is blended with the 'Story of Tom Sawyer,'" Stoddard later said.

By January 1874, however, Twain was getting tired of these marathon talks. "Stoddard & I have been talking & keeping a lonely vigil for hours," he scribbled to Livy one morning. "It is *so* unsatisfying." He loved his friend, but needed his wife: "I want *you*—& nobody else." He wrote her constantly, counting down the days until they saw each other again. He told her to have a bottle of Scotch ready when he arrived. He pictured himself ringing the bell of their home in Hartford—"then the turning of the bolt, & 'Who is it?'— then ever so many kisses—then you & I in the bath-room, I drinking my cock-tail & undressing, & you standing by—then to bed." It was time to go home. His business was done: he had copyrighted the English edition of *The Gilded Age*; his lectures had been a hit. Before he left for America on January 13, 1874, he would perform a pair of farewell shows in Liverpool. Hundreds of Britons packed into the hall to give their beloved American a hearty send-off. Twain presented Stoddard with a page of his "prompt notes" as a gift—an aide-mémoire he used at the lectern, scrawled with mnemonic symbols—and inscribed it, "We're done with *this*, Charles, forever!"

It made a fitting memento for his faithful secretary, who had seen the lectures so many times he nearly knew them by heart. They spent their final night together in the usual way, drinking and talking well past midnight. Whatever happiness Twain felt at going home gradually faded as the hour advanced, and his usual melancholy returned. "He sank into a sea of forebodings," wrote Stoddard, who watched helplessly as Twain slid into a nightmare trance, revisiting his terror of the poorhouse, envisioning his future as "friendless, forsaken, despised"—until a comforting thought came to him. He knew what he would do if he failed as a writer. "I'll become a teacher of elocution!" he declared, and rang a clerk for a copy of the Bible. What followed was perhaps the most surreal of the many odd moments that occurred that winter. Twain read the book of Ruth while Stoddard listened, astonished. The man he had seen drawling onstage for more than a month now spoke with the oratorical fluency

Twain's "prompt notes" for his lecture "Roughing It on the Silver Frontier."
The icons helped him remember his talking points, starting from the
top left with Lake Tahoe. On the right is Twain's message to Stoddard:
"We're done with this, Charles, forever!"

of an Episcopal minister. The western twang was gone. The words flowed beautifully, "in a style that would have melted the hardest heart." "He seemed to forget my presence and lose himself in the simple beauty of the story," Stoddard remarked.

It was a story about loyalty, the virtue Twain most valued in others. Perhaps this explained his "soul-deep" feeling in reading it; perhaps the verses recalled some incident of his Presbyterian upbringing. Mostly, it gave his ravening mind something more sustaining to chew on. In the morning, he sailed home. He would be returning to a life entirely unlike the one he had imagined. The next few years would be happy, successful, and hugely productive. He wouldn't spend them in a poorhouse but in the eccentric, extravagant home he and Livy had just built in Hartford. He would publish *The Adventures of Tom Sawyer* and begin writing *Adventures of Huckleberry Finn*. He would become a regular contributor to the *Atlantic* and a favorite of Howells. He would take his seat at the table of the eastern aristocracy, and expand his mass appeal. And he would see an old friend become a bitter enemy.

BRET HARTE LOOKED EXHAUSTED. An "old-young man," a journalist called him, his face prematurely wrinkled, his eyes heavy. By 1874, he was no longer the Next Big Thing, the literary heartthrob who fascinated the nation with tales of gunslingers and gold seekers. He was a pale echo of his past self, doing anything he could to survive. His cratering finances had forced him onto the lecture circuit. He hated public speaking, but he had no choice. He needed money to survive. So while Twain put down roots in Hartford and embarked on the most creative period of his life, Harte wandered the continent like a traveling salesman, surviving blizzards and broken-down trains, sleeping in hotels and Pullman cars, playing to crowds from Toronto to Topeka.

People came out to see a real live westerner. He could sense their disappointment the moment he took the stage. He wore fancy suits, not the coarse garb of his characters. "[I]f I had been more herculean in proportions, with a red shirt and top boots, many of the audience would have felt a deeper thrill," he recalled. They felt even fewer thrills in the hour or so that followed, as Harte planted himself on the podium and proceeded to read a prepared text. If Twain liked to break down the wall between him and his listeners, Harte did the opposite. He put up as many barriers as he could. He spoke in a languid monotone, rarely looking up. He hadn't learned any lessons from his disastrous performance at Harvard in the summer of 1871—and these days he didn't have the luxury of shrugging it off. He had to keep touring, even in the face of withering criticism. From late 1872 through early 1875, he performed. An "exceedingly dull affair," groaned a journalist in St. Louis. "Harte as a lecturer is a dead failure," judged another in Des Moines.

Twain had a more nuanced view. "He has an excellent lecture . . . & reads it execrably," he said after seeing Harte perform in Hartford. The talk was called "The Argonauts of '49," and in it, Harte narrated the saga of the world-historical event that had inspired his best writing: the gold rush. Yet this wasn't the same gold rush as the one described in "The Luck of Roaring Camp"—it was more heroic than ironic, more triumphant than absurd. Harte had lost his sense of early California as a cosmic joke. He now eulogized the pioneers with the same rhetoric he once ridiculed. In fact, his description of the miners of 1849—an "Argonautic brotherhood" of "jauntily insolent" young Americans—sounded curiously like another frontier fraternity: the Bohemians of the Pacific coast.

The lost literary scene of San Francisco had been the only place Harte ever belonged. When he left, burning his bridges, he achieved a degree of glory unknown for a western writer, followed by an exceptionally brutal decline. He limped on in a kind of literary afterlife, lingering in the periphery of the public eye. He became the living fulfillment of Twain's worst fears: not just bankrupt, but "friendless, forsaken, despised." People used to hang on his every word; now they hammered at all his failures and flaws. The most hurtful attacks came from California, where, in late 1872, the *San Francisco Chronicle* ran a front-page article by a former friend of Harte's that accused him of embezzling money from the *Overland Monthly* during his tenure as editor.

Harte was furious. "I have been lately pretty well abused from unexpected sources but I think the enclosed caps the climax," he wrote Twain, who had remained loyal since their reconciliation. "I don't mind his slander; that I can refute—but how am I to make this dog know that he is a dog and not a man?" Not everything the dog said was easy to refute, however. Perhaps Harte didn't steal from the *Overland*—but the *Chronicle* piece also charged him with being a "borrower of considerable sums," and "a cool ignorer of the gracious loaners," facts no one could deny. Indeed, his endless debts and lackadaisical approach to repaying them did incalculable harm to his reputation. He made it worse by lashing out at his creditors, complaining of their "hoggishness."

His delusions grew. He pretended to be rich, even as evidence of his ruin mounted. He continued to insist on special treatment, even as the quality of his writing plummeted. His biggest liability was his pride. When a Chicago magazine wanted to make him its editor, he killed the deal by demanding an exorbitant salary. When John H. Carmany at the *Overland Monthly* asked him to return to San Francisco to resume control of the magazine, he used it as an excuse to whine about California's recent treatment of him. "I do not see how I could make the Overland's 'Sanctum' the literary Mecca of the West, after the Prophet had been so decidedly renounced by his disciples," he wrote.

Even the *Atlantic* tried to give him a second chance. In 1874, the magazine considered bringing Harte back on an exclusive basis. Unfortunately, his ego got in the way. The crisis came when he insisted on being paid $500 for a story. Maybe in 1871, Harte could've commanded such prices—but no longer. Still, Howells promised to read the piece and consult his publishers. A week later, the editor returned with a counteroffer: $150. Harte bristled at the insult. "[S]ince my arrival East, I have never received so small an offer for any story," he huffed. "I don't blame you, my dear Howells . . ." he added condescendingly, "but I do wish you lived out of a literary atmosphere which seems to exclude any vision of a broader literary world beyond."

This exchange permanently terminated Harte's relationship with the *Atlantic*. It also paved the way for another westerner to join the magazine's distinguished ranks. The same month Harte threw his tantrum, Twain submitted "A True Story, Repeated Word for Word as I Heard It." The piece was based on a conversation with Livy's sister's cook, a former slave, about seeing her husband and children sold at auction. Twain put her heartbreaking tale on paper in its original dialect. As in "Jim Smiley and His Jumping Frog," he enclosed the story in a frame. The white narrator sits on the porch with his black servant, Aunt Rachel, whom he describes as a "cheerful, hearty soul." She laughs easily, and with such genuine joy, that the narrator can't help wondering at her happiness. "Aunt Rachel, how is it that you've lived sixty years and never had any trouble?" he asks. Her smile disappears, and she begins the tragic yarn that puts the narrator's question to shame.

Howells judged the result "extremely good." He was especially impressed by Twain's ear for "black talk"—a talent drawn from his memories of listening to slaves in antebellum Missouri. It lent the text a rugged verisimilitude of the kind the editor was keen to promote in his pages. It also treated a subject of great contemporary significance. By 1874, Reconstruction was in retreat. The brief postwar experiment in redeeming the sins of the South had begun to lose steam. A federally imposed regime in the states of the former Confederacy had enabled ex-slaves to vote, travel, hold office, and own property, but a confluence of factors conspired against it—including a violent insurgency by the Ku Klux Klan and other groups. Southerners would succeed in scuttling Reconstruction and re-establishing white supremacy. Northerners, eager to heal the wounds of the war, would find it easy to forget the evils of slavery.

"A True Story" would remind them. It appeared in the *Atlantic* in November 1874, and Howells liked it so much that he immediately gave Twain another commission. "Our Bret Harte negotiation *did* fall through," the editor explained to one of his publishers, "but I've more than made good the loss by securing Mark Twain for a series of sketches next year." This would be "Old Times on the Mississippi," a seven-part serial about Twain's experiences as a steamboat pilot. Like "A True Story," it belonged to Twain's ongoing transmutation of his personal past into literary gold.

Meanwhile, Harte entered the last leg of his downward spiral. His writing had deteriorated to the point of self-parody; his life had become an unsustainable mix of poverty and pride. His lies, to himself and others, were unraveling. When a Boston paper reported that he might have to take a job at the US Custom House in New York to support his family, he felt the need to deny it publicly. "I have always found my profession sufficiently lucrative," Harte declared, even as his creditors took him to court. Yet Twain stood by his friend. He tried to help. He lent him money. He persuaded Elisha Bliss to give him a contract for a novel that took years to produce and fared catastrophically poorly when published. He even collaborated with him on a play.

This wasn't purely charity on Twain's part. Writing for the stage could be very lucrative, and the standards weren't especially high. Twain had dramatized *The Gilded Age* without much trouble, and earned a small fortune from it. Harte had also tried breaking into the theater world, with less success. He wrote a baggy, bewildering gold rush melodrama called *Two Men of Sandy Bar* that got devastating reviews. The *New York Times* pronounced it "the most dismal mass of trash that was ever put into dramatic shape before a New-York audience."

But Twain liked it. One character in particular grabbed him: a Chinese laundryman played in yellowface by an actor named Charles Thomas Parsloe Jr., who, despite being onstage for only five minutes, made audiences howl with laughter by saying things like "Me no likee" and bobbing across the boards in clogs and a coolie hat. When Harte proposed joining forces, Twain recommended they write a new play with this "delightful Chinaman" as the protagonist, and enlist Parsloe for the part. "Harte came up here the other day & asked me to help him write a play & divide the swag, & I agreed," Twain wrote Howells on October 11, 1876.

Over the following months, Harte made multiple trips to Hartford. By this point he and his family were living in New York, only three or four hours away by train. The co-writers camped out in the study on the top floor of Twain's house, happily isolated from the domestic bustle below. They built the plot, fleshed out the scenes. They wouldn't be doing their best work. They were slumming, trying to cash in on the national fascination with the Far Western frontier they had helped create. The result was a convoluted bit of dime-novel drama, set in a California mining camp. They called it *Ah Sin*, after the Chinese hero of Harte's famous poem "The Heathen Chinee."

Harte's days as a slow, fastidious writer were over. He couldn't spare those extra hours searching for *le mot juste*. He was in survival mode. "He worked rapidly and seemed to be troubled by no hesitations or indecisions," Twain recalled. Alcohol helped. A neighbor who stopped by in November found Harte and Twain hard at work in the study, with "bottles of spirits" nearby. Twain was no teetotaler, but Harte had become a drunk. One night in early December, Harte took a break from the play to finish a story for the *New York Sun*. It was due the next day, but he didn't seem especially stressed. He enjoyed a leisurely dinner with his hosts, shared a couple of post-prandial cocktails with Twain, and then retired to his room to write. He took a bottle of whiskey with him and, around five in the morning, rang for the butler to bring him another. At nine he came down for breakfast, the story finished, two quarts of booze in his bloodstream and "not even tipsy," Twain remembered.

Liquor didn't magically restore Harte's literary powers. But it did ease his writer's block. It reconciled him to the tedium of turning out mediocre work on deadline for money—to "working over old material into new shape," as the *Alta California* put it. Fortunately, the success of his venture with Twain depended less on the quality of the script than it did on the presence of a bankable star, and in mid-December, Harte went to New York to get Parsloe on board. The actor didn't make it easy. He failed to show at their first meeting, and then acted insufferably superior at their next. Once, Harte had been the highest-paid writer in the country. Now he sat patiently while an entertainer whose chief distinction was a talent for irredeemably racist caricature treated him like a serf. Harte's clothes were ragged. His pants were coming apart at the hem. Still, he prevailed with Parsloe. "I read him those portions of the 1st & 2d acts that indicated his *role*, and he expressed himself satisfied with it," Harte wrote Twain on December 16. "As nearly as I could judge he was pleased."

Harte's tone suggested a man humbled by circumstances. He almost certainly knew that *Ah Sin* offered his last best hope of salvation, and this inspired a new kind of resolve. "He was a man who could never persuade himself to do a stroke of work until his credit was gone," Twain observed. Then he could "work harder . . . than any man I have ever seen." Harte's letter to Twain displayed his diligence. He provided the details of the Parsloe meeting, and described his continued tinkering with the manuscript. He asked after Twain's health and gave his love to Livy.

But this closeness wouldn't last. In Twain's recollection, Harte made an insufferable houseguest. He wouldn't stop making snide remarks. He ridiculed everything, all day. At some point, he turned his satirical sights from the furniture and the flatware to a more precious feature of the household: Livy. Whatever he said was "slight and vague and veiled," Twain recalled, but sufficiently insulting to provoke. Twain had no patience for uncharitable words about his wife. Moved to anger, he became implacably malevolent.

He was nothing if not thorough. First he called Harte "a shabby husband." Then "a born bummer," a "tramp," a "loafer," an "idler," a "sponge," a wearer of rags, a delinquent debtor, and, above all, an ingrate. "[Y]ou are not charged anything here for the bed you sleep in, yet you have been very smartly and wittily sarcastic about it," he seethed. "[Y]ou sneer at everything in this house, but you ought to be more tender, remembering that everything in it was honestly come by and has been paid for."

Possibly Twain said all this in person. Possibly he put it in a letter, or said none of it at all. The above account, given thirty years later in his autobiography, might be a composite, or pure fantasy. But the final split definitely took place in late February 1877. Twain wrote Harte a note, now lost, that said some unkind things. Harte took a few days to cool off before answering. Then, on March 1, he composed a long reply. "I'm not anxious to write this," he began. "But there are a few things I must say to you."

The ensuing pages had the strained, quivery quality of someone trying to keep his cool. Harte didn't want to go completely berserk. He had signed a contract dividing the profits from *Ah Sin* three ways with Twain and Parsloe, and still hoped to see some money from it. But he couldn't resist airing his grievances. He started by accusing Twain of sabotaging his novel. He blamed its poor sales on Twain's monopolizing the publisher's resources. "Either Bliss must confess that he runs his concerns solely in *your* interest, and that he uses the names of other authors to keep that fact from the public, or else he is a fool." Next, he attacked Twain for refusing to lend him more money. Twain had offered Harte a weekly stipend of $25, plus room and board in Hartford, to write another play together. Harte found the idea insulting. It struck him as a scheme to exploit his poverty by making him Twain's indentured servant. Harte concluded with stern words about *Ah Sin*. He demanded that Twain stop "marring it" with unauthorized revisions, and insisted he be consulted on all future decisions.

The letter enraged Twain. He couldn't even finish it. "I have read two pages of this ineffable idiotcy [*sic*]—it is all I can stand of it," he scrawled on the back in pencil. Harte had made another major miscalculation. He had wanted to put his partnership with Twain on a fairer footing, and ended up destroying it instead. In the coming months, Twain took *Ah Sin* wholly into his own hands. He rewrote the play until he "left hardly a foot-print of Harte in it," he told Howells. He infested rehearsals, bombarding the actors with notes. He kept Harte in the dark, and abused him so loudly that even Livy grew concerned. "[D]on't say harsh things about Mr. Harte," she told him. "We are so desperately happy . . . and he is so miserable, we can easily afford to be magnanimous toward him." It was no use. Twain's wrath was immune to reason. In his early forties, he still had the temper of a ten-year-old.

He was regressing in more ways than one. *Ah Sin* would show him not only at his meanest but also at his most mercenary. Seizing the production from Harte, Twain pushed it in the direction he hoped would be most profitable. When a journalist visited a rehearsal, he saw Parsloe in costume as Ah Sin. "Look at him," Twain said, "ain't he a lost and wandering Chinee by nature? See those two front teeth . . . just separated far enough to give him the true Mongol look." This was a far cry from 1864, when Twain had watched a gang of hooligans assault a Chinese laundryman and courageously tried to publicize the incident in the *San Francisco Call*. Thirteen years later, Twain was putting on a play those same thugs would love. *Ah Sin* premiered in Washington on May 7, 1877, and opened on Broadway on July 31. Its title character wasn't just gap-toothed but a liar, a thief, and an imbecile. He yapped in pidgin, got mocked and beaten, and frequently humiliated himself. "The Chinaman is killingly funny," Twain bragged, hopeful about its box-office success. Adding to the insult, he insisted his portrait was accurate. The first night in New York, Twain came onstage after the conclusion of the performance to announce that what the viewer had just seen was "as good and as natural and consistent a Chinaman as he could see in San Francisco."

Whether he actually believed this, or simply said it to conceal the cynicism of trying to profit from pandering to people's bigotry, didn't make *Ah Sin* any less of a moral failure. The "Chinese question" was becoming a national issue, and Twain couldn't have chosen a worse time to weigh in. Only a week before, a race riot had broken out in San Francisco. It started on the night of July 23, 1877, when eight thousand workers gathered outside City Hall to show support for the railroad strikes that had flared throughout the country that summer. The Panic of 1873 had produced a long depression, sharpening the class antagonisms of the Gilded Age. California was in especially bad shape. The decade following the arrival of the transcontinental railroad had been a never-ending nightmare of crisis, stagnation, and unemployment. Closer integration with the East had made the region more vulnerable to financial tremors elsewhere in the country. Immigrants flocked to California in record numbers, hoping to escape the depression, only to find equally bleak conditions when they arrived. Local shocks, like the failure of San Francisco's all-powerful Bank of California in the summer of 1875, made matters worse. The golden days of the 1860s were gone—and, as always, some people blamed the Chinese for their suffering.

This element made itself felt at the rally. Hecklers cried anti-Chinese slogans. Hoodlums pummeled a Chinese passerby. "On to Chinatown!" someone shouted, and a mob of hundreds spun off from the crowd and went on a rampage. They sang and swore and screamed, "indulging in the wildest species of Indian yells," a journalist wrote. They set fire to Chinese homes and cut the hoses of the firemen who came to extinguish them. They pried cobblestones from the street and broke the windows of Chinese laundries. They killed four Chinese people, and inflicted $20,000 in damage before a combined force of city police, state militia, and vigilantes pushed them back.

Not far from where the mayhem took place, Harte had written the poem that became "The Heathen Chinee." In 1870, he had tried to satirize anti-Chinese prejudice. By 1877, Chinatown was burning, and the hero of that poem—Ah Sin—was onstage three thousand miles away, reincarnated as a cretinous coolie played for cheap laughs. For both Harte and Twain, *Ah Sin* represented a betrayal not just of their principles but of their Bohemianism—of the outsider ethos that imbued San Francisco's literary boom. The play foundered. It hung on through the fall before closing permanently. A "most abject & incurable failure," Twain reported to Howells on October 15, 1877. "I'm sorry for poor Parsloe, but for nobody else concerned."

Poor Parsloe would be fine. He had found his niche as a "stage Chinaman," and it would keep him steadily employed for years to come. Harte wouldn't be so lucky. By late 1877, he was nearly sunk—"floating on the raft made of the shipwreck of his former reputation," in the words of one Boston paper—and he knew it. He felt "run over in flesh and spirit," he said: racked by a hacking cough, consumed with anxiety about how to support his wife and children. Yet he hadn't entirely lost his instinct for survival. Even before *Ah Sin* fell through, he had been trying to get a job at an American consulate overseas. In June 1877, he almost succeeded in landing one—in China.

Twain did everything he could to block it. He even enlisted Howells in the effort. Howells's wife, Elinor, was President Rutherford B. Hayes's cousin, and Howells himself had been a prominent Hayes supporter during the campaign. Twain wanted Howells to urge the president not to hire Harte. "I think your citizenship lays the duty upon you of doing what you can to prevent the disgrace of literature & the country which would be the infallible result of the appointment of Bret Harte to any responsible post," Twain wrote. Elinor passed Twain's denunciation on to Hayes's son. An answer from Washington followed soon after: "Father has read the letters and directs me to tell you there is no danger of [Harte's] appointment."

Harte kept pushing, however. He rallied his few remaining friends, and pleaded his case to powerful Republicans who had pull with the president. By the spring of 1878, he had succeeded in putting himself back in the running. President Hayes wrote Howells directly, asking his opinion, saying he had "heard sinister things" from Twain. Howells responded with a carefully worded reply. He didn't sugarcoat Harte's reputation regarding "solvency and sobriety." But he still felt "great affection for the man," and sympathized with his plight. "It would be a godsend to him, if he could get such a place; for he is poor, and he writes with difficulty and very little."

Nine days later, on April 18, 1878, the assistant secretary of state summoned Harte for a meeting in Washington, DC. The official produced a map of Germany and pointed to a town on the Rhine called Crefeld, a major exporter of silks and velvets. The State Department needed a commercial agent there to supervise the shipment of goods to the United States. The position paid an annual salary of $2,500, plus a portion of the export duties collected. "[W]ith all my disappointments, this seemed like a glimpse of Paradise," Harte told his wife. A month later, he officially accepted. He would go alone, sending money home until he could move the whole family to Europe.

Harte sailed on June 27, 1878. Twain had a fit when he found out. "Harte is a liar, a thief, a swindler, a snob, a sot, a sponge, a coward," he wrote Howells. Moreover, Twain felt "snubbed." President Hayes "should not have silently ignored my testimony," he groused, unaware of Howells's behind-the-scenes role in helping Harte get the job. "If he had only been made a home official, I think I could stand it; but to send this nasty creature to puke upon the American name in a foreign land is too much." At least there was one consolation: Twain wouldn't have to see Harte again. He never returned to America, and never brought his family to Europe. When he left in 1878, he left forever.

AFTERLIFE

There was a certain irony in sending Bret Harte abroad to represent the United States. He was a contrarian, a critic, a Bohemian. His best work was about outcasts and underdogs, people on the fringe. He resembled them, despite his refined facade. In San Francisco, he had found a community of fellow misfits, and when he left, he wouldn't find anything like it again. As Mark Twain became a ubiquitous presence in postwar America, Harte grew ever more estranged from it. He withdrew into himself, and severed his friendships one by one. He was "a man without a country," Twain said, and by the time Harte departed for Europe, he had already been living in internal exile for years.

Charles Warren Stoddard suffered a similar fate. In 1878, he returned to San Francisco after five years away. He looked different: balder, heavier, with a thick brown beard obscuring what remained of his boyish face. That summer, he would turn thirty-five. His literary career was largely finished and, like Harte, he had himself to blame. Back in 1873, he had published *South-Sea Idyls*, his comic chronicle of the Pacific Islands. It was the best thing he ever wrote, and it brought him his first national fame. Then he disappeared. He drifted through Europe and the Middle East for half a decade, squandering his talent on lackluster letters for the *San Francisco Chronicle* that earned him barely enough to live.

Aside from his stint in London as Twain's secretary, Stoddard traveled aimlessly. He grew his beard, drank cheap wine. He met young artists in Rome and Paris and Munich. He kept in touch with Twain, and found reminders of his friend everywhere he went. "I find no English speaking people who have not heard of you and know something about you," he wrote from Venice. "Surely your success has been astonishing." In 1875, he read the first of Twain's "Old Times on the Mississippi" articles in the *Atlantic Monthly*, and remembered their late nights at the Langham Hotel together—"the old times when we used to sit up over the fire in the corner room and you drew such graphic off hand pictures of the Mississipp'."

He felt happy for Twain, but couldn't help feeling forlorn about his own situation. Abroad, he could escape the burden of being a good son, a good student, even a good writer. But he was still lonely and anxious, and permanently poor. His *Chronicle* correspondence paid little. He hoped to boost his income by collecting his travel writings into a book, and asked for Twain's help. Twain tried to get Elisha Bliss on board, but "he shook his head—says he has got more books than customers, & doesn't want any more of the former." Times were tough. The depression brought on by the Panic of 1873 had hurt the publishing business. Ever loyal, Twain came up with another idea: a consulship. "Stoddard's got no worldly sense," Twain wrote Howells. "He is just the stuff for a consul." For his part, Howells promised to "leg like a centipede" on behalf of their mutual friend. But nothing ever came of it, and by the summer of 1877, Stoddard was on his way home. He scrounged up enough money to buy his steamer ticket to Philadelphia, and spent seven months in the East before taking an overland train to San Francisco.

"You will find me changed, I fear, and most likely not for the better," Stoddard warned a friend. All those years of wandering had hardened him. He was less meek, more self-assured. "My enthusiasm has boiled down," he said; "there is more grit in me than of old." Those qualities that made his *South-Sea Idyls* so charming— the childish sense of wonder, the easy pleasure in pretty things— had mellowed with age. But there were certain things he hadn't outgrown, like his inability to settle down. He still felt adrift. "I have torn up my roots so often that they do not strike into any soil with much vigor," he wrote.

San Francisco had changed almost as much as he had. The city had been a refuge in the 1860s, but now it looked more like a dumping ground. People from other parts of the country washed up on its shores looking for work, swelling the ranks of the poor. By 1877, San Francisco's unemployment rate was as high as 25 percent. Stoddard's parents lived south of Market Street, a sprawling neighborhood that bore the brunt of the bad economy. Among its flophouses and slums, jobs were scarce and crime was commonplace. "Bankruptcy, suicide and murder and robberies were the order of the day," recalled one workingman.

The city's literary fortunes had undergone an equally steep decline. The last remnants of the Bohemian scene had vanished. The *Overland Monthly* finally closed its doors in 1875. A group called the Bohemian Club, started in 1872, had briefly offered hope of keeping San Francisco's creative energies alive. It grew out of a Sunday salon hosted by James F. Bowman, a friend of Harte and the rest of the old set, and became a society for writers and journalists. Soon artists, actors, and musicians joined. Businessmen were strictly barred from admission. "Weaving spiders come not here," declared the club motto.

Stoddard joined before he left town in 1873. By the time he returned in 1878, the club had moved into roomier, more respectable quarters, and its membership had grown to include many of the mercantile types it had once excluded. The reason for this reversal was simple. As one early member recalled, they had bills to pay: "It was soon apparent that the possession of talent, without money, would not support the club." Bankers and industrialists and entrepreneurs trickled in. By the time Oscar Wilde stopped by in 1882, the transformation was complete. "I never saw so many well-dressed, well-fed, business-looking Bohemians in my life," he remarked.

San Francisco's Bohemia had never existed in an economic vacuum. No matter how loudly Harte abused California's capitalists, the literary flowering he led wouldn't have been possible without the prosperity of the 1860s. At the Bohemian Club, however, hypocrisy reached new heights. By becoming "Bohemians," California's postwar parvenus could playact at glamorous poverty. They could pretend that art, not money, was what united them. They could indulge their creative impulses within a safely circumscribed setting, in members-only performances known as High Jinks, and later at their annual encampments at the Bohemian Grove, their retreat on the Russian River. In the twentieth century, the club would welcome William Randolph Hearst and Richard Nixon. It became an enclave of elite men, the ultimate insider institution—and a grotesque parody of the original Bohemia that inspired its name.

Stoddard visited the club regularly after his return to San Francisco. He was broke, and often had to skip breakfast and lunch. But at the club he could drink for free, and usually find someone willing to take him to dinner. His friend Ina Coolbrith was another beneficiary. The all-male Bohemians elected her as an honorary member—although as a woman, she still needed an invitation to enter. More helpfully, they also arranged fund-raisers on her behalf.

She was grateful. Like Stoddard, she needed all the help she could get. They saw each other in 1878 for the first time in five years. While Stoddard couldn't stand still, Coolbrith had the opposite problem: she couldn't move. The restraints keeping her in place had recently grown stronger. In 1874, her older sister Agnes died, leaving two children behind. Coolbrith took them in. She now supported a household of five. Selling poems to magazines wouldn't be enough to make ends meet. So she took a job as a librarian in Oakland, and found a house nearby for her family. She worked twelve hours a day, six days a week, for a salary of $80 a month—less than half of what Harte earned in Germany doing considerably lighter work for the State Department. A "living tomb," she called it, and she would remain there for eighteen years.

It wasn't all misery, however. Schoolchildren filled the library, and she loved to recommend reading for them. One of her young patrons was Jack London. He first came into the library as a ten-year-old, and pulled a book on Pizarro's conquest of Peru off the shelf. Coolbrith praised his choice, and London never forgot it. "[Y]ou were the first one who ever complimented me on my choice of reading matter," he told her twenty years later. "Nobody at home bothered their heads over what I read." He held her in awe: "You were a goddess to me . . . No woman has so affected me to the extent you did."

Coolbrith created a little world. "Why, we used to come to the library just to look at her—she was so beautiful!" remembered a visitor. "She sat in her chair as though on a throne," said another. Between cataloguing and cleaning, and cultivating new generations of readers, she also found time to write. She finally published her first book in 1881, *A Perfect Day, and Other Poems*. "Miss Coolbrith's admirers would have preferred to see her work come from one of the great publishing houses of the East," remarked Ambrose Bierce, but the book nevertheless found its way into the hands of eastern critics. Their response was favorable, if restrained. "Without having a large vocabulary or a great range of expression, this poetess makes pleasant music on a few strings," judged the *New York Times*. She mailed a signed copy to Stoddard, who gave a warmer verdict. "I know of no living poetess in either England or America who is your superior," he replied. That year, Stoddard would leave San Francisco, return to Hawaii, and later live in Indiana, Kentucky, Washington, DC, and Massachusetts—teaching English literature, writing articles and books, and never quite finding a permanent home.

But at least he had his freedom. He and Coolbrith stayed in

touch, and her letters often raged at the unfairness of how her life
had turned out:

> My relatives? O, how infinitely better off I would be had I
> none! What have any of them ever done but hurt me? Look at
> the long years I gave . . . while you . . . and Harte, were out in
> the world, and lived, I knew only the four walls in which I
> worked and the house where I ate and slept, and the path
> which lay between these two!

California became loathsome to her. It became a cage, the monotonous backdrop for her "convict-life." "How I hate Californians!
Maybe human nature is the same elsewhere, but I doubt it," she
wrote Stoddard. Still, she kept writing. Eventually, California would
claim her as one of its greatest writers, and the last remaining link
to its literary golden age. In 1915, at a ceremony held at the Panama-
Pacific International Exposition in San Francisco, she became the
state's first poet laureate. Now seventy-four and severely arthritic,
she walked slowly to the stage, and turned to face the crowded
auditorium:

> I feel that the honor extended me today is meant not so much
> because of any special merit of my own, as in memory of that
> wonderful group of early California writers with which it
> was my fortune to be affiliated, and of which I am the sole
> survivor.

Harte died in 1902, Stoddard in 1909, Twain in 1910. She had
written a manuscript of reminiscences, but it burned in the earthquake and fire that incinerated San Francisco in 1906. By then she
had returned to Russian Hill. "I took frequent 'notes,'" she said, "I
had . . . *volumes* of them." Later, when a publisher asked her to re-
produce them, she declined: "Were I to write what I know the book

would be too sensational for you to publish; but were I to write what I think proper, it would be too dull to sell."

After the blaze died down, she walked to what remained of Anton Roman's old bookstore. There, on the second floor, the *Overland Monthly* had been born. That night, Harte came to her in a dream. He took her back to the shop, and they stood in the rubble. "There is nothing left for us now," he said. "We'll have to go away and leave it to those who are coming after us." She died in 1928, and was buried in an unmarked grave.

WHAT MADE THE BOHEMIAN EXPERIMENT so extraordinary was that it happened where it did. On a distant frontier barely removed from its days of gold digging and gunfighting, a literary scene emerged that invigorated the region, fascinated the country, and, through Harte and Twain, gave America two of its most popular writers. The Bohemians showed that great writing could grow anywhere: that its origins could be remote, its subjects crude, so long as it told stories worth telling. They helped awaken America to the fact of its bigness, to its infinite canvas of incident and character and slang.

Their methods inspired future generations. The use of the vernacular led later writers to take a deeper interest in dialect, in how English evolved in different corners of the country. The use of frontier humor disrupted the distinction between high and low, and unleashed the imaginative possibilities of popular art. These innovations helped pry American literature away from its provincial origins in New England and push it into a broader current—toward the discovery of a vast, varied continent composed of countless local cultures.

What distinguished Twain from the others wasn't simply raw talent. It was his relentlessness. For Harte, Stoddard, and Coolbrith, Bohemia had meant the best years of their lives. For Twain, it meant

the years that made him a writer and put him on the path to greatness. Harte never figured out how to be a westerner in the East.
Stoddard and Coolbrith never overcame the loss of a circle that
soothed their solitude and fired their creativity. But Twain transplanted himself to eastern soil, and took root. He married into a rich
and respectable family. He settled in Hartford and joined the lofty
society of Nook Farm. He befriended Howells and clawed his way
into the cultural elite. And throughout, he remained recognizably
himself. His clothes grew more elegant, but his language still crack-
led with yarns and jokes and hoaxes, and delicious drawling slang.
He experimented constantly, speculating in everything from science
fiction to historical novels to detective stories. Not all of his risks paid
off, but they kept him in constant motion. He never stopped looking
for new lines of attack, and never relinquished the westernness that
gave his writing its original force. The Bohemian moment in San
Francisco had been brief. Through Twain, it achieved a lasting
legacy.

ACKNOWLEDGMENTS

Franklin Walker's pioneering *San Francisco's Literary Frontier* (1939) was the starting point for this book. I'm grateful to Charles Fracchia, founder of the San Francisco Museum and Historical Society, for introducing it to me. Charles made other helpful suggestions, and gave me the courage to head into the archives, where my research began. I'm indebted to Hoke Perkins and the staff of the Alderman Library at the University of Virginia; to David Kessler, Susan Snyder, and the staff of the Bancroft Library at the University of California, Berkeley; to Robert Hirst, general editor of the Mark Twain Papers and Project, also at the Bancroft; to Natalie Russell and the staff of the Huntington Library in San Marino, California; to Dorothy Lazard of the Oakland History Room at the Oakland Public Library; to Liz Phillips in the Department of Special Collections at the University of California, Davis; to Patricia Keats at the Society of California Pioneers; to Kathleen Correia at the California History Room of the California State Library in Sacramento; to Amy McDonald at the Duke University Archives; and to the staff of the San Francisco History Center at the San Francisco Public Library.

The many authors whose work I relied on are detailed in the notes. But several deserve special mention. Gary Scharnhorst's work on Bret Harte was an essential resource and an inspiration throughout. The late

Carl Stroven and Roger Austen provided a wealth of material on Charles Warren Stoddard. Josephine DeWitt Rhodehamel and Raymund Francis Wood introduced me to Ina Coolbrith. And Ron Powers, whose writing on Mark Twain is a national treasure, helped teach me how to think about history.

I wrote this book in the New York Public Library's Frederick Lewis Allen Memorial Room. Thanks to Jay Barksdale for making my time there possible. I'm also indebted to the Archives Research Fellowship, which enabled me to explore aspects of Twain's life that I didn't have the chance to discuss in the book. The library's Irma and Paul Milstein Division of United States History, Local History, and Genealogy was indispensable, along with the Microforms Reading Room, the Rare Book Division, the Henry W. and Albert A. Berg Collection of English and American Literature, and the Miriam and Ira D. Wallach Division of Art, Prints and Photographs. Thomas Lannon of the Manuscripts and Archives Division provided research help throughout.

My agent, Joy Harris, inspired me to pursue this project, and kept me afloat with regular infusions of enthusiasm and expert counsel. I'm forever grateful to her. My editor, Lindsay Whalen, steered me masterfully through the writing of the manuscript, and always pushed me to improve. I feel fortunate to have had her at my side.

Meg Flaherty contributed to this book in every way possible. She helped with the research, the writing, the thinking, the structure. She helped track down obscure dates, went digging through reels of microfilm, and made big-picture recommendations that improved the manuscript immeasurably. Thanks to Cris Beam and the Hertog Research Assistantship Program in the Writing Program of the School of the Arts at Columbia University for putting us together.

T. J. Stiles, Patty O'Toole, and Mark Danner lent crucial moral support. This book owes much to their advice and example, as role models for my life and writing. Carol Field and Susan McGovern offered insights drawn from their deep knowledge of San Francisco. Adam and Noah Pritzker helped keep me human when long days in the library threatened to turn me into a robot. Rachel Nolan and Will Payne were perceptive readers, and their revisions made this book much better. Moira Weigel was an invaluable editor, interlocutor—and more. My parents were a constant source of edits, suggestions, wisdom, love, and encouragement. They also had the foresight to fall in love and move to San Francisco in time for me to be born there, the first in a long list of debts I can never hope to repay.

NOTES

For simplicity's sake, I refer to Samuel Langhorne Clemens as Mark Twain throughout. "Mark Twain" was more than just a pen name. He used it in public and in private. He signed letters "Mark" and "Sam," and his friends knew him by both names.

Several online resources were helpful for my research. These were Readex America's Historical Newspapers, JSTOR, Google Books, Twain quotes.com, the Mark Twain Project Online, the Making of America archive at the University of Michigan, and the California Digital Newspaper Collection from the Center for Bibliographic Studies and Research, University of California, Riverside.

PEOPLE

BH	Bret Harte (b. Francis Brett Harte)
CWS	Charles Warren Stoddard
IC	Ina Coolbrith (b. Josephine Donna Smith)
OLC	Olivia Langdon Clemens (b. Olivia Louise Langdon)
SLC	Mark Twain (b. Samuel Langhorne Clemens)
WDH	William Dean Howells

BOOKS

Mark Twain

AMT Harriet Elinor Smith, ed., *Autobiography of Mark Twain: The Complete and Authoritative Edition*, vol. 1 (Berkeley: University of California Press, 2010).

ET&S   Edgar Marquess Branch and Robert H. Hirst, eds., *The Works of Mark Twain: Early
          Tales & Sketches*, vol. 1, 1851–1864, and vol. 2, 1864–1865 (Berkeley: University of
          California Press, 1979–1981).

MCMT   Justin Kaplan, *Mr. Clemens and Mark Twain* (New York: Simon & Schuster, 1983
          [1966]).

MTAL   Ron Powers, *Mark Twain: A Life* (New York: Free Press, 2006 [2005]).

MTB   Albert Bigelow Paine, *Mark Twain: A Biography*, vols. 1–3 (New York: Harper &
          Brothers, 1912).

MTL   Edgar Marquess Branch, Michael B. Frank, and Kenneth M. Sanderson, eds., *Mark
          Twain's Letters*, vol. 1, 1853–1866. Harriet Elinor Smith and Richard Bucci, eds., vol.
          2, 1867–1868. Victor Fischer and Michael B. Frank, eds., vol. 3, 1869, and vol. 4, 1870–
          1871. Lin Salamo and Harriet Elinor Smith, eds., vol. 5, 1872–1873. Michael B. Frank
          and Harriet Elinor Smith, eds., vol. 6, 1874–1875 (Berkeley: University of California
          Press, 1988–2002).

MTLO   Victor Fischer, Michael B. Frank, and Harriet Elinor Smith, eds., *Mark Twain's Let-
          ters*, 1876–1880 (Berkeley: University of California Press, 2007). Accessible via Mark
          Twain Project Online, http://www.marktwainproject.org.

MTN   Frederick Anderson, Michael B. Frank, and Kenneth M. Sanderson, eds., *Mark
          Twain's Notebooks and Journals*, vol. 1, 1855–1873 (Berkeley: University of California
          Press, 1975).

MTR   Mark Twain, *Roughing It*, ed. Harriet Elinor Smith and Edgar Marquess Branch
          (Berkeley: University of California Press, 1996 [1872]).

TAMT   Charles Neider, ed., *The Autobiography of Mark Twain* (New York: HarperPerennial,
          1990 [1959]).

TIHOT   Gary Scharnhorst, ed., *Twain in His Own Time: A Biographical Chronicle of His Life,
          Drawn from Recollections, Interviews, and Memoirs by Family, Friends, and Associates*
          (Iowa City: University of Iowa Press, 2010).

Bret Harte

BHAN   Axel Nissen, *Bret Harte: Prince and Pauper* (Jackson: University Press of Mississippi,
          2000).

BHGS   Gary Scharnhorst, *Bret Harte: Opening the American Literary West* (Norman: Univer-
          sity of Oklahoma Press, 2000).

Charles Warren Stoddard

CRP   "Confessions of a Reformed Poet," an unpublished autobiography by Charles Warren
          Stoddard. The manuscript is held by the Bancroft Library, University of California,
          Berkeley. For page numbers, I refer to the typescript copy that accompanies the man-
          uscript. Because these numbers reset for each chapter, I have included the chapter
          information as well.

CSCWS   Carl Stroven, "A Life of Charles Warren Stoddard" (unpublished PhD diss., Duke
          University, 1939).

GP   Roger Austen, *Genteel Pagan: The Double Life of Charles Warren Stoddard*, ed. John
          W. Crowley (Amherst: University of Massachusetts Press, 1991).

Ina Coolbrith

ECW   Ina Coolbrith, "Personal Reminiscences of Early California Writers," an address
          given on April 10, 1911, to the Pacific Coast Women's Press Association in San Fran-
          cisco, held by the Bancroft Library, Berkeley, California.

ICCWS   Ina Coolbrith, "Charles Warren Stoddard," an address given in 1923 [?] in Oakland,
          held by the Bancroft Library, Berkeley, California.

ICHC   Ina Coolbrith, "introduction" to *The Heathen Chinee: Plain Language from Truthful James* (San Francisco: Book Club of California, 1934), n. pag.

ICLL   Josephine DeWitt Rhodehamel and Raymund Francis Wood, *Ina Coolbrith: Librarian and Laureate of California* (Provo, UT: Brigham Young University Press, 1973).

Other

SFLF   Franklin Walker, *San Francisco's Literary Frontier* (Seattle: University of Washington Press, 1970 [1939]).

COLLECTIONS

BANC   Bancroft Library, University of California, Berkeley.

HUNT   Huntington Library, San Marino, California.

UVA   Clifton Waller Barrett Library, Albert and Shirley Small Special Collections, University of Virginia, Charlottesville, Virginia.

OAK   Oakland History Room, Oakland Public Library.

The notes are organized by paragraph. For each note I've listed the page number, followed by the first few words of the paragraph.

INTRODUCTION

1   **The Civil War began** 750,000 deaths: J. David Hacker, "A Census-Based Count of the Civil War Dead," *Civil War History* 57.4 (Dec. 2011), pp. 307–348.

1   **If America belonged** More than half of all Californians in 1850 were in their twenties, according to Earl Pomeroy, *The Pacific Slope: A History of California, Oregon, Washington, Idaho, Utah, and Nevada* (Reno: University of Nevada Press, 2003 [1965]), pp. 40–41. *"Pioneers! O Pioneers"*: Walt Whitman, *Complete Poetry and Collected Prose*, ed. Justin Kaplan (New York: Library of America, 1982), pp. 371–375.

2   **When Whitman looked** Jefferson's idea of the West: Gordon S. Wood, *Empire of Liberty: A History of the Early Republic, 1789–1815* (Oxford, UK: Oxford University Press, 2009), pp. 357–359. For a discussion of western expansionism, see Henry Nash Smith, *Virgin Land: The American West as Symbol and Myth* (Cambridge, MA: Harvard University Press, 1978), pp. 15–33. Jefferson used the phrase "empire of liberty" several times; for an early example, see his 1780 letter to George Rogers Clark, included in Julian P. Boyd et al., eds., *The Papers of Thomas Jefferson*, vol. 4 (Princeton, NJ: Princeton University Press, 1950), pp. 237–238. *"The future lies that way to me . . ."*: Henry David Thoreau, "Walking," in *The Writings of Henry David Thoreau*, vol. 9 (Boston: Houghton Mifflin, 1893), p. 266. ·

2   **Mark Twain was** Until 1847, San Francisco was known as Yerba Buena. Gold rush growth of SF: Roger W. Lotchin, *San Francisco, 1846–1856: From Hamlet to City* (Champaign: University of Illinois Press, 1997 [1974]), pp. 3–30.

3   **By the time** Financing new frontiers: Rodman W. Paul, "After the Gold Rush: San Francisco and Portland," *Pacific Historical Review* 50.1 (Feb. 1982), pp. 20–21, and SFLF, pp. 9–12. Champagne: SFLF, p. 13.

3   **They also sustained** Early literary life: Michael Kowalewski, "Romancing the Gold Rush: The Literature of the California Frontier," *California History* 79.2 (Summer 2000), pp. 207–210, and SFLF, pp. 17–54. The gold rush generation produced a vast amount of letters, diaries, and other documents about early California. The most famous of these early firsthand accounts was written by Louise Amelia Knapp Smith Clappe under the pen name Dame Shirley in 1851–1852. For a complete listing of gold rush literature, see Gary F. Kurutz, *The*

California Gold Rush: A Descriptive Bibliography of Books and Pamphlets Covering the Years 1848–1853 (San Francisco: Book Club of California, 1997).

CHAPTER ONE

9 **What people remembered** Twain's drawl: Arthur McEwen, "In the Heroic Days," in TIHOT, p. 22; Henry J. W. Dam, "A Morning with Bret Harte," *McClure's* 4.1 (Dec. 1894), p. 47; MTAL, pp. 168–169; and William H. Rideing, "Mark Twain in Clubland," *Bookman* 31 (June 1910), pp. 379–382. Twain's seriousness: ibid. and G. K. Chesterton, *A Handful of Authors: Essays on Books and Writers*, ed. Dorothy Collins (New York: Sheed and Ward, 1953), pp. 10–15.

9 **On May 2, 1863** Mark Twain's first visit to SF: ET&S, vol. 1, pp. 248–249. Stagecoach journey from Virginia City to SF: Mark Twain, "Letter from Mark Twain," *Territorial Enterprise*, September 17, 1863, in ET&S, vol. 1, pp. 293–295.

10 **Now he fell** *"After the sage-brush..."*: MTR, p. 396. Activities during SF visit: SLC to Jane Lampton Clemens and Pamela A. Moffett, June 1, 1863, in MTL, vol. 1, pp. 255–256, and SLC to Jane Lampton Clemens and Pamela A. Moffett, June 4, 1863, MTL, vol. 1, pp. 256–257.

10 **He hadn't planned** Mid-May: SLC to Jane Lampton Clemens and Pamela A. Moffett, May 18, 1863, MTL, vol. 1, pp. 252–254. *"I am going to the Dickens..."* and *"[W]hen I go down Montgomery..."*: SLC to Jane Lampton Clemens and Pamela A. Moffett, June 1, 1863, MTL, vol. 1, p. 255. SF population in 1863: SFLF, p. 90.

11 **Spring turned to summer** *"It seems like going back to prison..."*: SLC to Jane Lampton Clemens and Pamela A. Moffett, June 4, 1863, MTL, vol. 1, p. 256. Twain returned to Virginia City on July 2, 1863: ET&S, vol. 1, p. 254.

11 **On February 3, 1863** Mark Twain, "Letter from Carson City," *Territorial Enterprise*, February 3, 1863, in ET&S, vol. 1, pp. 194–198.

11 **This debut didn't** The other pen names of Sam Clemens included W. Epaminondas Adrastus Blab and Thomas Jefferson Snodgrass. Premature birth and *"When I first saw him..."*: MTAL, p. 8.

12 **The origins of his** Origin of "Mark Twain": MTAL, pp. 118–119, and Paul Fatout, "Mark Twain's Nom de Plume," *American Literature* 34.1 (March 1962), pp. 1–7.

12 **By 1863, he had** Twain's first known published item is "A Gallant Fireman," which appeared in his brother Orion's *Western Union* (later the *Hannibal Journal*) on January 16, 1851: ET&S, vol. 1, pp. 61–62. *"very wild and mischievous"*: "Mark Twain's Boyhood: An Interview with Mrs. Jane Clemens," in TIHOT, p. 1. In the same interview, Jane recounts how her son begged to leave school, and that she "concluded to let him go into a printing office to learn the trade." See also MTB, vol. 1, pp. 74–76. Twain probably began his apprenticeship in the fall of 1847, in the office of Henry La Cossitt's *Hannibal Gazette*: ET&S, vol. 1, p. 5. Cigar, pipe, and off-color songs: from a letter by Pet McMurry, a journeyman in the printer's office of the *Missouri Courier* who worked alongside Twain, quoted in MTB, vol. 1, p. 77. The rival editor scorched by Twain was J. T. Hinton; see MTAL, pp. 53–55.

12 **Twain's irreverence** Hannibal's transformation: ibid., pp. 47, 57–58.

13 **By the time** Expanding print landscape: ibid., pp. 46–47; Henry Nash Smith, *Virgin Land: The American West as Symbol and Myth* (Cambridge, MA: Harvard University Press, 1978), pp. 87–88; William James Linton, *The History of Wood-Engraving in America* (Boston: Estes and Lauriat, 1882), pp. 27–33. Statistics on numbers of newspapers: Bruce A. Bimber, *Information and American Democracy: Technology in the Evolution of Political Power* (Cambridge: Cambridge University Press, 2003), pp. 52–53.

13 **The newspaper revolution** Role of newspapers in the gold rush: H. W. Brands, *The Age of Gold: The California Gold Rush and the New American Dream* (New York: Doubleday, 2002), pp. 70, 124–126, 130. Literacy in the Far West: SFLF, pp. 7, 14; Earl Pomeroy,

The Pacific Slope, pp. 34–35, 42, 153; and Sanford Winston, *Illiteracy in the United States* (Chapel Hill: University of North Carolina Press, 1930), pp. 16–17. Literary paper as sign of flush times: MTR, p. 339. Literature's significance for farmers and miners: SFLF, p. 120.

14 **Twain arrived in** Twain's departure for Nevada: MTAL, pp. 101–102.

14 **So he climbed** Coyotes and jackrabbits: MTR, pp. 12, 30. *"The country is fabulously rich...":* SLC to Pamela A. Moffett and Jane Lampton Clemens, October 25, 1861, MTL, vol. 1, p. 132.

14 **After a failed stint** First day of work: MTAL, p. 110; C. C. Goodwin, "As I Remember Them," in TIHOT, p. 17. Virginia City: Bernard DeVoto, *Mark Twain's America* (Lincoln: University of Nebraska Press, 1997 [1932]), pp. 122–125; Paul Fatout, *Mark Twain in Virginia* City (Bloomington: Indiana University Press, 1964), pp. 54–60; and MTAL, pp. 110–111.

15 **Virginia City's lawlessness** *Enterprise* journalism: Effie Mona Mack, *Mark Twain in Nevada* (New York: Charles Scribner's Sons, 1947), pp. 207–211, and MTAL, pp. 111–117. For more Nevada writing from the Comstock era, see Lawrence I. Berkove, ed., *The Sagebrush Anthology: Literature from the Silver Age of the Old West* (Columbia: University of Missouri Press, 2006).

15 **Virginia City taught Twain** *"an unmitigated lie...":* SLC to Orion and Mary E. Clemens, October 21, 1862, MTL, vol. 1, p. 242. "Petrified Man" probably appeared in the *Territorial Enterprise* on October 4, 1862. Since there are no extant files of the *Enterprise* from these years, the surviving articles are those reprinted in other papers. Twain's rivalry with G. T. Sewall: ET&S, vol. 1, pp. 155–156.

16 **Newspapers throughout Nevada** At least twelve newspapers in California and Nevada reprinted "Petrified Man." Of these, eight reprinted it without comment; see ET&S, vol.1, p. 158. *"I could not have gotten...":* quoted ibid., p. 156. Courtship of mining companies: MTAL, p. 114. *"I am the most conceited ass...":* SLC to Jane Lampton Clemens and Pamela A. Moffett, August 19, 1863, in MTL, vol. 1, p. 264.

16 **Yet his swagger** *"Not a settler...":* quoted in Earl Pomeroy, *The Pacific Slope*, pp. 124–125.

16 **The Comstock** Virginia City's colonial status, and SF's dominance of the Far West: SFLF, pp. 9, 92–93, 351, and Earl Pomeroy, *The Pacific Slope*, pp. 124–126. More newspapers per capita than any other American city: ibid., pp. 158–159. Mark Twain's first letter to the *San Francisco Morning Call* would appear on July 9, 1863.

17 **By the 1860s** Gold production in California peaked in 1852 and then sharply declined: see "Appendix A: Gold Production," in Rodman W. Paul, *California Gold: The Beginning of Mining in the Far West* (Cambridge, MA: Harvard University Press, 1947), p. 345. Impact of Comstock and Civil War: SFLF, pp. 10–11, 90, 97–98; Earl Pomeroy, *The Pacific Slope*, pp. 77–113; James F. Carson, "California: Gold to Help Finance the War," *Journal of the West* 14.1 (Jan. 1975), pp. 35–38; Thomas R. Walker, "Economic Opportunity on the Urban Frontier: Wealth and Nativity in Early San Francisco," *Explorations in Economic History* 37.3 (2000), pp. 258–277; Kevin Starr, *Inventing the Dream: California Through the Progressive Era* (Oxford, UK: Oxford University Press, 1986 [1985]), p. 131; and David J. St. Clair, "The Gold Rush and the Beginnings of California Industry," *California History* 77.4 (Winter, 1998/1999), pp. 185–208.

17 **The Civil War would** Origins of transcontinental railroad: Richard White, *Railroaded: The Transcontinentals and the Making of Modern America* (New York: W. W. Norton, 2011), pp. 17–22, and David Haward Bain, *Empire Express: Building the First Transcontinental Railroad* (New York: Penguin, 2000 [1999]), pp. 3–118. Messianic rhetoric and anticipation: William Deverell, "Redemptive California? Re-thinking the Post–Civil War," *Rethinking History* 11.1 (March 2007), pp. 65–66.

18 **Any citizen** July 4 festivities: *San Francisco Evening Bulletin*, July 6, 1863.

19   **The news from** First news of Gettysburg in SF: *San Francisco Evening Bulletin*, July 6, 1863. First news of Vicksburg in San Francisco: *San Francisco Bulletin*, July 7, 1863. Growing exhaustion with the war: SFLF, pp. 108–109. Bad turnout and 35 cases of public drunkenness: *San Francisco Evening Bulletin*, July 6, 1863.

19   **King knew how** King at the Metropolitan: ibid. King: Kevin Starr, *Americans and the California Dream, 1850–1915* (Oxford, UK: Oxford University Press, 1986 [1973]), pp. 99–105. California politics during the Civil War: Gerald Stanley, "Civil War Politics in California," *Southern California Quarterly* 64.2 (Summer 1982), pp. 115–132; Benjamin Franklin Gilbert, "California and the Civil War: A Bibliographical Essay," *California Historical Society Quarterly* 40.4 (Dec. 1961), pp. 291–293; and Steven M. Avella, "California," in David S. Heidler and Jeanne T. Heidler, eds., *Encyclopedia of the American Civil War: A Political, Social, and Military History* (New York: W. W. Norton, 2000), p. 340.

19   **Before speaking that day** Reading and reception of poem: *San Francisco Evening Bulletin*, July 6, 1863. For the full text of the poem, see Bret Harte, *The Writings of Bret Harte*, vol. 20 (Boston: Houghton Mifflin, 1914), pp. 328–330. George R. Stewart Jr., *Bret Harte: Argonaut and Exile* (Port Washington, NY: Kennikat Press, 1959 [1935]), p. 116, speculates that Harte stayed home out of shyness.

20   **Not that he wasn't** A stylish overcoat sporting a lamb collar: "Bret Harte's Early Days in San Francisco," *San Francisco Morning Call*, May 25, 1902. A felicitous flash of color: TAMT, pp. 163–164. Smile and agreeable voice: Charles A. Murdock, "Francis Bret Harte," in *California Writers Club Quarterly Bulletin* 2.2 (June 1914), p. 1. Many contemporaries commented on Harte's aloofness. According to the poet Joaquin Miller, Harte "did not mix greatly with men; nor did he talk much": see Joaquin Miller, "He Writes for the Saturday Review His Reminiscences of Bret Harte," *New York Times*, May 31, 1902.

21   **And there was much** Harte married Anna Griswold on August 11, 1862. Their first son, Griswold, was born a year later. Family and job history: BHAN, pp. 64–71, and BHGS, p. 18.

21   **This shy, soft-spoken** *"vagrant keels"*: Bret Harte, "The Legend of Monte del Diablo," in *The Luck of Roaring Camp and Other Writings*, ed. Gary Scharnhorst (New York: Penguin, 2001), p. 4. *"district poorhouse"*: Bret Harte, "Bohemian Papers: The City Hall," *Golden Era*, March 29, 1863.

21   **Few things escaped** *"the corrosive touch..."*: William Dean Howells, "Editor's Easy Chair," *Harper's Monthly Magazine* 108.643 (Dec. 1903), p. 155. *"singular fraternity"* and *"free from the trammels of precedent"*: Bret Harte, "The Rise of the 'Short Story,'" in *The Luck of Roaring Camp and Other Writings*, ed. Gary Scharnhorst, p. 254. See also Bret Harte, "Bohemian Days in San Francisco," ibid., pp. 268–285.

22   **Harte had always wanted** Harte recalled this story later in life. All quotes: Henry J. W. Dam, "A Morning with Bret Harte," p. 42. As Axel Nissen points out in BHAN, p. 273, the journalist interviewing Harte got his birth year wrong, so it's possible that Harte published the poem at sixteen, in 1852. Background on Harte's parents: BHGS, pp. 3–4, and BHAN, pp. 16–18. Harte's father died in 1845; see BHAN, p. 19.

22   **But he did** Harte left school at thirteen: BHAN, p. 23, and BHGS, pp. 5–6. *"girlish pink-and-whiteness"* and *"Fanny"*: ICHC. *"Gilded Vice"* and *"Gorgeous Villainy"*: Harte's letter to Miss Bessie Ward, September 19, 1874, UVA.

23   **It was a part** Harte embarked for California with his sister Maggie on February 20, 1854. See BHAN, p. 24, and BHGS, p. 6. *"no better equipment"*: Henry J. W. Dam, "A Morning with Bret Harte," p. 40. Holing up in his garret: "Bret Harte's Early Days in San Francisco," *San Francisco Morning Call*, May 25, 1902. Harte worshipped Dickens his entire life; see BHAN, pp. 21, 40, and BHGS, p. 48. Twain accused Harte of being a "deliberate imitator of Dickens"; many others, including William Dean Howells, noted the similarities between Harte and Dickens.

23   **He also loved** Harte's love for *Don Quixote*: Henry J. W. Dam, "A Morning with Bret Harte," p. 40. Wandering years: BHGS, pp. 6–10, and BHAN, pp. 40–46. Many of Harte's

contemporaries commented on his smallpox. It's not entirely clear when he contracted it. Henry Kirk Goddard remembered seeing Harte during his time in Oakland, and commented on his smallpox scars: see BHAN, p. 41. *"somewhat pathetic figure"*: Charles A. Murdock, "Francis Bret Harte," p. 2. More details of Harte in Humboldt: Charles A. Murdock, "Bret Harte in Humboldt," *Overland Monthly* (Sept. 1902), pp. 301–302; Charles A. Murdock, *A Backward Glance at Eighty: Recollections & Comment* (San Francisco: Paul Elder, 1921), pp. 73–74; BHGS, p. 10. *"He was simply untrained..."*: Charles A. Murdock, *A Backward Glance at Eighty*, p. 73.

23   **He always felt** *"seek distinction..."* and *"I am fit..."*: Harte's entry for December 31, 1857, in his 1857–1858 diary, BANC.

24   **This declaration would** *"Perhaps I may..."*: Harte's December 31, 1857, diary entry. Harte's career at the *Northern Californian*: BHAN, pp. 52–53. For an example of Harte's writing from this period, see "Wanted—A Printer," which appeared in the October 19, 1859, issue of the *Northern Californian* and is reprinted in Bret Harte, *The Writings of Bret Harte*, vol. 20, pp. 118–119. Issues of the *Northern Californian* during Harte's tenure are held by HUNT. *"poor boy's college"*: MTAL, p. 47. Harte contributed prose and poetry to the *Golden Era* during 1857–1858 and published a poem in the New York–based *Knickerbocker* magazine in January 1858; see BHAN, pp. 49–51.

24   **On the morning** Indian Island massacre: *Northern Californian*, February 29, 1860; Lynwood Carranco, "Bret Harte in Union (1857–1860)," *California Historical Society Quarterly* 45.2 (June 1966), pp. 99–112; *New York Times*, April 12, 1860; Les W. Field, *Abalone Tales: Collaborative Explorations of Sovereignty and Identity in Native California* (Durham, NC: Duke University Press, 2008), p. 51; BHAN, pp. 55–56; BHGS, pp. 13–14.

25   **The massacre shocked** Harte's editorial appeared in the *Northern Californian*, February 29, 1860.

25   **Here was the nightmarish** *"Indian Wars"*: James J. Rawls, *Indians of California: The Changing Image* (Norman: University of Oklahoma Press, 1984), pp. 161–172. Indian children as indentured servants: ibid., pp. 87–94. *"white civilizer"* and *"barbarity"*: *Northern Californian*, February 29, 1860. Harte's paternal grandfather, Bernard Hart (the "e" was added to the family name later) was a British-born Jew who emigrated to the United States in 1780; see BHAN, pp. 13–16.

26   **Harte's impassioned broadside** *"seriously threatened..."*: Charles A. Murdock, *A Backward Glance at Eighty*, p. 79. The notice of Harte's resignation and departure for SF appeared in the *Northern Californian*, March 29, 1860, as quoted in BHAN, pp. 55–56. The killers were businessmen and landowners, whose names were widely known to the community: *San Francisco Chronicle*, February 28, 2004. *"too much of a gentleman..."*: Joaquin Miller, "He Writes for the Saturday Review His Reminiscences of Bret Harte," *New York Times*, May 31, 1902.

26   **The Indian Island massacre** Harte's arrival in SF in the spring of 1860: BHGS, p. 14. The city had at least fifty newspapers in 1860, according to the US newspaper directory maintained by the Library of Congress. *Golden Era*: SFLF, pp. 116–127. Until the passage of international copyright legislation in 1891, European writers were widely pirated by American publishers. *"Many times the Era..."*: *Golden Era*, December 16, 1860, quoted in SFLF, p. 120.

27   **The *Era* could count** Lawrence's campaign to urbanize the *Era*: SFLF, p. 120. Changing face of the city: Earl Pomeroy, *The Pacific Slope*, p. 126, and Roger W. Lotchin, *San Francisco, 1846–1856*, p. xxxvii. The plush hotels: construction on the Lick House began in late 1861, according to James R. Smith, *San Francisco's Lost Landmarks* (Sanger, CA: Word Dancer Press, 2005), p. 210. Seventeen-course dinners in South Park: Amelia Ransome Neville, *The Fantastic City: Memoirs of the Social and Romantic Life of Old San Francisco* (Boston: Houghton Mifflin, 1932), p. 134. Teakwood tables: ibid., p. 194.

27   **Joe Lawrence hoped** Rollin M. Daggett, one of the *Era*'s cofounders, remembered that Harte "would waste more time over a two stick item than I would take for a column," as

quoted in BHAN, p. 60. Lawrence's grandfatherly warmth: Joaquin Miller, "Joseph E. Lawrence," *San Francisco Morning Call*, September 4, 1892, and Charles Warren Stoddard, *Exits and Entrances: A Book of Essays and Sketches* (Boston: Lothrop, 1903), pp. 243–244. Harte's early pieces for the *Era*: BHAN, pp. 59–60, and BHGS, pp. 16–17. Harte began writing his "Bohemian" column in May 1860; see "Town and Table Talk: The Bohemian at the Fair," *Golden Era*, September 23, 1860; "Town and Table Talk: The Bohemian on 'Things,'" *Golden Era*, September 30, 1860; "Town and Table Talk: The Bohemian Does the Cheap Shows," *Golden Era*, October 14, 1860; "Town and Table Talk: The Bohemian on Balls," *Golden Era*, October 28, 1860. Ocean zephyrs: Bret Harte, "Bohemian Days in San Francisco," p. 284. The legend of Harte setting his pieces into type directly is discussed in BHAN, p. 60, and repeated in TAMT, p. 163. *"a new and fresh..."*: ibid.

28 **If California were** Jessie Benton Frémont's Black Point home: BHAN, pp. 61–62. Her love of the Bay's sights and sounds: from her letter to Elizabeth Blair Less, June 14, 1860, in Jessie Benton Frémont, *The Letters of Jessie Benton Frémont* (Champaign: University of Illinois Press, 1993), Pamela Herr and Mary Lee Spence, eds., pp. 229–231. Like living in the bow of a ship: ibid., p. 230. *"true city," "very good opera," "lots of private parties"*: ibid. Fog bells: Adam Goodheart, *1861: Civil War Awakening* (New York: Vintage, 2012 [2011]), p. 224. Beautiful, brilliant, and tremendously self-confident: Sally Denton, *Passion and Principle: John and Jessie Frémont, the Couple Whose Power, Politics, and Love Shaped Nineteenth-Century America* (Lincoln: University of Nebraska Press, 2009 [2007]), pp. 64–65.

28 **Her father** Benton's career in the Senate: Henry Nash Smith, *Virgin Land*, pp. 22–34. *"nor even anywhere..."*: Mark Twain, *The Adventures of Tom Sawyer* (Hartford, CT: American Publishing Company, 1881), p. 178. *"realize the grand idea..."*: from a speech Benton gave in 1849, as quoted in Henry Nash Smith, *Virgin Land*, p. 28. *"The nations of Europe..."*: Thomas Hart Benton, *Selections of Editorial Articles from the St. Louis Enquirer, on the Subject of Oregon and Texas* (St. Louis: Missourian Office, 1844), p. 23.

29 **His daughter would** Jessie's similarities to her father: Sally Denton, *Passion and Principle*, pp. 45–46. Marriage, reconciliation with Thomas Hart Benton, and John Charles Frémont's travels: ibid., pp. 65–105. Frémont's reports: ibid., pp. 84–86, 103–104, and Tom Chaffin, *Pathfinder: John Charles Frémont and the Course of American Empire* (New York: Hill and Wang, 2002), pp. 136–147, 241–249.

29 **Furnished with thrilling** In March 1846, Frémont raised an American flag on Gavilán Peak (now Fremont Peak) near Monterey; see Sally Denton, *Passion and Principle*, pp. 120–122. His run for president: ibid., pp. 222–265.

30 **One can imagine** Jessie Benton Frémont's reception of Harte: Jessie Benton Frémont, *Souvenirs of My Time* (Boston: D. Lothrop, 1887), pp. 203–204. *"I have taken a young..."*: from Jessie Benton Frémont's letter to Thomas Starr King, January 16, 1861, in Jessie Benton Frémont, *The Letters of Jesse Benton Frémont*, p. 234.

30 **As 1860 ground** *"I do not measure..."*: quoted in Adam Goodheart, *1861*, p. 248. King's campaign: ibid., pp. 242–251, and Kevin Starr, *Americans and the California Dream*, pp. 97–105.

31 **Harte, too, answered** The flag Harte made in 1861 still survives, held by BANC. An accompanying note at the Bancroft by Maud Eberts provides the details of its history. King often read Harte's poetry at his speeches; see BHAN, pp. 69–70. *"patriot pride"* and *"clashing steel"*: from Bret Harte's 1862 poem "Our Privilege," included in Bret Harte, *The Writings of Bret Harte*, vol. 12 (Boston: Houghton Mifflin, 1896), p. 12. King gave his lectures on American poetry in early 1863; he describes them in October 29, 1862, and February 10, 1863, letters to James T. Fields, both held by HUNT. *"The state must be Northernized..."*: letter from Thomas Starr King to James T. Fields, October 29, 1862. King's sermons and *"Yosemites in the soul"*: Kevin Starr, *Americans and the California Dream*, pp. 100–104.

32 **This revelation struck** The story and *"wonderful and apart"*: ECW.

32   **In later life** Rhyme came naturally to her: as a child, she once told her schoolteacher that she preferred to write in rhyme because it was "easier," as she recalled in ECW. *"Her whole life has been a poem"*: Joaquin Miller, quoted in Kate M. Kennedy, "Ina Coolbrith Day," *Overland Monthly* 49.4 (April 1907), p. 341. *"half rapture and half pain"*: from Coolbrith's poem "How I Came to Be a Poet," quoted in ICLL, p. 65.

32   **Her first memories** Coolbrith's early life: ICLL, pp. 3–26; Ina Lillian Cook, "Ina Donna Coolbrith: A Short Account of Her Life," *Westward* 1 (May 1928), pp. 3–5; and Mira Maclay, "A Talk with Ina Coolbrith," *Oakland Tribune Magazine*, March 2, 1924. *"chloroform in print"*: MTR, p. 107.

33   **A dark secret** Coolbrith's family on the overland trail: ICLL, pp. 28–39. Her memories of the journey: Marian Taylor, "Ina Coolbrith, California Poet," *Overland Monthly* 64.4 (Oct. 1914), pp. 328–329, and George Wharton James, "Ina Donna Coolbrith: An Historical Sketch and Appreciation," *National Magazine* 26.3 (June 1907), pp. 316–318. *"world-wide carpet"*: MTR, p. 29.

33   **At the foot** *"one of the most beautiful creatures…"* and *"Here is California…"*: from a speech at a luncheon given in Coolbrith's honor in San Francisco on April 24, 1927, quoted in Mildred Brooke Hoover et al., eds., *Historic Spots in California*, 5th ed. (Stanford, CA: Stanford University Press, 2002), p. 282.

33   **Or so Ina remembered** Family's arrival in Los Angeles: ICLL, pp. 51–57. Descriptions of early Los Angeles: John Joseph Stanley, "Vigilance Movements in Early California," in Gordon Morris Bakken, ed., *Law in the Western United States* (Norman: University of Oklahoma Press, 2000), pp. 65–66, and Kevin Starr, *Inventing the Dream*, pp. 13–14. *"[T]his is nominally…"*: ibid., p. 14.

34   **Yet there was another** Ina was said to have opened a ball on the arm of Don Pio Pico, the last governor of the Mexican territory of Alta California before the American conquest; see ICLL, pp. 57–58, and Marian Taylor, "Ina Coolbrith, California Poet," p. 330. Coolbrith published her first poem, "My Childhood's Home," in the *Los Angeles Star*, August 30, 1856. A selection of her early poetry, and the praise she earned from local editors, can be seen in a scrapbook of her verse held by OAK. *"a sorrow dwells in my young heart"*: from "To Nelly," published in the *Los Angeles Star*, July 11, 1857, quoted in ICLL, p. 59. *"warm, rich personality…"*: quoted ibid., p. 60.

34   **In 1858, a Californian** *"a young girl of genius"* and *"an enviable reputation"*: scrapbook of Coolbrith's verse, OAK. Marriage, attempted murder, and divorce: ICLL, pp. 60–72.

35   **Worse, she suffered** It's unclear when the child was born, whether it was a boy or a girl, and how long it lived. ICLL, p. 415, cites three sources: testimony from Coolbrith's grandniece, cousin, and close friend. All three women waited until the 1950s to make their statements. Coolbrith first published "The Mother's Grief" in the *Californian*, March 25, 1865, and included it in two subsequent collections: *A Perfect Day* and *Songs from the Golden Gate*. *"To-day no shafts…"*: "The Mother's Grief," in Ina Donna Coolbrith, *A Perfect Day and Other Poems* (San Francisco: John H. Carmany, 1881), p. 33.

35   **Tragedy changed her** *"Only twenty…"*: from "Twenty-two," an unpublished poem written for the twenty-second birthday of her grandniece, quoted in ICLL, p. 77. Coolbrith's move to San Francisco: ibid., pp. 77–80.

35   **She became Ina Donna Coolbrith** Coolbrith's early days in SF: ibid., pp. 80–83. *"Some of the best men…"*: Bret Harte, "The Argonauts of '49," in *The Luck of Roaring Camp and Other Writings*, ed. Gary Scharnhorst, p. 233. Coolbrith's memory of seeing King for the first time and hearing Harte's poetry: ECW. An advertisement in the *Daily Evening Bulletin*, November 3, 1862, provides the details of the event.

36   **That fall** Quoted Seneca: Amelia Ransome Neville, *The Fantastic City*, p. 62. California as the new Canaan: Kevin Starr, *Americans and the California Dream*, p. 100. John Frémont was appointed the commander of the newly created Department of the West on July 25,

1861. *"I have worked..."*: letter from Thomas Starr King to James T. Fields, October 29, 1862, HUNT. King must have met Stoddard in late 1862, since Stoddard's first poem in the *Golden Era* appeared in September 1862 and King began his lectures on New England poets in early January 1863; see CSCWS, p. 52.

36 **Chileon Beach's shop** Experiences as a bookstore clerk: CRP, chap. 2, pp. 1–2. Memories of Nicaragua: Charles Warren Stoddard, *In the Footprints of the Padres* (San Francisco: A. M. Robertson, 1902), pp. 14–22.

37 **One day, California's** All quotes and details: CRP, chap. 2, pp. 7–8.

37 **At first glance** The contrast between Harte's penmanship and Stoddard's can be seen in written correspondence from their respective collections at BANC and UVA. Stoddard's poor spelling persisted into his old age, and became a joke among his friends. "It seems rather in his praise than otherwise that he wrote a largely illegible, beautiful-looking hand, and if you had any particular trouble with a given word, you found that it was misspelled," wrote William Dean Howells in 1917.

37 **What people loved** *"invincible charm"*: ICCWS.

38 **There would always** Stoddard's sexuality and boyhood trials: GP, pp. 4–14, 23–25. *"The Love Man"*: Charles Phillips, "Charles Warren Stoddard," *Overland Monthly* 51.2 (Feb. 1908), p. 135. In 1869, the Austro-Hungarian journalist Karl Maria Kertbeny published two anonymous pamphlets protesting the proposed introduction of Prussia's anti-sodomy law into the new North German Confederation. These marked the first use of the word "homosexuality"; see Manfred Herzer and Hubert Kennedy, "Kertbeny, Karl Maria," in Timothy F. Murphy, ed., *Reader's Guide to Lesbian and Gay Studies* (Chicago: Fitzroy Dearborn, 2000), pp. 325–326. Stoddard's discovery of Whitman's "Calamus" poems: GP, pp. 35, 45–46. *"the pensive aching to be together"*: Walt Whitman, *Leaves of Grass, 1860: The 150th Anniversary Facsimile Edition*, ed. Jason Stacy (Iowa City: University of Iowa Press, 2009), p. 22.

38 **Stoddard first came** Stoddard's boyhood: GP, pp. 6–15, and CSCWS, pp. 2–41. Stoddard first arrived in San Francisco with his family on January 6, 1855, on the *Sierra Nevada* from Nicaragua; see "Arrival of the Sierra Nevada," San Francisco *Daily Placer Times and Transcript*, January 8, 1855. *"a natural tendency..."*: Charles Warren Stoddard, *In the Footprints of the Padres*, p. 101. *"enchanting music"* and *"beautiful women in bewildering attire"*: ibid., p. 64. Stoddard's father belonged to the 1856 Committee of Vigilance, which conducted lynchings and deportations, and ruled San Francisco for three months before relinquishing power. Stoddard remembers the executions of Cora and Casey in "Veteran Recalls Vigilante Days," undated clipping, BANC.

39 **In California** Thirteen thousand people: SFLF, pp. 89–90. More discreet gamblers and prostitutes: Roger W. Lotchin, *San Francisco, 1846–1856*, pp. 207, 271. Gristmills, breweries, etc.: GP, p. 16, and *San Francisco Municipal Reports: 1859–1860* (San Francisco: Towne & Bacon, 1860), p. 155.

39 **The fast-growing city** *"the cradle and the grave..."*: Charles Warren Stoddard, *Exits and Entrances: A Book of Essays and Sketches* (Boston: Lothrop, 1903), p. 242. The *Golden Era* first published Stoddard on September 21, 1862; see CSCWS, p. 52. *"No member of my family..."* and story of submitting first poem: CRP, chap. 1, p. 7. Origins of "Pip Pepperpod": ibid., p. 8.

40 **After this harrowing** For the year following Stoddard's *Era* debut in September 1862, he would contribute a poem to almost every issue; see CSCWS, p. 53. *"It is because..."*: letter from Thomas Starr King to Charles Warren Stoddard, January 10, 1863, HUNT. King's constructive criticisms: CRP, chap. 2, p. 8, and CSCWS, pp. 54–55. *"city life..."*: CRP, chap. 2, p. 8.

40 **If Stoddard proved** Twain wrote the article on June 19, 1863, and it probably appeared in the *Virginia City Territorial Enterprise* between June 21 and 24. Three months later, on September 27, 1863, the *Golden Era* reprinted it as "Mark Twain—More of Him," the form in which it appears in ET&S, vol. 1, pp. 304–312. All quotes: ibid., p. 311.

41 **Lawrence's hopes for** *"simply palatial"*: Joaquin Miller, "Joseph E. Lawrence," *San Francisco Morning Call*, September 4, 1892. Description of Lawrence: ibid.; Charles Warren Stoddard, *Exits and Entrances*, p. 243; and SFLF, pp. 119–120, 122.

41 **By the summer** Ina Coolbrith, "June," *Golden Era*, June 7, 1863.

42 **No matter that** Australian coal gas and Alaskan ice: Earl Pomeroy, *The Pacific Slope*, p. 123. California agriculture: ibid., pp. 94–95, and Roger W. Lotchin, *San Francisco, 1846–1856*, p. 47. From 1848 to 1853, nearly all flour consumed in California was imported into SF. Industry: ibid., pp. 64–67.

42 **Harte led the charge** *"street music"*: Bret Harte, "Town and Table Talk: Glances over My Left Shoulder from a Corner Window, and Cogitations Generally," *Golden Era*, July 8, 1860. *"There are moments..."*: Bret Harte, "Town and Table Talk: The Bohemian's 'Sensation' Play," *Golden Era*, November 25, 1860. For the best of Harte's later "Bohemian" columns, see "A Rail at the Rail," *Golden Era*, April 12, 1863, and "Back Windows," *Golden Era*, March 8, 1863.

42 **Harte made an** For an overview of Bohemia's origins, see Roy Kotynek and John Cohassey, *American Cultural Rebels: Avant-Garde and Bohemian Artists, Writers, and Musicians from the 1850s through the 1960s* (Jefferson, NC: McFarland, 2008), pp. 5–20. *"Bohemia has never..."*: Bret Harte, "Town and Table Talk: The Bohemian Concerning," *Golden Era*, November 11, 1860.

CHAPTER TWO

45 **On September 8** Virginia City in the summer of 1863: MTAL, pp. 123–124. *"infernal racket"* and *"O, for the solitude..."*: "'Mark Twain's' Letter," *San Francisco Morning Call*, July 9, 1863, included in ET&S, vol. 1, pp. 254–258. Twain describes the fire in his next letter, in *San Francisco Morning Call*, July 30, 1863, included in ET&S, vol. 1, pp. 259–261, and in a letter to Jane Lampton Clemens and Pamela A. Moffett, August 5, 1863, in MTL, vol. 1, pp. 261–262. Twain's cold: ET&S, vol. 1, p. 270.

45 **Twain made the most** Joked about it in the *Call*: "'Mark Twain's' Letter," *San Francisco Morning Call*, July 30, 1863, included in ET&S, vol. 1, pp. 259–261. Two weeks at Tahoe: ibid., p. 270. *"a voice..."* and *"an impalpable..."*: *Virginia City Territorial Enterprise*, August 19, 1863, included in Mark Twain, *Mark Twain of the Enterprise: Newspaper Articles and Other Documents, 1862–1864*, ed. Henry Nash Smith and Frederick Anderson (Berkeley: University of California Press, 1957), p. 69. See also ET&S, vol. 1, pp. 270–283. *"Everybody knows me..."*: SLC to Jane Lampton Clemens and Pamela A. Moffett, August 19, 1863, in MTL, vol. 1, p. 264.

46 **He came to San Francisco** Twain's stagecoach trip and arrival in SF: Mark Twain, "Letter from Mark Twain," *Virginia City Territorial Enterprise*, September 17, 1863, included in ET&S, vol. 1, pp. 291–295. *"How to Cure a Cold"*: *Golden Era*, September 20, 1863, included ibid., pp. 296–303.

47 **Fortunately, the** *Golden Era's* Dropping out of City College: CRP, chap. 2, p. 8.

47 **In the fall** *"a kind of wildwood..."*: Charles Warren Stoddard, *Exits and Entrances*, p. 239. *"almost as quiet..."*: CRP, chap. 2, p. 8. Stoddard's arrival and Brayton Academy: CSCWS, pp. 60–61. Only an hour or so by ferry: George H. Harlan and Clement Fisher Jr., *Of Walking Beams and Paddle Wheels: A Chronicle of San Francisco Bay Ferryboats* (San Francisco: Bay Books, 1951), p. 19.

48 **Before the semester** House in Oakland: CRP, chap. 3, p. 2. The Oakland Creek is now known as the San Antonio Creek, the Oakland Estuary, or the Oakland Inner Harbor.

48 **"Harte used to"** *"Harte used to have this room"*: CRP, chap. 3, p. 2. *"Much as I longed..."*: ibid., p. 3.

48 **The two men** Autograph album: CRP, chap. 2, p. 9. Many of the entries were published in "Notable Autographs," the *Californian: A Western Monthly Magazine* 1.4 (April 1880),

pp. 353–357. *"gifted owner"*: ibid., p. 353. *"I might have . . ."* and *"seemed to look . . ."*: Charles Warren Stoddard, *Exits and Entrances*, p. 254. Stoddard's blue eyes: GP, p. 156.

49 **In time, they** Harte's poem for Stoddard, "Mary's Album," is also included in Bret Harte, *The Writings of Bret Harte*, vol. 20, pp. 306–307.

49 **This bit of cynicism** *"throw the shadow . . ."*: Charles Warren Stoddard, *Exits and Entrances*, p. 255.

49 **Harte's inscription aside** *"I conned my . . ."*: CRP, chap. 3, p. 7. *"at the long . . ."*: ibid., p. 3.

50 **Fortunately, there was** "Once a week I could return to the bosom of my family and revel in the pageant of the streets that were so picturesque and peculiar in those days," Stoddard wrote in CRP, chap. 2, p. 9. The ferry from Oakland landed near Davis Street between Vallejo and Broadway, according to *San Francisco Municipal Reports for the Fiscal Year 1862–63* (San Francisco: Charles F. Robbins, 1863), p. 204. This was a few blocks south of where Clarke's Point stood, a rocky promontory below Telegraph Hill where traders once landed.

50 **Stoddard agonized over** For more on Stoddard's academic struggles, see CRP, chap. 3, pp. 5–8, and CSCWS, pp. 62–64. Twain dropped out of school and became a printer's apprentice after his father died in March 1847; see MTB, vol. 1, pp. 74–75. Bret Harte ended his schooling at thirteen; see BHAN, p. 23. Coolbrith most likely attended school in St. Louis from 1846 to 1851, and in Los Angeles from 1855 to 1858; see ICLL, pp. 25–64. *"Education consists . . ."*: Mark Twain, *Mark Twain's Notebook*, ed. Albert Bigelow Paine (New York: Harper & Brothers, 1935), p. 346.

50 **By this standard** Literary migration to SF: SFLF, pp. 146–175. Webb: ibid., pp. 133–135; George R. Stewart Jr., *Bret Harte*, pp. 119–120; and L. Anne Clark Doherty, "Webb, Charles Henry," *American National Biography Online*, February 2000, http://www.anb.org.ezp -prod1.hul.harvard.edu/articles/16/16-01729.html. Boom in journalism: Louis M. Starr, *Bohemian Brigade: Civil War Newsmen in Action* (New York: Knopf, 1954), p. 9. *"I was quartered . . ."*: *New York Times*, April 2, 1862.

51 **In San Francisco** Webb arrived in San Francisco on April 20, 1863. He came to the city as a correspondent for the *New York Times*, and joined the *San Francisco Evening Bulletin* as its literary editor. His arrival: SFLF, pp. 133–134. Description of Webb: ECW and Charles Warren Stoddard, "In Old Bohemia II: The 'Overland' and the Overlanders," *Pacific Monthly* 19.3 (March 1908), p. 261. *"decorative impediment . . ."*: ibid.

51 **Webb began his** For a selection of Webb's columns, signed under the pseudonym Inigo, see *Golden Era*, July 24, 1863; August 16, 1863; August 30, 1863; September 27, 1863; November 8, 1863; November 22, 1863; November 29, 1863.

51 **No newcomer aroused** *"caught the eye . . ."*: Charles Warren Stoddard, "La Belle Menken," *National Magazine* 21.5 (Feb. 1905), pp. 477–478. In his article, Stoddard includes the drawing that he claims was used as Menken's publicity picture. A photograph of Menken that may have circulated at the time is included in Renée M. Sentilles, *Performing Menken: Adah Isaacs Menken and the Birth of American Celebrity* (Cambridge: Cambridge University Press, 2003), p. 164. *"[I]f she is half . . ."*: Charles Henry Webb, "Things," *Golden Era*, August 16, 1863.

52 **By the time** Scene at the premiere and *"We doubt . . ."*: *Daily Alta California*, August 25, 1863. Maguire's Opera House in San Francisco had a chandelier with twenty gas burners: Karyl Lynn Zietz, *The National Trust Guide to Great Opera Houses in America* (New York: John Wiley & Sons, 1996), p. 35.

52 **Menken didn't disappoint** For an overview of Menken's *Mazeppa*, see "Tom Maguire, Napoleon of the Stage: III. Man of Affairs," *California Historical Society Quarterly* 21.1 (March 1942), p. 59, and SFLF, pp. 169–170. Her reception in SF: Renée M. Sentilles, *Performing Menken*, pp. 179–181, and Twain's review in "Letter from Mark Twain," *Virginia City Territorial Enterprise*, September 17, 1863, included in *Mark Twain of the Enterprise*, pp. 78–80.

52 **Everyone went to** "Grace" was a word often used in connection with Menken. For one example, see *Golden Era*, August 30, 1863. Whispering crowds: Charles Henry Webb, "Things," *Golden Era*, August 30, 1863. *"if the performance . . .": San Francisco Evening Bulletin,* quoted in Renée M. Sentilles, *Performing Menken,* p. 180. *"Prudery is obsolete": Sacramento Daily Union,* quoted ibid. *"People who have . . .":* Charles Henry Webb, "Things," *Golden Era,* August 30, 1863.

53 **Menken so thoroughly** All quotes: "Letter from Mark Twain," *Virginia City Territorial Enterprise,* September 17, 1863, included in *Mark Twain of the Enterprise,* pp. 78–80.

53 **Stoddard felt differently** Stoddard's fascination with Menken: Charles Warren Stoddard, "La Belle Menken," pp. 477–488. *"out of the common run":* ibid., pp. 477–478. *"willowy elasticity"* and *"idealized duality of sex": Golden Era,* September 13, 1863, quoted in Renée M. Sentilles, *Performing Menken,* p. 182. Cigarettes: ibid., p. 216. In 1862, Menken married her third husband, Robert Henry Newell, who wrote satirical articles under the pseudonym Orpheus C. Kerr. Newell joined her in the Far West and wrote for the *Golden Era;* they divorced in 1865. *"half-feminine masculinity":* Charles Warren Stoddard, "La Belle Menken," p. 478. *"physique . . . made whole":* from Stoddard's December 1866 entry in his "Thought Book" (1865–1867), BANC, and quoted in GP, p. 24.

52 **Menken's sensuality wasn't** The term "Bohemians" originally came from Paris, where it described the young loafers who began haunting the cafés of the Latin Quarter in the 1830s. They took their name from the kingdom of Bohemia, once thought to be the homeland of Gypsies, and embraced lives of art and vice. In the late 1850s, the word migrated to New York, where it came to refer to a group centered on Pfaff's. See Joanna Levin, *Bohemia in America, 1858–1920* (Stanford, CA: Stanford University Press, 2009), pp. 16–22, and Roy Kotynek and John Cohassey, *American Cultural Rebels,* pp. 15–20. Description of Clapp: Elihu Vedder, *The Digressions of V: Written for His Own Fun and That of His Friends* (Boston: Houghton Mifflin, 1910), p. 232; Junius Henri Browne, *The Great Metropolis: A Mirror of New York* (Hartford, CT: American Publishing Company, 1869), pp. 152–153; and William Dean Howells, *Literary Friends and Acquaintance: A Personal Retrospect of American Authorship* (New York: Harper & Brothers, 1901), pp. 69–70. *"It attacked . . .":* ibid., p. 70.

54 **Menken joined the** *"precedent"* and *"new free forms":* Walt Whitman, *Complete Poetry and Collected Prose,* p. 14. Menken's love of Whitman: Renée M. Sentilles, *Performing Menken,* pp. 147–149; SFLF, p. 170; and Adah Isaacs Menken, "Swimming Against the Current," *Golden Era,* November 15, 1863. *"Swimming against . . .":* ibid.

54 **The New York Bohemians** The *Era* often republished articles from the New York press about the Pfaffians; see Joanna Levin, *Bohemia in America,* p. 113, and *Golden Era,* June 3, 1860. *"fellows of infinite humor and rare fancy": Golden Era,* August 12, 1860. *"Bohemian Capital":* Bret Harte, "Town and Table Talk: The Bohemian's 'Christmas,'" *Golden Era,* December 23, 1860.

54 **There was also** *"eccentricities . . .":* Fitz Hugh Ludlow, "A Good-Bye Article," *Golden Era,* November 22, 1863. The Pfaffians who traveled to San Francisco in 1863 included Fitz Hugh Ludlow, Ada Clare, and Robert Henry Newell.

55 **The legacy of** By 1860, 39 percent of SF's population was female. Compare this with 1852, when, according to the census, only 15 percent was female. The gender imbalance persisted for decades; as late as 1900, men still made up 55 percent of the population. See Philip J. Ethington, *The Public City: The Political Construction of Urban Life in San Francisco, 1850–1900* (Berkeley: University of California Press, 2001 [1994]), p. 47. *"nomads"* in the *"vast beehives": Golden Era,* February 17, 1861. *"natural resting place"* and *"living tide":* Bret Harte, "Bohemian Feuilleton: Hotel Life," *Golden Era,* April 21, 1861.

55 **If San Francisco's fluid** "Bohemian" as working writer: Joanna Levin, *Bohemia in America,* pp. 67, 249; see also Earl Pomeroy, *The Pacific Slope,* pp. 158–159: "[N]o other American city supported so many newspapers and writers in proportion to the total population or prized so much its associations with the arts and artists." *"small portion . . .":* Bret Harte,

"Town and Table Talk: Glances over My Left Shoulder from a Corner Window, and Cogitations Generally," *Golden Era*, July 8, 1860. Percentage of foreign-born male citizens: Philip J. Ethington, *The Public City*, p. 50. See also Barbara Berglund, *Making San Francisco American: Cultural Frontiers in the Urban West, 1846–1906* (Lawrence: University Press of Kansas, 2007), pp. 4–5. Mexican and Chinese clothing: Amelia Ransome Neville, *The Fantastic City*, p. 47. *"bustling . . ."*: Bret Harte, "Bohemian Days in San Francisco," p. 277.

56 **There was another** Seeing the Far West for the first time: Wallace Stegner, "Thoughts in a Dry Land," *Where the Bluebird Sings to the Lemonade Springs: Living and Writing in the West* (New York: Penguin, 1992), pp. 52–55. For eyewitness accounts of gold rush–era California, see Gary F. Kurutz, *The California Gold Rush*. For pre–gold rush narratives, see Joshua Paddison, ed., *A World Transformed: Firsthand Accounts of California before the Gold Rush* (Berkeley, CA: Heyday, 1999), pp. 167–305. *"to about twice . . ."* and *"I said we . . ."*: SLC to Jane Lampton Clemens, October 26, 1861, in MTL, vol. 1, p. 137.

57 **This was what** *"westernization of the perceptions"*: Wallace Stegner, "Thoughts in a Dry Land," p. 54. Thomas Starr King on giant sequoias: letter to James T. Fields, June 26, 1862, HUNT.

57 **The seemingly obvious** Eastern views of the West: Henry Nash Smith, *Virgin Land*, pp. 216–249. *"semi-barbarous citizens"*: quoted ibid., p. 219.

57 **This theory of progress** *"struggling up to civilization"*: letter from Thomas Starr King to James T. Fields, October 29, 1862, HUNT.

58 **These weren't unusual** Fireside Poets: James H. Justus, "The Fireside Poets: Hearthside Values and the Language of Care," in A. Robert Lee, ed., *Nineteenth-Century American Poetry* (London: Vision Press, 1985), pp. 146–165.

58 **New England had dominated** *"We have listened . . ."*: Ralph Waldo Emerson, "The American Scholar," in Carl Bode and Malcolm Cowley, eds., *The Portable Emerson* (New York: Penguin, 1981 [1946]), p. 70.

58 **The New York Bohemians** *"solemn Philistines"*: quoted in Roy Kotynek and John Cohassey, *American Cultural Rebels*, p. 17.

59 **In October 1863** Harte's story was called "The Legend of Monte del Diablo." The *Atlantic Monthly*'s October 1863 issue also included Emerson's poem "Voluntaries" and Thoreau's essay "Life Without Principle." Thoreau had died the year before. *"I am sure . . ."*: a letter from Thomas Starr King to James T. Fields, January 31, 1862, HUNT. *"a fresh mind . . ."*: Jessie Benton Frémont's letter to James T. Fields, October 26, 1862, quoted in BHAN, p. 71.

59 **A Californian writing** *"pushing, bustling . . ."*: Bret Harte, "The Legend of Monte del Diablo," included in *The Luck of Roaring Camp and Other Writings*, ed. Gary Scharnhorst, p. 12. *"deceitful lure"*: ibid., p. 13.

59 **As blasphemous as** *"the greatest disgrace . . ."*: Henry David Thoreau, "Life Without Principle," in *Atlantic Monthly* 12.72 (Oct. 1863), p. 487. *"a rush . . ."* and *"a general jail-delivery . . ."*: Ralph Waldo Emerson, "Considerations by the Way," in *The Conduct of Life* (Boston: Ticknor and Fields, 1860), p. 224.

59 **These patronizing appraisals** *"bustling Yankee"*: Bret Harte, "Bohemian Papers: The Mission Dolores," *Golden Era*, March 22, 1863. *"romantic and dramatic . . ."*: Bret Harte, "The Rise of the 'Short Story,'" p. 255.

60 **Harte's *Atlantic* coup** *"Your young friend . . ."*: quoted in BHGS, p. 20. For more of Harte's early fiction dealing with pioneer California, see "The Work on Red Mountain," which later became "M'Liss," and "Notes on Flood and Field," both included in *The Writings of Bret Harte*, vol. 1 (Boston: Houghton Mifflin, 1896).

60 **Twain, on the other** Twain's four features in the *Era* were "How to Cure a Cold," *Golden Era*, September 20, 1863; "Mark Twain—More of Him" and "The Lick House Ball," *Golden Era*, September 27, 1863; and "The Great Prize Fight," *Golden Era*, October 11, 1863. Heady dose of high society: Mark Twain, "The Lick House Ball," *Golden Era*, September 27, 1863, included in ET&S, vol. 1, pp. 313–319. It's not clear exactly when or how

Twain acquired the nickname Washoe Giant; it appears in Charles Henry Webb, "Things," *Golden Era*, November 8, 1863, as well as in Fitz Hugh Ludlow, "A Good-Bye Article," *Golden Era*, November 22, 1863.

61 **On October 28** "A Bloody Massacre near Carson" appeared in *Virginia City Territorial Enterprise*, October 28, 1863, included in ET&S, vol. 1, pp. 320–326.

61 **The story caused** Power of *Sacramento Daily Union*: SFLF, pp. 110, 120, and Charles Carroll Goodwin, *As I Remember Them* (Salt Lake City: Salt Lake Commercial Club, 1913), p. 79. *"I Take It..."* and *"dividend cooking"*: quoted in ET&S, vol. 1, p. 320. *"The only..."*: ibid., pp. 320–321.

61 **The reaction was swift** For the reaction to Twain's article, see ET&S, vol. 1, pp. 320–323, and Richard G. Lillard, "Contemporary Reaction to 'The Empire City Massacre,'" *American Literature* 16.3 (Nov. 1944), pp. 198–203. All quotes from Richard G. Lillard, "Contemporary Reaction to 'The Empire City Massacre.'"

62 **Although unrepentant in public** *"All this worried..."*: Dan De Quille, as interviewed in Archibald Henderson, *Mark Twain* (1910), included in TIHOT, pp. 38–39. See Richard G. Lillard, "Contemporary Reaction to 'The Empire City Massacre,'" p. 203, for a summary of the references to Twain's hoax in the Nevada and California press. The *Virginia City Daily Morning Union* discussed it as late as October 29, 1866. For more on the dark side of Twain's reputation, see Arthur McEwan, "In the Heroic Days" (1893), included in TIHOT, p. 22, and George E. Barnes, "Mark Twain as He Was Known during His Stay on the Pacific Slope," included ibid., p. 47.

62 **He was always** *"He liked..."*: William Dean Howells, *My Mark Twain*, ed. Marilyn Austin Baldwin (Baton Rouge: Louisiana State University Press, 1967 [1910]), p. 37. Twain's contemporaries left a substantial written record of his loyalty as a friend and his viciousness as an enemy; in MTAL, p. 33, Ron Powers writes that Twain saw friendship as "a value of nearly sacred proportions." *"In attack he was fiery..."*: Dan De Quille, "Salad Days of Mark Twain," included in TIHOT, p. 28.

62 **By late 1863** *"As a literary..."*: *Alta California*, September 20, 1863. This article refers to the "celebrities" writing for the *Era*, counting Twain, Harte, and Webb among its star contributors. *"graceful and elegant"*: Charles Henry Webb, "Things," *Golden Era*, September 27, 1863. *"[S]o loudly..."*: Charles Henry Webb, "Things," *Golden Era*, October 25, 1863.

63 **This kind of puffery** The groundbreaking ceremony for the Central Pacific Railroad took place in Sacramento on January 8, 1863; see David Haward Bain, *Empire Express*, pp. 122–124.

64 **Building a better** Coolbrith's early days in San Francisco: ICLL, pp. 80–83. *"unpitying world"* and *"shafts of enmity..."*: Ina Coolbrith, "Unrest," published in the *Los Angeles Star* in 1862 after she arrived in San Francisco, excerpted in ICLL, p. 82.

64 **She first met** *"slender, delicate...,"* *"We were little more...,"* *"petted and spoiled..."*: ICCWS. *"ideal Poet..."*: ICHC. Frequent mood swings: ICCWS. Soul-expiring sighs: Charles Phillips, "Charles Warren Stoddard," *Overland Monthly* 51.2 (Feb. 1908), p. 137, and GP, p. 10. *"moonstruck vacuity"*: ICHC.

65 **Like the other** *"the tribe"*: ICCWS. *"The friendship..."*: IC to CWS, May 4, 1872, HUNT. The collections of their correspondence held by HUNT and BANC offer invaluable insights into their relationship. One common thread is Coolbrith's good-natured teasing of Stoddard for not answering her letters promptly. As time went on, Coolbrith's tone grew perceptibly less playful and occasionally even bitter: by 1879, it's no longer clear if she's kidding when she calls him "bad, fickle, unloving." In a letter from March 20, 1868, and another from October 14, 1870, both held by HUNT, Coolbrith threatens to box Stoddard's ears "soundly." The second letter, written while Stoddard was in Tahiti, is worth excerpting at length: "Don't you come back here! Don't you dare to! Who do you suppose would come to see you—except to box your ears soundly and tell you how much they—loved you and had missed you, Charlie—god bless your dear heart!"

65 **In December 1863** *"seedling..."*: Ina Coolbrith, "December," *Golden Era*, December 20, 1863. *"Bret and I..."*: Charles Henry Webb, "Things," November 8, 1863. For more of the buzz in the *Era* about a new paper, see Bret Harte, "About the Inigo Boy," *Golden Era*, November 15, 1863, and Charles Henry Webb, "Things," *Golden Era*, November 29, 1863.

65 **They shared a single** All quotes: Bret Harte, "Things," *Golden Era*, November 8, 1863. For more on the shift in San Francisco's literary climate, see SFLF, pp. 177–184.

66 **In early 1864** The first issue of the new journal, the *Californian*, appeared on May 28, 1864, and advertised itself as not only the "Best Journal on the Pacific Coast" but also the "Equal of Any on This Continent!" It also listed its offices at 728 Montgomery Street. This is the Genella Building, built in the early 1850s by the merchant Joseph Genella on the site of the first meeting of Freemasons in California. Miraculously, it is still standing. At the time, the *Golden Era* was at 543 Clay Street, about two blocks away.

66 **On February 26** The account of King's illness and death comes from his friend Robert Bunker Swain's *Address Before the First Unitarian Society of San Francisco in Memory of Their Late Pastor, Rev. Thomas Starr King, March 15, 1864* (San Francisco: Frank Eastman, 1864), pp. 23–28.

66 **Twenty thousand people** King's funeral: Kevin Starr, *Americans and the California Dream*, pp. 104–105; *Daily Evening Bulletin*, March 5, 1864, and March 7, 1864; and *Golden Era*, March 6, 1864.

67 **Of course, his** Stoddard's poem: Charles Warren Stoddard, "Dirge," *Golden Era*, March 6, 1864. *"gentle Teacher..."*: Ina Coolbrith, "Starr King," *Golden Era*, March 13, 1864. See also Charles Henry Webb's column in *Golden Era*, March 6, 1864. *"A star..."*: Bret Harte, "Relieving Guard," *Golden Era*, March 13, 1864. Later, Harte would write two more poems for King: "At the Sepulchre," to commemorate the dedication of a monument to King in 1864, and "His Pen" in 1865.

67 **A fitting eulogy** *"Every sufferer..."*: a letter from Thomas Starr King to Charles Lyman Strong, August 3, 1863, HUNT. The Yosemite peak is called Mount Starr King, elevation 9,092 feet. In 1869, Josiah Whitney recorded the height of Thomas Starr King's giant sequoia in the Calaveras Grove as 283 feet. King's statue in the Capitol: Adam Goodheart, *1861*, p. 380. Statue's removal and *"I wasn't sure..."*: Kimberly Geiger, "National Statuary Hall," *San Francisco Chronicle*, October 25, 2006. The legislator who introduced the resolution was Dennis Hollingsworth, a Republican state senator from Riverside County.

68 **Two months after San Francisco** Twain's previous visit to SF lasted from September 8, 1863, until mid-October. By October 19, 1863, he was in Carson City, Nevada, reporting on the First Annual Fair of the Washoe Agricultural, Mining, and Mechanical Society. Blistering from the sun: Mark Twain, "'Mark Twain' in the Metropolis," published in the *Virginia City Territorial Enterprise* between June 17 and June 23, included in ET&S, vol. 2, pp. 9–12. Oysters, salmon, and fowl: ibid. *"the most cordial..."* and parties: MTR, p. 396. *"I had longed..."*: ibid.

68 **Recently, Nevada had** Lager beer, Limburger cheese, smell of sagebrush, barren scenery: Mark Twain, "'Mark Twain' in the Metropolis," p. 10.

68 **The Civil War loomed** For an overview of the Carson City Sanitary saga, see James E. Caron, *Mark Twain: Unsanctified Newspaper Reporter* (Columbia: University of Missouri, 2008), pp. 148–155. Thomas Starr King's work for the Sanitary Commission: Adam Goodheart, *1861*, p. 380. For a breakdown of funds contributed by California to the Sanitary Commission, see Charles J. Stillé, *History of the United States Sanitary Commission* (Philadelphia: J. B. Lippincott, 1866), pp. 539–541. The copy of the *Virginia City Territorial Enterprise* with Twain's hoax is no longer extant, but is quoted in a letter from the ladies of Carson City to the editors of the *Territorial Enterprise*, published in the *Virginia City Daily Union*, May 25, 1864, included in MTL, vol. 1, p. 289. *"to aid..."*: ibid.

69 **This hoax delivered** Context for Twain's miscegenation hoax: MTAL, p. 138, and Mark Twain, *Mark Twain of the Enterprise*, pp. 196–197.

69   **The fallout would be severe** Carson City ladies' letter in *Virginia City Daily Union*, May
     25, 1864, in MTL, vol. 1, p. 289. *Enterprise's* refusal to print the letter, and *Daily Union*
     publishing it for three days in a row: ibid. Ostracized Mollie: MTAL, p. 138. *"I am sorry . . .",*
     "not sober," "I suppose . . .," and *"I cannot submit . . .":* SLC to Mary E. Clemens, May 20, 1864,
     in MTL, vol. 1, p. 288. Twain did publish somewhat of an apology in the *Territorial Enter-*
     prise on May 24, 1864, included in MTL, vol. 1, p. 297. He also wrote a half-contrite letter
     to one of the aggrieved ladies; see SLC to Ellen G. Cutler, May 23, 1864, in MTL, vol. 1,
     p. 296. She didn't find it satisfactory, however, and her husband, William K. Cutler, chal-
     lenged Twain to a duel; see *MTL*, vol. 1, p. 301.

70   **Meanwhile, Twain opened** Reuel Colt Gridley: SLC to Jane Lampton Clemens and Pamela
     A. Moffett, May 17, 1864, in MTL, vol. 1, pp. 281–287. Twain would later recount the story
     of Gridley and his flour sack in *Roughing It*. Twain's attack on the *Daily Union: Virginia*
     City Territorial Enterprise, May 18, 1864, included in MTL, vol. 1, p. 287. The *Union*
     responded on May 19, 1864; see MTL, vol. 1, pp. 289–290. Twain replied in the *Enterprise*,
     provoking more responses from the *Union*; see MTL, vol. 1, pp. 290–291.

70   **The inner devils** *"insulting":* SLC to James L. Laird, May 21, 1864, in MTL, vol. 1, p. 290.
     J. W. Wilmington replied directly to Twain on May 21, 1864; see MTL, vol. 1, p. 292. *"cow-*
     ardly sneak," "without alternative," "satisfaction due to a gentleman": SLC to James L. Laird,
     May 21, 1864, in MTL, vol. 1, p. 292. *"Mr. Wilmington has . . .":* James L. Laird to SLC, May
     21, 1864, in MTL, vol. 1, p. 294. Twain's response: SLC to James L. Laird, May 21, 1864, in
     MTL, vol. 1, p. 293. Laird's final refusal: James L. Laird to SLC, May 23, 1864, in MTL, vol.
     1, p. 295. Twain published the letters in the *Territorial Enterprise*, May 24, 1864. *"unmiti-*
     gated liar," "an abject coward," and *"fool":* ibid., included in MTL, vol. 1, p. 295. Twain's
     departure for SF: MTL, vol. 1, p. 302. By the time he left Virginia City, he faced at least
     three potential dueling partners: James L. Laird, J. W. Wilmington, and William K. Cut-
     ler. Twain believed he would soon face more challenges from other husbands of the Carson
     City ladies; see MTL, vol. 1, p. 298.

71   **The reasons are unclear** *"afraid of the grand jury," "Washoe has long . . .,"* and his plan to
     return East: SLC to Orion Clemens, May 26, 1864, in MTL, vol. 1, p. 299. *"The indigna-*
     tion . . .": Gold Hill *Daily News*, May 30, 1864, in MTL, vol. 1, p. 302.

72   **Not exactly a** *"It cannot be said . . .":* George E. Barnes, "Mark Twain as He Was Known
     during His Stay on the Pacific Slope," in TIHOT, p. 47. Twain omits the incident from
     Roughing It (1872). For later accounts, see Mark Twain, "How I Escaped Being Killed in a
     Duel," in *Tom Hood's Comic Annual for 1873*, ed. Tom Hood (London: Fun, 1872), pp. 90–91,
     and AMT, pp. 296–298.

72   **On November 8, 1863** Ward's arrival, debut, and background: MTAL, pp. 129–130, and
     SFLF, pp. 158–162. Lincoln reading Ward aloud to his cabinet: Doris Kearns Goodwin,
     Team of Rivals: The Political Genius of Abraham Lincoln (New York: Simon & Schuster,
     2005), p. 481.

73   **A tall, thin man** Ward's appearance: Don C. Seitz, *Artemus Ward: A Biography and Bibliog-*
     raphy (New York: Harper & Brothers, 1919), p. 148; *Artemus Ward's Mormon Entertainment:*
     Opinions of the New York Press (New York: Chaplin, Bromell, Scott & O'Keefe, 1865), p. 23;
     and SFLF, p. 161. Ward first found fame through a series of newspaper sketches, collected
     in the best-selling *Artemus Ward: His Book*. *"praps":* Charles Farrar Browne, *Artemus Ward:*
     His Book (New York: Carleton, 1862), p. 79. *"faseshus":* ibid., p. 24. Ward's lecture style: *San*
     Francisco Daily Evening Bulletin, November 14, 1863; Dan De Quille, "Artemus Ward,"
     San Francisco Examiner, February 26, 1888, included in Lawrence I. Berkove, ed., *The Sage-*
     brush Anthology, p. 247; Mark Twain, "How to Tell a Story," in *How to Tell a Story and*
     Other Essays (Hartford, CT: American Publishing Company, 1901 [1897]), pp. 8, 11–12; and
     SFLF, p. 161.

73   **"The point of his lecture"** *"The point . . .":* San Francisco *Daily Evening Bulletin*, November
     14, 1863. Many critics objected to the absence of a moral purpose in Ward's lecture. They

were particularly annoyed by the fact that Ward dressed like a gentleman yet had nothing elevating or edifying to say. See SFLF, pp. 161–162, and Bret Harte, "Artemus Ward," *Golden Era*, December 27, 1863. *"humor that belongs..."* and *"that fun..."*: ibid. For the *Golden Era*'s glowing review of Ward's debut, see *Golden Era*, November 15, 1863.

73 **Harte had hit** Origins of "tall talk": Kenneth S. Lynn, *Mark Twain and Southwestern Humor* (Boston: Little, Brown, 1959), pp. 23–45.

74 **Twain absorbed their** Twain's relationship to Southwestern humor: ibid., pp. 140–173; Bernard DeVoto, *Mark Twain's America*, pp. 3–99. "Pikes" on the Pacific coast: Kevin Starr, *Americans and the California Dream*, pp. 192–193; G. R. MacMinn, "'The Gentleman from Pike' in Early California," *American Literature* 8.2 (May 1936), pp. 160–169; and David Carkeet, "The Dialects in *Huckleberry Finn*," *American Literature* 51.3 (Nov. 1979), p. 325.

74 **Artemus Ward also owed** Ward's stint in Virginia City: MTAL, pp. 129–134. Ward arrived on December 18, 1863, and left on December 29, 1863.

75 **Twain and Ward** Twain's first appearance in the *New York Sunday Mercury* and his first appearance in NY press: James E. Caron, *Mark Twain*, pp. 165–166. *"leave sage-brush obscurity..."*: SLC to Jane Lampton Clemens, January 2[?], 1864, MTL, vol. 1, p. 268.

CHAPTER THREE

77 **"The birds"** *"The birds..."*: Mark Twain, "'Mark Twain' in the Metropolis," p. 11.

77 **He benefited from** The *Californian*'s debut: SFLF, pp. 178–182.

78 **But creating** *"forty-eight..."* and *"seemed no..."*: Charles Henry Webb, "Things," *Californian*, May 28, 1864. In the same column, Webb explained the magazine's name: "'The Californian' sounds plain, practical, and expressive. It is comprehensive, and commits the paper to no particular field [of] literature, politics, or religion, leaving, on the contrary, a free field open to it for the discussion of all." Harte's pieces were "Neighborhoods I Have Moved From" and "The Ballad of the Emeu."

79 **Progress had always** *"bullet to a man's heart..."*: *Californian*, August 13, 1864. See also "The Morals of the Age," *Californian*, August 6, 1864, and "A Mistake Corrected," *Californian*, September 10, 1864.

79 **Reading the reports** Coolbrith and the Civil War: ICLL, p. 83. All quotes: Ina Coolbrith, "Christmas Eve, 1863," *Golden Era*, December 27, 1863.

80 **Life in San Francisco** Anonymous contributions to *Californian*: ICLL, p. 85. Scene with Webb and all quotes: ECW.

80 **What Webb feared** Webb's fears: ECW. "He told me afterwards that for months he lived in mortal terror of being called down by some exchange on a plagiarized poem!" Coolbrith recalled. "You see I was still not exempt from suspicion." Poem for her composition class: ECW. The editor was John Rollin Ridge, also known as Yellow Bird, who published a popular novel about a legendary Mexican bandit, *The Life and Adventures of Joaquin Murieta*, in 1854.

81 **The meeting with** *"He had a mother..."*: ECW.

81 **Coolbrith would bring** *"Cheeks of an..."*: Ina Coolbrith, "In the Pouts," *Songs from the Golden Gate* (Boston and New York: Houghton Mifflin, 1907 [1895]), p. 73.

81 **She had tamed** All quotes: Ina Coolbrith (as Meg Merrill), "Not an Intercepted Letter," *Californian*, February 4, 1865.

82 **By remarrying** Meeting Harte and all quotes: ECW. Later in life, Coolbrith recalled "joshing" with Twain when he was "a lanky red-headed journalist" at the *Call*; see SFLF, p. 362, and "Ina Coolbrith of California's 'Overland Trinity,'" *New York Sun*, December 7, 1919.

82 **One day while** All quotes: ECW.

82 **Francis Brett Harte** First time she saw Thomas Starr King speak: ICLL, p. 83. Harte's stern regimen of rewriting: Noah Brooks, "Bret Harte in California," *Century Magazine* 58.3 (July 1899), p. 447, and Noah Brooks, "Bret Harte: A Biographical and Critical Sketch,"

Overland Monthly 40.3 (Sept. 1902), pp. 201–202, 206. In the latter, Brooks writes, "Undoubtedly, when [Harte] re-wrote a story many times, he contrived to shorten it with each successive draft. Artists of less genius would have maimed while they condensed; Harte's 'boiling down' never gave his work the appearance of writing that had been often re-written and often worked over for the mere sake of reducing its volume."

83 **Coolbrith found him** Later, Coolbrith would recall "what handsome men lived in San Francisco in the old days." "It was hard to tell whether Frank Harte or Charlie Stoddard was the better-looking," she remembered; see SFLF, p. 362. *"manly"*: ICHC. Harte's flattering remark: BH to IC, May 31, 1865, BANC. *"Every man . . ."*: BH to IC, June 3, 1865, BANC. Harte's letter was in response to Coolbrith's "Fragment from an Unfinished Poem"; see ICLL, pp. 85–86.

83 **By the summer** All quotes: "What the Press Says of It," *Californian*, June 4, 1864.

84 **The *Californian* made** *"the best interests of California"*: see advertisement for the *Californian* in *San Francisco Daily Evening Bulletin*, August 6, 1864. Climate too mild: "Defects of a Fine Climate," *Californian*, October 8, 1864. People too ignorant, culture too crude: "Home Culture," *Californian*, November 11, 1865. For more of the *Californian's* contrarian, critical, satirical spirit, see "Howling as One of the Fine Arts," June 4, 1864; "The Weakness and Divisions of the Protestant Churches in California," July 16, 1864; "Murder as a Mathematical Certainty," August 20, 1864; "The Wires Working," February 18, 1865; Bret Harte, "On the Decay of Professional Begging," June 17, 1865; "The Pioneers," September 16, 1865; "The Latest Views of an Honest Miner," November 25, 1865; "California Nomenclature," December 2, 1865. The December 3, 1864, issue of the *Californian* carried a portion of a new novel by Mary Elizabeth Braddon, along with an editorial critical of the genre, entitled "'Sensational Novels.'" *"to pander . . ."*: *Californian*, June 4, 1864. See also SFLF, pp. 180–181.

84 **Charles Warren Stoddard published** The poem was "Drowned! Drowned!!," published in the *Californian*, July 23, 1864. First year at Brayton Academy: CRP, chap. 3, pp. 4–8; CSCWS, pp. 60–64; GP, pp. 21–27.

85 **By the end** *"nervous wreck"*: CRP, chap. 3, p. 8. Stoddard's departure for Hawaii: CSCWS, pp. 78–79. Daydreams: CRP, chap. 3, p. 9. *"the whole current"*: ibid.

85 **By the time** *"Heaven on the half shell"*: Mark Twain, "'Mark Twain' in the Metropolis," p. 10. Extravagances: ibid. and MTR, p. 396. Plan to sell mining stock, and plummeting value: SLC to Orion Clemens, May 26, 1864, in MTL, vol. 1, pp. 299–301, and SLC to Orion Clemens and Mary E. Clemens, August 13 and 14, 1864, in MTL, vol. 1, pp. 307–309. See also MTAL, pp. 143–146.

85 **Once, in a vainer** Twain joining the *Morning Call*: James E. Caron, *Mark Twain*, p. 164, and MTAL, p. 144. Maguire's Opera House event: Mark Twain, "Parting Presentation," *Alta California*, June 13, 1864, in ET&S, vol. 2, pp. 5–8.

86 **In San Francisco he** Life with Steve Gillis: SLC to William Wright (Dan De Quille), July 15, 1864, in MTL, vol. 1, pp. 303–305; SLC to Jane Lampton Clemens and Pamela A. Moffett, September 25, 1864, in MTL, vol. 1, pp. 311–314; and MTB, vol. 1, pp. 253–256. Steve Gillis's appearance: MTB, vol. 1, p. 213.

86 **These diversions aside** A reporter for the *Call*: TAMT, pp. 155–157; MTB, vol. 1, pp. 257–258; and Edgar Marquess Branch, introduction to Mark Twain, *Clemens of the "Call,"* ed. Edgar Marquess Branch (Berkeley: University of California Press, 1969), pp. 1–35. For his *Call* articles, see ibid., pp. 40–278, and ET&S, vol. 2, pp. 31–61.

86 **It's hard to imagine** *"soulless drudgery"* and *"awful slavery . . ."*: TAMT, p. 156. See also James E. Caron, *Mark Twain*, pp. 164–165.

86 **To console himself** Mild hoaxing: "What a Sky-Rocket Did," *San Francisco Morning Call*, August 12, 1864, in ET&S, vol. 2, pp. 34–37. Albert S. Evans represented the city's more respectable classes, and feuded not only with Twain but with San Francisco Bohemia as a whole. He invented a character named Armand Leonidas Stiggers, a caricature of the

urban Bohemian. The *Californian* frequently ridiculed Evans in its pages. His rivalry with Twain: James E. Caron, *Mark Twain*, p. 196; ET&S, vol. 2, pp. 39, 329; Nigey Lennon, *The Sagebrush Bohemian: Mark Twain in California* (New York: Paragon, 1990), pp. 50–51; and Joanna Levin, *Bohemia in America*, pp. 116–117. *"He said that..."*: TAMT, p. 157.

87 **Discouraged, Twain almost** The friend was John McComb. His account is quoted in William Montgomery Clemens, *Mark Twain: His Life and Work, A Biographical Sketch* (San Francisco: Clemens, 1892), pp. 56–59. McComb says Twain claimed his salary as a pilot would be $300 per month. At the *Call*, he made between $100 and $140 per month. *"You have a style..."* and *"If you don't..."*: ibid., p. 58. *"unfettered..."*: Mark Twain, *Life on the Mississippi*, ed. James M. Cox (New York: Penguin, 1986 [1883]), p. 122.

87 **San Francisco broadened** *"fifty-six Chinese dialects"*: TAMT, p. 156.

88 **But San Francisco's greatest** *"sterling literary weekly"* and *"Some of the most..."*: *San Francisco Morning Call*, September 4, 1864, included in Mark Twain, *Clemens of the "Call,"* p. 63.

88 **He soon had** The building at 612 Commercial Street housed the offices of the *Golden Era*, the *San Francisco Morning Call*, and the annex of the local branch of the US Mint, where Harte worked; see Roy Morris Jr., *Lighting Out for the Territory: How Samuel Clemens Headed West and Became Mark Twain* (New York: Simon & Schuster, 2010), p. 158, and TAMT, pp. 161, 164. All quotes: Henry J. W. Dam, "A Morning with Bret Harte," p. 47.

88 **To Twain, Harte** All quotes: TAMT, pp. 163–164. Harte took over as editor of the *Californian* from September 10 to November 19, 1864; see ET&S, vol. 2, p. 67. Harte would also take over the following year, from April to December 1865, and then again from April to August 1866; see MTR, p. 699.

89 **It was a miracle** *"spoke in a slow..."*: Henry J. W. Dam, "A Morning with Bret Harte," p. 47.

89 **The meeting went** All quotes: SLC to Jane Lampton Clemens and Pamela A. Moffett, September 25, 1864, in MTL, vol. 1, p. 312.

89 **He would soon** *"It was true..."* and *"broad hints..."*: James J. Ayers, *Gold and Sunshine: Reminiscences of Early California* (Boston: Richard G. Badger, 1922), p. 224. *"It was like a father..."*: TAMT, p. 160. Long-delayed revenge: ibid., pp. 160–161. See also MTR, p. 404, and MTAL, p. 146. Barnes's account: George E. Barnes, "Mark Twain as He Was Known during His Stay on the Pacific Slope," p. 48.

90 **Losing his job** $25 a week at the *Call* versus $50 a month at the *Californian*: SLC to Jane Lampton Clemens and Pamela A. Moffett, September 25, 1864, in MTL, vol. 1, p. 312. *"It was a terrible..."*: George E. Barnes, "Mark Twain as He Was Known during His Stay on the Pacific Slope," p. 48. *"Mark was the laziest..."*: quoted in Nigey Lennon, *The Sagebrush Bohemian*, p. 49.

90 **For the next** Twain's nine pieces for the *Californian* were "A Notable Conundrum," October 1, 1864; "Concerning the Answer to That Conundrum," October 8, 1864; "Still Further Concerning That Conundrum," October 15, 1864; "Whereas," October 22, 1864; "A Touching Story of George Washington's Boyhood," October 29, 1864; "Daniel in the Lion's Den— and Out Again All Right," November 5, 1864; "The Killing of Julius Caesar 'Localized,'" November 12, 1864; "A Full and Reliable Account of the Extraordinary Meteoric Shower of Last Saturday Night," November 19, 1864; "Lucretia Smith's Soldier," December 3, 1864. These pieces are included in ET&S, vol. 2, pp. 66–133. *"deeply grieved..."*: Mark Twain, "Whereas," ET&S, vol. 2, p. 91. Twain treated the Civil War more directly in "Lucretia Smith's Soldier," about a woman who shames her lover into enlisting.

91 **Before Twain could dig** Steve Gillis's beatdown of the bartender: William R. Gillis, *Memories of Mark Twain and Steve Gillis* (Sonora, CA: The Banner, 1924), pp. 29–33; MTB, vol. 1, p. 265; and MTAL, p. 149. Twain left San Francisco on December 4, 1864; see ET&S, vol. 2, p. 134.

91 **If Gillis hadn't** *"queer vicissitudes"*: MTR, p. 405.

91 **In December 1864** Stoddard stayed in Nuuanu Valley, two miles from Honolulu. His lounging time and journey with Perry: CSCWS, pp. 79–82, and GP, pp. 27–30.

92   **Touring the island** Week at Hilo: CSCWS, p. 81. All quotes: Charles Warren Stoddard, "Kane-Aloha," *The Island of Tranquil Delights: A South Sea Idyl and Others* (Boston: Herbert B. Turner, 1905), pp. 260–261.

92   **Perry strongly disapproved** Stoddard calls Perry his "chaperone" throughout his sketch "Kane-Aloha." *"I cut loose . . ."*: from an unpublished autobiographical sketch, quoted in CSCWS, p. 82. *"We reveled in . . ."*: Charles Warren Stoddard, "Kane-Aloha," p. 268. *"We had certainly . . ."*: ibid., p. 271.

92   **What kind of transgression** Emotional parting: ibid., pp. 273–276. For an overview of Stoddard's views on the Pacific, see Paul Lyons, "From Man-Eaters to Spam-Eaters: Cannibal Tours, Lotus-Eaters, and the (Anti)Development of Late Nineteenth- and Early Twentieth-Century Imaginings of Oceania," *American Pacificism: Oceania in the U.S. Imagination* (New York: Routledge, 2006), pp. 122–123.

93   **Back home, he** *"never become . . ."*: CRP, chap. 3, p. 9. Stoddard would contribute seventeen poems to the *Californian* in 1865; see CSCWS, p. 87.

93   **He couldn't have** Eastern plagiarism and Webb's protests: *Californian*, February 4, 1865, and ET&S, vol. 2, p. 127. *"nearly bankrupted . . ."*: Charles Henry Webb (as John Paul), *John Paul's Book: Moral and Instructive: Consisting of Travels, Tales, Poetry, and Like Fabrications* (Hartford, CT: Columbian Book Company, 1874), p. 540. The *Californian* running out of money: MTAL, p. 153. The paper's offices moved to 532 Merchant Street, between Montgomery and Sansome Streets, as announced in the *Californian*, April 8, 1865.

93   **But the future** Celebrations in SF: *San Francisco Daily Evening Bulletin*, April 4, 1865.

94   **At 10:20 p.m.** Times of Lincoln's assassination and death: Edward Steers Jr., *The Lincoln Assassination Encyclopedia* (New York: HarperCollins, 2010), p. xxxviii. Mob attack on anti-Lincoln papers: *San Francisco Daily Evening Bulletin*, April 17, 1865.

94   **That night** Funeral procession: *San Francisco Daily Evening Bulletin*, April 19, 1865.

94   *I have read* Harte's reaction and all quotes: Bret Harte, "Our Last Offering," *Californian*, April 22, 1865.

95   **Everyone knew that** All quotes: ibid. Lincoln as "rail-splitter": Ronald C. White Jr., *A. Lincoln: A Biography* (New York: Random House, 2009), pp. 3–4, 321, 331.

96   **In the summer** Harte published thirteen "Condensed Novels" in the *Californian* between July 1865 and June 1866, later reprinted in F. Bret Harte, *Condensed Novels and Other Papers* (New York: G. W. Carleton, 1867), pp. 11–147. Parody of Dickens: "The Haunted Man," ibid., pp. 56–66. Parody of Braddon: "Selina Sedilia," ibid., pp. 29–39. Parody of Cooper: "Muck-a-Muck: A Modern Indian Novel, After Cooper," ibid., pp. 11–20.

96   **He showed less** No fiction during his years at the *Californian*: BHGS, pp. 25–26, and BHAN, p. 78. Birth of Francis King Harte: BHAN, p. 73. Feather duster on his back: Alvin Fay Harlow, *Bret Harte of the Old West* (New York: J. Messner, 1943), p. 225.

96   **His friends admired** All quotes: Charles Henry Webb, "Inigoings," *Californian*, February 10, 1866.

97   **Anna Griswold Harte** Anna Griswold Harte: Josephine Clifford McCrackin, "A Letter from a Friend," *Overland Monthly* 40.3 (Sept. 1902), pp. 222–225; BHAN, pp. 73, 91; Richard O'Connor, *Bret Harte: A Biography* (Boston: Little, Brown, 1966), p. 84; and BHGS, pp. 21–23. In 1941, Harte's grandson Geoffrey Bret Harte wrote, "My grandparents had little in common. In the final analysis, what my grandfather most wanted was peace in the home and this I believe he never got. In our age this problem would have been solved by divorce; in theirs such a course was unthinkable." Quoted BHGS, pp. 22–23. Photographs of Anna: ibid., p. 24, and BHAN, p. 168. *"positively plain"*: Elinor Mead Howells to Victoria and Aurelia H. Howells, March 17, 1871, in Elinor Mead Howells, *If Not Literature: Letters of Elinor Mead Howells*, ed. Ginette de B. Merrill and George Arms (Columbus: Ohio State University Press, 1988), p. 137.

97   **The *Californian* helped** Coolbrith's appearance: George Wharton James, "Ina Donna Coolbrith: An Historical Sketch and Appreciation," p. 315; ICLL, p. 113; and Charles Warren

Stoddard, "Ina D. Coolbrith," *Magazine of Poetry: A Quarterly Review* 1.1 (1889), p. 313. *"the ripe glow...":* ibid. Anna Griswold was from New York, the daughter of a wealthy businessman. *"might easily have...," "the contralto voice," "gentle melancholy,"* and *"Spanish and semitropical":* Charles Warren Stoddard, "Ina D. Coolbrith," p. 313. *"We used to shout...":* ICHC.

98 **Coolbrith gave Harte** Ina Coolbrith, "The Mother's Grief," *Californian,* March 25, 1865. Pair of meandering essays: Ina Coolbrith (as Meg Merrill), "Not an Intercepted Letter," *Californian,* February 4, 1865, and Ina Coolbrith (as Meg Merrill), "Meg Merrilliana: A Declaration of First Love," *Californian,* March 4, 1865. *"Unfortunately, I seldom...":* ibid.

98 **Coolbrith would never** Menken's marriages: Michael Foster and Barbara Foster, *A Dangerous Woman: The Life, Loves, and Scandals of Adah Isaacs Menken, 1835–1868, America's Original Superstar* (Guilford, CT: Lyons, 2011), p. 307. *"Why doesn't some...":* IC to CWS, May 25, 1874, HUNT. *"How grand the Bay...":* Ina Coolbrith (as Meg Merrill), "Meg Merrilliana: A Declaration of First Love," *Californian,* March 4, 1865.

100 **On December 4, 1864** Twain's arrival at Jackass Hill: MTAL, p. 149. *"forlorn remnant":* TAMT, p. 176. Twain's memories of mining country: ibid., pp. 175–177, and MTR, pp. 391–395, 412–420. See MTR, p. 704, for information on Jackass Hill. In 1864, California produced $24 million worth of gold; in 1865, it produced $17.9 million. Compare this with the gold rush peak of $81.2 million in 1852. See "Appendix A: Gold Production" in Rodman W. Paul, *California Gold,* p. 345.

100 **The cabin at Jackass Hill** *"headquarters of all Bohemians...":* quoted in Roy Morris Jr., *Lighting Out for the Territory,* p. 168. Harte's stay at Jackass Hill: BHAN, pp. 43–46, and TAMT, pp. 162–163. *"ragged and hungry":* quoted in Charles Carroll Goodwin, *As I Remember Them,* p. 93. Jim Gillis demanding his money back: ibid.

100 **Twain was in** Early days in Jim Gillis's cabin: MTAL, pp. 150–151; MTB, vol. 1, pp. 266–270; and MTN, pp. 68–78. His last piece for the *Californian* was "Lucretia Smith's Soldier" on December 3, 1864; his next would be "An Unbiased Criticism," on March 18, 1865.

101 **But rural California** Byron, Shakespeare, and Dickens: MTN, p. 70. Jim Gillis: Bernard DeVoto, *Mark Twain's America,* pp. 169–172; MTAL, p. 150; and TAMT, pp. 181–182. *"stand up before...," "enjoying each...,"* and *"monstrous fabrications":* ibid.

101 **In Angel's Camp** Traveling to Angel's Camp in late January 1865: MTN, pp. 71–72. Twain's attempt at mining: William R. Gillis, *Memories of Mark Twain and Steve Gillis,* pp. 37–38, and MTB, vol. 1, pp. 270–273. *"marooned miners":* TAMT, p. 176. *"T.—Age 38...":* MTN, p. 74. *"beans & dishwater"* and *"Hellfire, General Debility...":* ibid., p. 78. *"Coleman with his jumping...":* ibid., p. 80.

102 **The story involved** *"austere facts"* and *"was not telling...":* Mark Twain, "Private History of the 'Jumping Frog' Story," in *Collected Tales, Sketches, Speeches, and Essays,* vol. 2, p. 153. Albert Bigelow Paine, in MTB, vol. 1, p. 271, claims that the narrator of the story was Ben Coon, identified in Twain's notebook as a riverboat pilot from Illinois whom he met at Angel's Camp; see MTN, p. 75. However, Twain never definitively identified the tale's narrator; see ibid.

102 **Quite possibly they** Provenance of jumping frog tale: Roger Penn Cuff, "Mark Twain's Use of California Folklore in His Jumping Frog Story," *Journal of American Folklore* 65.256 (April–June 1952), pp. 155–158; Hennig Cohen, "Twain's Jumping Frog: Folktale to Literature to Folktale," *Western Folklore* 22.1 (Jan. 1963), pp. 17–18; Bernard DeVoto, *Mark Twain's America,* pp. 172–175; and Oscar Lewis, *The Origin of "The Celebrated Jumping Frog of Calaveras County"* (San Francisco: Book Club of California, 1931), pp. 5–27. A version of the story had appeared in the *Sonora Herald* in 1853, written by James W. E. Townsend, who had worked for both the *Virginia City Territorial Enterprise* and the *Golden Era.* It's possible that Twain read it in the *Herald,* heard it from Townsend, or first discovered it much earlier, in Missouri.

102 **Twain adored the story** *"one gleam..."* and *"quoted from..."*: SLC to James N. Gillis, January 26, 1870, in MTL, vol. 4, p. 36. Twain returned to San Francisco on February 26, 1865; see MTN, p. 82. *"offences against public decency"*: "California Nomenclature," *Californian*, December 2, 1865; see also "The Pioneers," *Californian*, September 16, 1865. *"He said the men...," "half unconsciously...,"* and *"It was as graphic..."*: Henry J. W. Dam, "A Morning with Bret Harte," p. 47.

103 **Twain mimicked the** Discovering Ward's letters: MTN, p. 82. *"Write it..."*: quoted in MTB, vol. 1, p. 277. See also ET&S, vol. 2, pp. 264–265.

103 **Even with the deadline** Twain's delays: ET&S, vol. 2, pp. 265–269. "The idea of writing the Jumping Frog Story only very slowly took shape in my mind," he explained in 1897. Twain's return to SF literary life: MTAL, pp. 152–153.

103 **He wasn't the same** Mark Twain, "An Unbiased Criticism," *Californian*, March 18, 1865, in ET&S, vol. 2, pp. 134–143.

103 **He was experimenting** For a selection of Twain's pieces from this period, see ET&S, vol. 2, pp. 134–261. Twain began writing for the *Enterprise* again in June 1865: Edgar Marquess Branch, introduction to ET&S, vol. 1, p. 30. Most of his *Enterprise* letters are lost, but a handful remain. For a selection of his anti-police articles, see Mark Twain, "Thief Catching," *Virginia City Territorial Enterprise*, December 19, 1865, included in Mark Twain, *Mark Twain's San Francisco*, ed. Bernard Taper (Berkeley, CA: Heyday, 2003 [1963]), pp. 157–158; Mark Twain, "The Black Hole of San Francisco," *Territorial Enterprise*, December 29, 1865, included ibid., pp. 171–173; and Mark Twain, "What Have the Police Been Doing?" *Territorial Enterprise*, reprinted in *Golden Era*, January 21, 1866, included ibid., pp. 189–191. Twain also wrote about the police for the *San Francisco Dramatic Chronicle*, and produced a couple of parodies of children's literature for the *San Francisco Youths' Companion*; see James E. Caron, *Mark Twain*, pp. 202–208, and MTB, vol. 1, p. 264. *"Mark Twain is still..."*: *San Francisco Examiner*, February 10, 1866, quoted in Fred Kaplan, *The Singular Mark Twain: A Biography* (New York: Anchor, 2005 [2003]), p. 137.

104 **Twain had always** Moralist of the Main: MTAL, p. 153. *"All right..."*: Mark Twain, *The Adventures of Huckleberry Finn* (New York: Harper & Brothers, 1918 [1885]), p. 297.

104 **As a prankster** Praise from *Gold Hill News*: "The Californian," *Gold Hill News*, July 5, 1863, quoted in Edgar Marquess Branch, introduction to ET&S, vol. 1, p. 31.

105 **He also earned** *"foremost"* and *"among..."*: "American Humor and Humorists," *New York Round Table*, September 9, 1865, quoted in Edgar Marquess Branch, introduction to ET&S, vol. 1, p. 32. Rising eastern profile: ibid., pp. 32–33, and ET&S, vol. 2, p. 268. *"To my thinking..."*: Charles Henry Webb, "Letter from San Francisco," *Sacramento Union*, November 3, 1865, quoted in Edgar Marquess Branch, introduction to ET&S, vol. 1, p. 33.

CHAPTER FOUR

109 **The American frontier** Daniel Boone wrestling bears: Robert Morgan, *Boone: A Biography* (Chapel Hill, NC: Algonquin, 2007), pp. xiv–xvi. Davy Crockett battling a twelve-foot catfish: from the 1836 edition of *Davy Crockett's Almanack*, discussed in Michael A. Lofaro, introduction to James Atkins Shackford, *David Crockett: The Man and the Legend*, ed. John B. Shackford (Lincoln: University of Nebraska Press, 1994 [1956]), p. xii. Utah grasshoppers: C. Grant Loomis, "Hart's Tall Tales from Nevada," *California Folklore Quarterly* 4.3 (July 1945), p. 238, and Bernard DeVoto, *Mark Twain's America*, p. 150. Arkansas corn: Thomas Bangs Thorpe, "The Big Bear of Arkansas," in *Southern Frontier Humor*, eds. M. Thomas Inge and Ed Piacentino, p. 134. *"borderland of fable"*: Bernard DeVoto, *Mark Twain's America*, p. 149. See also Richard Slotkin, *Regeneration Through Violence: The Mythology of the American Frontier, 1600–1860* (Norman: University of Oklahoma Press, 2000 [1973]).

110 **These forms found** Mark Twain, "Jim Smiley and His Jumping Frog," *New York Saturday Press*, November 18, 1865, included in ET&S, vol. 2, pp. 282–288.

110   **The path to publication** Two incomplete drafts: "The Only Reliable Account of the Celebrated Jumping Frog of Calaveras County" and "Angel's Camp Constable," both written
between September 1 and October 16, 1865. See ET&S, vol. 2, pp. 262–281.

111   **Money always made** John Marshall Clemens's bad business sense: MTAL, pp. 9–10, 14–15,
20, 23, 38. Wages from *Virginia City Territorial Enterprise* and *San Francisco Dramatic
Chronicle*: SLC to Orion and Mary E. Clemens, October 19 and 20, 1865, in MTL, vol. 1, p.
324. Between July and December 1865, Twain wrote only seven articles for the *Californian*;
see ibid., p. 325. He published "Advice for Good Little Boys" in the *San Francisco Youths'
Companion*, July 1, 1865, and "Advice for Good Little Girls" in the same magazine on either
July 1 or July 8, 1865; see ET&S, vol. 2, pp. 240–245. He also published three letters in the
Napa County Reporter, from November to December 1865; see ibid., pp. 297–299, 371–375,
380–384, 481–512.

111   **In *Roughing It*** "*slinking,*" "*I slunk from...,*" and "*I felt meaner...*": MTR, pp. 405–406.
His reminiscences in *Roughing It* may be a composite of two periods of financial hardship:
the first in 1864, before his departure for Jackass Hill, and the second in 1865, after his return to SF. See MTR, p. 701. "*There is now...,*" "*the end of his credit,*" and "*Having become...*": "A Sheik on the Move," *San Francisco Morning Call*, October 29, 1865. "*I put the
pistol...*": from a marginal note in Twain's copy of *Letters of James Russell Lowell*, dated
April 21, 1909, quoted in MTL, vol. 1, p. 325. He recalled his near suicide as an "experience
of 1866," but it probably took place in late 1865, before the publication of "Jim Smiley and
His Jumping Frog."

112   **Unhappiness forced him** "*I never had but...*": SLC to Orion and Mary E. Clemens, October
19 and 20, 1865, in MTL, vol. 1, pp. 322–323.

113   **This epiphany marked** "*drop all trifling...*": ibid., p. 324.

113   **His new self-knowledge** "*I am utterly...*" and "*If I do not...*": ibid. "*It is only now...*": ibid.,
p. 323. Praise from *New York Round Table* and its effect in SF: Edgar Marquess Branch,
"Introduction," in ET&S, vol. 1, pp. 32–33, and ET&S, vol. 2, p. 268.

113   **Out of this crisis** Twain probably wrote the final version of the story between October 16
and 18, 1865, and sent it on the Pacific Mail steamship that departed San Francisco on October 18; see ET&S, vol. 2, p. 269. Carleton passing the item to Clapp: ibid., p. 270; MTN, p.
80; and MTB, vol. 1, pp. 277–278.

114   **Twain modeled the** Southwestern frame: Kenneth S. Lynn, *Mark Twain and Southwestern
Humor*, pp. 64–65, and Hennig Cohen and William B. Dillingham, "Introduction" in *Humor of the Old Southwest*, ed. Hennig Cohen and William B. Dillingham (Athens: University of Georgia Press, 1994 [1964]), pp. xxix–xxxi. See also James E. Caron, *Mark Twain*, pp.
28–32.

114   **At first, "Jim Smiley"** Use of Pike County dialect: David Carkeet, "The Dialects in *Huckleberry Finn*," p. 326. All quotes: Mark Twain, "Jim Smiley and His Jumping Frog," *New
York Saturday Press*, November 18, 1865, in ET&S, vol. 2, pp. 284–285.

115   **Twain inverts the** Twain's inversion of Southwestern conventions: Kenneth S. Lynn, *Mark
Twain and Southwestern Humor*, pp. 145–147.

115   **"Jim Smiley and"** "*set all New York*" and "*I have been asked...*": Richard Ogden, "Letter
from New York," written December 10, 1865, published in *Alta California*, January 10,
1866, quoted in ET&S, vol. 2, p. 271. Eastern praise: ibid. "*No reputation...*": Edward H.
House, "Mark Twain as a Lecturer," *New York Tribune*, May 11, 1867, included in
TIHOT, p. 64.

116   **By the end** "*an English graft*": Bret Harte, "Our Last Offering," *Californian*, April 22, 1865.

117   **No one recognized** "*those New York people...*": SLC to Jane Lampton Clemens and Pamela
A. Moffett, January 20, 1866, in MTL, vol. 1, p. 327.

117   **Harte followed Twain's** "*[I]t will never...*": Henry J. W. Dam, "A Morning with Bret
Harte," p. 48. Harte reprinted the story as "The Celebrated Jumping Frog of Calaveras
County" in the *Californian*, December 16, 1865. For an overview of the changes introduced

by either Harte or Twain, see ET&S, vol. 2, pp. 667–668. *"Though I am..."* and *"I wouldn't..."*: SLC to Jane Lampton Clemens and Pamela A. Moffett, January 20, 1866, in MTL, vol. 1, p. 328.

117 **It began innocently** Origins of *Outcroppings*: BHAN, pp. 80–81, and Bret Harte, "My First Book," in *The Bell-Ringer of Angel's and Other Stories* (Boston: Houghton Mifflin, 1894), pp. 321–327. *"chill wind"* and *"attaining..."*: ibid., p. 324. *"practical business men..."*: ibid., p. 325.

118 **These happened to** Ina Coolbrith contributed "Cupid Kissed Me," "The Mother's Grief," "A Lost Day," and "In the Pouts." Charles Warren Stoddard contributed "At Anchor," "A Fancy," "Through the Shadows," and "Mars." Charles Henry Webb contributed five poems. *"monotonous climate"*: preface to Bret Harte, ed., *Outcroppings: Being Selections of California Verse* (San Francisco: A. Roman, 1866), p. 3.

118 **Predictably, Outcroppings provoked** Response to *Outcroppings*: BHAN, pp. 81–82; BHGS, pp. 27–28; SFLF, pp. 214–217; and Bret Harte, "My First Book," pp. 328–333. *"Bret Harte has given..."*: *San Francisco Dramatic Chronicle*, December 7, 1865. *"contains as little..."*: *Sacramento Union*, December 20, 1865. *"the very trashiest..."*: quoted in BHGS, p. 28. See ibid. for more reviews: a "Bohemian advertising medium" (*San Francisco American Flag*); "purp-stuff" (*Gold Hill News*); "a mutual admiration society" (*Pajaro Times*).

119 **Harte had started** *"One of the most..."* and *"He affects..."*: *Virginia City Territorial Enterprise*, reprinted in *San Francisco Examiner*, January 19, 1866. *"Methinks..."*: Bret Harte, "Tailings: Rejections of California Verse," *Californian*, December 23, 1865, quoted in SFLF, p. 217. For more of the Bohemian counterattack, see *Californian*, December 9, 1865; December 16, 1865; December 23, 1865; and December 30, 1865.

119 **The two camps** Industrialized interior: Earl Pomeroy, *The Pacific Slope*, pp. 46–47, 53.

119 **The struggle over** Self-censorship in California: Bret Harte, "Bohemian Days in San Francisco," pp. 268–269, and Bret Harte, "From California," *Springfield Republican*, May 5, 1866, included in Bret Harte, *Bret Harte's California*, ed. Gary Scharnhorst (Albuquerque: University of New Mexico Press, 1990), pp. 28–30.

120 *Outcroppings'* **critics feared** *"to foster Eastern..."*: Bret Harte, "My First Book," p. 322.

120 **Yet the eastern** Eastern response to *Outcroppings*: "Eastern Assays of California Outcroppings," *Californian*, January 20, 1866, and BHGS, p. 27. *"abused beyond..."*: letter from BH to Anton Roman, quoted BGHS, p. 28. *"We know all..."* and *"poetical asses"*: SLC to Jane Lampton Clemens and Pamela A. Moffett, January 20, 1866, in MTL, vol. 1, pp. 328–329. A competing volume to *Outcroppings* was eventually published as *Poetry of the Pacific* (San Francisco: Pacific, 1867); see MTL, vol. 1, pp. 330–331.

120 **By early 1866** *"'Deep Diggings,' in..."*: *Sacramento Bee*, January 15, 1866. *"rare good taste"*: quoted in BHGS, p. 28.

121 **Inside a quiet** Coolbrith's parlor: Charles Warren Stoddard, "Ina D. Coolbrith," p. 313, and Charles Warren Stoddard, "In Old Bohemia II: The 'Overland' and the Overlanders," pp. 268–269. The address of Coolbrith's house was 1302 Taylor Street, between Washington and Jackson Streets, as provided in Henry G. Langley, *San Francisco Directory*, 1867–1868; see ICLL, p. 81. *"She was the center..."*: Joaquin Miller, "California's Fair Poet," *San Francisco Morning Call*, August 21, 1892. *"Those eyes..."*: George Wharton James, "Ina Donna Coolbrith," *National Magazine* 26.3 (June 1907), p. 315. *"Miss Coolbrith..."*: "Outcroppings," *Nation*, December 7, 1865, quoted in "Eastern Assays of California Outcroppings," *Californian*, January 20, 1866.

122 **Her parlor gave** The architectural variety of SF is described in Amelia Ransome Neville, *The Fantastic City*, p. 192: "In residence districts one found a varied assortment of architectural freaks, and downtown still had a haphazard aspect, with low frame structures, surviving from the fifties, scattered among well-built business blocks." *"hill of Memories"*: Ina Coolbrith, "From Russian Hill," in *Wings of Sunset* (Boston and New York: Houghton Mifflin, 1929), p. 15.

122   **Harte came often** Decline of the *Californian* and Webb's departure: SFLF, pp. 180, 184, and MTR, p. 699. Webb left San Francisco on April 18, 1866. Harte edited the paper until August 1, 1866, when he was replaced by James F. Bowman. The *Californian* survived for another two years; its final issue appeared on November 21, 1868.

122   **Charles Warren Stoddard also became** *"I was nowhere..."*: Charles Warren Stoddard, "In Old Bohemia II," p. 269. Leaving Brayton Academy: CSCWS, p. 86. *"It was now evident..."*: CRP, chap. 3, p. 9. *"restful room"*: Charles Warren Stoddard, "In Old Bohemia II," p. 269. In CRP, chap. 4, p. 4, Stoddard says that Harte had by this point become his "guide, philosopher and friend." *"He would jump..."*: an interview in the *Santa Barbara Morning Press*, October 31, 1908, included in the Stoddard clippings at BANC. *"In mood he..."* and *"I used to say..."*: ICCWS.

123   *Outcroppings* **brought them** *"the abuse which..."*: CRP, chap. 4, p. 2. *"the worst specimens..."*: *Virginia City Territorial Enterprise*, quoted in *San Francisco Evening Bulletin*, January 6, 1866. *"no satisfaction"* and *"It was in reality..."*: ICCWS.

123   **In 1866, shortly** Stoddard's compliment-fishing campaign: CSCWS, pp. 91–94; GP, pp. 32–34; and CRP, chap. 4, pp. 3–5. *"I was hoping..."*: CRP, chap. 4, p. 3.

123   **Incredibly, most replied** *"I am much..."*: Ralph Waldo Emerson to CWS, quoted in CSCWS, p. 93. *"I have read..."*: Alfred Tennyson to CWS, December 28, 1866, quoted ibid. *"quite struck"*: Herman Melville to CWS, quoted in GP, p. 33. *"of the very..."*: John Stuart Mill to CWS, quoted ibid. *"an apology for..."*: Oliver Wendell Holmes to CWS, quoted in CRP, chap. 4, p. 4.

124   **But Stoddard was** *"ethereal unreality"*: ICHC. *"as much out..."*: BH to Henry Whitney Bellows, September 15, 1866, quoted in BHAN, p. 89. Stoddard beginning to plan his book: CRP, chap. 4, p. 4, and GP, p. 34.

124   **Twain could relate** *"[p]oor, pitiful...,"* *"scribbling...,"* and *"blinded..."*: SLC to Orion and Mary E. Clemens, October 19 and 20, 1865, in MTL, vol. 1, p. 323. *"I loved him..."*: ICCWS. *"He was refined..."*: AMT, p. 161.

124   **By 1866, he** Origins of Twain's Hawaii trip: MTAL, pp. 159–160, and MTL, vol. 1, p. 331. *"I am so sorry...,"* *"the cream of the town,"* *"Where could..."*: SLC to Jane Lampton Clemens and Pamela A. Moffett, January 20, 1866, MTL, pp. 329–330.

125   **He wouldn't make** Twain departed San Francisco on the *Ajax* on March 7, 1866. For his agreement with the *Sacramento Union*, see SLC to William R. Gillis, March 3[?], 1866, and SLC to Jane Lampton Clemens and Pamela A. Moffett, March 5, 1866, in MTL, vol. 1, pp. 332–334. *"I am tired..."*: SLC to Orion and Mollie Clemens, December 13, 1865, ibid., p. 326. See also MTN, pp. 94–95.

125   **In his four months** See Mark Twain, *Letters from the Sandwich Islands: Written for the Sacramento Union by Mark Twain*, ed. G. Ezra Dane (Stanford, CA: Stanford University Press, 1938). These letters formed the basis for an unpublished book, later absorbed into chaps. 62–78 of *Roughing It*. *"I have not written..."*: SLC to Mollie Clemens, May 22, 1866, in MTL, vol. 1, p. 341. Historical background on Hawaii and overview of Twain's trip: MTN, pp. 95–108. Twain's Hawaii notebooks: ibid., pp. 110–237.

125   **In the midst** *Hornet* disaster and Twain: David Zmijewski, "The *Hornet*: Mark Twain's Interpretations of a Perilous Journey," *Hawaiian Journal of History*, vol. 33 (1999), pp. 55–67; SLC to Jane Lampton Clemens and Pamela A. Moffett, June 27, 1866, in MTL, vol. 1, pp. 347–349; Mark Twain, "My Début as a Literary Person," *Century Magazine* 59.1 (Nov. 1899), pp. 76–88; and MTAL, pp. 161–162. Twain's article appeared on the front page of the *Sacramento Union*, July 19, 1866.

126   **He was on fire** Twain demanding $300 from *Sacramento Union*: Mark Twain, "My Début as a Literary Person," p. 77. His magazine piece appeared as "Forty-Three Days in an Open Boat," *Harper's New Monthly Magazine* 34.199 (Dec. 1866), pp. 104–113, although *Harper's* misidentified him as "Mark Swain." The article benefited enormously from the fact that Twain accompanied three of the *Hornet* survivors back to the United States. This

gave him the opportunity to interview them, and to copy the contents of two of their journals.

126 **His motive, as always** Ward's earnings at San Francisco debut: Edward P. Hingston, *The Genial Showman: Reminiscences of the Life of Artemus Ward, and Pictures of a Showman's Career in the Western World* (London: John Camden Hotten, 1871), p. 299. Ward's lucrative career: Mark Twain, "Artemus Ward Lecture," in Mark Twain, *Mark Twain Speaking*, ed. Paul Fatout (Iowa City: University of Iowa Press, 2006 [1976]), p. 45. After his return to SF, Twain worked on turning his *Union* letters into a book manuscript. He had abandoned the project by June 1867; see MTN, pp. 103, 176–177. Origins of first lecture: Fred W. Lorch, *The Trouble Begins at Eight: Mark Twain's Lecture Tours* (Ames: Iowa State University Press, 1968), pp. 25–26, and MTR, pp. 533–534.

126 **One rainy evening** All quotes: George E. Barnes, "Mark Twain as He Was Known during His Stay on the Pacific Coast," in TIHOT, p. 60.

127 **Happily, Twain obeyed** Marketing campaign: MTAL, p. 163, and MTR, p. 533. *"A SPLENDID ORCHESTRA . . ."* and *"The Trouble . . ."*: from an advertisement in the *Daily Alta California*, September 28, 1866.

127 **Twain's promotional push** Advance sales: Paul Fatout, *Mark Twain on the Lecture Circuit* (Bloomington: Indiana University Press, 1960), p. 36. *"We have no . . ."*: *San Francisco Morning Call*, September 30, 1866, quoted ibid., p. 36. *"Those who wish . . ."*: *San Francisco Evening Bulletin*, October 2, 1866, quoted ibid., p. 37. Rumors: ibid., p. 36, and Fred W. Lorch, *The Trouble Begins at Eight*, p. 26.

128 **Several years later** *"the most distressed . . ."* and *"I grieved that . . ."*: MTR, p. 533.

128 **On the evening** Descriptions of premiere: Paul Fatout, *Mark Twain on the Lecture Circuit*, p. 38; Fred W. Lorch, *The Trouble Begins at Eight*, p. 29; and *San Francisco Evening Bulletin*, October 3, 1866. *"It is perhaps fortunate . . ."*: ibid. *"the regular opera . . ."*: quoted in Paul Fatout, *Mark Twain on the Lecture Circuit*, p. 38. *"a big claque"*: Bailey Millard, "Mark Twain in San Francisco," *The Bookman: A Magazine of Literature and Life* 31.4 (June 1910), p. 371.

128 **At eight o'clock** Crowd's reaction and Twain's first moments onstage: Fred W. Lorch, *The Trouble Begins at Eight*, p. 29, and MTAL, p. 168. *"I was in the middle . . ."*: MTR, p. 535.

128 **For seventy-five minutes** *"brilliant success"* and *"word painting"*: *San Francisco Evening Bulletin*, October 3, 1866. Description of lecture: ibid.; Fred W. Lorch, *The Trouble Begins at Eight*, pp. 30–32; Paul Fatout, *Mark Twain on the Lecture Circuit*, pp. 42–43, 47; and MTAL, pp. 167–169. The audience was especially impressed with Twain's eloquent description of the eruption of the Kilauea volcano in Hawaii.

130 **Even Harte came** All quotes: Bret Harte, "From California," *Springfield Republican*, October 27, 1866, included in Bret Harte, *Bret Harte's California*, ed. Gary Scharnhorst, p. 104. The first series of James Russell Lowell's collected *Biglow Papers* appeared in 1848; the second series appeared in 1867.

130 **He captured** *"I think I recognize . . ."*: Bret Harte, "From California," *Springfield Republican*, October 27, 1866, included in Bret Harte, *Bret Harte's California*, ed. Gary Scharnhorst, p. 104.

131 **Twain's total take** $400: Fred W. Lorch, *The Trouble Begins at Eight*, p. 33. Twain's tour through California and Nevada: *ibid.*, pp. 35–41, and Paul Fatout, *Mark Twain on the Lecture Circuit*, pp. 45–56.

131 **The climax came** Performances in Virginia City and Carson City: Fred W. Lorch, *The Trouble Begins at Eight*, pp. 40–41, and Paul Fatout, *Mark Twain on the Lecture Circuit*, pp. 54–55. *"hurricane of applause"*: Steve Gillis, quoted ibid., p. 54. Carson City invitation: MTAL, p. 166; SLC to Abraham V. Z. Curry and Others, November 1, 1866, in MTL, vol. 1, p. 363; and SLC to Henry G. Blasdel and Others, November 1, 1866, ibid., pp. 364–365.

132 **Back in San Francisco** Return to SF and second lecture: MTAL, p. 170; Fred W. Lorch, *The Trouble Begins at Eight*, pp. 43–45; Paul Fatout, *Mark Twain on the Lecture Circuit*, pp. 58–60. *"be heartily . . ."*: *San Francisco Dramatic Chronicle*, quoted ibid., p. 60. Courts claiming share of proceeds for forfeited bond: Gary Scharnhorst, "Mark Twain's Imbroglio

with the San Francisco Police: Three Lost Texts," *American Literature*, 62.4 (Dec. 1990), p. 691.

132 **Fortunately, he soon** Twain's commission with the *Alta California*: MTAL, pp. 170–171, and MTL, vol. 1, p. 370. Hopes for Hawaii book: MTL, vol. 2, pp. 3–4.

132 **On the evening** Twain's final lecture and all quotes: *Alta California*, December 15, 1866, reprinted in Fred W. Lorch, *The Trouble Begins at Eight*, pp. 49–50, and MTL, vol. 1, p. 373.

133 **Five days later** Twain departed SF on December 15, 1866; see MTL, vol. 2, p. 1. *"than any newspaper…"* and *"fraternity"*: SLC to Jane Lampton Clemens and Family, December 15, 1866, in MTL, vol. 1, p. 373. *"Lincoln of our literature"*: William Dean Howells, *My Mark Twain*, p. 84.

CHAPTER FIVE

135 **It had been** Date of Twain's arrival in NY: MTAL, p. 174. For his impressions of the city, see his letters in *Alta California*, March 28, 1867; July 7, 1867; July 21, 1867; and August 11, 1867. NY as nerve center of new economy: Sven Beckert, *The Monied Metropolis: New York City and the Consolidation of the American Bourgeoisie, 1850–1896* (Cambridge: Cambridge University Press, 2003 [2001]), pp. 145–195. *"no man dreamt…"* and *"original barbarism"*: Mark Twain, "The Sex in New York," *Alta California*, July 21, 1867.

135 **Twain had a talent** *"fidgety, feverish restlessness"*: Mark Twain, "New York," *Alta California*, August 11, 1867.

136 **While Twain elbowed** Construction of Central Pacific in early 1867: David Haward Bain, *Empire Express*, pp. 315–322. Chinese workers: ibid., pp. 208–209, 221–223. Pacific Railway Act of 1862 and its amendment in 1864: ibid., pp. 104–118, 178–180, and Richard White, *Railroaded*, pp. 17–27.

136 **Meanwhile, California anxiously** Reading boom: John Tebbel, *Between Covers: The Rise and Transformation of Book Publishing in America* (New York and Oxford: Oxford University Press, 1987), pp. 79–88; Hellmut Lehmann-Haupt, in collaboration with Lawrence C. Wroth and Rollo G. Silver, *The Book in America: A History of the Making and Selling of Books in the United States*, 2nd ed. (New York: R. R. Bowker, 1951), pp. 195–201; and MTAL, pp. 175–176. Coolbrith in the *Galaxy* and *Harper's Weekly*: ICLL, p. 88. From January 1866 to November 1867, Harte wrote letters about California for the *Boston Christian Register* and the *Springfield Republican*; see Bret Harte, *Bret Harte's California*, ed. Gary Scharnhorst.

136 **Scaling the heights** Stoddard's first book: CRP, chap. 4, pp. 4A–5; CSCWS, pp. 94–97; MTL, vol. 2, pp. 30–31.

137 **Before leaving for** *"Your book will…"*: SLC to CWS, April 23, 1867, in MTL, vol. 2, pp. 29–30. *"My Young Friend…"*: SLC to CWS, April 27, 1867, in MTL, vol. 2, p. 36.

137 **Twain's sympathy for** Twain's hopes for Hawaii book: SLC to Edward P. Hingston, January 15, 1867, in MTL, vol. 2, pp. 8–9. Heavy traffic: Mark Twain, "The Overgrown Metropolis," *Alta California*, March 28, 1867. Winter: Mark Twain, "The Dreadful Russian Bath," *Alta California*, April 5, 1867, and "New York Weather," *Alta California*, June 30, 1867. Twain and Webb in NY: MTL, vol. 2, pp. 6–7; TAMT, pp. 198–199; and MTAL, p. 177.

138 **In February 1867** In a letter to John McComb, February 2[?]–7, 1867, summarized in "California Authors," *Alta California*, March 15, 1867, Twain made it clear that he expected Carleton to publish his book; see MTL, vol. 2, pp. 12–14. Scene with Carleton: TAMT, pp. 199–200. *"Well, what can…"*: ibid., p. 200.

138 **When Twain mentioned** All quotes: ibid.

138 **This encounter inspired** All quotes: ibid., pp. 200–201.

139 **Carleton had a rough** *"looked so disreputable"*: quoted in MTL, vol. 2, p. 13. Carleton wasn't the only publisher to refuse Twain's manuscript; see MTL, vol. 2, p. 14. Harte's book with Carleton, *Condensed Novels and Other Papers*, was announced as early as February 1867; see MTL, vol. 2, p. 13.

139   **Twain was furious** All quotes: SLC to CWS, April 23, 1867, in MTL, vol. 2, p. 30.
139   **Eventually Webb offered** Webb's offer: TAMT, p. 201. Manuscript revisions: MTAL, p. 179. On May 1, 1867, Webb printed 1,000 copies of *The Celebrated Jumping Frog of Cala-veras County, and Other Sketches.* A second printing of an additional 552 copies took place 20 days later; see Kevin MacDonnell, "The Primary First Editions of Mark Twain," *Firsts: Collecting Modern First Editions* 8.7/8 (July/August 1998), p. 32.
140   **Sadly, the pages inside** Typos in the text and Twain's dissatisfaction: SLC to BH, May 1, 1867, in MTL, vol. 2, pp. 39–40. Twain later said that he expected *The Celebrated Jumping Frog* to sell 50,000 copies. It only sold about 4,000; see MTL, vol. 2, p. 58. *"excellent style"*: Mark Twain, "Personal," *Alta California*, June 10, 1867. *"It is full . . ."*: SLC to BH, May 1, 1867, in MTL, vol. 2, p. 39.
140   **Fortunately, he was** Twain's lecture plans in NY: MTL, vol. 2, pp. 40–42; TAMT, pp. 223–226; and Fred W. Lorch, *The Trouble Begins at Eight*, pp. 60–64. During a brief visit to his home state of Missouri in the spring of 1867, he had given his Hawaii lecture to audiences in St. Louis and Hannibal, as well as in Keokuk, IA, and Quincy, IL; see ibid., pp. 52–59.
141   **Seven years later** Twain's lecture debut in NY: ibid., pp. 64–65, and MTL, vol. 2, pp. 42–44. *"For an hour and fifteen . . ."*: TAMT, p. 226. *"It was certainly . . ."* and *"needs to be . . ."*: Edward H. House, "Mark Twain as a Lecturer," pp. 65–66.
141   **That night, Twain** Origins of Twain's interest in the *Quaker City* excursion: MTAL, pp. 183–185, and MTL, vol. 2, pp. 14–17. Prospectus: MTL, vol. 2, pp. 381–384. *"Send me . . ."*: SLC to Proprietors of the *San Francisco Alta California*, March 2[?], 1867, in MTL, vol. 2, p. 17. Departure of *Quaker City*: ibid., p. 62. Final passenger list: ibid., pp. 385–387.
142   **Twain's impatience served** *"A man has no . . ."*: Mark Twain, *A Connecticut Yankee in King Arthur's Court* (New York and London: Harper & Brothers, 1889), p. 191.
142   **In the summer** Stoddard probably went to Yosemite in June or July 1867. Anton Roman published his *Poems* in early September 1867; see CSCWS, pp. 96–97.
142   **Even at his** Response to Stoddard's *Poems*: SFLF, pp. 230–232; GP, pp. 34–35; CSCWS, pp. 97–98; and CRP, chap. 4, pp. 7–13. *"the pet of the literary 'Ring'"*: *San Francisco Dramatic Chronicle*, quoted ibid., p. 7. *"imitation spasms"*: "Some of the Smaller Poets," *Nation* 5.127 (Dec. 5, 1867), p. 452. *"the incubus of imitation . . ."*: "Reviews," *Round Table* 7.155 (Jan. 11, 1868), p. 24.
143   **Unlike Twain, Stoddard** *"mere wind-fall . . ."*: CRP, chap. 4, p. 8.
143   **Stoddard needed a new** Stoddard's Catholic baptism: Charles Warren Stoddard, *A Troubled Heart and How It Was Comforted At Last* (Notre Dame, IN: Joseph A. Lyons, 1885), pp. 111–113. *"From the steps . . ."*: ibid., p. 113. Conversion: CSCWS, pp. 101–108; SFLF, pp. 232–233; and GP, pp. 35–37. *"I couldn't be anything . . ."*: CWS to James Whitcomb Riley, April 8, 1891, quoted GP, p. 36.
144   **Catholicism also helped** CWS to James Whitcomb Riley, April 8, 1891: "I couldn't help it, you see; it was born in me and was the only thing that appealed to my temperament. I believe a man's religion is nessessarily [*sic*] a matter of temperament." Quoted in GP, p. 36. *"Shun all Humans . . ."*: from Stoddard's "Thought Book," section 24, July 15, 1866, quoted in CSCWS, p. 105.
144   **This was easier** All quotes: ICCWS.
144   **Their time together** Stoddard's acting career: CSCWS, pp. 109–113. *"natural and self-possessed"*: *Sacramento Daily Union*, March 14, 1868, quoted ibid., p. 111. Rich, deep voice: ICHC.
145   **Unfortunately, his talent** *"That feller . . ."*: Charles Warren Stoddard, "Over the Foot-Lights," *Atlantic Monthly* 34.202 (Aug. 1874), p. 170. Stoddard's trials as an actor: ibid., pp. 169–174. The other plays offered by Stoddard's company in Sacramento included *The Merchant of Venice*; see CSCWS, p. 111.
145   **His friends did** All quotes: IC to CWS, March 11, 1868, HUNT.
146   **Harte wasn't much** All quotes: BH to CWS, March 16, 1868, UVA.

146 **When Harte's** *Condensed Novels* Appearance of *Condensed Novels* and reception: BHGS,
pp. 34–35, and BHAN, pp. 83–84. Harte's letters disavowing Carleton's changes: for example, BH to Mr. Bush, November 22, 1867, quoted BHAN, p. 84. *"charming parodies...":*
"Reviews and Literary Notices," *Atlantic Monthly* 21.123 (Jan. 1868), p. 128.

147 **Harte hated his** *"deformed brat...":* BH to James T. Fields, October 30, 1868, quoted in
M. A. DeWolfe Howe, *Memories of a Hostess: A Chronicle of Eminent Friendships, Drawn
Chiefly from the Diaries of Mrs. James T. Fields* (Boston: Atlantic Monthly Press, 1922), p.
233. Death of son: BHGS, p. 33.

147 **For the past** Harte reviewed Stoddard's *Poems* favorably in "Literary Gossip," *Daily Alta
California,* January 13, 1867, quoted in CRP, chap. 4, p. 10. Harte also reviewed the book for
the *Springfield Republican.* *"tuneful mob"* and *"hardness...":* Bret Harte, "From Califor-
nia," *Springfield Republican,* October 12, 1867, in Bret Harte, *Bret Harte's California,* p. 142.
"The curse of California...": BH to J. L. VerMehr, February 2, 1868, BANC. *"twitter...":*
Bret Harte, "From California," *Springfield Republican,* October 12, 1867, in Bret Harte,
Bret Harte's California, p. 142.

148 **Anton Roman understood** Anton Roman: BHAN, p. 92, and Hellmut Lehmann-Haupt,
The Book in America, pp. 216–217. Founding the *Overland:* Charles Warren Stoddard, "In
Old Bohemia II: The 'Overland' and the Overlanders," p. 264; Anton Roman, "The Beginnings of the *Overland:* As Seen by the First Publisher," *Overland Monthly* 32.187 (July
1898), pp. 72–74; Anton Roman, "The Genesis of the *Overland Monthly*," *Overland Monthly*
40.3 (Sept. 1902), pp. 220–222.

149 **First he needed** *"lean too much..."* and *"a magazine that would...":* ibid., p. 220.

149 **Predictably, Harte didn't** Harte's reservations: ibid., pp. 220–221, and W. C. Bartlett,
"*Overland* Reminiscences," *Overland Monthly* 32.187 (July 1898), p. 41. *"threw cold wa-
ter...":* Anton Roman, quoted in BHGS, p. 37. *"in his bones":* W. C. Bartlett, "*Overland*
Reminiscences," p. 41. A copy of the prospectus Roman circulated to secure advertisements
is reprinted in Anton Roman, "The Beginnings of the *Overland,*" p. 73. Roman's pitch to
Harte: ibid., p. 74. Roman later claimed that he found at least half of the *Overland*'s pieces
for the first six issues. However, one of the men Roman hired as Harte's assistant, W. C.
Bartlett, recalled that he and several others agreed to write "successive papers for six
months, if such contributions were actually necessary to the life of the Monthly," and remembered this as a "turning point" in the negotiations with Harte; see W. C. Bartlett,
"*Overland* Reminiscences," p. 41.

149 **But the most** *"the central position..."* and the map: Anton Roman, "The Genesis of the
Overland Monthly," pp. 220–221. The Pacific Mail Steamship Company began regular
transpacific service from San Francisco in 1867; see E. Mowbray Tate, *Transpacific Steam:
The Story of Steam Navigation from the Pacific Coast of North America to the Far East and
the Antipodes, 1867–1941* (New York: Cornwall Books, 1986), pp. 23–27.

150 **Harte accepted** *"I am trying...":* BH to Henry W. Bellows, quoted in BHGS, p. 38. *"The
Overland marches...":* BH to CWS, quoted ibid., p. 37. Roman and Harte's trip: Anton Roman, "The Genesis of the *Overland Monthly*," p. 221.

151 **When the first** Harte and the cover design: SLC to Thomas Bailey Aldrich, January 27,
1871, in MTL, vol. 4, pp. 317–318. *"recognizes his rival..."* and *"coming engine...":* Bret
Harte, "Etc.," *Overland Monthly* 1.1 (July 1868), p. 99.

151 **Twain loved the** *"prettiest fancy...":* Twain to Thomas Bailey Aldrich, January 27, 1871, in
MTL, vol. 4, p. 317. Twain's return to SF: MTL, vol. 2, p. 205. Twain wrote fifty letters for
the *Alta California* about the excursion, one for the *Naples Observer* (reprinted by the *Alta
California*), one for the *New York Herald,* and six for the *New York Tribune;* see Daniel
Morley McKeithan, introduction to Mark Twain, *Traveling with the Innocents Abroad:
Mark Twain's Original Reports from Europe and the Holy Land,* ed. Daniel Morley Mc-
Keithan (Norman: University of Oklahoma Press, 1958), p. ix. The *Alta California* pub-
lished the last of its Twain letters on May 17, 1868; see ibid., p. 301.

of an Earthquake, Measure of a Man (Princeton, NJ: Princeton University Press, 2007), pp. 52–53. The suppressed report estimated the property damage at $1.5 million; the chamber's telegram put the cost at $300,000.

161   **Harte couldn't have** *"with a little more . . .":* Bret Harte, "Etc.," *Overland Monthly* 1.5 (Nov. 1868), p. 480. *"dignified dons . . .":* Noah Brooks, "Early Days of 'The Overland,'" *Overland Monthly* 32.187 (July 1898), p. 10. See also Noah Brooks, "Harte's Early Days: Reminiscences by Noah Brooks, Who Knew Him in California," *New York Times,* May 24, 1902; Noah Brooks, "Bret Harte in California," p. 450; and BHGS, p. 42.

162   **Harte couldn't help** Henry George's background and personality: SFLF, pp. 294–302. See also Henry George, "What the Railroad Will Bring Us," *Overland Monthly* 1.4 (Oct. 1868), pp. 297–306.

162   **George began with** *"What is the railroad . . .":* ibid., p. 298. *"The locomotive . . ."* and *"When liveries . . .":* ibid., p. 303.

163   **Later, George would** *"In California there . . .":* ibid., p. 305.

CHAPTER SIX

165   **The connection couldn't** The telegram announcing the delay arrived on the afternoon of May 7, 1869; see *Daily Alta California,* May 8, 1869, and *San Francisco Daily Evening Bulletin,* May 7, 1869. Reasons for delay: David Haward Bain, *Empire Express,* pp. 648–652.

165   **At sunrise, cannon** Celebration on May 8: *San Francisco Daily Evening Bulletin,* May 8, 1869, and *Daily Alta California,* May 9, 1869.

166   **By the time** Celebration on May 10: *Daily Alta California,* May 11, 1869, and *San Francisco Daily Evening Bulletin,* May 10, 1869. One of the illuminated signs held during that evening's festivities read "The Pacific Railroad, Uncle Sam's Waistband—He would burst without it." See also SFLF, pp. 3–5. National celebration: David Haward Bain, *Empire Express,* pp. 666–667. Stagecoach from St. Louis to SF: Philip L. Fradkin, *Stagecoach: Wells Fargo and the American West* (New York: Simon & Schuster Source, 2002), p. 31. Traveling from NY to SF by steamer required taking a ship to Aspinwall, Panama, then a railroad across the isthmus, and finally another ship from Panama City to SF. The journey could last as few as 21 days, but more often it took about a month; see ET&S, vol. 2, p. 169, and MTL, vol. 6, p. 41. Transcontinental railroad travel time: ibid. *"a victory over space":* San *Francisco Daily Evening Bulletin,* May 8, 1869.

166   **The railroad didn't** "The *Overland* for June crosses the continent on the completed Pacific Railroad," Harte wrote in the June 1869 issue of the *Overland Monthly.* It had his poem "What the Engines Said," a whimsical take on the transcontinental link. It also included another one of his gold rush stories, "Miggles." The eastern papers that reprinted Harte's fiction included the *Springfield Republican, New York Evening Post,* and the *Hartford Courant;* see BHGS, p. 47. James T. Fields's offer: ibid., pp. 48–49.

167   **Dime novels were** Dime novels and explosion of popular literature: John Tebbel, *Between Covers,* pp. 73–75; Hellmut Lehmann-Haupt, *The Book in America,* pp. 194–196; and Gary Scharnhorst, "'All Hat and No Cattle': Romance, Realism, and Late Nineteenth-Century Western American Fiction," in Nicolas S. Witschi, ed., *A Companion to the Literature and Culture of the American West* (New York: Blackwell, 2011), pp. 282–284. Formation of "Wild West": ibid., pp. 282–285.

167   **This set the scene** *"the trammels of English . . .":* Bret Harte, "The Rise of the 'Short Story,'" p. 251. *"inchoate poetry":* ibid., p. 257.

167   **He did so subtly** Harte's technique: William F. Conner, "The Euchring of Tennessee: A Reexamination of Bret Harte's 'Tennessee's Partner,'" *Studies in Short Fiction* 80.17 (Spring 1980), pp. 113–120. A man stranded in the wilderness: Bret Harte, "The Outcasts of Poker Flat," *The Luck of Roaring Camp and Other Writings,* ed. Gary Scharnhorst, pp. 27–37. A father reunites with his estranged son: Bret Harte, "Mr. Thompson's Prodigal," *The Luck*

of Roaring Camp and Other Writings, ed. Gary Scharnhorst, pp. 79–86. *"snapper"*: Mark Twain, "How to Tell a Story," p. 8.

168 **The** *Overland* **stories** *"the Western predilection..."*: Bret Harte, "Mr. Thompson's Prodigal," *The Luck of Roaring Camp and Other Writings*, ed. Gary Scharnhorst, p. 79. Harte's wryness: ICHC and ECW. *"You could never..."*: William Dean Howells, "Editor's Easy Chair," p. 156.

169 **Ever since the** *"He was an exacting..."*: Charles Warren Stoddard, "In Old Bohemia II: The 'Overland' and the Overlanders," p. 265.

169 **But sharp editing** *"Why do you waste..."*: quoted ibid., p. 266. Stoddard's departure for Hawaii: CSCWS, pp. 118–120, and GP, pp. 39–41.

169 **His friends hated** All quotes: IC to CWS, January 9, 1869, HUNT.

170 **Harte, she discovered** *"a born actor..."*: ICHC.

170 **One day Coolbrith** Harte's religious critics: BHGS, p. 50. All quotes from the scene: ECW.

171 **They took care** *"Harte was good..."*: ibid. Harte helping Coolbrith with household tasks and trying to find her paying work: ibid. Society of California Pioneers gig: BH to IC, August 17, 1868, BANC, and George Wharton James, "Ina Donna Coolbrith: An Historical Sketch and Appreciation," p. 320.

171 **Most important, he** *"I was quite..."*: BH to IC, January 28, 1869, BANC. *"Is it because..."*: BH to IC, undated, BANC. Ringing on Saturday afternoon: BH to IC, May 3, year unknown, BANC. *"I must have..."*: ibid. Sending messenger: two undated letters from BH to IC, BANC.

171 **He was equally** New title and extra syllable: BH to IC, undated, BANC. *"What do I..."*: Ina Coolbrith, "The Years," *Overland Monthly* 4.2 (Feb. 1870), p. 161.

172 **Harte always wanted** All quotes: ECW.

172 **Yet the one** Anna Griswold Harte: Josephine Clifford McCrackin, "A Letter from a Friend," pp. 222–224. *"How my heart..."*: quoted ibid., p. 223.

173 **In June 1869** Roman's sale of the *Overland*: BHGS, pp. 50–51. Harte announced his demands in a letter to John H. Carmany, June 7, 1869, BANC. *"Of my ability..."* and *"If I do not..."*: BH to John H. Carmany, June 8, 1869, BANC.

173 **Carmany surrendered** Harte quit his job at the US Mint in August 1869. John H. Carmany would later recall that "the importance of [Harte's] remaining with the magazine was a constant subject of anxious thought on my part"; quoted in BHGS, p. 51.

173 **In 1869, as** *"The Eastern press..."*: quoted in MTL, vol. 3, p. 321.

174 **It had been** Arrival in NY and trip to Hartford to see Bliss: MTAL, pp. 240–241. Book delays: Elisha Bliss Jr. to SLC, February 10, 1869, in MTL, vol. 3, pp. 98–100; SLC to Elisha Bliss Jr., February 14, 1869, ibid., p. 98; and Elisha Bliss Jr. to SLC, April 14, 1869, ibid., pp. 193–194. See also MCMT, pp. 102–104. Battle with board of directors: MTL, vol. 3, pp. 170–171, and TAMT, pp. 207–208. Publication would be postponed again: Elisha Bliss Jr. to SLC, July 12, 1869, in MTL, vol. 3, p. 286. *"After it is done..."*: SLC to Elisha Bliss Jr., July 22, 1869, in MTL, vol. 3, p. 285.

174 **Bliss got the** Bliss's replies to Twain's angry letter: Elisha Bliss Jr. to SLC, July 30[?], 1869, in MTL, vol. 3, p. 287, and Elisha Bliss Jr. to SLC, August 4, 1869, in MTL, vol. 3, pp. 292–294. Bliss registered the copyright for *The Innocents Abroad* on July 28, 1869. Book's appearance: Mark Twain, *The Innocents Abroad, or The New Pilgrims' Progress* (Hartford, CT: American Publishing Company, 1869), and MTAL, p. 275. *"trimmed & trained..."*: SLC to Thomas Bailey Aldrich, January 27, 1871, in MTL, vol. 4, p. 316.

175 **In a typically Twainian** Meeting Livy and proposal: MTAL, pp. 229–230, 241–245; MCMT, pp. 65–66, 76–83.

175 **Predictably, her answer** Twain's first courtship letter to Livy was SLC to Olivia L. Langdon, September 7 and 8, 1868, in MTL, vol. 2, pp. 247–249. 184 letters: MTAL, p. 245; Victor Fischer and Michael B. Frank, introduction to MTL, vol. 3, pp. xxv–xxvi; and Mark Twain, *The Love Letters of Mark Twain*, ed. Dixon Wecter (New York: Harper & Brothers, 1949).

Nearly half of Twain's courtship letters have been lost. The last of them was written on January 20, 1870, shortly before his marriage to Livy in February. On the envelope of this letter, Livy wrote, "184th—Last letter of a 17-months' correspondence"; see Resa Willis, *Mark and Livy: The Love Story of Mark Twain and the Woman Who Almost Tamed Him* (New York: Routledge, 2004 [1992]), p. 51. For a calendar of the courtship letters, see MTL, vol. 3, pp. 473–480. *"Don't read a word..."*: SLC to Olivia L. Langdon, December 31, 1868, in MTL, vol. 2, pp. 369–370.

176 **Fortunately, it never** Livy's assent, and her parents' conditional approval: SLC to Mary Mason Fairbanks, November 26 and 27, 1868, ibid., pp. 283–288. *"I am so happy..."*: SLC to Joseph H. Twitchell, November 28, 1868, ibid., p. 294. Livy's editorial input: MTL, vol. 3, p. 179; SLC to Mary Mason Fairbanks, March 24, 1869, in MTL, vol. 3, p. 176; SLC to Olivia L. Langdon, May 13, 1869, in MTL, vol. 3, pp. 225; and MTAL, p. 271. *"scratch out..."*: SLC to Susan L. Crane, March 9 and 31, 1869, in MTL, vol. 3, p. 181.

176 **It worked** Copies sold and royalties: MTL, vol. 4, p. 280, and MTAL, p. 277. Reviews: Louis Budd, ed., *Mark Twain: The Contemporary Reviews* (Cambridge: Cambridge University Press, 1999), pp. 34–89. *"There is an amount..."*: William Dean Howells, "Reviews and Literary Notices," *Atlantic Monthly* 24.146 (Dec. 1869), pp. 765–766.

176 **The *Atlantic*'s support** Subscription publishing: John Tebbel, *Between Covers*, pp. 166–169. Twain's use of the model: Bruce Michelson, *Printer's Devil: Mark Twain and the American Publishing Revolution* (Berkeley: University of California Press, 2006), pp. 17–18, 82–88, and MTAL, pp. 176, 234–235.

177 **Upscale Americans had** The years after the Civil War saw a surge of Americans traveling to Europe, as the rising American middle class took advantage of improved transatlantic routes. "Everybody was going to Europe," as Twain recalled in *The Innocents Abroad*. See Jeffrey Steinbrink, "Why the Innocents Went Abroad: Mark Twain and American Tourism in the Late Nineteenth Century," *American Literary Realism, 1870–1910* 16.2 (Autumn 1983), pp. 278–286. *"old connoisseurs..."*: Mark Twain, *The Innocents Abroad*, p. 263. Relic hunter crawling up the Sphinx: ibid., pp. 473–474. *"The gentle reader..."*: ibid., p. 164.

178 **The familiar spectacle** *"mournful wreck"*: ibid., p. 132.

178 **This declaration of independence** Harte, in his review of *Innocents* for the *Overland Monthly*, detected in Twain's book "that ungathered humor and extravagance which belong to pioneer communities"; see Bret Harte, "Current Literature," *Overland Monthly* 4.1 (Jan. 1870), p. 101. *"continuous incoherence"*: William Dean Howells, "Reviews and Literary Notices," *Atlantic Monthly* 24.146 (Dec. 1869), p. 766.

178 **It made for** Twain's lecture tour began on November 1, 1869, in Pittsburgh; his last performance was on January 21, 1870, in Jamestown, NY. The tour took him through towns in New York, Pennsylvania, and New England, as well as to Washington, DC. See Fred W. Lorch, *The Trouble Begins at Eight*, pp. 105–110. More than fifty towns: MTAL, p. 277. For an example of Twain's personal appeals to newspaper editors, see SLC to Whitelaw Reid, August 15, 1869, in MTL, vol. 3, p. 303. As many as two thousand advance copies: Elisha Bliss Jr. to SLC, August 4, 1869, in MTL, vol. 3, p. 293.

179 **One would of course** *"He praised the book..."*: SLC to Charles Henry Webb, November 26, 1870, in MTL, vol. 4, p. 248. Problem with distributor: ibid. *"wrote me the..."*: ibid., p. 249. Harte's letter is no longer extant.

179 **Yet Harte still** *"six hundred and fifty..."*: Bret Harte, "Current Literature," *Overland Monthly* 4.1 (Jan. 1870), p. 100. Favorable notice of *The Luck of Roaring Camp and Other Sketches* in "New Books," *Buffalo Express*, April 30, 1870; see MTL, vol. 4, p. 250.

180 **Sometime in the early** Twain's margin notes in *The Luck of Roaring Camp and Other Sketches*: Bradford A. Booth, "Mark Twain's Comments on Bret Harte's Stories," *American Literature* 25.4 (Jan. 1954), pp. 492–495. *"nearly blemishless"*: ibid., p. 493. *"Dickens..."*: ibid., p. 494. *"showy, meretricious..."*: TAMT, p. 163. *"artificial reproduction"*: ibid., p. 397. *"a dialect which..."*: ibid., pp. 162–163. *"truthful pictures..."*: "New Publications," *New York*

Times, April 30, 1870. Contract for *Roughing It*, prepared on July 15, 1870: MTL, vol. 4, pp. 565–566.

180 **Sometimes this bothered** Persuading Livy's parents: MTAL, pp. 260–262, 266–267; MCMT, pp. 88–92; and TAMT, pp. 247–248. *"six prominent men"*: ibid., p. 247. *"The friends I had..."* and *"did not..."*: SLC to CWS, August 25, 1869 [2010 edition], accessed online via Mark Twain Project Online, University of California, Berkeley.

181 **On February 2, 1870** Wedding: MTL, vol. 4, pp. 42–49; MTAL, pp. 280–281; and MCMT, pp. 112–113. Wedding cards: MTL, vol. 4, p. 57. *"Tell me..."*: SLC to CWS, February 6[?], 1870, in MTL, vol. 4, p. 62.

181 **Stoddard would stay** *"did more for me..."*: interview in the *Santa Barbara Morning Press*, October 31, 1908, included in the Stoddard clippings at BANC.

182 **In the summer** Stoddard's Hawaii trip in 1868–1869: CSCWS, pp. 120–126, and GP, pp. 41–44. He returned to SF in July 1869. *"You will easily..."*: SLC to Walt Whitman, March 2, 1869, quoted in GP, p. 43. No response from Whitman to Stoddard's *Poems*: ibid., p. 35. *"Now my voice..."*: SLC to Walt Whitman, March 2, 1869, quoted ibid., p. 42. *"Those tender..."*: Walt Whitman to SLC, June 12, 1869, quoted ibid., p. 43.

182 **"A South-Sea Idyl"** Charles Warren Stoddard, "A South-Sea Idyl," *Overland Monthly* 3.3 (Sept. 1869), pp. 257–264. *"petted in..."*: ibid., p. 260. *"hating civilization"*: ibid., p. 259.

182 **Harte loved the** *"Now you have..."*: quoted in CRP, chap. 6, p. 7. *"mustang humor"*: William Dean Howells, "Introductory Letter," in Charles Warren Stoddard, *South-Sea Idyls* (New York: Charles Scribner's Sons, 1907 [1873]), p. vi. *"If you want..."*: Charles Warren Stoddard, "A South-Sea Idyl," p. 258. *"who dared..."*: quoted in GP, p. 44. Stoddard sent the piece to Whitman on April 2, 1870. *"beautiful & soothing"*: Walt Whitman to CWS, April 23, 1870, in Walt Whitman, *Selected Letters of Walt Whitman*, ed. Edwin Haviland Miller (Iowa City: University of Iowa Press, 1990), p. 149.

183 **Harte wanted the** Charles Warren Stoddard, "Barbarian Days," *Overland Monthly* 4.4 (April 1870), pp. 327–335. Charles Warren Stoddard, "How I Converted My Cannibal," *Overland Monthly* 3.5 (Nov. 1869), pp. 455–460. For other of Stoddard's South Sea sketches, see CSCWS, p. 129. *"It's time..."*: BH to CWS, April 24, 1870, quoted ibid., p. 129.

183 **Of course, the** Stoddard's plans to return to the Pacific: GP, pp. 45–48, and Charles Warren Stoddard, *The Island of Tranquil Delights*, pp. 13–14.

184 **He anchored himself** Bierce arrived in SF in late 1866 or early 1867. His former commander, Major General William B. Hazen, had promised him a captain's commission, but when he arrived at the Presidio, he discovered a letter with a commission for only second lieutenant. Angrily, Bierce resigned. See Roy Morris Jr., *Ambrose Bierce: Alone in Bad Company* (Oxford, UK: Oxford University Press, 1998 [1996]), pp. 101–115. Stoddard would use the nickname Biercy in their letters; see M. E. Grenander, "Ambrose Bierce and Charles Warren Stoddard: Some Unpublished Correspondence," *Huntington Library Quarterly*, 23.3 (May 1960), pp. 261–292. Bierce's appearance: Roy Morris Jr., *Ambrose Bierce*, p. 124, and Richard O'Connor, *Ambrose Bierce: A Biography* (Boston: Little, Brown, 1967), p. 75. Bierce and Coolbrith: ICLL, p. 97. Bierce and Harte: BHAN, p. 94, and BHGS, pp. 36, 52. Bierce and Stoddard: GP, pp. 38–39.

184 **In print he** Bierce also published poems and prose pieces during the final years of the *Californian*; see Roy Morris Jr., *Ambrose Bierce*, pp. 115–116. But Bierce's local literary career really began when he became the "Town Crier" of the *San Francisco News Letter* in December 1868. His columns: ibid., pp. 118–127; SFLF, pp. 250–255; and Ambrose Bierce, *A Sole Survivor: Bits of Autobiography*, ed. S. T. Joshi and David E. Schultz (Knoxville: University of Tennessee Press, 1998), pp. 87–105.

184 **This ruthlessness reflected** Bierce was struck by a bullet from a Confederate sharpshooter on June 23, 1864, during the Battle of Kennesaw Mountain; see Roy Morris Jr., *Ambrose Bierce*, pp. 88–89. His war experience: ibid., pp. 21–89; Richard O'Connor, *Ambrose Bierce*, pp. 22–45; and Carey McWilliams, *Ambrose Bierce: A Biography* (Boston: Albert & Charles

Boni, 1929), pp. 28–64. *"To the amiable ..."*: Ambrose Bierce (as Ursus), "Grizzly Papers, No. 1," *Overland Monthly* 6.1 (Jan. 1871), p. 94. Bierce wrote five essays for the *Overland*, which he called the "Grizzly Papers," and signed under the pseudonym Ursus; see Roy Morris Jr., *Ambrose Bierce*, pp. 127–128. The *Overland* would also publish Bierce's first short story, "The Haunted Valley," in July 1871.

185   **The gold rush had** Industrialization of gold mining: Martin Ridge, "Why They Went West: Economic Opportunity on the Trans-Mississippi Frontier," *American West* 1.3 (May 1964), pp. 48–50, and Earl Pomeroy, *The Pacific Slope*, pp. 45–47. Corporate agriculture and land monopoly: Kevin Starr, *Inventing the Dream*, pp. 131–132, 164–165.

185   **No single event** Suez Canal: SFLF, p. 351.

186   **There were bigger** California's challenges after 1869: Ira B. Cross, *A History of the Labor Movement in California* (Berkeley: University of California Press, 1974 [1935]), pp. 60–65; Robert Knight, *Industrial Relations in the San Francisco Bay Area, 1900–1918* (Berkeley: University of California Press, 1960), pp. 12–14; Kevin Starr, *Americans and the California Dream*, pp. 130–134; SFLF, pp. 296–297; William Deverell, *Railroad Crossing: Californians and the Railroad, 1850–1910* (Berkeley: University of California Press, 1994), pp. 34–40. Seven thousand San Franciscans out of work: ibid., p. 36.

186   **The heads of** Nob Hill palaces: Richard Rayner, *The Associates: Four Capitalists Who Created California* (New York: W. W. Norton, 2008), pp. 118–119.

186   **Meanwhile, the slow** *"social wrecks"*: Walter Mulrea Fisher, *The Californians* (London: Macmillan, 1876), p. 72. Hoodlums: Kevin Starr, *Americans and the California Dream*, p. 133. Rising anti-Chinese racism: ibid., p. 132; Neil Larry Shumsky, "Dissatisfaction, Mobility, and Expectation: San Francisco Workingmen in the 1870s," *Pacific Historian* 30.2 (March 1986), pp. 21–27; and Robert Knight, *Industrial Relations in the San Francisco Bay Area*, pp. 14–17. *"The cause of her death ..."*: San Francisco News Letter, October 8, 1870, quoted in Roy Morris Jr., *Ambrose Bierce*, pp. 119–120.

187   **The rising tide** Bierce's version of events: Roy Morris Jr., *Ambrose Bierce*, p. 127. Conversely, Twain later claimed that Harte wrote the poem "for his own amusement" and "threw it aside, but being one day suddenly called upon for copy he sent that very piece in"; see BHGS, p. 52. Bret Harte, "Plain Language from Truthful James," *Overland Monthly* 5.3 (Sept. 1870), pp. 287–288.

188   **"Plain Language from"** *"We are ruined ..."*: Bret Harte, "Plain Language from Truthful James," *Overland Monthly* 5.3 (Sept. 1870), p. 288. *"did as the ..."*: Henry J. W. Dam, "A Morning With Bret Harte," p. 43. "The Heathen Chinee" as satire: Margaret Duckett, "Plain Language from Bret Harte," *Nineteenth-Century Fiction* 11.4 (March 1957), pp. 241–260.

188   **"The Heathen Chinee"** Reception of "The Heathen Chinee": BHGS, pp. 51–58; BHAN, pp. 111–112; and Richard O'Connor, *Bret Harte*, pp. 122–123. *"an explosion of delight"*: TAMT, p. 165. *"doubled their orders"*: John H. Carmany, "'The Publishers of the *Overland*': Remarks of Hon. J. H. Carmany," p. 12, in a supplement appended to *Overland Monthly* 1.2 (Feb. 1883). Harte's *Poems*: BHGS, pp. 57–58.

188   **Within months, Harte** *"Harte does soar ..."*: SLC to Charles Henry Webb, November 26, 1870, in MTL, vol. 4, p. 248. Twain's struggles with *Roughing It*: MTAL, pp. 289–290.

189   **Yet he didn't** *"was no less ..."* and *"finer, higher work"*: ICHC. The pirated edition was published in 1870 by the Chicago-based Western News Company, with accompanying illustrations by Joseph Hull; the images are available at the University of Virginia's website at http://etext.virginia.edu/railton/roughingit/map/chiharte.html.

189   **This was only** Impact of "The Heathen Chinee" on "Chinese question": BHGS, pp. 54–55; Gary Scharnhorst, "'Ways That Are Dark': Appropriations of Bret Harte's 'Plain Language from Truthful James,'" *Nineteenth-Century Literature* 51.3 (Dec. 1996), pp. 377–399; and David Scott, *China and the International System, 1840–1949: Power, Presence, and Perceptions in a Century of Humiliation* (Albany: State University of New York Press, 2008), pp. 60–63.

Although the Page Act of 1875 specifically prohibited Communists, prostitutes, and people with mental or physical handicaps from entering the United States, the law was used to target Chinese immigrants; see John Seonnichsen, *The Chinese Exclusion Act of 1882* (Santa Barbara, CA: Greenwood, 2011), pp. 55, 61.

189   **Harte had every** Worst poem he ever wrote: MTL, vol. 4, p. 250. *Putnam's* offer: BHGS, p. 58. *"the lowest and least..."* and *"I have propositions..."*: BH to F. P. Church, October 18, 1870, BANC. The *New York Tribune, Scribner's,* and the *Boston Commercial Bulletin* all made offers for Harte's contributions; see BHGS, pp. 58–59.

190   **The most intriguing** Fields, Osgood, and Company sent its offer on June 21, 1870; see BHGS, p. 60, and BHAN, p. 112. University appointment and salary: BH to Fields, Osgood, and Company, September 16, 1870, included in Bradford A. Booth, "Bret Harte Goes East: Some Unpublished Letters," *American Literature* 19.4 (Jan. 1948), p. 321. *"It has long been..."*: Ambrose Bierce, "Town Crier," *San Francisco News Letter,* August 20, 1870, included in Ambrose Bierce, *A Sole Survivor: Bits of Autobiography,* ed. S. T. Joshi and David E. Schultz, p. 101. Incorporated in 1868, the University of California remained in Oakland until moving to Berkeley in 1873. *"Can you do..."*: Bradford A. Booth, "Bret Harte Goes East," p. 321.

190   **The timing worked** Delay caused by regent: Noah Brooks, "Bret Harte in California," p. 450. Harte's decision to decline the UC position: BH to Charles Henry Webb, November 20, 1870, BANC.

191   **By late 1870** It's unclear when Harte made the decision to leave California. On September 16, 1870, he told Fields, Osgood, and Company that he was "still anxious to make my home in the East." On November 5, 1870, he wrote William Dean Howells of the "conviction being strong upon me that I should be somewhere near Boston at this date"; see William Dean Howells, *Life in Letters of William Dean Howells,* vol. 1, ed. Mildred Howells (New York: Russell & Russell, 1968 [1928]), p. 158. Although this letter suggests Harte wanted to be in Boston, he had made no formal arrangement with any periodical by the time he left SF. John H. Carmany, in "'The Publishers of the *Overland*': Remarks of Hon. J. H. Carmany," p. 13, recalled that he made a last-ditch effort to keep Harte at the *Overland* by raising his salary to $5,000 a year and giving him a one-quarter stake in the magazine. Harte, however, remembered it differently. According to his March 5, 1871, letter to Ambrose Bierce, Harte was the one who made the offer, and Carmany declined; see Bradford A. Booth, "Bret Harte Goes East: Some Unpublished Letters," pp. 324–325. *"played out"* and *"The tourists..."*: from Harte's response to an 1870 proposal from the *New York Tribune* to become its San Francisco correspondent, quoted in BHGS, p. 58.

191   **Harte urged his** *"[H]e was constantly..."*: ECW. Portfolio of poems: ICLL, pp. 109–110. In an undated letter to Coolbrith held by BANC, Harte writes, "I shall write tonight to Fields, Osgood & Co, and should like to send them your poems." The *Springfield Weekly Republican* of February 17, 1871, calls Stoddard "the only notable and original literary genius in California" since "Bret Harte has left," and mentions his latest South Sea sketch in the *Overland. "John D. Coolbrith"*: "New Publications," *Cincinnati Daily Gazette,* February 4, 1871.

191   **Someday, perhaps, she** *"that dear old circle"*: ECW. *"unprecedented sharps..."* and *"sudden soaring..."*: ICCWS.

192   **Unlike Coolbrith, Stoddard** Stoddard's hope that Harte would help his career in the East: CSCWS, pp. 150–151. *"I know there..."*: CWS to Walt Whitman, April 2, 1870, included ibid., p. 136. On July 7, 1870, Stoddard sailed for Tahiti. Trip: ibid., pp. 138–146, and GP, pp. 48–53. *"'railroaded'..."*: Charles Warren Stoddard, *Exits and Entrances,* p. 239. *"No one who..."*: ibid., p. 252.

192   **On February 2** Harte's departure: *Alta California,* February 2, 1871; BHAN, p. 112; BHGS, p. 63. Telegraph Hill: Bret Harte, "Town and Table Talk: The Bohemian Concerning," *Golden Era,* November 11, 1860.

NOTES

CHAPTER SEVEN

197 **Mark Twain felt** *"Do you know ..."*: SLC to John Henry Riley, March 3, 1871, MTL, vol. 4, p. 338.

198 **He was right** Harte's transcontinental journey: BHGS, pp. 63–64, and BHAN, pp. 113–114. A sampling of press coverage: *New York Daily Tribune*, February 10, 1871; *Leavenworth (KS) Bulletin*, February 11, 1871; *Quincy (IL) Whig*, February 11, 1871; *Yankton (SD) Press*, February 15, 1871; *New York Evening Express*, February 21, 1871.

198 **Chicago felt good** Chicago poaching SF's markets: Ira B. Cross, *A History of the Labor Movement in California*, p. 62. *Lakeside Monthly* offer: BHGS, p. 64, and *Springfield Weekly Republican*, February 17, 1871.

198 **Inexplicably, he failed** Carriage excuse: *Boston Daily Journal*, February 20, 1871; *Daily State Gazette* (Trenton, NJ), February 18, 1871; and *Cincinnati Commercial*, February 23, 1871. Harte later repeated the carriage story in New York to his friend Noah Brooks; see Noah Brooks, "Harte's Early Days: Reminiscences by Noah Brooks, Who Knew Him in California," *New York Times*, May 24, 1902. The source for the story of Mrs. Harte's tantrum is Josephine Clifford McCrackin, Harte's *Overland* assistant, who learned of it from a friend at the *Lakeside Monthly*; see Josephine Clifford McCrackin, "A Letter from a Friend," p. 224. Harte himself never confirmed this account. On March 3, 1871, he wrote McCrackin a letter blaming the incident on "the childishness and provincial character of a few of the principal citizens of Chicago."

198 **Whether Bret's ego** Chicago departure and visits to Syracuse and New York City: BHGS, p. 65. The Hartes arrived in Boston on February 24, 1871.

198 **The assistant editor** Howells at the station: William Dean Howells, "Editor's Easy Chair," p. 154. *"a child ..."* and *"pressed forward ..."*: ibid.

199 **Over the course** Harte's tour of Boston: BHGS, pp. 65–67. *"an English graft"*: Bret Harte, "Our Last Offering," *Californian*, April 22, 1865. More indigenous fare: Bret Harte, "The Rise of the 'Short Story,'" pp. 250–257. In 1871, the Howells family lived at 3 Berkeley Street in Cambridge. *"Why, you couldn't ..."*: quoted in William Dean Howells, "Editor's Easy Chair," p. 154. Pretty girls dawdling outside: ibid., p. 155. Harte's portrait appeared on the cover of *Every Saturday* on January 14, 1871, along with a flattering editorial and the full text of his story "Tennessee's Partner." Howells arranged this publicity coup, as *Every Saturday* was owned by James R. Osgood and Company, the successor to Fields, Osgood, and Company after James T. Fields retired from the partnership in December 1870. See BH to WDH, January 24, 1871, included in Bradford A. Booth, "Bret Harte Goes East: Some Unpublished Letters," pp. 322–323. *"a perfect furore ..."* and *"All the young ..."*: letter from Elinor Mead Howells to Aurelia H. Howells, January 29, 1871, quoted in BHAN, p. 5.

199 **Harte induced nearly** Harte's visit to the Saturday Club: BHGS, pp. 65–66, and Anne Fields's diary, as excerpted in Edward Waldo Emerson, *The Early Years of the Saturday Club, 1855–1870* (Boston: Houghton Mifflin, 1918), pp. 384–385. The Saturday Club met at the Parker House, a hotel on Beacon Hill. *"had a spice ..."*: William Dean Howells, "Editor's Easy Chair," p. 155.

200 **The main event** February 28 dinner: Susan Goodman and Carl Dawson, *William Dean Howells: A Writer's Life* (Berkeley: University of California Press, 2005), p. 136, and BHGS, p. 66. *"so many we ..."*: John Fiske to his mother, March 2, 1871, included in John Fiske, *The Letters of John Fiske*, ed. Ethel F. Fiske (New York: Macmillan, 1940), p. 200. "Everyone wore his best bib and tucker, the house is well arranged for entertaining, and the supper was delicious," Fiske wrote. *"overliterary"*: William Dean Howells, "Editor's Easy Chair," p. 155. *"I was so wined ..."*: BH to Ambrose Bierce, March 5, 1871, included in Bradford A. Booth, "Bret Harte Goes East: Some Unpublished Letters," p. 324.

200   **The hostess felt** *"[T]he party!..."*: Elinor Mead Howells to Victoria and Aurelia H. How-
      ells, March 17, 1871, included in Elinor Mead Howells, *If Not Literature: Letters of Elinor
      Mead Howells*, ed. Ginette de B. Merrill and George Arms, p. 138. Details of party: ibid., pp.
      137–143, and Susan Goodman and Carl Dawson, *William Dean Howells*, p. 136. Howells
      assumed the editorship of the *Atlantic* from James T. Fields in July 1871. Falling circulation
      and decline in quality of contributors: Ellery Sedgwick, *A History of the Atlantic Monthly,
      1857–1909: Yankee Humanism at High Tide and Ebb* (Amherst: University of Massachusetts
      Press, 2009 [1994]), pp. 127, 134.

201   **This experimental spirit** Howells's background: Susan Goodman and Carl Dawson, *Wil-
      liam Dean Howells*, pp. 1–138. Howells's review of *Innocents*: William Dean Howells, "Re-
      views and Literary Notices," *Atlantic Monthly* 24.146 (Dec. 1869), pp. 764–766. *"the
      earnests..."*: William Dean Howells, "Editor's Easy Chair," p. 153.

201   **What would this** *"intense ethicism..."*: William Dean Howells, "Literary Boston as I
      Knew It," in *Literary Friends and Acquaintance: A Personal Retrospect of American Author-
      ship*, p. 117. *"soil," "air," "the newest kind..."*: William Dean Howells, "Editor's Easy Chair,"
      p. 153. *"finest poetry..."*: quoted in Ellery Sedgwick, *A History of the Atlantic Monthly,
      1857–1909*, p. 121. Howells's realism: ibid., pp. 120–123.

202   **On March 6, 1871** Harte's agreement with the *Atlantic*: BH to James R. Osgood, March 6,
      1871, BANC. In 1871, a congressman's salary was $5,000 a year; see John J. Patrick et al.,
      The Oxford Guide to the United States Government (Oxford, UK: Oxford University Press,
      2001), p. 561. *"may still claim..."* and *"He tarried..."*: Louise Chandler Moulton, quoted in
      BHGS, p. 68.

202   **Howells welcomed the** *"witchery of that..."*: William Dean Howells, "Editor's Easy
      Chair," p. 159. Scene with Harte on the train and "mock heartbreak": ibid.

203   **Twain had a plan** *"I must & will keep..."* and *"I will 'top'..."*: SLC to Orion Clemens, March
      11 and 13, 1871, in MTL, vol. 4, pp. 350–351. Twain bought a one-third stake in the *Buffalo
      Express* in August 1869, with a loan from Livy's father, Jervis, and became its managing
      editor; see Victor Fischer and Michael B. Frank, introduction to MTL, vol. 3, p. xxvii, and
      MTAL, pp. 274, 283–284. By late 1870, his involvement in the *Express* had steadily dimin-
      ished, and he visited the offices only once a week; see SLC to Charles Henry Webb, Novem-
      ber 26, 1870, in MTL, vol. 4, p. 248. *Express* offices: MTL, vol. 3, p. 306.

203   **How had it** Langdon's birth and Livy's fever: MCMT, p. 122. Doctors and nurses: SLC to
      John Henry Riley, March 3, 1871, in MTL, vol. 4, p. 338. *"You do not know..."* and *"I be-
      lieve..."*: SLC to Elisha Bliss Jr., March 17, 1871, ibid., pp. 365–366.

203   **Needless to say** The July 1870 contract for *Roughing It* said the manuscript was due on
      January 1, 1871. Slow progress: MCMT, pp. 121–122. *"In three whole..."*: SLC to Elisha Bliss
      Jr., March 17, 1871, in MTL, vol. 4, p. 365. The name of the parody was "The Three Aces."
      It appeared in the *Buffalo Express* on December 3, 1870, under the name Carl Byng. On
      January 7, 1871, *Every Saturday* identified Twain as the author; see ibid., p. 303. *"I am
      not..."*: SLC to the editor of *Every Saturday* (Thomas Bailey Aldrich), January 15, 1871,
      ibid., p. 304. A week later, after his temper had cooled, Twain wrote Aldrich a more subdued
      letter asking him not to publish his earlier message in *Every Saturday*. By then, however, it
      was too late; see SLC to Thomas Bailey Aldrich, January 22, 1871, ibid., p. 305.

204   **Anger made him** Aside from his stalled progress on *Roughing It*, Twain had other profes-
      sional frustrations in this period. In 1870, he had dreamed up a book about a diamond strike
      in South Africa, and hired a friend, John Henry Riley, to travel to the region and undertake
      the preliminary research. Riley sailed for South Africa in January 1871, but the project
      never panned out, and Riley died a year later; see MTAL, p. 292. In March 1871, Twain
      published a hastily arranged pamphlet called *Mark Twain's (Burlesque) Autobiography*. It
      was a critical and commercial failure; see ibid., pp. 298–299.

204   **One thing was** Leaving Buffalo: SLC to John Henry Riley, March 3, 1871, in MTL, vol. 4,
      pp. 337–340; SLC to Orion Clemens, March 4, 1871, ibid., pp. 341–346; SLC to Orion

Clemens, March 10, 1871, ibid., pp. 348–349; and SLC to Jane Lampton Clemens and Family, March 15, 1871, ibid., p. 361. Hartford and Nook Farm: MCMT, pp. 139–142.

205 **But first, the** Livy's worsening condition: SLC to Elisha Bliss Jr. and Orion Clemens, March 20, 1871, in MTL, vol. 4, pp. 367–369, and SLC to Elisha Bliss Jr., March 17, 1871, ibid., pp. 365–367. *"I had rather die . . ."* and *"I want to get clear . . ."*: ibid., p. 365.

205 **The farmhouse belonged** Twain and his family spent nearly twenty summers at Quarry Farm, from 1871 to 1889. The books he wrote there include *Tom Sawyer, Huckleberry Finn*, and *A Connecticut Yankee in King Arthur's Court*. Quarry Farm: ibid., pp. 366–367, and MTAL, p. 298. Twain walking there several times a week: SLC to Orion Clemens, April 8, 9, and 10, 1871, ibid., p. 376. Majestic setting: SLC to John Brown, April 27, 1874, in MTL, vol. 6, p. 121; and SLC to Joseph H. and Harmony C. Twichell, June 11, 1874, ibid., p. 158. *"a foretaste of heaven"*: SLC to Joseph Twichell, October 2, 1879, in MTLO. Getting back to work: MTAL, p. 298, and MCMT, pp. 135–136.

205 **He relied on** Book's composition: Franklin R. Rogers, introduction to *Roughing It*, in *The Works of Mark Twain*, vol. 2 (Berkeley: University of California Press for the Iowa Center for Textual Studies, 1972), pp. 4–21. Goodman's arrival: MTL, vol. 4, p. 379. "He is going to read my MSS critically," Twain wrote Orion on April 18, 1871; see ibid., p. 378. Goodman's visit: MTAL, pp. 298–299. *"I knew it! . . ."* and *"Mark . . ."*: MTB, vol. 1, pp. 435–436.

206 **Goodman's visit lifted** *"booming along"*: SLC to Orion Clemens, April 8, 9, and 10, 1871, in MTL, vol. 4, p. 376. Livy's recovery: SLC to Mary Mason Fairbanks, April 26, 1871, ibid., p. 381. Healthy baby Langdon: SLC to Orion Clemens, April 4, 1871, ibid., p. 372. Superhuman pace and two-thirds done: SLC to Elisha Bliss Jr., May 15, 1871, ibid., pp. 390–393. *"a red-hot interest"* and *"Nothing grieves . . ."*: ibid., p. 391.

206 **All this confidence** *"curious new world"*: MTR, p. 1. Passing references to the *Golden Era*, the *Californian*, and Bret Harte: ibid., p. 405.

207 **The book's freewheeling** Filler and the exigencies of subscription publishing: MTAL, pp. 302–303. *"It was a driving . . ."*: MTR, p. 391.

208 **By the fall** Departure for Hartford and renting a house: MTAL, p. 304.

208 **It's unclear who** In mid-1871, Twain sent Harte a photograph of baby Langdon at six and a half months. "The most determined singer in America sends his warm regards to the most notorious one," the inscription read, signed Langdon Clemens. It's possible that the two men met before this, or that Harte wrote the first letter; see SLC to BH, June 7–September 28, 1871, in MTL, vol. 4, pp. 397–398. The details of the Keeler lunch come from William Dean Howells, who discussed the event at least three times: in a May 7, 1902, letter to Aldrich, quoted in MTL, vol. 4, pp. 485–486; in "Editor's Easy Chair," pp. 156–157; and in William Dean Howells, *My Mark Twain*, pp. 7–8. Twain's first visit to the *Atlantic* offices in 1869: ibid., pp. 5–6.

208 **Fortunately, this was** *"nothing but careless . . ."*: William Dean Howells, "Editor's Easy Chair," p. 156. *"This is the dream . . ."*: ibid.

209 **Later, Howells claimed** *"betrayed his enjoyment . . ."*: William Dean Howells, *My Mark Twain*, p. 8. This was Howells's final account of the lunch, written in 1910. He made no mention of Twain's reaction to Harte's comment in his two earlier accounts.

209 **Only nine months** *"not quite au fait . . ."*: Elinor Mead Howells to Victoria and Aurelia H. Howells, March 17, 1871, in Elinor Mead Howells, *If Not Literature: Letters of Elinor Mead Howells*, ed. Ginette de B. Merrill and George Arms, p. 137. *"was not much of a talker"*: William Dean Howells, "Editor's Easy Chair," p. 155.

209 **His first test** *"You could hardly . . ."*: quoted in BHGS, pp. 73–74. *"dignity and fitness"*: ibid., p. 73. Harte's poem was entitled "The Old Major Explains." An hour to write and apology to Fields: BH to James T. Fields, May 13, 1871, BANC. Lowell's invitation: BHGS, p. 74, and BHAN, p. 116.

210 **This time, Harte** Phi Beta Kappa gathering: *Boston Daily Advertiser*, June 30, 1871, and *New York Daily Tribune*, June 30, 1871. Harte's clothing: Mrs. Thomas Bailey Aldrich,

Crowding Memories (Boston: Houghton Mifflin, 1922 [1920]), p. 142. Harte's delivery: *Boston Daily Advertiser*, June 30, 1871, and *Albany Evening Journal*, July 11, 1871. The poem was "The Lost Beauty," first published in 1862; see BHGS, p. 74. *"a jingle so trivial..."*: William Dean Howells, "Editor's Easy Chair," p. 158. *"The thoughtful portion..."*: the *Washington Capital*, as reprinted in the *Albany Evening Journal*, July 11, 1871. *"Bret Harte's 'Fizzle' at Harvard"*: ibid. See also *New York Daily Tribune*, July 7, 1871; *Cincinnati Daily Gazette*, July 10, 1871; and *Columbian Register* (New Haven, CT), July 15, 1871.

210   **These disappointments put** Bret Harte, "The Poet of Sierra Flat," *Atlantic Monthly* (July 1871), pp. 115–120, also included in Bret Harte, *The Luck of Roaring Camp and Other Writings*, ed. Gary Scharnhorst, pp. 98–107. *"[S]carcely as striking..."*: *Philadelphia Inquirer*, June 19, 1871; see also *New York Evening Post*, June 22, 1871, and BHGS, p. 75.

211   **May, June, July** The *Albany Evening Journal* of July 11, 1871, described Harte's attitude at the Phi Beta Kappa ceremony as "plainly indifferent, not to say contemptuous." In *Crowding Memories*, p. 142, Mrs. Thomas Bailey Aldrich agreed, observing that Harte "did not recognize the dignity of the occasion." William Dean Howells took a more charitable view. Harte "took the whole disastrous business lightly, gayly, leniently, kindly, as that golden temperament of his enabled him to take all the good or bad of life"; see William Dean Howells, "Editor's Easy Chair," p. 158. *"It is a serious damage..."*: quoted in BHGS, p. 85.

211   **Beneath his insouciant** *"exodus from the exile"*: William Dean Howells, "Editor's Easy Chair," p. 154. Harte discussed his hatred for California with Anna Dickinson in Chicago; see Dickinson's letter to her mother, included in James Harvey Young, "Anna Dickinson, Mark Twain, and Bret Harte," *Pennsylvania Magazine of History and Biography* 76.1 (Jan. 1952), pp. 44–45. He expressed similar sentiments to M. E. W. Sherwood in Newport; see M. E. W. Sherwood, "Bret Harte: Mrs. Sherwood Writes Her Reminiscences, Dating from the Success of 'The Luck of Roaring Camp,'" *New York Times*, May 10, 1902. *"bewildered..."*: Noah Brooks, "Harte's Early Days: Reminiscences by Noah Brooks, Who Knew Him in California," *New York Times*, May 24, 1902. *"this noisy yet..."*: quoted in BHGS, p. 75. Harte's house hunting in upstate New York, New Jersey, and Connecticut: ibid., pp. 75–76. *"[W]hat have become..."*: BH to WDH, May 15, 1871, quoted ibid. Newport days: ibid., pp. 76–84. *"left Newport in debt..."*: TAMT, p. 387. *"gotten so little..."*: quoted in Charles Warren Stoddard, "In Old Bohemia II: The 'Overland' and the Overlanders," p. 266.

212   **All of Harte's** *"There was a happy..."*: TAMT, p. 166.

212   **Neither Charles Warren Stoddard** Harte did remain in touch with at least two Californians after going East, however, at least briefly. These were Josephine Clifford McCrackin, his *Overland* assistant, and Ambrose Bierce.

212   **Coolbrith never recovered** *"I had my own heartache..."*: quoted in Edward F. O'Day, "Varied Types XLI—Ina Coolbrith," *Town Talk*, September 30, 1911, clipping from the Coolbrith scrapbooks held by OAK. *"toiled and suffered..."*: ECW. *"[My] duties..."*: IC to CWS, January 26 [year unknown, but certainly before Stoddard's departure for Europe in 1873], HUNT. "I have written nothing by daylight for over a year," she told Stoddard. Commencement ode and *Overland* poems: ICLL, pp. 114–117, and OAK scrapbooks. Coolbrith published seven poems in the *Overland* in 1871. *"The sorrow..."*: Ina Coolbrith, "Two Pictures," *Overland Monthly* 7.2 (Aug. 1871), p. 130.

213   **She couldn't help it** *"I cannot sit..."*: Ina Coolbrith, "Marah," *Overland Monthly* 10.6 (June 1873), p. 545. Miller's daughter: ICLL, p. 120. Disappearance of father: ibid., pp. 124–125. *"The last of the brood..."*: IC to CWS, August 27, 1873, HUNT.

214   **Stoddard was no stranger** Harte's silence and Stoddard: CSCWS, pp. 150–151. "Many of Harte's old friends felt hurt at his silence after he left for the eastern states. He seemed to quite ignore California and Californians," Stoddard wrote in "In Old Bohemia II: The 'Overland' and the Overlanders," p. 266. Charles Warren Stoddard, "A Prodigal in Tahiti," *Atlantic Monthly* 30.181 (Nov. 1872), pp. 610–621. *"infinitely the best..."*: WDH to CWS, November 13, 1872, HUNT. *"Do send us..."*: WDH to CWS, October 25, 1872, HUNT.

214   **Encouraged, Stoddard powered** Departure for Samoa and decision to stay in Hawaii: CSCWS, pp. 158–161, and GP, pp. 55–57. Search for publisher: CSCWS, pp. 164–165, and GP, pp. 57–58. *"I have spoken..."*: WDH to CWS, January 3, 1873, HUNT.

214   *South-Sea Idyls* Charles Warren Stoddard, *South-Sea Idyls* (Boston: James R. Osgood, 1873). *"[B]arbarism has..."*: SLC to Walt Whitman, April 2, 1870, included in CSCWS, p. 136.

215   **This voice was** Reception of *South-Sea Idyls*: GP, pp. 61–63. *"[T]hey have each..."* and *"careless..."*: William Dean Howells, "Recent Literature," *Atlantic Monthly* 32.194 (Dec. 1873), pp. 740–741. *Chronicle* commission and departure: CSCWS, pp. 167–168.

215   **Coolbrith was in** *"When I received..."* and *"You cannot avoid..."*: IC to CWS, August 27, 1873, HUNT.

216   **Stoddard would remain** Salt Lake City: Charles Warren Stoddard, "Saints Alive!" *San Francisco Chronicle*, September 14, 1873. Chicago: Charles Warren Stoddard, "The Modern Babylon," *San Francisco Chronicle*, September 21, 1873. New York: Charles Warren Stoddard, "In Gotham," *San Francisco Chronicle*, October 19, 1873. *"I shall be among..."*: WDH to CWS, June 2, 1873, HUNT. Stoddard sent a photograph of himself to Howells before coming East. Howells responded that Stoddard's face "is expressive of everything that I liked best in your writings." *"More delightful..."*: William Dean Howells, "Editor's Easy Chair," *Harper's Monthly Magazine* 136.811 (Dec. 1917), p. 148.

216   **Stoddard liked the East** Departure for England and arrival in Liverpool: CSCWS, pp. 169–170. Finding Twain: Charles Warren Stoddard, "Mark Twain," *San Francisco Chronicle*, July 28, 1878, and SLC to CWS, October 16, 1873, in Victor Fischer, Michael B. Frank, Sharon K. Goetz, and Harriet Elinor Smith, eds., *Mark Twain's Letters Newly Published 1*, accessed online via Mark Twain Project Online, University of California, Berkeley.

217   **A big boost** Twain's fears: SLC to David Gray, June 10, 1880, in MTLO and MTAL, p. 321.

217   **Twain had nothing** *Roughing It*'s sales: Harriet Elinor Smith, foreword to MTR, p. xxvii. Royalties: MTAL, p. 318. Critical reception: ibid., p. 321, and MCMT, pp. 148–149. All quotes: William Dean Howells, "Recent Literature," *Atlantic Monthly* 29.176 (June 1872), p. 754.

217   **Twain felt relieved** *"I am as uplifted..."*: SLC to WDH, May 22–29 [?], 1872, in MTL, vol. 5, p. 95. In *My Mark Twain*, p. 15, Howells writes of Twain, "We were natives of the same vast Mississippi Valley; and Missouri was not so far from Ohio but that we were akin in our first knowledges of woods and fields as we were in our early parlance. I had outgrown the use of mine through my greater bookishness, but I gladly recognized the phrases which he employed for their lasting juiciness and the long-remembered savor they had on his mental palate."

218   **He also found** Growing friendship between Twain and Howells: SLC to WDH, March 18, 1872, in MTL, vol. 5, pp. 58–59; SLC to WDH, June 15, 1872, ibid., pp. 102–108; and SLC to WDH, March 13, 1873, ibid., pp. 317–319. For an overview of their relationship, see Susan Goodman and Carl Dawson, *William Dean Howells*, pp. 148–173.

218   **Over the years** *"Lincoln of our literature"*: William Dean Howells, *My Mark Twain*, p. 84. *"the superiority of the vulgar"*: William Dean Howells, *W. D. Howells as Critic*, ed. Edwin H. Cady (London and Boston: Routledge & Kegan Paul, 1973), p. 77.

219   **But that was** Deteriorating relationship between Harte and Howells: BHGS, pp. 76–77. *"a queer absent-minded..."*: Anne Fields's diary entry for January 12, 1872, reprinted in M. A. DeWolfe Howe, *Memories of a Hostess*, p. 240. *"catastrophe"*: quoted in BHGS, p. 86.

219   **No one could've** *"burned his ships"*: quoted in Anna Dickinson's letter of February 22, 1871, to her mother, included in James Harvey Young, "Anna Dickinson, Mark Twain, and Bret Harte," p. 45. Harte-Howells correspondence on "Concepción de Argüello": Bradford A. Booth, "Bret Harte Goes East: Some Unpublished Letters," pp. 328–331. *"my dear boy"*: BH to WDH, March 25, 1872, ibid., p. 328. *"Yankee Professors"* and *"I am careless..."*: ibid., p. 329.

219 **Even the affable** Howells's response, Harte's apology, and reconciliation: BHAN, p. 122. Bret Harte, "Concepción de Argüello": *Atlantic Monthly* 29.175 (May 1872), pp. 603–605. Expiration of contract: BHGS, pp. 85–89. Photograph from 1872 included ibid., p. 88. Harte's debts: ibid., pp. 77–78. *"He was utterly..."*: Noah Brooks, "Harte's Early Days: Reminiscences by Noah Brooks, Who Knew Him in California," *New York Times*, May 24, 1902.

220 **On June 13** Harte's arrival in Hartford: MTL, vol. 5, p. 105. Langdon's worsening health: SLC to Orion and Mollie Clemens, May 15, 1872, ibid., p. 86. Death of Langdon: MTAL, p. 319, and MCMT, p. 149.

220 **One cold morning** Carriage ride: TAMT, pp. 249–250. *"Yes, I killed him"*: William Dean Howells, *My Mark Twain*, p. 12. *"I have always felt..."*: TAMT, p. 249.

221 **He went to** *"sparkling sarcasms..."*: TAMT, p. 387. Harte's financial troubles and Twain's loan: ibid. Twain persuading Bliss to give Harte a book contract: BH to SLC, July 25, 1872, in MTL, vol. 5, p. 134. *"Tell Mrs. Clemens..."* and *"You ought to..."*: BH to SLC, June 17, 1872, ibid., pp. 105–106.

221 **Harte's own conjugal** Anna Griswold Harte's illness: BHGS, p. 79. Jessamy's illness: ibid., pp. 87–89. Move to Morristown: ibid., p. 87. *"sleepy dolce..."* and *"Could not you and I..."*: BH to SLC, July 25, 1872, in MTL, vol. 5, p. 134.

222 **On August 21, 1872** Twain's departure for England: MTAL, pp. 322–325, and MCMT, p. 151. *"I do miss him..."* and *"England is a subject..."*: quoted in Edith Colgate Salsbury, *Susy and Mark Twain: Family Dialogues* (New York: Harper & Row, 1965), p. 10. For Twain's early thoughts on England, see MTL, vol. 5, pp. 584–585.

222 **What he didn't** Twain's trip: "Mark Twain's 1872 English Journals" in MTL, vol. 5, pp. 583–629; SLC to OLC, September 11, 1872, ibid., pp. 154–158; SLC to OLC, September 15, 1872, ibid., pp. 159–160; SLC to OLC, September 22, 1872, ibid., pp. 169–170; SLC to OLC, September 25, 1872, ibid., pp. 178–182; SLC to OLC, October 3, 1872, ibid., pp. 188–190; SLC to OLC, October 12, 1872, ibid., pp. 196–197; SLC to OLC, October 25, 1872, ibid., pp. 199–204. State banquet: SLC to OLC, November 10, 1872, ibid., pp. 221–222. Dinner held by sheriffs of London: SLC to OLC, September 28, 1872, ibid., pp. 183–188. *"I was never..."* and *"I did not know..."*: ibid., p. 184. Twain's popularity in England: MCMT, pp. 151–153, and William Dean Howells, *My Mark Twain*, pp. 39–40.

223 **The English craze** English reception of Artemus Ward and Twain: MCMT, pp. 152–154; Dennis Welland, *Mark Twain in England* (London: Chatto & Windus, 1978), pp. 15–63; and Judith Yaross Lee, "The International Twain and American Nationalist Humor: Vernacular Humor as a Post-Colonial Rhetoric," *Mark Twain Annual* 6.1 (Nov. 2008), pp. 33–49. *"peculiar humor..."*: *Once a Week*, December 14, 1872, quoted ibid., p. 33. See also the English reviews of Twain's books in Louis J. Budd, ed., *Mark Twain: The Contemporary Reviews* (Cambridge: Cambridge University Press, 1999), pp. 82–83, 102–103.

223 **Flattered wasn't the** *"Too much company..."*: SLC to OLC, September 11, 1872, in MTL, vol. 5, p. 155. Tower of London: ibid. Westminster Abbey: "Mark Twain's 1872 English Journals," ibid., p. 600. Handel's *Messiah*: SLC to OLC, September 25, 1872, ibid., p. 179. *Spectator* letter: SLC to the editor of the London *Spectator*, September 20, 1872, ibid., pp. 163–168. *"I am not going abroad..."*: SLC to OLC, October 12, 1872, ibid., p. 196.

223 **He kept his** The full entourage accompanying Twain to England in May 1873 included Livy, their baby daughter Susy, Susy's nurse Nellie Bermingham, Livy's friend Clara Spaulding, and Samuel C. Thompson, a twenty-five-year-old former journalist who briefly served Twain as his personal secretary; see MTAL, p. 334. Thatched roofs: OLC to her sister, May 31, 1873, quoted in MTL, vol. 5, p. 371. Shakespeare's tomb: ibid., p. 388. Robert Browning and Anthony Trollope: ibid., p. 397, and SLC to Mary Mason Fairbanks, July 6, 1873, ibid., p. 402.

CHAPTER EIGHT

227 **By October 1873** *"I am blue and cross and homesick"*: undated letter by Livy, probably to her mother or sister, quoted in MTL, vol. 5, p. 457. Panic of 1873: Irwin Unger, *The Greenback Era: A Social and Political History of American Finance, 1865–1879* (Princeton, NJ: Princeton University Press, 1968 [1964]), pp. 213–226, and Richard White, *Railroaded*, pp. 82–84.

227 **One night after** Twain and Livy's reaction to the Panic of 1873: SLC to John Brown, September 22 and 25, 1873, in MTL, vol. 5, pp. 439–442; OLC to her mother, September 25, 1873, ibid., pp. 443–444; and MCMT, p. 168. More than $10,000: SLC to Thomas W. Knox, September 10, 1873, in MTL, vol. 5, p. 435. Twain lectured at the Queen's Concert Rooms in Hanover Square from October 13 to 18, 1873, with five evening performances and one matinee; see Fred W. Lorch, *The Trouble Begins at Eight*, pp. 139–143. Liverpool performance: ibid., p. 143, and Paul Fatout, *Mark Twain on the Lecture Circuit*, p. 182. Twain and his family departed Liverpool for New York on October 21, 1873.

228 **He wouldn't be gone** Dropping off Livy and family at Hartford: MTL, vol. 5, p. 458. Twain sailed for England from New York on November 8, 1873. Lying in his berth: SLC to OLC, November 10 and 17, 1873, ibid., p. 473. Back at the Langham: SLC to OLC, November 20, 1873, ibid., p. 478.

228 **He had returned** *The Gilded Age*'s composition: MCMT, pp. 159–167; MTAL, pp. 328–333; and Louis J. Budd, introduction to Mark Twain and Charles Dudley Warner, *The Gilded Age*, pp. xi–xxxi. By late April 1873, the manuscript was finished; Twain and Warner signed the contract with Elisha Bliss the following month.

228 **Ever since moving** Twain's view of postwar America: MCMT, pp. 154–170; Mark Twain, "Open Letter to Commodore Vanderbilt," *Packard's Monthly* (March 1869), pp. 89–91, and Mark Twain, "The Revised Catechism," *New York Tribune* September 27, 1871. *"an era of incredible rottenness"*: SLC to Orion Clemens, March 27, 1875, in MTL, vol. 6, p. 427.

229 **Twain's relationship** to this Twain and the new economy: MCMT, pp. 95–96, 158–159. *The Gilded Age* as first novel sold by subscription: MTL, vol. 5, p. 362. Twain's marketing efforts: SLC to Elisha Bliss Jr., November 5, 1873, ibid., pp. 461–470.

229 **This was why** Twain arranged for *The Gilded Age*'s publication in England by Routledge & Sons, and copyrighted the edition to protect his interests. See SLC to T. B. Pugh, July 27, 1873, in MTL, vol. 5, pp. 421–422; SLC to Elisha Bliss Jr., July 16, 1873, ibid., pp. 416–417; SLC to Charles Dudley Warner, July 16, 1873, ibid., pp. 417–418; and SLC to Elisha Bliss, July 27, 1873, ibid., pp. 420–421. Twain hired Stoddard as his secretary in October 1873, before escorting his family home to Hartford and returning to London in November; see CSCWS, pp. 173–175, and SLC to CWS, October 19, 1873, in MTL, vol. 5, pp. 456–458.

229 **Stoddard had little** *"I hired him..."*: AMT, p. 161. *"He seized me..."*: quoted in George Wharton James, "Charles Warren Stoddard," *National Magazine* (Aug. 1911), p. 669. *"long, long talks..."*: Charles Warren Stoddard, *Exits and Entrances*, p. 70.

230 **On December 1** Twain and Stoddard in London: Charles Warren Stoddard, "Mark Twain," *San Francisco Chronicle*, July 28, 1878; Charles Warren Stoddard, *Exits and Entrances*, pp. 64–74; George Wharton James, "Charles Warren Stoddard," pp. 662, 669–671; and Charles Warren Stoddard, "In Old Bohemia II: The 'Overland' and the Overlanders," pp. 262–263; and AMT, pp. 161–163. The London fog of the 1873–1874 winter: Philip Eden, *Great British Weather Disasters* (London: Continuum, 2008), pp. 68–74, and SLC to OLC, December 9, 1873, in MTL, vol. 5, p. 497. *"nearly broke my heart"*: SLC to OLC, December 13 and 15, 1873, ibid., p. 512.

230 **Finally, the time** Twain's 1873 performances in London: Fred W. Lorch, *The Trouble Begins at Eight*, pp. 140–149, and Paul Fatout, *Mark Twain on the Lecture Circuit*, pp. 179–188. Rubbing his hands: George Wharton James, "Charles Warren Stoddard," p. 669. *"The*

moment...": quoted ibid. *"delicious dialect of California": Evening Standard* (London), October 14, 1873, quoted in Paul Fatout, *Mark Twain on the Lecture Circuit*, p. 180.

230 **He opened with** Twain delivered his Hawaii lecture every evening from December 1 through December 5, 1873, with a matinee on December 3 and another on December 6. He switched to his *Roughing It* lecture on December 9, and continued it through December 20; see Fred W. Lorch, *The Trouble Begins at Eight*, pp. 143–144. Stoddard's observations: Charles Warren Stoddard, *Exits and Entrances*, pp. 67–68. *"still as statues...,"* faces in the crowd, and *"Bully audiences"*: SLC to OLC, December 16, 1873, in MTL, vol. 5, p. 521.

231 **Lecturing energized him** Negro spiritual, *"With fear and trembling..."* and *"Yours was so damned..."*: Charles Warren Stoddard, "In Old Bohemia II: The 'Overland' and the Overlanders," p. 263. *"knew the art..."*: quoted in George Wharton James, "Charles Warren Stoddard," p. 669. Stoddard remembered the cocktails being made from bourbon. But the active ingredient was almost certainly Scotch, per the recipe given in SLC to OLC, January 2, 1874, in MTL, vol. 6, p. 3: "a bottle of Scotch whiskey, a lemon, & some crushed sugar, & a bottle of *Angostura bitters*." "Ever since I have been in London I have taken in a wineglass what is called a cock-tail (made with those ingredients,) before breakfast, before dinner, & just before going to bed," he told Livy.

231 **Twain was a born** *"gorgeous seclusion"*: quoted in George Wharton James, "Charles Warren Stoddard," p. 662. *"Very, very..."*: ibid., p. 670.

232 **This wasn't the** *"his youth..."*: Charles Warren Stoddard, "In Old Bohemia II: The 'Overland' and the Overlanders," p. 263. Church bells: Charles Warren Stoddard, *Exits and Entrances*, p. 70. *"now talking..."*: quoted in George Wharton James, "Charles Warren Stoddard," pp. 669–670.

232 **A vivid panorama** *"I could have..."*: Charles Warren Stoddard, *Exits and Entrances*, p. 70.

232 **By 1873, Twain** Fit of remembering: MTAL, pp. 312–315, 351–352. *"The fountains..."* and *"faces..."*: SLC to William Bowen, February 6, 1870, in MTL, vol. 4, p. 50. Around 1868, Twain wrote "Boy's Manuscript," an early unpublished attempt to put his Hannibal memories into fictional form; see Mark Twain, *Huck Finn and Tom Sawyer among the Indians and Other Unfinished Stories*, ed. Dahlia Armon et al. (Berkeley: University of California Press, 1989), pp. 1–19, 265–266. This piece anticipates *The Adventures of Tom Sawyer*, which he began writing as early as 1872.

233 **These remembrances didn't** *Gilded Age* as autobiographical: MTAL, pp. 330–332, and MCMT, pp. 169–170. *"dyspeptic"* and *"the crude material..."*: WDH to Charles Dudley Warner, December 28, 1873, in MTL, vol. 5, p. 468. *"I merely put him..."*: TAMT, p. 25.

234 **In London, Stoddard** *"I trust I am..."*: Charles Warren Stoddard, *Exits and Entrances*, p. 70.

234 **By January 1874** *"Stoddard & I..."*: SLC to OLC, January 3, 1874, in MTL, vol. 6, p. 4. *"then the turning..."*: SLC to OLC, January 2, 1874, in MTL, vol. 6, p. 3. "Sometimes I get so homesick I don't know what to do," he told Livy on December 31, 1873; see MTL, vol.5, p. 543. The farewell shows in Liverpool took place on January 9 and 10, 1874; see Fred W. Lorch, *The Trouble Begins at Eight*, pp. 149–151. *"We're done..."*: SLC to CWS, January 9, 1874, in MTL, vol. 6, pp. 17–18. The "prompt notes" were for the *Roughing It* lecture, which he delivered on January 9. The following evening, he performed his Hawaii lecture, and, as an encore, read the jumping frog story aloud; see ibid., p. 20.

234 **It made a fitting** *"He sank into..."*: Charles Warren Stoddard, *Exits and Entrances*, p. 73. *"friendless, forsaken, despised"*: quoted in George Wharton James, "Charles Warren Stoddard," p. 670. *"I'll become..."*: ibid., p. 671. Oratorical fluency: ibid. *"in a style..."*: Charles Warren Stoddard, *Exits and Entrances*, p. 74.

236 **It was a story** *"soul-deep"*: quoted in George Wharton James, "Charles Warren Stoddard," p. 671. Twain and Livy moved into their new house at 351 Farmington Avenue in Hartford in September 1874; see MTAL, p. 360.

236 **Bret Harte looked** *"old-young man"* and heavy eyes: from a correspondent who saw Harte in Washington, printed in *Virginia City Territorial Enterprise*, December 6, 1874,

quoted in BHGS, p. 96. Wrinkles: Anne Fields's diary, quoted ibid. Exhausted: ibid., p. 101. Harte on the lecture circuit: ibid., pp. 90–114, and BHAN, pp. 126–134.

236 **People came out** *"[I]f I had been..."*: quoted in Henry J. W. Dam, "A Morning With Bret Harte," p. 50. Harte's lecture style: BHGS, p. 95. Harte lectured from late 1872 through early 1873, the spring and winter of 1873, early 1874, and the winter of 1874–1875. *"exceedingly dull affair"*: *St. Louis Republican*, reprinted in *Portland (ME) Daily Press*, October 28, 1873. *"Harte as a lecturer..."*: *Iowa State Register*, quoted in BHGS, p. 106.

237 **Twain had a** *"He has an..."*: SLC to Josephus N. Larned, March 22, 1873, in MTL, vol. 5, p. 320. Twain saw Harte perform in Hartford on January 3, 1873; see ibid., p. 321. *"Argonautic brotherhood"*: Bret Harte, "The Argonauts of '49," in *The Luck of Roaring Camp and Other Writings*, ed. Gary Scharnhorst, p. 237. *"jauntily insolent"*: ibid., p. 239.

237 **The lost literary** Accusation of embezzling: W. A. Kendall, "Frank Bret Harte," *San Francisco Chronicle*, December 15, 1872. Kendall was a poet and journalist associated with the Bohemians. Harte had included three of his poems in *Outcroppings*, and five of his poems in the *Overland Monthly*; see MTL, vol. 5, pp. 9–10. Harte would soon see another old California friend turn into an enemy. In 1873, Joe Lawrence, editor of the *Golden Era*, reprinted Harte's story "M'liss," which first appeared in the paper in 1863, and hired a local writer to write an additional 62 chapters to supplement Harte's first 16. Harte was outraged; see BHGS, pp. 98–99.

238 **Harte was furious** *"I have been..."* and *"I don't mind..."*: BH to SLC, December 26, 1872, in MTL, vol. 5, p. 318. *"borrower of..."* and *"a cool ignorer..."*: W. A. Kendall, "Frank Bret Harte," *San Francisco Chronicle*, December 15, 1872. *"hoggishness"*: BH to James R. Osgood, April 18, 1875, quoted in BHAN, p. 135.

238 **His delusions grew** Chicago magazine: BHGS, pp. 103–104. *"I do not see how..."*: BH to John H. Carmany, September 13, 1875, BANC.

238 **Even the *Atlantic*** Second chance at *Atlantic*: BHGS, pp. 108–110; BHAN, pp. 132–133; and Bradford A. Booth, "Bret Harte Goes East: Some Unpublished Letters," pp. 331–333. *"[S]ince my arrival"*: BH to WDH, September 8, 1874, quoted ibid., p. 332. *"I don't blame..."*: ibid., p. 333.

239 **This exchange permanently** Twain submitting "A True Story": SLC to WDH, September 2, 1874, in MTL, vol. 6, pp. 217–220. *"cheerful, hearty soul"* and *"Aunt Rachel..."*: Mark Twain, "A True Story, Repeated Word for Word as I Heard It," *Atlantic Monthly* 34.205 (Nov. 1874), p. 591.

239 **Howells judged the** *"extremely good"* and *"black talk"*: WDH to SLC, September 8, 1874, in MTL, vol. 6, p. 219.

240 **"A True Story"** *"Our Bret Harte..."*: WDH to Melancthon M. Hurd, November 7, 1874, in MTL, vol. 6, p. 266. Twain submitted his first installment in "Old Times on the Mississippi" to Howells on November 20, 1874; see ibid., pp. 294–295. The series appeared in the *Atlantic Monthly* between January and August 1875. Later, the articles became chaps. 4–17 of *Life on the Mississippi* (1883).

240 **Meanwhile, Harte entered** *"I have always found..."*: from Harte's letter, dated January 11, 1875, in *Boston Transcript*, January 14, 1875. Creditors suing Harte: BHAN, p. 135, and BHGS, pp. 115–116. Twain lent Harte as much as $3,000, according to his autobiography: TAMT, p. 386. Elisha Bliss signed a book contract with Harte for a novel in September 1872. Harte didn't finish *Gabriel Conroy* until June 1875, and, in the meantime, regularly asked Bliss for advances. The novel appeared serially in *Scribner's* between November 1875 and August 1876, and Bliss published it as a single volume in September 1876. The reviews were devastating, and it sold 4,000 copies in its first year. See SLC to Elisha Bliss Jr., July 28, 1872, in MTL, vol. 5, pp. 133–135; SLC to WDH, May 22, 1876, in MTLO; and BHGS, pp. 90, 114–117.

240 **This wasn't purely** Twain's stage adaptation of *The Gilded Age*: MTAL, pp. 352–354, 358–360. Reviews of *Two Men of Sandy Bar*: BHGS, pp. 121–122. *"the most dismal..."*:

"Amusements: Bret Harte's New Drama: 'The Two Men of Sandy Bar' at Union Square Theater," *New York Times*, August 29, 1876.

241   **But Twain liked** Twain seeing *Two Men of Sandy Bar*: SLC to BH, September 7–11, 1876, in MTLO. Parsloe's popularity: BHGS, pp. 124–125. *"Me no likee"*: Bret Harte, *Two Men of Sandy Bar: A Drama* (Leipzig: Bernhard Tauchnitz, 1877), p. 88. Wood shoes and coolie hat: ibid., p. 9. *"delightful Chinaman"*: TAMT, p. 388. Beginning of collaboration with Harte: ibid. *"Harte came up..."*: SLC to WDH, October 11, 1876, in MTLO.

241   **Over the following** At the time, Harte and his family were living in New York. After Twain and Harte had their initial meeting in early October 1876, Harte returned to Hartford for visits in late October, early November, late November, and early December; see SLC to WDH, October 11, 1876, in MTLO, and SLC to George Bentley, December 5, 1876, ibid. Composition of *Ah Sin*: TAMT, pp. 389–390.

241   **Harte's days as** *"He worked rapidly..."*: TAMT, p. 390. *"bottles of spirits"*: Isabella Beecher Hooker's diary, quoted in BHGS, p. 125. Harte's drinking: ibid., p. 96. Harte's visit in early December 1876: SLC to George Bentley, December 5, 1876, in MTLO and TAMT, pp. 388–389. *"not even tipsy"*: ibid., p. 389. Harte's story was "Thankful Blossom: A Romance of the Jerseys, 1779," published in four weekly installments in the *New York Sun*, beginning on December 3, 1876.

242   **Liquor didn't magically** *"working over..."*: *Alta California*, quoted in BHGS, p. 112. Harte and Parsloe: Margaret Duckett, *Mark Twain and Bret Harte* (Norman: University of Oklahoma Press, 1964), pp. 124–125. *"I read him..."*: BH to SLC, December 16, 1876, ibid., p. 124. Harte's ragged clothes: TAMT, p. 395. In his autobiography, Twain claimed that Harte dragged his feet in getting the play to Parsloe: "Harte had been procrastinating; the play should have been in Parsloe's hands a day or two earlier than this, but Harte had not attended to it"; see ibid.

242   **Harte's tone suggested** *"He was a man..."*: TAMT, p. 388.

242   **But this closeness** In his autobiography, Twain claims incorrectly that he and Harte wrote *Ah Sin* in a "fortnight" at the Hartford house. Their collaboration took place over a longer period of time, as Harte made multiple visits. *"slight and vague and veiled"*: TAMT, p. 390.

243   **He was nothing** All quotes: ibid., pp. 390–391.

243   **Possibly Twain said** The precise cause of the break between Harte and Twain remains a mystery, but there are clues scattered throughout their correspondence. In Harte's letter of December 16, 1876, he refers jokingly to his "heterodoxy" and begs Livy's forgiveness: "I feel her gentle protests to my awful opinions all the more remorsefully that I am away." On February 27, 1877, Twain complained to his sister of the "smouldering rage" he had felt recently "over the precious days & weeks of time which Bret Harte was losing for me"; see SLC to Pamela A. Moffett, February 27, 1877, in MTLO. For more on the possible causes of their estrangement, see Margaret Duckett, *Mark Twain and Bret Harte*, pp. 130–142. *"I'm not anxious..."*: BH to SLC, March 1, 1877, ibid., p. 134.

243   **The ensuing pages** Twain signed the contract for *Ah Sin* on December 30, 1866, while Harte and Parsloe both signed on January 5, 1877; see ibid., pp. 127–129. *"Either Bliss must..."*: BH to SLC, March 1, 1877, ibid., p. 135. *"marring it"*: ibid., p. 136.

244   **The letter enraged** *"I have read..."*: quoted ibid., p. 137. *"left hardly..."*: SLC to WDH, August 3, 1877, in MTLO. Twain's changes to *Ah Sin*: Margaret Duckett, *Mark Twain and Bret Harte*, pp. 146–151, and MTAL, pp. 403–404. *"[D]on't say harsh..."*: OLC to SLC, July 29, 1877, quoted ibid., pp. 405–406.

244   **He was regressing** *"Look at him... "*: "Twain and Harte's New Play," *San Francisco Argonaut*, May 19, 1877, quoted in Gary Scharnhorst, "'Ways That Are Dark': Appropriations of Bret Harte's 'Plain Language from Truthful James,'" pp. 391–392. *Ah Sin* played in Washington from May 7 to May 12, 1877, in Baltimore from May 14 to May 19, and reached New York on July 31; see BHGS, p. 128. *"The Chinaman is killingly funny"*: SLC to William Dean Howells, August 3, 1877, in MTLO. *"as good..."*: quoted in Margaret Duckett, *Mark*

Twain and Bret Harte, p. 153. See also "The Drama: The Heathen Chinee," *New York Tribune*, August 1, 1877.

245   **Whether he actually** San Francisco riot of 1877: *San Francisco Daily Evening Bulletin*, July 24, 1877, and July 25, 1877; *Alta California*, July 24, 1877; Kevin Starr, *Americans and the California Dream*, p. 132; and Robert Edward Lee Knight, *Industrial Relations in the San Francisco Bay Area, 1900–1918*, pp. 15–16. Failure of Bank of California: Ira B. Cross, *A History of the Labor Movement in California*, pp. 69–70.

245   **This element made** *"On to Chinatown!"* and *"indulging..."*: *Alta California*, July 24, 1877.

246   **Not far from** Failure of *Ah Sin*: Margaret Duckett, *Mark Twain and Bret Harte*, p. 158. *"most abject..."* and *"I'm sorry for..."*: SLC to WDH, October 15, 1877, in MTLO.

246   **Poor Parsloe would** Parsloe: "An Actor Stricken With Paralysis," *New York Times*, November 19, 1894, and "Death List of a Day: Charles Thomas Parsloe," *New York Times*, January 23, 1898. *"floating on the raft..."*: quoted in BHGS, p. 132. *"run over in..."*: quoted ibid. Harte's campaign for a consulate: ibid., pp. 134–138. Harte may have been hoping to secure a position overseas as early as 1876; see SLC to WDH, June 21, 1877, in MTLO and TAMT, p. 398.

246   **Twain did everything** *"I think your..."*: SLC to WDH, June 21, 1877, in MTLO. *"Father has read..."*: Birchard A. Hayes to Elinor Mead Howells, July 9, 1877, in BHAN, p. 158.

247   **Harte kept pushing** Harte's Republican friends: BHGS, p. 137. *"heard sinister things"*: Rutherford B. Hayes to WDH, April 5, 1878, in BHAN, p. 161. *"solvency and sobriety," "great affection..."* and *"It would be..."*: WDH to Rutherford B. Hayes, April 9, 1878, in BHGS, pp. 137–138, and Susan Goodman and Carl Dawson, *William Dean Howells*, p. 162.

247   **Nine days later** Harte's meeting with Assistant Secretary of State Frederick W. Seward: BHGS, pp. 158–159, and BHAN, p. 161. *"[W]ith all my..."*: BH to Anna Griswold Harte, April 19, 1878, ibid. Harte accepted the post on May 11, 1878. Crefeld is now known as Krefeld.

247   **Harte sailed on** Harte's departure: BHAN, pp. 161–162. All quotes: SLC to WDH, June 27, 1878, in MTLO.

AFTERLIFE

249   **There was a certain** *"a man without a country"*: TAMT, p. 396.

249   **Charles Warren Stoddard suffered** Stoddard in 1878: CSCWS, pp. 201–204.

250   **Aside from his** Stoddard's travels in Europe and the Middle East: ibid., pp. 178–196, and GP, pp. 67–84. *"I find no English..."* and *"Surely your success..."*: CWS to SLC, December 12, 1874, in MTL, vol. 6, p. 365. *"the old times..."*: CWS to SLC, February 24, 1875, ibid., p. 418.

250   **He felt happy** Stoddard first asked for Twain's help in publishing a book in a letter from February 24, 1875. He asked again in 1876, in a letter now lost, prompting Twain's reply. *"he shook his head..."*: SLC to CWS, September 20, 1876, in MTLO. In the same letter, Twain proposed the idea of a consulship to Stoddard. *"Stoddard's got no..."* and *"He is just..."*: SLC to WDH, September 21, 1876, in MTLO. *"leg like a..."*: WDH to SLC, October 8, 1876, in MTLO. Stoddard's return to America: CSCWS, pp. 197–201.

250   **"You will find"** All quotes: CWS to unknown, March 8, 1877, in George Wharton James, "Charles Warren Stoddard," p. 661. See also CSCWS, pp. 321–324.

251   **San Francisco had changed** Unemployment rate and depression: William Deverell, *Railroad Crossing*, p. 38, and Robert Knight, *Industrial Relations in the San Francisco Bay Area, 1900–1918*, pp. 14–15. *"Bankruptcy..."*: William Deverell, *Railroad Crossing*, p. 37. Stoddard's parents lived at 42 Hawthorne Street; see CSCWS, p. 204.

251   **The city's literary fortunes** The *Overland Monthly* ceased publication in 1875, but was revived in 1883; see ICLL, p. 163. The new magazine never lived up to its predecessor. "[T]he present corps of contributors do not equal the old," Coolbrith told Stoddard; see IC to CWS, September 18, 1883, HUNT. Origins of Bohemian Club: Roy Kotynek and John Cohassey, *American Cultural Rebels*, pp. 28–29; Andrew McF. Davis, "High Jinks," *Californian: A*

Western Monthly Magazine 1.5 (May 1880), pp. 418–422; and Charles Warren Stoddard, "In Old Bohemia: Memories of San Francisco in the Sixties," pp. 639–641.

251 **Stoddard joined before** The club's first location was on Sacramento Street between Kearny and Montgomery. In 1877, the club moved into better rooms at 430 Pine Street. *"It was soon..."*: Edward Bosqui's diary, quoted in G. William Domhoff, "Bohemia Betrayed: Sellout to the Social Register," in César Graña and Marigay Graña, *On Bohemia: The Code of the Self-Exiled* (New Brunswick, NJ: Transaction, 1990), p. 639. *"I never saw..."*: Roy Morris Jr., *Declaring His Genius: Oscar Wilde in North America* (Cambridge, MA: Harvard University Press, 2013), p. 140.

252 **Stoddard visited the** Impecunious Stoddard at the club: GP, p. 89, and CSCWS, pp. 204–209, 218–219. Coolbrith's election as honorary member and fund-raisers: ICLL, pp. 119, 124–125, 135, 224, 276.

252 **She was grateful** Death of Coolbrith's sister Agnes: ICLL, p. 122. Decision to become librarian: ibid., pp. 125–126. Hours and salary: pp. 131–132.. *"living tomb"*: SLC to CWS, August 31, 1882, HUNT.

253 **It wasn't all** Schoolchildren: ICLL, pp. 149–151. All quotes: Jack London to IC, December 13, 1906, in Jeanne Campbell Reesman, *Jack London: A Study of the Short Fiction* (New York: Twayne, 1999), p. 6.

253 **Coolbrith created a** *"Why, we used..."*: ICLL, p. 151. *"She sat in her..."*: Henry Kirk, quoted ibid., p. 150. Ina D. Coolbrith, *A Perfect Day, and Other Poems* (San Francisco: John H. Carmany, 1881). *"Miss Coolbrith's admirers..."*: Ambrose Bierce, *San Francisco News Letter*, undated clipping in the Coolbrith scrapbooks held by OAK. *A Perfect Day* was reviewed in the *Chicago Inter-Ocean*, the *Boston Transcript*, and the *Philadelphia Times*; these reviews are quoted in an advertisement for the book included in the *Californian* 6.32 (Aug. 1882). *"Without having..."*: "New Books," *New York Times*, June 20, 1881. Inscribed copy to Stoddard: ICLL, p. 156. *"I know of no..."*: CWS to IC, May 6, 1881, BANC. In October 1881, Stoddard left SF. He would return briefly in 1885 on his way to Notre Dame, where he taught for a year and a half. He didn't see SF again until 1905, and he died in Monterey, CA, four years later. See CSCWS, pp. 220–313, and GP, pp. 93–167.

253 **But at least** *"My relatives?..."*: IC to CWS, February 15, 1898, HUNT.

254 **California became loathsome** *"convict-life"*: ibid. *"How I hate..."*: IC to CWS, October 28, 1898, HUNT. On June 29, 1915, at the Panama-Pacific International Exposition Congress of Authors and Journalists, Coolbrith received the poet laureate's crown; see ICLL, pp. 310–316; Marian Taylor, "Congress of Authors and Journalists at the Panama-Pacific International Exposition," *Overland Monthly* 66.5 (Nov. 1915), pp. 439–447; and Josephine Clifford McCrackin, "Ina Coolbrith Invested With Poets' Crown," ibid., pp. 448–450. *"I feel that the..."*: quoted in ICLL, p. 314.

254 **Harte died in** Memoir manuscript and its destruction: ICLL, pp. 245–246, 254, 258. *"I took frequent..."*: ICHC. *"Were I to write..."*: quoted in Carlton Kendall, "California's Pioneer Poetess," *Overland Monthly and Out West Magazine* 87.8 (Aug. 1929), p. 230. According to a 1919 article in *Physical Culture* by George Wharton James, available at http://www.twain quotes.com/Bradley/bradley.html, Twain sent three autographed photographs of himself to help raise money for Coolbrith after her house burned down, and later sat for more portraits.

255 **After the blaze** Coolbrith's dream and quotes: *San Jose Mercury*, November 21, 1907, in a scrapbook held by OAK. Coolbrith is buried in Mountain View Cemetery in Oakland. Her grave remained unmarked until 1986, when the Ina Coolbrith Circle placed a headstone on the site.

INDEX

ILLUSTRATION CREDITS

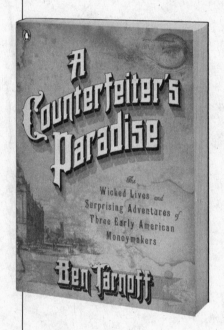